Hellenic Studies 84

HOMER'S THEBES

Recent Titles in the Hellenic Studies Series

HOMER'S THEBES

EPIC RIVALRIES AND THE
APPROPRIATION OF MYTHICAL PASTS

by
Elton T. E. Barker
Joel P. Christensen

CENTER FOR HELLENIC STUDIES
Trustees for Harvard University
Washington, DC
Distributed by Harvard University Press
Cambridge, Massachusetts, and London, England
2020

Names: Barker, Elton T. E. (Elton Thomas Edward), 1971- author. | Christensen,
  Joel (Joel P.), author.
Title: Homer's Thebes : epic rivalries and the appropriation of mythical pasts /
  Elton Barker, Joel Christensen.
Description: Washington : Center for Hellenic Studies, 2020. | Includes
  bibliographical references and index.
Identifiers: LCCN 2019021516 | ISBN 9780674237926
Subjects: LCSH: Homer--Criticism and interpretation. | Thebes (Greece)--In
  literature.
Classification: LCC PA4037 .B375 2019 | DDC 883/.01--dc23
LC record available at https://lccn.loc.gov/2019021516

Contents

Acknowledgements

THE IDEAS IN THIS BOOK were first launched in a waterlogged basement in Queens, New York City, in the spring of 2007, although our partnership had first emerged in the similarly watery surrounds of the Venice International University *Seminar on Literature and Culture in the Ancient Mediterranean* (2003–2004). There we enjoyed the rare resources of both time and money to hear lectures by and receive advice from Alessandro Barchiesi, Walter Burkert, Ettore Cingano, Irad Malkin, Piotr Michalowski, Dirk Obbink, David Sider, and Richard Thomas (among others). Our first publication together on Archilochus (Barker and Christensen 2006), produced as a direct result of that seminar, set out the beginnings of the methodological framework used in this book. Other articles have appeared over the years. The argument and much of the content of Chapter 1 made a first appearance as "On Not Remembering Tydeus: Agamemnon, Diomedes and the Contest for Thebes," in *Materiali e discussioni per l'analisi dei testi classici* no. 66 (2011):9–44; Chapter 2 draws on our contribution ("Even Heracles Had to Die: Homeric 'Heroism', Mortality and the Epic Tradition," pp. 249–277) to the special issue edited by Christos Tsagalis, "Theban Resonances in Homeric Epic," *Trends in Classics* 6, no. 2 (2014); and an early foray into Thebes took the form of "Oedipus of Many Pains: Strategies of Contest in the Homeric Poems," *Leeds International Classical Studies* 7, no. 2 (2008):1–30, which provides the basis for Chapter 3. The form and substance here differ substantially from their earlier incarnations, by virtue of engaging with the latest scholarship, being made to serve the argument of this book, and not least of all reflecting a welcome maturity in our thinking.

We have learned much taking our ideas on the road. For the insightful and thought-provoking comments that we have received along the way (and helped shaped this book), we thank our audiences at Columbia University, Texas Tech University, the University of Missouri, the Celtic Conference in Classics, the Academy of Athens, and the universities of St. Andrews, Lampeter, Oxford, and Cambridge. Many colleagues have provided advice and support over the course of this book's long gestation period. In particular we would like to thank: Justin Arft, Ettore (Willy Boy) Cingano, Erwin Cook, Casey Dué, Mary Ebbott, Marco Fantuzzi, Tom Hawkins, Malcolm Heath, Adrian Kelly, Kyriaki Konstantinidou,

Acknowledgements

Irini Kyriakou, David Larmour, Don Lavigne, Aleydis Van de Moortel, Sheila Murnaghan, Leonard Muellner, Chris Pelling, Benjamin Sammons, Matthew Santirocco, Giampiero Scafoglio, David Sider, Zoe Stamatopoulou, and Christos Tsagalis. We are extremely grateful also to Zachary Elliott and Taylor G. Mckinnon for their assistance with bibliography and editing. Taylor also helped to produce both indices. We have benefitted substantially from the institutional support and research assistance provided by Christ Church (Oxford), The Open University, New York University, the University of Texas at San Antonio, the University of Siena (Italy), the Center for Hellenic Studies, and Brandeis University. Finally, we owe a large debt to the CHS editorial team, especially Jill Curry Robbins and the rest of the production staff.

Finally, and most importantly, we are indebted to the patience, kindness, and love of our partners, Kyriaki and Shahnaaz, and to the inspiration and new life that we have gained from our children Maya, Aalia, and Iskander.

Note on Text and Translations

PASSAGES FROM THE HOMERIC POEMS are quoted from T.W. Allen's *editio maior* of the *Iliad* (1931) and P. Von der Mühll's Teubner *Odyssey* (1962) respectively. Those from Hesiod are from M. L. West's *Theogony* (1966), F. Solmsen's *Works and Days* (1970), and R. Merkelbach's and M. L. West's *Fragmenta Hesiodea* (1967). Quotations from the Theban fragments come from the editions of M. Davies (1988) and A. Bernabé (1996). Unless otherwise stated, translations are our own, for which we have generally opted for usefulness over elegance. In transliterating proper names we have used a hybrid system, preferring Latinized forms for names that are widely familiar but a more precise transliteration of the Greek for those less so: thus Achilles and Oedipus (rather than Akhilleus and Oidipous), but Kyknos and *The Ehoiai* (rather than Cycnus and *The Ehoeae*). We ask the reader's forbearance for any irregularities in this system (e.g. Herakles).

Introduction

Why Thebes?

You tell the events of Thebes,
he tells of the Phrygians' battle-shouts;
but I tell of my conquests.
No horse has destroyed me,
nor foot soldier, nor ships,
but another new army
strikes me from its eyes.

Anacreontea, fr. 26[1]

WHEN WE FIRST STARTED WORKING on this book, just over a decade ago, very little had been written on the topic of Theban epic and even less on Theban myth in Homer. Since then, however, in addition to our articles of 2008, 2011 and 2014, there has been a spate of publications on non-Homeric archaic Greek hexameter epic, encompassing both the other Trojan War poems (the so-called "epic cycle": West 2013; Fantuzzi and Tsagalis 2014; Davies 2016; cf. Burgess 2001) and the poems related to Thebes and Theban myth (Davies 2014; cf. Tsagalis 2008). As part of this burgeoning interest in Homer's epic rivals, the mythical archaeology of Thebes has come under particular scrutiny (e.g. Berman 2013; 2015), as well as the use of Theban myth in Homer (e.g. Tsagalis

---

[1] Σὺ μὲν λέγεις τὰ Θήβης,
ὃ δ' αὖ Φρυγῶν ἀυτάς,
ἐγὼ δ' ἐμὰς ἁλώσεις.
οὐχ ἵππος ὤλεσέν με,
οὐ πεζός, οὐχὶ νῆες,
στρατὸς δὲ καινὸς ἄλλος
ἀπ' ὀμμάτων με βάλλων.

All translations are our own.

2014), which is the central concern of this book. Given this proliferating bibliography, it is fair to ask: why Thebes, why now?

The city of Thebes has always been of interest to scholars working within mythographical and literary traditions, precisely because its presence looms large in our corpus of extant textual and especially non-textual sources. Looming even larger is the absence of a monumental epic to encapsulate its story in the manner that the *Iliad* and *Odyssey* do for the Troy story.[2] Myths set in Thebes or involving Theban characters occupy a significant portion of the surviving plays of Athenian tragedy (as well as testimonies of lost plays), and feature prominently in epinician and lyric poetry from the sixth and fifth centuries BCE. Yet none of the epics that purportedly detailed the strange origins under Cadmus, the labors of the Theban Herakles, and the two wars for the city walls have survived (save for a few unclear fragments). While the loss of Thebes' rich epic heritage may be put down to historical accident, given the city's importance in myth and history, the impact that these epics might have had continues to attract scholarly attention.

Some of this attention may be due to the absence itself—we love mysteries, and it is tempting to reframe the fragments that we do have in order to tell the stories that we want to hear about Thebes. In itself, however, this is insufficient to account for the refocusing of a critical lens onto the Theban epic over the past decade. In part, the renewed interest in Thebes relates to a trend in recent scholarship to reconsider fragmentary works more generally, especially with a view to paying due attention to their contextualization in, and reframing by, later sources. More importantly, however, the study of epic fragments has been revolutionized by oral theory. All examples of Greek hexameter epic poetry, whether the "complete" poems of Homer or Hesiod, or fragmentary remains from alternative traditions (such as those related to Thebes), as well as other performance-based poetry, like lyric or elegy, are now subject to analysis in terms of their shared language and motifs.

Before setting out this methodological approach in more detail below, we first want to consider Thebes' epic credentials. The clearest evidence for thinking about Thebes in epic terms comes from a passage of the *Works and Days* where Hesiod pairs Thebes with Troy (156–165):

> Αὐτὰρ ἐπεὶ καὶ τοῦτο γένος κατὰ γαῖα κάλυψεν,
> αὖτις ἔτ᾽ ἄλλο τέταρτον ἐπὶ χθονὶ πουλυβοτείρῃ
> Ζεὺς Κρονίδης ποίησε, δικαιότερον καὶ ἄρειον,
> ἀνδρῶν ἡρώων θεῖον γένος, οἳ καλέονται

---

[2] Willcock 1977:xi regrets the loss of *Thebais* precisely because it "would have provided the best of all possible parallels to the *Iliad*." On reconstructions of the Theban poems, see note 9 below.

2

ἡμίθεοι, προτέρη γενεὴ κατ' ἀπείρονα γαῖαν.
καὶ τοὺς μὲν πόλεμός τε κακὸς καὶ φύλοπις αἰνὴ
τοὺς μὲν ὑφ' ἑπταπύλῳ Θήβῃ, Καδμηίδι γαίῃ,
ὤλεσε μαρναμένους μήλων ἕνεκ'Οἰδιπόδαο,
τοὺς δὲ καὶ ἐν νήεσσιν ὑπὲρ μέγα λαῖτμα θαλάσσης
ἐς Τροίην ἀγαγὼν῾ Ἑλένης ἕνεκ' ἠυκόμοιο.

But when also this race he had hidden beneath the earth,
again still another, the fourth on the fruitful earth
Zeus the son of Cronos made, more just and brave,
a divine race of hero-men, who are called
semi-divine, the race prior to ours, throughout the boundless earth.
Evil war and dread battle destroyed them,
some at seven-gated Thebes in the land of Cadmus,
when they fought for the flocks of Oedipus,
others when it had led them in their ships over the great deep sea
to Troy for lovely-haired Helen.

This passage has long been recognized as disrupting Hesiod's depiction of a cosmic fall from grace, which charts a serial decline from a golden age society of easy living and righteous behavior to the present day world of his audience, an "iron age" characterized by hard graft and corruption. Prior to his description of that world, Hesiod inserts "a divine race of hero-men, who are called semi-divine" (ἀνδρῶν ἡρώων θεῖον γένος, οἳ καλέονται / ἡμίθεοι). Here, Thebes and Troy are paired as a way of denoting this heroic age, as the sites where major conflicts took place. These conflicts, while bearing witness to the characteristic feature of this age—men who were "more just and brave"—also have the instrumental effect of wiping out the race of heroes, which leaves the world populated by mere mortal men. This grim existence of having to scrape out a living is the scenario envisaged and explored in the *Works and Days*. Hesiod's poem, then, provides a cosmological frame for thinking about the "generation of hero men" and their relation to the world of the present, where there are no more heroes anymore.

At the same time this passage suggests a metapoetic reflection on, and rivalry with, heroic epic as a genre. One of the few remaining fragments from the so-called heroic epic poem the *Cypria*, apparently from its proem, sets out how Zeus planned to rid the world of heroes through conflict at Troy, in order to relieve Earth of her burden of men (fr. 1.4: κουφίσαι ἀνθρώπων παμβώτορα σύνθετο γαῖαν). While the *Iliad*'s proem is conspicuously less explicit, there are hints of such a narrative in the reference to Zeus' plan, the focus on conflict (between Achilles and Agamemnon), and the description of the myriad souls of heroes being sent to Hades (*Iliad* 1.1-9)—heroes here being almost a generic marker for this kind of epic (ἡρώων, 4).[3] Later on, at more or less the midpoint of the poem, Homer pans back from the fighting to situate his narrative of the fall of Troy in the context of the disappearance of this heroic world, using the striking description of "semi-divine" (ἡμίθεοι). We say "striking" because the only other occurrence of ἡμίθεοι in the whole of the hexameter epic corpus is in our passage from Hesiod, where it serves to delineate further the generation of heroes. This "divine race of hero men" (ἀνδρῶν ἡρώων θεῖον γένος) turns out to be only *semi*-divine (ἡμίθεοι); that is to say, crucially, these heroes are mortal.[4] This is the point of the passage in Hesiod, which, as we have seen, describes their annihilation at Thebes and Troy; it is also the force of the passage in the *Iliad*, where Homer describes the action of his epic from the perspective of a much later age when the heroes of Troy are dead and buried. Along with the evidence from the fragment of the *Cypria*, the impression is that heroic epic, as a genre, not only celebrated the great deeds of men but also dramatized the destruction of the race of heroes, as if part of some broader evolutionary narrative.

What that broader evolutionary system might look like has been articulated by Barbara Graziosi and Johannes Haubold who have shown how Homer's *Iliad* and *Odyssey* fit into a putative cosmic history mapped out by four extant hexameter epic poems. This history begins with Hesiod's *Theogony*, which describes the origins of the cosmos itself (including the birth of the gods) and explains how Zeus came to rule supreme (and will rule forever); it culminates in the *Works and Days*, which provides an epic view of ordinary life in its divine framing of the human business of working hard and pursuing justice.[5] In between these two poles are the Homeric poems. The *Iliad* covers the story of the end of the "race of heroes." What is important here is that the *Iliad* is not only set in the now bygone heroic era; to a certain extent it also *accounts for* its destruction. Through its protagonist Achilles, the *Iliad* charts a movement from a world full of gods to a world of men. The poem's first movement is dominated by "godlike Achilles," especially his interaction with a number of divine figures. In Achilles' final appearance, it is his status as "the son of Peleus" to which Priam appeals and by which he contemplates their common mortality; the gods are conspicuously absent (since even the boundary-crossing Hermes recuses himself from

---

[3] On ways of reading the connection between the proems of the *Iliad* and *Cypria* (such as it survives), see: Finkelberg 2000; Marks 2002; Barker 2008.

[4] The use of ἡμίθεοι in conjunction with heroes in Hesiod may be charged: Nagy 1999 [1979]:159-160, who argues that "semi-divine" is "more appropriate to a style that looks beyond epic." See Haubold 2000:4-8 for limitations on the "hero" as leader in Homer.

[5] Graziosi and Haubold 2005. Cf. Clay 2003; and Mackie 2008:34-40.

the scene); the poem itself ends with the burial of this other, very mortal hero, Hektor. Along the way, we see Achilles slaughter countless numbers of Trojans, who (we are led to be believe for the first time in the war) have only been enticed out of their walls by his initial absence and a mistaken belief that Zeus now favored them. By the poem's end, then, the fate not only of Troy but also of the heroes who fought there is sealed. That is not to say that some heroes do not make it home: the *Odyssey* picks up the tales of those who did. But, as this poem shows, they have to undergo a kind of transformation to make it home. The *Odyssey* begins this process with its very first word—this poem will be about the *man* (ἄνδρα, 1.1) Odysseus. It continues with a pared-back divine apparatus that casts into relief human agency and responsibility. In turn, its investigation of what constitutes appropriate behavior for mortals is picked up by the intense interrogation of justice in Hesiod's *Works and Days*.[6]

Whether poems about Thebes similarly situated their narratives within such a cosmological framework is impossible to say in the light of the fragmentary remains, but this question and the related issue about the degree of their Panhellenic appeal is a concern to this book for a very good reason. Hesiod's passage clearly pairs Thebes and Troy in the destruction of the race of heroes. The pairing is not limited to the idea of these two cities as the sites of total war, where the heroes perished. Given what we have just said about the *Iliad*'s depiction of the Trojan War and the *Odyssey*'s post-war vision, to pair the two cities is also suggestive of comparable narrative traditions, as if we should expect heroic epics about Thebes (which we don't have) as well as those about Troy (which we do). From a Hesiodic perspective, then, the wars and traditions about Troy and Thebes are notionally equivalent, in that they both serve to relate the extinction of this former race of heroes. It is also true that the two cities share a certain cognitive distance. In Hesiod they already exist on the margins of time, as if belonging to the (already) doomed race of heroes. In later performance contexts, too, Troy and Thebes enjoy a degree of separation from their audiences: where Troy is the city that is forever doomed to fall, Thebes is the city that is forever under siege.[7] Thus, although only fragments of a Theban tradition remain, in contrast to the tradition of the Troy story represented for us by the *Iliad* and *Odyssey*,[8] these fragments tend to be grouped together to form functionally equivalent epics. The resulting poems—namely the *Oedipodea*,

---

[6] For justice in Homer and Hesiod, see the classic debate between Adkins 1970 and Lloyd-Jones 1971, recently revisited by Allan 2006.

[7] See Zeitlin 1986 and Chapter 6, "Burying the Seven and Heroic Remains," below. Troy's non-Greekness may have facilitated its adoption and popularity: see Easterling 2005:57 and further in Chapter 6 below.

[8] For the fragments, cf. Chapter 4, 28–42.

Thebais, Epigonoi, and *Alcmeonis*—are reconstructed from later representations (especially tragedy), references in works of historiography, comments of the scholastic tradition, and the story patterns of Homer's epics.[9]

One pressing issue for us has been how to negotiate such a notional equivalence of these two cities, when it is only Homer's poems about the war at Troy and the return home that have survived. If Hesiod's invocation of the cities of Thebes and Troy were the only pairing of these two cities, it might be possible to understand it as merely a broad reference to a heroic mythical past. But the cities—and their attendant motifs—are compared and contrasted throughout early Greek poetry. Pindar, for example, pairs the marriages of Cadmus-Harmonia and Peleus-Thetis (*Pythian* 3.86–105) as golden-age unions that precipitate the wars of heroic extinction around Thebes and Troy. Anacreon, too, (fr. 26 cited above) contrasts the affairs at Thebes (τὰ Θήβης) and the wars in Phrygia (Φρυγῶν αὐτάς) with his own non-martial poetry (ἐμάς). In Attic tragedy, Thebes is established as the "other" city always under siege, a counterpoint to Troy, the city always sacked. At the same time, however, it may well be mistaken to consider Hesiod's association of Thebes and Troy, at any rate, as a pairing of equal members. As we will discuss later in the book (e.g. Chapters 4 and 5), early Greek poetry often provides lists and doublets that culminate in the most significant entry—a case of last is better. Here, Hesiod's diction and presentation does little to betray that one city may be more important than the other apart from the sequencing that positions Helen's Troy as coming after Oedipus' Thebes. What is interesting, as we shall see (e.g. Chapters 2, 3 and 4), is that the temporal priority of the Theban conflict is consistently exploited by the Homeric poems to lend greater weight and significance to the events around Troy.[10] What Thebes had started—the destruction of the race of heroes—Troy finishes off. Or, to put that differently, Thebes is insufficient to do the job itself.

A brief survey of the use of the name and label "Thebes" in the *Iliad* serves to show the underlying importance of this city to Homer, or, perhaps better, the anxiety felt in this narrative about an epic siege of (another story of) another epic siege. It will also help to anticipate the content and form of the approach that we follow in this book (cf. Barker and Christensen 2011). When Agamemnon describes the walls of Thebes as "sacred" (ἱερὰ τείχεα Θήβης, 4.378), his words evoke descriptions elsewhere in the *Iliad* of other walls and other cities. The

---

[9]   Pausanias even claims that the *Thebais* was best, after the *Iliad* and the *Odyssey* (Pausanias IX 9.5). For reconstructions of the Theban epic tradition see Davies 2014; cf. Cingano 1992, 2000, and 2004. For the suggestion that there were multiple epics about Thebes: Wehrli 1957; Torres-Guerra 1995a and 1995b; cf. Huxley 1969. On the *Thebais*'s place in the construction of an "epic cycle," see Burgess 2001.

[10] On Theban myth in the Homeric tradition, see Barker and Christensen 2008: 2011 and Nagy 1990:414–416; see also Ebbott 2010:240–242; Arft 2014.

epithet "sacred" is used most often in the *Iliad* to denote the city of Troy itself: its use here by Agamemnon might indicate poetic tension, especially since elsewhere in extant poetry Thebes *is* described by this epithet.[11] Clearly, Thebes can be described, like Troy, as being a "sacred" city. Yet the one time when *a* Thebes is described as sacred in the *Iliad*, it is another city altogether. As early as book 1 Achilles declares that he has sacked Thebes—but this is neither Boiotian Thebes nor the similarly famous Egyptian Thebes, but Thebê, "the sacred city of Eetion" (Θήβην, ἱερὴν πόλιν Ἠετίωνος, *Iliad* 1.366). The immediate qualification suggests Homer's care in defining this city for his audience. This *other* "Thebes" is further elaborated in book 6 when Andromache describes its sack by Achilles and the death of her father, the aforementioned Eetion (*Iliad* 6.414–20). Significantly, Andromache's description of this Thebes also includes the epithet "lofty-gated" (Θήβην ὑψίπυλον), which is used otherwise *only* of Troy.[12] The redeployment of Thebes' epithet as "sacred" to denote another (not) Thebes, the elevation of that other (not) Thebes to the lofty heights of Troy, and its sack (already) by the hero of this narrative, all suggest a sustained assault by the *Iliad* on its rival city-under-seige.

There is a further significance underlying the description of Troy and Thebes as "lofty-gated" (ὑψίπυλος) and holy (ἱερή). Both terms would seem to suggest security, either physical (as in gates that are high and difficult to breach) or conceptual (as in cities that come under the protection of the gods). Yet that is not how these terms are deployed in the *Iliad*. As Corinne Pache has observed, the adjective "high-gated" (ὑψίπυλος) is used in the *Iliad* *only* in the context of the *sacking of a city*, either in fact, as with Andromache's Thebes (6.416), or in intention, as with Troy (the gods prevent its actual sack in this poem: 16.698 and 21.544). Furthermore, while the epithet "holy" applies to a number of cities (including Plakaian Thebes, as we have seen), the only two cities to have walls that are specifically described as "holy" are Troy and Boiotian Thebes, when Agamemnon recalls how Tydeus gathered men to attack

---

[11] Kirk 1985:369 *ad* 378 notes, "The walls of Thebes are 'holy', according to T because they had been built through the power of Amphion's lyre; but more probably because ἱερός is a conventional epithet applied fairly indiscriminately to different places (primarily to Troy, cf. Ἴλιος ἴρη (etc.), 20x *Il*., but also e.g. to Euboea at 2.535)." In the *Homeric Hymn to Apollo* the description of "holy Thebes" (ἱερῇ ἐνὶ Θήβῃ, 426) seems to refer to a pre-populated site of the famous city—a pre-epic Thebes, as it were, when gods still frequented the world of men. Cf. the "sacred city" (ἱερὸν ἄστυ) of Thebes mentioned in athletic victor epigram of the third century BCE (Ebert 1972, no. 64, 7). Quintus of Smyrna refers to the "famous city of Thebes" (Θήβης κλυτὸν ἄστυ, 4.544).

[12] It occurs in a repeated contrary-to-fact proposition: "Then the sons of the Achaeans would have taken *lofty-gated* Troy [had not]" (Ἔνθά κεν ὑψίπυλον Τροίην ἕλον υἷες Ἀχαιῶν, *Iliad* 16.698 = 21.544). Tsagalis 2008:21–22 attributes the use of the epithet ὑψίπολις for Andromache's Thebes to the influence of seven-gated (Boiotian) Thebes, since "Hypoplakian Thebes was an unimportant and small city, which could not have been famous for being 'high-gated' (ὑψίπυλος)" (21).

"the sacred walls of Thebes" (ἱερὰ τείχεα Θήβης, *Iliad* 4.378). "The holiness of the city walls," Pache writes, "provides no protection and is brought into play at a city's most distressing moments."[13] The same point emerges from the description of Thebes in the Catalogue of Ships as "the strong-founded citadel" (ἐϋκτίμενον πτολίεθρον, *Iliad* 2.505). This account is already curious in that it is "*lower* Thebes" ('Υποθήβας) which is described—as if Thebes were the city-that-ought-not-to-be-named. This Hypothebai, which must refer to the settlement "below the city" that survived the sack of the Epigonoi, is nevertheless described as "well built." For Geoffrey Kirk, the epithet "well-built" (ἐϋκτίμενος) "does not accord with a particularly low status for Hupothebai, but seems to be applied somewhat arbitrarily."[14] As Pache argues, however, its application is far from arbitrary, since, "as in Andromache's description of her own fallen city of Placaean Thebes as 'high-gated,' 'well-built' lower Thebes also calls our attention to what once was but is no longer there… The epithet ἐϋκτίμενος thus calls attention not to the present condition of Hypothebai, but to the glorious past of Thebes and the ominous fall of its supposedly impregnable walls."[15]

Thus deeply embedded in the imagery and very language of heroic epic poetry is the memory of these two cities, Troy and Thebes. Their well-built, lofty, and holy epithets serve as reminders of their previous security and sanctity and bring their current predicament to the fore. Or, rather, in Homer they serve to commemorate Thebes' (already complete) fall and anticipate Troy's (endlessly deferred) sack. The picture is further complicated by the *Iliad*'s marginalization of Thebes through the substitution of an alternative Thebes (Plakaian) and the supplement of another (Hypothebai).

The ultimate replacement of Thebes as a city (worthy) of epic song may also be behind the *Iliad*'s redeployment of these epithets in the first place. Troy's place in the tradition as "holy" is explained in its foundational story, where king Laomedon contracted Apollo and Poseidon to build the city's defenses.[16] Thebes' defensive constructions were arguably even more famous: its walls and seven gates function as a metonym of its fame and the stories of the wars that surrounded it.[17] As Singor 1992 has shown, the *Iliad* inverts the logic of the Trojan tale by depicting the Achaeans constructing a wall around their ships, with the result that it is the besieging Achaeans who become the besieged. The fact that the Achaean wall is conceived and built during the course of the

---

[13] Pache 2014:283, 285.

[14] Kirk 1985:194.

[15] Pache 2014:284.

[16] For the building of the walls by the gods, see Pindar *Olympian* 8.30–46; Hellanicus *FGrHist* 4 F 2 and Metrodorus of Chios, fr. 3 (=Schol. Gen. ad *Iliad* 21.444). Cf. Apollodorus 2.103.

[17] Pache 2014:291 suggests that the seven Achaeans sent against the Trojans recall the seven gates and champions of Thebes (ἕπτ᾽ ἔσαν ἡγεμόνες φυλάκων, *Iliad* 9.85).

narrative (indeed, in one night, it seems) is suggestive of a motif that is not germane to the war at Ilium but a conceit of the *Iliad*. Indeed, its presence in the Troy tradition is specifically limited to this poem: not only does Apollo breach it like a child kicking over a sandcastle; when Homer pans out to situate his poem in epic history, we are told that the wall was destroyed without trace by the pro-Achaean Poseidon in anger at the Achaeans' lack of sacrifices (in a replay of his "original" anger at Laomedon's foundation of Troy).[18] If we already suspect that the trope of the Achaeans under seige belongs to a Theban tradition, the fact that this hastily constructed wall is at one point specified as having "seven" gates—like the famous wall of Thebes—would seem to confirm the *Iliad*'s sack of Thebes and ransacking of its motifs. The *Iliad*'s challenge to Thebes is not so much through the wall itself as through the narrative sleight of hand, in which the fame of the Theban wall is repurposed to magnify the stakes of this version of the Trojan War, where the Achaeans' very survival seems at stake.

It is clear from the *Iliad* and the *Odyssey* that the pairing of Thebes and Troy was not simply a feature of Hesiod's cosmic history. Homer's epics also appear to have intimate knowledge of events around Thebes.[19] Unlike most critics working with the references to Thebes, we are not intent on determining whether or not this knowledge comes from a lost Theban epic (or epics) or from a diffusion of Theban mythical material in multiple poetic genres and artistic forms over time.[20] Nor are we interested in relating these references to the remaining fragments of hexameter poetry from a purported Theban epic tradition for the purpose of reconstructing poems along the lines of Homer's. Other readers have done much to shed light on the possible content and themes of such nominal epics; our stance on the remnants of Theban epic remains decidedly agnostic. Not only do we not know for certain which Theban details were available for ancient audiences of Homer, we cannot be sure that they were presented in an epic form comparable to our *Iliad* and *Odyssey*.

Our response to the question *Why Thebes?*, then, is to assert that the references to this city's history in Homer's poems can help us better understand the epics about Troy. Accordingly, the chief concern of this book will be to investigate what the use of Theban material in the Homeric epics tells us

---

[18] See Clay 2011:59; cf. Pache 2014:293.

[19] See West 2012:29: "The way [the *Iliad*] refers to subsidiary episodes of the [Theban] saga suggests knowledge of an ample epic narrative, and there are certain lines that [it] may have adapted from [its] source." For the Homeric agonistic awareness of Theban traditions, see Pache 2014:295–296. Sammons 2014:297 remarks that it is striking that the references to Theban myths are restricted in scope. Ebbott 2010 compares the references to Theban myths (for her, the epics) to broken "hyperlinks" (cf. Ebbott 2014:319–320).

[20] For this question, see Tsagalis 2014:239–246 who concludes that oral epics were "known" to "Homer". Cf. Pache 2014; *contra*, Burgess 2009:61–70.

about *Homeric poetics*; that is, we are interested in identifying and exploring the strategies the *Iliad* and *Odyssey* employ both to develop their own themes and to distinguish themselves from rival mythological and poetic traditions. We do not deny that stories about Thebes may have explored common themes and issues shared with our epics, perhaps even in similar ways—indeed, we make a stab at identifying and discussing what some of those themes and issues might have been in Chapter 4. But our premise is that the Homeric poems selectively (re)present Theban narratives and (re)deploy Theban references in ways that amplify their own pre-eminence. In this way, our primary aim is to explore what the use of Theban myth within Homeric epic can tell us about that tradition's view of its own mythic past—how, in other words, Homeric poetry uses other story traditions to tell its own tales. As such, this book is not truly about Theban myth; rather, it is about the strategies and aesthetics of Homeric poetry. This is *Homer's* Thebes.

Still, why talk about Thebes in Homer *now*? After all, while new research has done much to bring to light (or, at any rate, bring together) hexameter fragments of Theban material, the references to Thebes in Homer are well recognized and have been in plain view since the fixation of the poems themselves. The answer lies in the growing maturity and progressive alignment of two strands of Homeric scholarship—the oral theory of Parry and Lord and the idea of poetic competition. Over the past decade the study of epic poetry has been revitalized by a focus on the ways in which meaning is generated in each oral performance both by drawing on a long established repertoire of phrases, scenes and stories ("traditional referentiality") and by playing off it for particular effect ("agonistics"). Our work enters the debate by focusing on the importance of oral-traditional poetics and poetic rivalry for thinking about the use of Thebes within Homer's poems. Indeed, we believe that an investigation of Homeric poetics, as informed by its use of other narrative traditions, can shed new light on the poetic culture that helped decisively shape the epics we have received from antiquity. By presenting a series of case studies, this book probes how much we can say about the imperfectly known contexts of Homeric performance based on the evidence internal to the poems themselves. In particular, we will be concerned to read Homer's Theban representations vis-à-vis the often cited, but little investigated, contemporary Panhellenic developments that were taking place in the period of the Homeric poems' likely composition.

In the rest of this introduction we set out the literary and cultural perspectives that frame our work. To begin with, we discuss the various ways in which scholars have approached reading Homeric epic in the wake of the oral-formulaic theory introduced and advanced by Milman Parry and Albert Lord. While recent studies applying the models of allusion, neoanalysis, and intertextuality have all made contributions to our understanding of Homer's poems, we make the case that traditional referentiality and resonance can better bring to light the strategies each poem employs in dealing with Thebes. In the second part, we discuss the cultural phenomena of competition and Panhellenism that we see as most pertinent for understanding the development of Homeric poetry in its negotiation of Thebes. Such cultural features operated alongside, and shaped the conditions of, the performance of Greek epic. In particular, as we discuss throughout this book, the relationship between the poetic traditions centered around Thebes and Troy was framed and defined by agonism; in turn, the cultural forces of Panhellenism helped to sharpen poetic competition, and, as we will argue in the final chapters, were in part responsible for Troy's ultimate eclipse of Thebes.

Methodologies

It is *de rigueur* to start a book on early Greek hexameter poetry with an outline of the assumptions that underpin what one means when writing "Homer." In this section that is what we will attempt to do, although we believe that—no matter the particular theoretical position that one holds—a great deal of the work on *interpreting* Homer is reconcilable, as Malcolm Willcock suggested over two decades ago.[21] It has been one of our advantages as collaborators that over our years of working together we have changed our minds about the Homeric question (and rarely at the same time or in the same direction). Such a tension has forced us to keep in mind different ways of thinking about Homer—from being an individual poet working within, to being a metonym representing an authoritative retelling of, the tradition of Troy—and to conceptualize the issues at stake with greater clarity. There remain ways in which what one believes about the nature of the epics and their composition has an impact on what we (can) say about the poems and how we (can) say it. While we do not wish to get bogged down with trying to resolve irresolvable questions of authorship, this introduction needs to consider both the cultural background upon which Homer's poems draw and the terminology that we use to explore how they function.

In our first work on this subject (Barker and Christensen 2008:2–9), we emphasized two broad trends in the study of Homer. One treats Homer as an author-genius in much the same way as one would a Herman Melville or Ezra Pound, following the ancient biographical tradition which posits "Homer" alternately as having temporal and/or cultural priority over his rivals (see on

---

[21] Willcock 1997:175; cf. Kelly 2012:221 for a nod to this before an assertion that the stakes still matter.

allusion and neoanalysis below). The other, which lays more emphasis on the "traditional" nature of the Homeric poems and the importance of oral poetics, presents a range of "Homers" of varying degree of fixity and textuality (see on traditional referentiality). The implied polarity is a somewhat artificial one, but the range of current interpretive responses to Homer makes it more pressing to distinguish one perspective from another.

Our first assumption when approaching the Homeric epics, following John Miles Foley and others, is that the epics are "orally-derived"—their composition betrays elements of the spoken word, such as repeated formulae, type scenes, and linear narration.[22] It is the quality and extent of this orality that is often at issue in interpretations.[23] On the one hand, the "textuality" of the epics cannot be denied: at some point the Homeric poems were recorded in writing and subsequently passed on as written texts, which is the form in which we have received them (albeit via a long and precarious tradition of physical transmission very different from our own: the manuscript codex). On the other hand, we understand these texts as having been repeated in performance long before they reached the form we have now. Such different layers of textuality—from the putative recitation of oral performance to the material reproducibility of the written word—can constitute the primary interest of academic investigations of epic. This, however, is not at all our foremost concern. Instead, we are mainly interested in what the texts we have *do* with the material they treat as part of the past.

In accepting the *Iliad* and the *Odyssey* as oral-derived texts, we must also face hotly debated issues around conventional versus intentional meaning as well as oral versus literary aesthetics. Throughout our work on these topics over the years we have returned to Foley's theory of "traditional referentiality" and the idea of "resonance" as articulated by Barbara Graziosi and Johannes Haubold 2005. There are two primary reasons why we believe that these approaches are the most appropriate means for addressing the question of how the Theban references in the Homeric poems work. The first concerns the relationship between a particular instantiation of a story and its larger storytelling traditions. As we noted before, stories set around Troy and Thebes share what Jonathan Burgess has called a "mythological substructure."[24] This means that they draw from familiar language, motifs, and themes for sometimes very different ends. The

---

[22] For the term "oral-derived" see Foley 1988. Cf. Martin 1989:1–8 for a concise articulation of the importance of recognizing the orality and performance culture of the epics.

[23] See Arft and Foley 2015:10–15 for an overview of the complex relationship between literacy and orality in artistic production.

[24] Burgess 2001:3. On this, see also Arft 2014:399–400 whose re-articulation of traditional referentiality has been useful. Cf. Foley and Arft 2015.

second relates, as Foley and Justin Arft have written, to the idea that individual poems emerge from larger traditions as "instances" not "artifacts" (2015). Only once they are transcribed do they become artifactual, at which point they should be treated both as oral poems *and* as fixed texts; that is, they present additional layers of interpretive complexity because they carry the echoic associations of multiple oral performances, while at the same time also constituting for us as readers the physical fixity of a single text. Such tensions were likely latent for the first "readers" of the poems who were also exposed to living oral traditions; as modern interpreters, we must labor intensely to develop approximate understandings of the effects of the poems' oralities, while also remaining vigilant and attentive to the opportunities afforded by our own literacies.

This is not to say that other approaches, which treat Homer's poems as *literature*—in the sense of having been composed in writing as fixed texts, and referencing other fixed texts—have little to contribute; on the contrary, what might be thought of as "conventional" literary criticism of Homer has produced some of the most enlightening and thought-provoking analyses of the poems. Nevertheless, we have found that taking the claims of oral theory seriously has forced us to confront our own assumptions when "reading" an oral poem; it has certainly helped us listen to Homer's recasting of Thebes in new and productive ways. Before explaining in more detail what our understanding of oral theory looks like and how it might function in practice, we first give a brief overview of different literary approaches to Homer in order to identify some of the assumptions underpinning them and their influence on interpretation.[25]

Allusion

In a recent book, Bruno Currie has responded to the renewed emphasis on the orality of Homer by reasserting the importance of allusion (cf. Currie 2006), on the basis that "individual poems may be fixed enough to serve as an object of allusion."[26] For Currie, it is possible to identify moments when one literary artifact refers directly—or *alludes*—to another, even within traditional art forms like oral-derived poems, "when they involve elements that appear to be typical or

---

[25] For discussion of these methods with an emphasis on motif transference, see Burgess 2006. For a brief overview of the terms used, see Edmunds 2016:1–8; cf. the very in-depth presentation of Currie 2016:4–38.

[26] Currie 2016:12. Shortly afterwards Currie offers a somewhat bewildering circularity: "If fixed texts are a precondition for specific, unidirectional allusion, so the demonstration of specific, unidirectional allusion, if it can be made, will imply the presence of fixed texts in this tradition. In short, nothing prohibits us from believing in discrete and sufficiently stable poems, some of which would be capable of alluding to others, rather than multiform 'traditions' reciprocally influencing each other throughout the archaic period" (2016:16).

non-formulaic."[27] It is not our object here to contest Currie's analysis point by point; individually, his detailed study helpfully draws attention to some of the ways in which Homer's poems intersect and interact with potential rivals. It is the premise itself, which refers to this engagement as allusion, that, to our minds, seems ill-founded and misleading.. For one thing, his definition of allusion relies on *argumenta ex silentio*—how can we know which repeated elements are not typical or non-formulaic, when so little of this kind of (hexameter heroic epic) poetry survive? For another, to think in terms of allusion is to posit not only a direct and intentional relationship between two texts, but also to establish a hierarchical relationship, with one text (the "target" for the allusion) made prior to the other (the "source" of the allusion).

This second point refers to the idea of allusion as it is often conceptualized within general literary theory, when applied to *literature*—works that are self-consciously written down as texts and written within a literary-based (reading) culture—outside of the Homeric poems. Here allusion tends to mean the direct and intentional quotation of or reference to a motif or even phrase from an earlier text/author by a specific author.[28] As such we find it problematic to apply allusion to Homer for at least two reasons. First, since we have no certain evidence for the content of "texts" prior to the Homeric epics, and no evidence for a cultural tradition of intentional allusion, allusion is aesthetically an anachronistic concept with which to think about oral poetry (though it can still be useful heuristically for identifying and thinking through different kinds of intertextual relations).[29] Second, the emphasis that it places on direct reference between two texts (text B is referring to text A) and intentionality (author B is deliberately referring to author A) seems particularly ill-suited to the dynamics of oral-derived poetry, no matter what one thinks about the idea of intentionality as a useful heuristic device for literary analysis more generally. What we mean is that, so far as one is able to tell from comparative analysis, oral poetry—which we can define more broadly as works that are composed in performance before an audience—places greater demands on the audience to recognize the intertextual relations and (re)construct meaning from it.

Figure 1.1 below is our attempt to provide a schematic representation of how allusion works. While undoubtedly over-simplistic, we find it helpful for drawing attention to how allusion takes insufficient account of the critical

---

[27] Currie 2016:11. Cf. Currie 2006:5. Currie draws on the neoanalytical work of Usener 1990:7–8; Kullman 1960 and the typological studies of Fenik 1968. For a criticism of this, see Kelly 2012:228: "the targeted element is still to be isolated from normal Homeric usage in order to reveal its 'interaction' with another text/poem."

[28] For allusion and intention, with critiques of the stance, see Hinds 1998:47–51; Heath 2002:59–97.

[29] Cf. Fowler 2000:116 for the objection that allusion limits what a reader can do; cf. Lyne 1994:187; and Barker and Christensen 2006:12–13.

contribution of audience to meaning-making, assumes a fixed text with an intentional author for Homeric poetry, and also posits a reference to a more or less fixed prior text.

Allusion, as a manner of understanding the technique of an author and/ or the cultural framework for artistic production, can play an important role in interpretation if the critic has these rather limited goals. But, by placing the emphasis on authorial intent, it ignores altogether the importance of audiences in the process of (re)constituting the text. As such it seems to us insufficient as a theoretical approach for thinking about Homer.

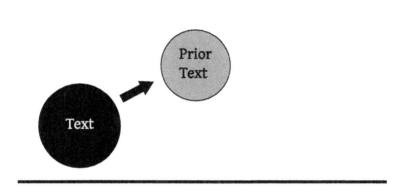

Figure 1.1. Allusion: 'Text' refers to a prior 'text' (by authorial design).

Neoanalysis

Allusion, insofar as it assumes a particular reference in one text to another particular text, has long been of interest to neoanalysis.[30] As Currie notes, allusion appears to be specifically focused on issues of poetics—how a specific poet does a specific thing—whereas neoanalysis writ large embraces mythological frameworks, typologies, motif transference, and issues of structure (2016:23). But the basic artistic assumptions that attend allusion are also central to neoanalysis: as a general rule, adherents of the approach have used rigorous textual

---

[30] For an expanded version of neoanalysis, see Currie 2016:22–29. On this, cf. Edmunds 2016:31. For examples of neoanalysis, see Kakridis 1949 and 1971; Kullman 1960 with an overview in Willcock 1997:174–189. Cf. Danek 1998; Currie 2006. On its contributions to the analysis of Homer more generally, see e.g. Burgess 2001; Montanari, Rengakos, and Tsagalis 2011. For a discussion of the creation of an earlier scene as a source for the *Iliad*, see Tsagalis 2008:239–271 on Thetis' lament and the broader tradition. Marks 2008:9–11 criticizes neoanalysis for a diachronic approach that betrays a "source and recipient model" (10).

criticism along with insights from oral theory to argue that other epics were known to the composer(s) of the *Iliad* and *Odyssey* and were influential in shaping their forms.[31]

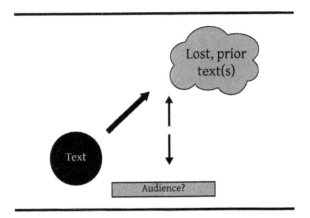

Figure 1.2. Neoanalytical Allusion: Intentional reference to
a prior text known to audience.

Initially, then, neoanalysis may appear somewhat more promising than conventional literary approaches, since it attempts to explain the source of problematic material independently of the Homeric text and thereby provide new perspectives on the ways in which the Homeric poems are crafted. Indeed, neoanalysis has been important for challenging the assumption that grants priority to Homer, and for drawing attention to the broader background to the Homeric poems. Even so, while neoanalytical studies have identified patterns repeated in the Homeric epics and (lost) texts in ways that have improved our understanding of Homeric structure, composition and aesthetics, nevertheless, their overall aim remains the establishment of the priority of one tradition over another.[32] (See Figure 1.2, opposite, for an image of neoanayltical modelling. The broken arrow indicates an unknown relationship between the act of "transference" and audience reception.) That is to say, the relationship between these oral poems is still configured in terms of a set hierarchy (e.g. the *Aithiopis* as prior to the *Iliad*) with a direct (and intentional) one-to-one mapping between

---

[31] "Oral theory gave neoanalysis a way to explain how Cyclic poems, generally agreed to have been recorded in written form after the *Iliad* was recorded, could have been the source of motifs in the *Iliad*." Edmunds 2016:5. Cf. Tsagalis 2008:67, 135. Kelly 2007:12n42 notes the possible uses of neoanalytical readings in oral-based inquiry. On the kind of neoanalytical reading that has much to offer oral theory, see Danek 1998.

[32] Kelly 2012:227 suggests that for the most part with neoanalysts "the aim is still to establish the priority of the non-Homeric material."

them (e.g. in its representation of the death of Hektor, the *Iliad* refers directly to the *Aithiopis*'s depiction of the death of Memnon). In addition, as Jonathan Burgess has noted, the complex system of "precise correspondences" identified by many neoanalytical arguments does not survive intact if "we drop the assumption that epic intertextuality was implemented through texts" (2009:61).[33] The level of specificity and correspondence assumed by neoanalytical studies relies on levels of fixity and repetition characteristic of literary texts and not oral traditions.

Intertextuality

Faced by the intractable problem of the so-called intentional fallacy, many literary critics have preferred a different method (and term) to mark the interplay between two texts without positing either authorial intention or a source-recipient model. Intertextuality is the theory that attempts to describe the relationship between two (or more) texts, without implying priority of one over the other or an author consciously making that connection (and asserting how it should be interpreted) themselves. Until recently, explicit articulations of intertextuality in the realm of classical studies had largely been restricted to Latin literature: it is no coincidence that the rich evidence supplied by the late Roman Republic and early Principate of a highly literate and referential literary culture should prove amenable to applications of this particular theoretical method.[34] More recently, however, "intertextuality" as a term to describe the cross-reference or even "quoting" (Tsagalis 2008:xii) between different types of hexameter epic material has gained traction. Whereas in 1987 Pietro Pucci radically (for the time) talked about the intertextuality of the *Iliad* and *Odyssey* (specifically where the *Odyssey* seems to be engaging self-consciously with an *Iliad* precedent), the method is now applied to similar references and topoi among lost traditions (like those of the epic cycle) and myth in general.[35] As Currie again notes, the evolutionary development of Homeric epic as posited by Gregory Nagy (and others), although "incompatible with unidirectional allusion, remains accommodating to a very differently conceived bidirectional intertextuality" (2016:17).[36] Such "bidirectionality" is, indeed, significant—but the oral background provides for much more than that.

---

[33] Burgess (1997; 2015) is even less positive about Homeric quotation of lost epic poems, but he remains impressed with the typological and motif-transference contributions of what he refers to as "post-neoanalysis," in particular the work of Kullmann 1960.

[34] E.g. Fowler 2000 and Lyne 1994.

[35] For intertextuality in Homer, in addition to Pucci 1987, see Rutherford 2001; Schein 2002; Currie 2006:7–15; Burgess 2009:56–71.

[36] Cf. Bakker 2015:158. On Nagy's evolutionary model, see Ch. 6 nn7 and 90.

It is often the case that Homerists conflate the terms allusion and intertext (as we ourselves have been guilty of in prior work), which can result in somewhat dizzying and none-too-distinct academic prose. In attempting to reconcile neoanalysis, allusion, and intertextuality, Jonathan Burgess pointedly writes: "Whereas classic neoanalysis has reserved discernment of motif transference to the scholar, it is more probable that the reflection would be recognized by a mythologically informed audience. In this case, motif transference is more than coincidental, casual, or merely vestigial. It is significant allusion, at least in the matter that oral intertextuality can be understood in the Archaic Age" (2009:71). Burgess, here, makes a salient point and, incidentally, demonstrates that Homerists will frequently refer to the same phenomena with different language. He credits the contributions of neoanalysis by shifting the responsibility for meaning making from the scholar sniffing out arcana to the ancient audience steeped in mythological narratives. Here, the "allusion" is the indication of that other tradition, the transference of motif that increases meaning.

In his work on the Trojan War in myth, Burgess has positioned Homeric epic as a particularly "self-conscious" version of "cyclic myth and cyclic epic" (2006:148–149).[37] Such self-consciousness is, as Margalit Finkelberg 1998:154–155 and Christos Tsagalis 2008:xii suggest, perhaps a unique characteristic of the Homeric epics.[38] (Given the lack of available evidence, it is impossible to say either way: but we would agree that Homeric epic does come across as particularly cannibalistic of rival traditions.) But the term *intertextuality* is not merely convenient for those who use it in reference to Homer: it also evokes deep metaphors of weaving as part of the creative art—present even in Homer—that imply, through the word "intertext," a "system of interwoven fabrics whose constituent parts are interrelated."[39]

Generally speaking, this understanding of the intertextual process applies well to the use of and interaction between broad images, motifs, and poetic structures in an oral poetic milieu. (See the representation of meaning-making in Figure 1.3 below.) Yet intertextuality remains problematic from a conceptual perspective if it relies on specific phrasing, or what a modern reader might understand as "quotation." The programmatic statement that sets out the case against thinking in terms of intertextuality is Gregory Nagy's assertion that

---

[37] He has also called this "mythological intertextuality;" see Burgess 2012:168; cf. Currie 2016:12.

[38] More recently, Margalit Finkelberg has adapted terms from Burgess 2009 to identify Homeric epic as "Meta-Cyclic," either "acknowledging the Cycle tradition and making it part of his own narrative or disacknowledging it and tampering with it" (2015:135). She concludes that "Homer does not simply appropriate the other versions of the Trojan saga or challenge their authority: he absorbs the Cycle tradition with the purpose of superseding it" (2015:138).

[39] Tsagalis 2008:xii; see also Bakker 2013:149–160 and Burgess 2006:177 for "motif transference" as a "type of intertextuality."

"when we are dealing with the traditional poetry of the Homeric (and Hesiodic) compositions, it is not justifiable to claim that a passage in any text can refer to another passage in another text" (1979:42).[40] For Nagy, the very orality of the Homeric poems—in the sense that they are composed (and recomposed) "in performance" at each and every performance—disqualifies them from being (able to be) thought about in terms that imply discrete and definable relations between finished (and finite) products—*inter-texts*. In response, Burgess has attempted to reframe what he means when he applies the term "intertextuality" to a performance culture (2012:169–170), by emphasizing that "correspondence of material" (structures, motifs, even phrases) need not indicate "poem-to-poem intertextuality" (a phrase we interpret as meaning fixed-text to fixed-text); instead, in the contexts of performance before a knowledgeable audience, "early epic is potentially allusive." Burgess concludes that a "text-less intertextuality" emerges from close readings of specific phrases, reflecting "not one text influencing another, but the traditional articulation of an episode being reflected by a secondary articulation of it" (2012:181).

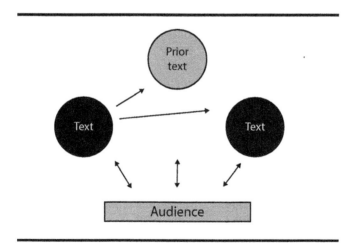

Figure 1.3. Intertextuality: Reference of text to prior text (and internal reference) is identified and processed through audience reception.

The approaches that we have so far outlined are underpinned by a common set of assumptions: first, that there is a relation between actual and fixed texts; and, second, that this relationship is hierarchical and mono-directional. Of these

[40] Cf. Currie 2016:10 for a critique of this claim as emerging from "dichotomous thinking." In earlier work (2016:89n1; cf. Barker and Christensen 2014) we suggest that intertextuality is appropriate primarily for fixed texts and less so for oral epic poetry.

methods we are most sympathetic to applications of intertextual readings. Our primary discomfort—beyond the rather mundane one of nomenclature and the emphasis on *text*—is that, in the case of early Greek poetic traditions (specifically, but not limited to, hexameter epic), we must face vague and undefined inheritances that appear to have established fleeting "intertexts" over time. The plurality of intertexts and the repetition of performances add quantitative and qualitative complexity to oral-derived epic's array of potential meaning. In addition, as we have emphasized in earlier work, models and methods that assume stability and fixity in poetic traditions are insufficient for representing the multidirectional and a-hierarchical engagements possible in living performance traditions, to which we turn now.

Oral-Poetic Frames: Traditional Referentiality

One of the advantages that literary/textualist approaches to Homer have is that they sidestep issues relating to the context of oral performance, the role of the bard in the production of poetic verse from a traditional repository of knowledge, and the competency of—or, better, the range of competencies among—the audience for interpreting and reconstructing the meaning of that composition. Yet this interpretive move merely substitutes one difficult unknown with another. There is an uncomfortable circularity in claiming that an author (or tradition) was sophisticated enough to deploy a meaningful structure, device, or allusion because *we* detect the use of that structure, device, or allusion in an oral-derived text.

Whether or not orally-derived epic implies or warrants a separate aesthetic interpretive framework has been a central feature of Homeric debate ever since the implications of Milman Parry and Albert Lord's oral theory began to be worked out.[41] At first, Parry's focus on formulaic expression and Lord's emphasis on composition in performance challenged hard-held beliefs central to the literary criticism of the time that privileged certain ideas of intention and originality. In a way, Homerists had to contend with post-modern notions of restricted expression and audience reception without the benefit of either the philosophical concepts or technical vocabulary that would become well known a

---

[41] For seminal works on oral theory, see M. Parry 1971 and Lord 1960. Cf. Foley 1988. For surveys see M. W. Edwards 1997 and Russo 1997. For criticism informed by oral theory see, for example, Whallon 1969; A. A. Parry 1973; Austin 1975; and especially Rutherford 1986:162 with n87; 1996:58–61. For the classic description of the operation of themes in oral poetry see Lord 1960:68–98. Foley 1988 prefers the terminology of "oral-derived," while the importance of recognizing orality is noted by Martin 1989:1–8. For literary-based objections to oral perspectives, see the bibliography cited by Kelly 2007:1, to which may be added Heiden 2008a:10n9.

generation later.[42] With the rise in broader studies on orality alongside advances in linguistics and literary theory, we can say with some confidence that not only does oral poetry—with or without an author—offer a range of interpretive interventions similar to that of "written" poetry (indeed, the dichotomy is largely false anyway), but also that the complex overlays of meaning and interpretation available to oral-derived poems may well exceed those of single-authored literary texts.[43]

However, these acknowledgements are still not enough to correct cultural and disciplinary prejudices about what interpretation means and what its results might look like. According to Robert Lamberton (1986:21) the existence if not preeminence of nonliteral meanings of the poems was taken for granted by Homer's earliest interpreters, showing that interpreting poetry "engaged the reader in an active role." And yet, one of these earliest interpreters is also one of the first to privilege the author's control over meaning over audience engagement. In his *Ion*, Plato (through the figure of Socrates) cross-examines a rhapsode (Ion of the dialogue's name) about how to interpret Homer in a way that best respects the poet's "intention" (*dianoia*). As Lamberton notes, Socrates' suggestion in the *Protagoras* (347e)—where he expresses a desire to interrogate an author for meaning—shares a strong affinity with Enlightenment literary tastes and Hellenistic editorial principles (299–300). In many ways, Plato's model has dominated literary approaches (especially by classicists) ever since, with the exception of more recent approaches that are informed by both postmodern literary theory and studies in orality.

As an alternative to this model of trying to recover authorial intention, we have found the orality models articulated by John Miles Foley 1988, 1991, 1999, Barbara Graziosi and Johannes Haubold 2005, and Egbert Bakker 2013, among others, to be more or less effective in both challenging our (literary-based) assumptions and offering new ways of thinking about how Homer's poetry works. Foley describes the difference in basic cognitive framing implied by the adoption of his traditional referentiality:

---

[42] Burgess 2009:56 admits that the "fluidity of oral narrative is certainly susceptible to a post-modern analysis in which everything potentially connects in an endless association of texts." But he worries that "the infinite regress of this approach...limits its utility."

[43] In a recent article, Edmunds 2016:4 contrasts intertextuality with traditional referentiality or resonance: he argues that the latter "dissolves formular diction in a great sea," whereas the former "with the assumption of some degree of textual fixation within ongoing oral traditions" may function well as "intertextuality without texts" to explain "correspondences between the proems of the *Iliad* and the *Cypria*." Edmunds argues that intertextuality can be pursued in early Greek epic if there are two conditions: one is that oral song traditions must be aware of one another; another is that one (in his case the *Iliad*) is not and does not rapidly gain precedence as the "standard" (2016:7).

The key difference lies in the nature of tradition itself: structural elements are not simply compositionally useful, nor are they doomed to a "limited" area of designation; rather they command fields of reference much larger than the single line, passage, or even text in which they occur. Traditional elements reach out of the immediate instance in which they appear to the fecund totality of the entire tradition, defined synchronically and diachronically, and they bear meanings as wide and deep as the tradition they encode...Traditional referentiality, then, entails the invoking of a context that is enormously larger and more echoic than the text or work itself, that brings the lifeblood of generations of poems and performances to the individual performance or text.[44]

Foley proposes that meaning in an oral tradition is essentially metonymic—that through synecdoche the relationship between the particular instance and traditional convention produces meaning that is "inherent."[45] While some of the language deployed in this definition is rather too fuzzy for our liking, we endorse the emphasis placed on the audience's role in producing meaning. According to Foley, the audience uses "extratextual" knowledge to interpret the performance of oral poetry in much the same way that many modern critics allow a literate reader to draw on prior and external knowledge in reading a text. Accordingly, Foley presents reader response approaches, or Receptionalism, as a model to be compared with his theory of *traditional referentiality*.[46] The perspective of receptionalism is invaluable for any genre that has its origins in performance.

In their version of this theory, Graziosi and Haubold suggestively draw on aural language, using the term "resonance" to denote the echoic reverberation that occurs when a traditional motif is deployed. If that motif reaffirms what is known (say, for example, that Troy will be sacked), it harmonizes the

---

[44] Foley 1991:7. Cf. Foley 2002:114–17. Cf. Kelly 2012:222–223; critique of this at Scodel 2002:11–12. See Danek 2002:13–19 for an appraisal of the method. See Currie 2016:4–7 for a misrepresentation of traditional referentiality that conflates allusion and intertextuality. For traditional referentiality applied to Thebes, see Arft 2014.

[45] Foley 1991:9–11. Dué 2002:2: "The traditionality of Homeric poetry allows the phrases, in the words of Lord, to 'resound with overtones from the dim past whence they came.' In other words, the traditional themes and phraseology carry with them powerful associations for a traditional audience, the 'echoes' of many past performances. Words can resonate within their context, recalling by association countless other song traditions." Muellner 1996:15: "a given traditional theme can carry with it ideas that poet and audience have learned to associate with it elsewhere."

[46] 1991:37–60. Foley draws on the work of Iser 1974. Hainsworth 1970:92 distinguishes this as an essential feature of any approach to Homer: "Invisible though it is in the printed text, the audience is a partner and contributor to the performance." For a more literary application of reader response, see Taplin 1992:2–7.

current poem-in-performance with the tradition, which, in turn, helps to lend it authority; if, on the other hand, the applied motif suggests an act or idea alien to or at odds with the tradition (say, for example, "swift-footed Achilles" rising to speak in the assembly), the resulting dissonance arrests the audience's attention and alerts them to what makes this poem-in-performance different (and why they should listen to it). In this way, resonance works economically and flexibly to endow Homeric poetry with "a sense of richness and meaning."[47]

A slightly different (again) reading of Foley's work has led Egbert Bakker to coin the terms *interformularity* and *intertraditionality*, in a clear and deliberate fusion of the literary idea of intertextuality with Foley's theory of traditional referentiality.[48] For Bakker, we can talk about the intertextuality of an oral poem if it "takes place within and is enabled by the formulaic system" (158). In this dynamic engagement of phrases and motifs, "The more restricted an expression, the more specific the context in which it is uttered, and the higher the point at which it can be placed on the scale" (159). Such a "scale of increasing interformularity" is useful for understanding the dynamic engagement of motifs and phrases through repetition within a *given tradition*. When these repetitions take place across *different epic traditions*, he labels them as moments of *intertraditionality*. By understanding "the continuum of increasing specificity" as "quintessentially cognitive" he again importantly draws attention to the dynamic between poet and audience. Recognizing (and understanding) interformularity and intertraditionality "is based on the judgment of the performer/poet and the audience as to the degree of similarity between two contexts: the more specific a formula and/or the more restricted its distribution, the greater the possible awareness of its recurrence and of its potential for signaling meaningful repetition" (159).

Taken together, these terms and concepts furnish us with a range of descriptive approaches for interpreting the Homeric poems that give due weight to both the medium (their orality) and the cultural context (their traditionality) of this kind of poetic creation. In addition to allowing us to talk about the orality of Homer in an informed and structured manner, however, two further critical trends encourage our adoption of traditional referentiality as a mode and method of analysis. First, studies in linguistics and cognitive science lend support to the notion that communication relies on shared inheritances with particular offshoots. A model that we have found useful for thinking with in this context

---

[47] Graziosi and Haubold 2005:53. Foley often uses the term "resonance" in a descriptive fashion. See Foley 1999, e.g. 6, 20, 164. Special thanks to Justin Arft for this citation (and many useful references and discussions).

[48] Bakker 2013. These approaches have been developed in our earlier articles: for these methodological statements see, Barker and Christensen 2008:6–9; 2011:9–12; and 2014:16–19.

of linguistic and cultural diffusion is the concept of the rhizome—the latest, and more nuanced, version of a linguistic tree. According to Deleuze and Guattari (1987:21), "Unlike trees or their roots, the rhizome connects any point to any other point, and its traits are not necessarily linked to traits of the same nature; it brings into play very different regimes of signs and even nonsign states...The rhizome operates by variation, expansion, conquest, capture, offshoots." As an analogical model for language and cultural diffusion, the rhizome is attractive because it focuses less on center and periphery (and thus less on hierarchy and authority), and instead values—or, better, draws attention to—connectivity and the potential for adaptation and change. In addition, since the rhizomes' roots and connections are hidden beneath the ground, it also functions well as a metaphor for the remains of an oral tradition whose "roots" and origins are obscure and irrecoverable.

Second, the dynamic model of an audience contributing meaning to narrative is one to which critics using cognitive science in literary studies increasingly turn.[49] At its base, linguistic and cognitive studies on the operation of metaphor (Lakoff and Johnson 1980; Turner 1996) have emphasized the ways in which "meaning making" takes place in a recipient's mind, creating a bond between the story or message projected and the one received. In expanding this basic idea to the study of narrative, Mark Turner emphasizes that a parable (story) is projected upon a target, but that both sources (parable and target) reflect back on one another to create a story. What cognitive science teaches us is not only that narrative is a fundamental function of the human brain at a neurobiological level, but that it depends by and large on input from external sources (other people) as well.[50] In a literary context, too, stories may be uttered by individuals, but their meaning is forged in the minds of audiences.

Given that "oral poetry works like a language, only more so" (Foley 2002:127), it is not surprising that several studies have used cognitive science to think anew about the language of Homeric poetry and have posited that its composition-in-performance emerges from the same structures and dynamics that condition "natural language."[51] For example, the widely observed phenomenon of repetition as a structuring element characteristic of Homeric poetry

---

[49] As Cánovas and Antović write, "it seems to us that [the] approach to oral composition in performance may be revived...and appreciated even better as ahead of its time, if it were viewed through the lenses of the cognitive sciences" (2016:4). For the cognitive turn and the novel, see Zunshine 2006; Zlatev 2008.

[50] For questions about the evolutionary development of the human capacity for narrative, see Ledoux 2002 and Gottschall 2012:26–31.

[51] Homeric language as composed of intonation units that correspond to the hexameter cola: Bakker 1997. Cf. Sifakis 1997; Foley 1999.

has been linked to cognitive analyses of everyday language,[52] while William Duffy and William Short (2016) have suggested that modern theories of cognitive metaphor can aid our understanding of how audiences may have conceived of epic (and their relationship to it). Other studies have more daringly examined the composition of the language itself, and, in turn, the poems. Cristobal Cánovas and Mihailo Antović have demonstrated that oral formulaic theory is functionally equivalent to usage-based cognitive grammar (2016:85) and that both descriptive categories depend on universals of human cognition. Similarly, Michael Drout has used evolutionary biology and cognitive psychology to argue that their evidence supports the development and "stability" of multiforms within oral traditions. He aptly describes our inability to "grasp multiformity" as a "cognitive weakness" (2011:448)—one that we would attest is reinforced by cultural paradigms which (over)emphasize stability, textuality, and authorship. According to Drout, by looking for similarity mental systems create a feedback loop in communities that leads to "increasing complexity as lineages ramify through cultural space and interact with each other" (2011:467). Such a feedback loop by definition includes the audience, who are perceived as working alongside performers in the creation of meaning through multiple iterations.

The epics that we possess may, in these terms, be understood as a synchronic fossilization of the diachronic process of reception and re-composition over time.[53] Absent from most text-based approaches is a recognition of the effect that this durative aspect may have had on both audiences and poems.[54] The question is: how do we deal with the (more-or-less) synchronic evidence of engagement with, "allusion" to, and "intertextuality" with, absent poems (or only partially extant and understood poetic traditions) in the diachronic plane?

We have been grappling with such shifting terms and concepts for the past decade and more. And, while we remain committed to the idea expressed by Willcock—that the approaches to Homer *do* have more in common with and more to teach each other than not—we have also become more alert to how drawing distinctions between methods is at times critical, not just for communicating

---

[52] For repetition, see Minchin 1996; for ring composition and orality from a cognitive perspective, see Person 2016.

[53] See Drout 2011:467 for individual multiforms as a spare "fossil record" of culture.

[54] Edmunds concludes that a specifically oral intertextuality is "plausible" and stronger than relying on Foley's "immanent art" (2016:20); Tsagalis' metaphor of the oral palimpsest to describe the way the poetic tradition functions is borrowed from Foley who describes its potential "to be 'erased' and rewritten in accordance with traditional structure and within the limits of the multiform idiom" (Foley 1990:31, cited by Tsagalis 2008:xi). In both cases, however, these authors and others are working with poems and remnants of poems that present a certain degree of fixity and whose "cross-references" they posit as happening in the same synchronic plane.

what we think Homeric poetry is, but especially for understanding *what it does*.[55] Being careful to separate out approaches, moreover, helps to frame one of the questions that we think the following studies might be able to answer—namely, how and why did our Homeric epics become preeminent?[56] For reasons that should be clear, we shy away from the language of neoanalysis because it assumes traditions prior to the *Iliad* shaping our *Iliad* in a mono-directional way; we avoid allusion too, where possible, because in literary studies the term tends to convey an intentionality that is bound up with the figure of a single author and a relationship between fixed texts. In addition, while we find the application of the term intertextuality to oral-derived poetry attractive when we have specific texts that may refer to one another (such as the *Iliad* and *Odyssey*, potentially), we feel that it is insufficiently flexible—too fixed on and tied to a direct one-to-one correspondence—to be able to take into account the dynamism of poetry composed in performance.

Therefore, despite varyingly effective challenges to the language and assumptions of traditional referentiality, or "resonance," this is the language that, along with its attendant framework, we use in this book for the following reasons. First and foremost, the ideas of traditional referentiality and resonance shift the focus of study away from the authority of the poet or the intention behind his design towards instead the interaction between audience and singer in the construction of meaning over and about a language and a tradition that they share in common.[57] Second, these approaches draw on a natural language analogy, which presupposes that motifs, structures and even particular phrases are regularly used in similar contexts over time in repeated performances. Intertexuality "works" for the Homeric epics in performance if we assume that the contents of the items being analyzed were more or less performed in the same story context and in the same way. (In this sense our approach aligns with what Jonathan Burgess has called mythological intertextuality.) Not only does

---

[55] Kelly 2012:221; cf. Edmunds 2016:5.

[56] As Burgess 2001 (*passim* but especially 117–126) makes clear, the Homeric epics became influential later than is commonly supposed; cf. Burgess 2012:170. Cf. Kelly 2007:10n33 for the warning that accepting Homeric poetry "as the norm of poetic composition in the Archaic period" causes us to relegate other forms of epic to an inferior position; and Edmunds 2016:7–8.

[57] We are not advocating here that thinking about the "design" of the Homeric poems is fruitless: in his (still unsurpassed) commentary on *Iliad* 24, Colin Macleod (1982) demonstrated the manifold echoes in that book with the beginning of the poem ("ring composition"), while Bruce Heiden (2008a) has argued convincingly for a "three movement" structure of the *Iliad,* which draws attention to the significant dynamic (and mismatch) between Zeus articulating his plans at the end of a movement (*Iliad* 8 and 15) and Achilles coming to his own decisions at the beginning of the next (in *Iliad* 9 and 16). Indeed, we could describe our analysis of Homer's Thebes in terms of their design on downgrading of this rival tale. Our point, rather, is that we choose to stress the structures within the poem rather than the poet's presumed intentions.

resonance allow us to embrace a healthier agnosticism about what other poems might have contained; it allows us to foreground a multiplicity of performed narratives over time, any and all of which can be subject to analysis and discussion.

When dealing with the Homeric epics as "transcripts" at the end of a dynamic tradition such as we have just described, talking about resonance encourages the acknowledgement that multiple poems provided multiple points and levels of engagement for different audiences over time. It is also the argument of this book that the prolonged and repeated experience of epic poetry in communities also involves identity formation and cultural expression: oral poetry developed as part of Greek culture that was increasingly competitive and which used forms of poetry for self-definition and prestige.

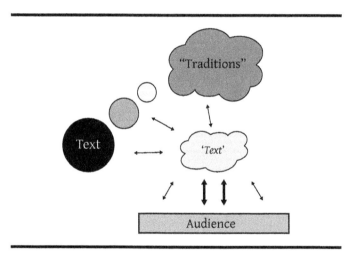

Figure 1.4. Traditional Referentiality: A particular text arises out of overlapping traditions—audiences make associative meanings between the text, prior iterations, and what they know of the traditions.

Rivalry and Panhellenism

Do you say to me concerning Thebes and its seven gates
that it is the only place where mortal women give birth to gods?

Sophocles fr. 773[58]

---

[58] Θήβας λέγεις μοι καὶ πύλας ἑπταστόμους,
οὗ δὴ μόνον τίκτουσιν αἱ θνηταὶ θεούς.

If traditional referentiality and resonance aid us in reading the Homeric poems by placing more emphasis on the plurality of potential responses that an audience might have, it is equally important to ponder the broader cultural framework out of which the poems emerged and in which they were shaped. Two trends in particular are instrumental for thinking about Homer's Thebes—the culture of rivalry and the development of Panhellenism. Both trends influence the form of the Homeric epics by conditioning the ways in which they respond to their own mythical and poetic traditions and the types of stories that they tell. In addition, we believe that the dynamics of competition and the process of aiming to achieve a Panhellenic reception hold an explanatory force when it comes to trying to understand complexity of the poems that we have received.[59]

Earlier, we introduced a vegetal metaphor—the rhizome—to describe the emergence of themes, structures, and poems from larger poetic traditions. Within the larger "organism" of early Greek myth and poetry, several traditions developed that shared the same language and aesthetics—even many of the same stories and what we would call poetic devices—while being localized physically in different regions and thematically in different story traditions (often emphasizing particular genealogies). Within this larger structure, which we will discuss shortly, the story traditions vied for attention and prominence. This is not to say that the different narrative traditions were directly in competition with each other, as pointedly recreated and reimagined in the so-called "Contest" (*Certamen*) between Hesiod and Homer; rather that competition was embedded in the very act of oral composition, where poems were created in performance and performers needed to arrest the attention of their listeners just in order to gain a hearing. As these creations were in turn adapted and remolded to appeal to each successive audience, so each new context favored the selection of more effective or engaging story traditions over others. This process was concentrated when performance competitions became institutionalized in the later Greek world.

While such a description must remain speculative given the scarcity of evidence, Homer nods towards such performance contexts in the *Odyssey*. These hints occur most obviously when the Ithacan bard, Phemios, sings about the (failed) *nostoi* of the Achaean heroes of Troy to entertain the suitors, or when the Phaiakian bard, Demodokos, regales the disguised Odysseus with epic-like songs about Achaeans fighting among themselves, the gods at (serious) play, and the sack of Troy. But the idea of poetic performance is there too, when Odysseus himself plays the singer of tales and for three whole books holds the Phaiakians

---

[59] Drout 2011:466 explores biological speciation as an analogy for individuation within a multiform oral tradition. He argues that individual representations will "appear discontinuous" because of a "pressure...to differentiate from each other."

entranced with his stories about monsters (Laistrygonians, Cyclopes, Scylla and Charybdis) and the supernatural (Circe and the underworld). Odysseus, of course, is instrumentalizing epic song, in the sense that he is singing for his homecoming (partly by keeping his hosts enchanted, partly, too, by providing them with paradigms by which to judge their own behavior). But his narrative serves to highlight how familiar motifs and stories can be adapted to suit a particular context (and audience). This, as well as the intersections with other narrative traditions—voyaging into unknown magical worlds recalls the adventures of the Argonauts, the meeting with the dead Herakles' *katabasis*, and so on—also reveals the strongly agonistic character of Greek poetry.[60] The internal world of the Homeric poems more generally reflects this competitive aesthetic, particularly in its questioning, and instantiation, of political behavior.[61]

The idea that the Homeric epics are closely related to each other goes back to antiquity, with Aristotle's judgment that the two poems complement each other to communicate not just the full experience of the Trojan War story but also the broadest range of human experience in general. From the simple idea that the two poems avoid repeating or referring to events related in the other (Monro's Law)—beginning with but going far beyond the fact that the *Iliad* narrates the war at Troy, while the *Odyssey* picks up the story of the return home—their relationship can easily be conceived of as agonistic.[62] In these terms, each poem bequeaths to its tradition not only the paradigmatic telling of the sack and return home respectively, but also different narrative styles and structures.[63] In earlier work, we have emphasized that this rivalry can also be

---

[60] See especially Collins 2004. Cf. Griffith 1990; Kurke 1999. Not all scholars agree. Scodel 2004 has effectively questioned the agonistic nature of Homeric poetry (see Burgess 2009:58).

[61] For the deeply competitive nature of Homer's world, see van Wees 1992 on values, and Martin 1989 and Parks 1990 on verbal dueling. Griffith 1990:188 identifies Greek cultural competition as "zero-sum" but later (191) proposes that the ambiguity of tales of judgment offers multiple possibilities for victory. For zero-sum in Homer, see Wilson 2002a:36–39; Scodel 2008:16–24, and Christensen 2018a. Elmer 2013. The idea of competition lies at the heart of the analysis of the Achaean agora in Barker 2009: see further Chapter 5.

[62] On poetic rivalry in the strategies enacted by the Homeric poems: see Pucci 1987 and, with an attempt to integrate oral theory, Tsagalis 2008. On the agonistic context of archaic Greek poetry, see Griffith 1990; cf. Lloyd 1987:50–108. Barker 2009 reads the *Odyssey*'s representation of debate as a response to (and complication of) the *Iliad*'s valorization of dissent. Hearing the other side—or, better, giving the space for the other side to be heard—is never that easy, and it is never without consequences.

[63] Lowe 2000. Where the author of *On the Sublime* attributed the different, more everyday style of the *Odyssey* to Homer's aging, Graziosi and Haubold 2005 see it rather as a further step in the evolution of the epic cosmos from the *Theogony* to the *Works and Days*. The proem's immediate focus on "man" positions the *Odyssey* at a stage further on from the *Iliad*'s tale of the death of the race of heroes, closer to a world of men, where the divine apparatus is all but stripped away in favor of stressing human responsibility.

conceived of as *intergeneric*, in the sense that it was likely a part of the poetic relationship between different narrative traditions, defined by performance context (e.g. sympotic vs. assembly) and poetic form (epic vs. elegy).[64] Our argument in this book draws on some of these same ideas but instead emphasize an *intrageneric* rivalry, using it as the framework through which to read how both the *Iliad* and the *Odyssey* use and redeploy material from the Theban tradition in the creation of their own narratives. This includes suppressing whatever themes or issues the Theban tradition had projected in favor of putting them at the service of the narrative ends of these two poems.[65] What sets this type of competition apart, we believe, is that it occurred as a *process over time*—at least for the duration over which both epics were being formed—and, quite likely, in multiple directions. That is to say, we see this rivalry not limited to one direction—the *Odyssey* responding to the *Iliad*, say, or the Homeric poems drawing on the Theban epics—but potentially in both directions simultaneously, as each discrete poetic production in each of its respective traditions sought to gain a foothold and an audience in a crowded marketplace of epic song. We have called this *dynamic rivalry* to denote this multidirectionality.

An important, and potentially decisive, step in this process is the emergence of the Homeric poems as common property for the whole Greek world—in others words, as a Panhellenic epic *koine*. As our work has developed, we have come to realize that the poems' narrative strategies, particularly their (re)use of other traditions, are intimately connected to the process by which they became adopted as Panhellenic narratives writ-large. As Christos Tsagalis has written: "'Homer' then reflects the concerted effort to create a Pan-Hellenic canon of epic song. His unprecedented success is due...not to his making previous epichoric traditions *vanish* but to his *erasing* them from the surface of his narrative while *ipso tempore* employing them in the shaping of his epics" (2008, xiii). Since our earlier approaches only partially acknowledged the importance of Panhellenism, this book needs to address how we think it frames poetic rivalry and the conditions that helped to shape the *Iliad* and the *Odyssey*. In Chapter 6 we will consider and discuss in some detail the role that Panhellenism plays in

---

[64] See Barker and Christensen 2006. Cf. Irwin 2005a for a similar analysis of the rivalry between martial elegy, Solon and Homeric epic.

[65] See Burgess 2001 passim but esp. 12–33. Burgess also criticizes Griffin's assertions persuasively that Homer's partial suppression of details from rival traditions is highly nuanced. See, for example, C.J. Mackie 1997. Cf. Finkelberg's reformulation of Homeric epic as "Meta-Cyclic", either "acknowledging the Cycle tradition and making it part of his own narrative or disacknowledging it and tampering with it" 2015:135. She concludes that "Homer does not simply appropriate the other versions of the Trojan saga or challenge their authority: he absorbs the Cycle tradition with the purpose of superseding it" (2015:138).

the eventual preeminence of Homeric epic. To anticipate that argument briefly here, our view is that a Panhellenic culture increased both the opportunities for rivalry and the incentives for engaging competitively with other traditions.

It was Anthony Snodgrass in 1971 who first outlined Panhellenism in its modern form. According to Snodgrass, Panhellenism refers to a historical process that indicates a gradual expression of shared "Greekness" through the embrace of common cult sites, agonistic aristocratic games, and the Homeric poems.[66] In antiquity, the idea of Panhellenism finds articulation only in later writers, and even then often problematically. The first expression of Panhellenism arguably comes in Herodotus, when the Athenians define "Greekness" as common blood, language, religious ritual, and customs (8.144.2): but, while this speech helps to articulate the lines of a Greek coalition against the Persian invader, it is given more as a show of loyalty by the Athenians than as a clear statement of Panhellenic unity—which Herodotus' narrative clearly demonstrates is never fully achieved.[67] Similarly, the very insistence of Isocrates on pushing the case for Panhellenic action rather betrays his lack of success in subordinating competing political motivations under the banner of a united Greek homeland. For all the flaws within these political attempts to exploit Panhellenism, modern scholars are right to identify it as an influential phenomenon implicit in the culturally shared entities identified above.[68] Constituent aspects of this Panhellenism were present at an early period in the generalization of local cult features and stories during migration and colonization (see Malkin 1998:140–145), in the development of Pan-Boiotian (see Larson 2007:8) and Pan-Ionian traditions, and in the transformation of Greek culture during the emergence of the city-state (see Nagy 1999 [1979] and 1990). Hesiod and Homer, as the foremost poets who (again according to Herodotus) "taught the Greeks their religion" (2.53.1–3), came to stand as representations of a shared Panhellenic song culture. Accordingly, part of the aesthetic of Homeric and Hesiodic poetry is the enforcement, and continual reinforcement, of a broader, more general cultural program—what Ian Rutherford has referred to as "Panhellenic Poetics" (2005:11). In the field of Homeric studies, Gregory Nagy more than anyone has explored the manifestations of a Panhellenic negotiation between local and broader traditions, and the repercussions for thinking about Homeric poetry

---

[66] For a stronger Hellenism emerging during the Persian Wars, see Hall 1989; Cartledge 1995. Cf. the longer discussion of Panhellenism in Chapter 6.

[67] See Barker 2009:196–197. Cf. Price 2001:71.

[68] On the somewhat different emphasis on Panhellenism in modern scholarship, see, e.g. Mitchell 2007.

that follow. For him, Panhellenism serves as a useful heuristic for appreciating the development of Homeric epic as *Greek* poetry.[69]

While there is debate about whether or not the epics reflect Panhellenism internally,[70] the various overlapping and intersecting strands of Panhellenic culture helps us to recognize that Homeric poetry partly emerges from many different local (epichoric) traditions.[71] This process of Panhellenic rivalry, moreover, was not one that occurred at single time, at a single place, or in a single direction. Instead, it is best conceived of as providing a general background for the reception of epic and a determining factor in the final forms of the Homer poems as we have them—as well as, arguably, the fragmentary form of the non-Homeric epic traditions. Fundamentally, it also helps to explain why the Homeric relationship with other poetic traditions should be geographical and political as well as poetic—a point to which we shall return in Chapter 6.

Swift-Footed Achilles, Again

To give a better idea of our methodology and to show the way in which it contrasts with but also complements the other approaches that we have outlined, we need an example of it in action. The one that we have chosen we have treated in a more limited fashion elsewhere—the case of "swift-footed Achilles" in the *Iliad*.[72] Achilles' first appearance in the narrative comes at a critical moment: the people are dying because of a plague sent by Apollo; in response to this existential crisis Achilles calls an assembly. Homer subsequently introduces Achilles' address to the assembly with the following line: "after taking his stand among them, he spoke to them, swift-footed Achilles" (τοῖσι δ' ἀνιστάμενος μετέφη πόδας ὠκὺς Ἀχιλλεύς, 1.58). The oddity with this description, which we have tried to bring out with our inelegant translation, is the labeling of Achilles

---

[69] Cf. Nagy 1999:7: "from the internal evidence of its contents, we see that this poetic tradition synthesizes the diverse local traditions of each major city-state into a unified Panhellenic model that suits most city-states but corresponds exactly to none." Rutherford 2005:11 calls this "Panhellenic poetics," which he describes as "the enterprise, through poetry, of reconciling and building connections between myths and genealogical traditions from different parts of Greece." Elmer 2013:274n2; cf. Scodel 2002:45–46. See González 2015:18 for Athens as becoming the dominant center of Homeric performance. Cf. Nagy 1996a:42.

[70] E.g. Finley 1954; see Ross 2005 for a "Proto-Panhellenism" in Homer; *pace* Cartledge 1993.

[71] See Nagy 1999 [1979] for an exploration of the Panhellenizing tendencies of Homeric epic and the local orientation of hero cult. Cf. Scodel 2002:4–46. Nagy 1990:70–79; Tsagalis 2011:217–218 and 236–238. For the *Odyssey*'s higher degree of "epichoric" material, see Tsagalis 2014:243. For the Homeric epics, along with Hesiod, as being more Panhellenic (as opposed to the more localized cyclic poems) see Nagy 2015:63.

[72] See Barker and Christensen 2008:8–9; this was originally inspired by Graziosi and Haubold 2005:51–53. See also the discussion in Dunkle 1997 and Foley 1991. Cf. Christensen 2015. For a similar comparison of different methodologies with reference to *Iliad* 10, see Dué 2011.

as "swift-footed" even though he is stationary (he was only getting to his feet anyway, and even that movement has been accomplished). It is not the only time that Achilles is described as "swift-footed" in Book 1. On a further four occasions Homer uses the line to introduce Achilles speaking, first in the assembly (1.84, 148, 215), then in his report to his mother (364); on each occasion, as before, Achilles is stationary.

In fact, in his summing up of the renewed crisis in the Achaean camp, Homer elaborates on the contrast between the usual swiftness of Achilles and his current raging inaction (1.488–492):

> Αὐτὰρ ὃ μήνιε νηυσὶ παρήμενος ὠκυπόροισι
> διογενὴς Πηλῆος υἱὸς <u>πόδας ὠκὺς Ἀχιλλεύς·</u>
> οὔτέ ποτ' εἰς ἀγορὴν πωλέσκετο κυδιάνειραν
> οὔτέ ποτ' ἐς πόλεμον, ἀλλὰ φθινύθεσκε φίλον κῆρ
> <u>αὖθι μένων</u>, ποθέεσκε δ' ἀϋτήν τε πτόλεμόν τε.

> But he raged, sitting there among the swift-wayed ships,
> The divine-born son of Peleus, *swift-footed Achilles.*
> Neither was he ever going to the assembly where men win glory,
> Nor ever into war; instead he was eating up his dear heart
> *Waiting there*, though he was full of desire for the battle-cry and war.

Here, the man of action and speed is marked out for everything he is *not* doing: neither was he going to the assembly, nor was he going into battle. The duration of this inaction is doubly marked too: the poem uses the imperfect iterative twice to develop the tension between his sustained *avoidance of frequenting* the assembly and his lingering *desire* to do so (πωλέσκετο... ποθέεσκε); it also repeats the indefinite temporal particle ποτε ("ever"), even though in reality only a short period of time can have passed since he has withdrawn to his ships. In effect, "swift-footed Achilles" is as stilled as the "swift-wayed ships" (νηυσὶ ὠκυπόροισι) among which he sits, ships that haven't moved for nigh on ten years. So striking is this passage that ancient scholars appear to have found it perplexing enough either to offer the explanation that "a hero is opposed to inaction" or to want to do away with it altogether.[73]

Why, then, is Achilles described as "swift-footed" in all of these instances, when he is simply standing to speak? Early responses to the articulation of oral-formulaic theory by Milman Parry (and then advanced by Albert Lord) pointed

---

[73] Schol. A ad *Iliad* 1.488 notes that Zenodotus athetized this entire passage. Schol A *ad Iliad* 1.492: "'He was longing': For the hero is opposed to inaction. He is especially desirous of honors for deeds" (<ποθέεσκε:> ἐχθρὸς γὰρ τῆς ἀργίας ὁ ἥρως, φιλότιμος δὲ περὶ τὰς πράξεις).

out problems (some sensible, others imagined). On the one hand, oral-formulaic theory provided an explanation for why Homer would use the description "swift-footed" to denote a hero who was motionless.[74] It was a turn of phrase, or *epithet*, that was particularly associated with the given hero, which sums up or encapsulates who they are. Achilles has the epithet "swift-footed" because essentially he *is* "swift-footed" or "swift of foot." Similarly he is also "divine-born" or the "son of Peleus," while Hektor is "of the shining helmet" and Odysseus is "much enduring," etc. At the same time, this particular epithet for Achilles is used here in accordance with the demands of the meter: that is to say, given the fact that epic hexameter is strictly limited (to six metrical feet), and given the fact that Homer, who was composing on the spot, wanted to describe Achilles standing to speak in the assembly, by the time he came to the end of the line he needed an epithet that would fit the remaining length. "Swift-footed" fits the bill on both counts. While providing a reason why "swift-footed" is used in these instances, however, the explanation hardly satisfies. It seems to imply that "swift-footed Achilles" is a conventional phrase used simply for metrical convenience without any meaning;[75] indeed, it could be argued to be the definition of meaning*less*, given the seeming incongruity with its usage here. And it is not merely the epithet that may be limited in its evocation of meaning. The beginning of the epic could simply be regarded as the deployment of a conventional type-scene (West 2013:83; Arend 1975:116–121).

The tension between recognizing the flexible economy of hexameter verse and the lingering dissatisfaction with a "poetry-by-numbers" reading of Homer has in large part driven Homeric scholarship for the last forty years, particularly with regard to the place of oral theory in studies of literary criticism. The challenge has been to think about ways in which units of utterance, like the epithet, can be both functional *and* contextually meaningful at the same time. Using this same example we can reflect on the different approaches to reading Homer that we set out above, and test them in their capacity to explain how this line might have been heard by ancient audiences of epic.

A neoanalytical reading of this particular epithet (and its use throughout the epic), for example, could help draw attention to its intra-textual, as well as its inter-textual, meaning. Although the evidence is fragmentary, we know

---

[74] See Dué 2011:171–173 for a good use of oral-formulaic theory. In our summary here, we are presenting a rather inaccurate view of the work of Parry and Lord, but one which is particularly common among their detractors.

[75] Parry (1971:146–72) allows for some particularized meaning where Lord (1960:66) appears less flexible. See Nagler 1974 and Vivante 1982 for attempts to reconcile oral poetics with the contextual meaning expected from a literary perspective. Recent work (Foley 1988 and 1991; Bakker 2005) illustrates that Homeric verse can be at once traditional and innovative. For Achilles' epithets, see Nagy 1999 [1979]:326; cf. Shive 1988.

from other poetic traditions that Achilles was renowned for his swiftness. In the *Cypria*, for example, he apparently overruns and wounds Telephos and ambushes Troilus, while in the *Aithiopis* he kills Penthesileia and Memnon: it is conceivable that the *Iliad* knows these episodes and alludes to them through the epithet "swift-footed," though without the evidence it is difficult to understand exactly how or with what effect, and it still doesn't explain the incongruous deployment of the epithet at the beginning of the *Iliad*. As the poem unfolds, of course, we *do* get to witness Achilles' swiftness (when, at length, he returns to battle), which might suggest that its usage in Book 1 is *intratextually proleptic*, in that it anticipates the hero's later actions in the epic (though these fleet-of-foot actions are themselves complicated, as we shall see in a moment). We are on safer ground with the *Odyssey*, since the close relationship, even *intertextuality*, between the two Homeric epics is well established.[76] During the games among the Phaiakians, a young prince mocks Odysseus and claims that "man has no greater glory as long as he lives / than what he can do with his own feet and hands" (οὐ μὲν γὰρ μεῖζον κλέος ἀνέρος, ὄφρα κεν ᾖσιν, / ἢ ὅ τι ποσσίν τε ῥέξῃ καὶ χερσὶν ἑῇσιν, *Odyssey* 8.146-147). The same theme is further articulated shortly afterwards, when the bard Demodokos sums up his tale of Ares and Hephaistos by declaring "Wicked deeds do not prevail: now the slow overcomes the swift / just as Hephaistos who is slow has caught Ares" (οὐκ ἀρετᾷ κακὰ ἔργα· κιχάνει τοι βραδὺς ὠκύν, / ὡς καὶ νῦν Ἥφαιστος ἐὼν βραδὺς εἷλεν Ἄρηα, *Odyssey* 8.329-330). It is possible to read these specific passages in direct relation to the *Iliad*—not least because in the Funeral Games of Patroklos we witness the allegedly sluggish Odysseus outsprinting all the Achaeans (though, of course, Achilles is not competing). From this perspective, one might want to say that the *Odyssey* is *alluding* to the *Iliad* by casting its hero as slow in body but mentally agile. Or, if one takes the idea of intertextuality seriously, one could equally read the *Iliad*'s opening depiction of a hero marked out by his epithet for being swift of foot deliberately removing himself from the action, as a response to the downplaying of physical prowess in the *Odyssey*.

So far we have drawn on a combination of neoanalysis, allusion, and intertextuality for interpreting the *Iliad*'s curiously still swift-footed hero. What, then, is the meaningful contribution of traditional referentiality and our emphasis on interpoetic (and intertraditional) rivalry? To take the former idea first: traditional referentiality allows us to hear any and all units of utterance—the

---

[76] See especially Pucci 1987. Tsagalis 2008:67–68 explores the engaging notion that the *Odyssey* may allude to poems that formed after it; his argument shows how oral poetry necessarily reflects rival song traditions in the performance that creates a single text from "*variae lectiones* on the level of myth" (68). For a thorough treatment of the *Odyssey*'s citation of itself and use of other traditions from a largely neoanalytical perspective: Danek 1998.

language, as well as the themes, type scenes and story patterns—of the specific poem-in-performance diachronically in and against past performances. Through this process of being continuously heard in relation to other songs, the poem accrues meaning; or, to put that differently, by virtue of the listening out for what units resonate with others, and *how*, the audience gives meaning to the poem. Of course, the performers' intentions and certainly their design play an important role in the creation of meaning; but audience experience of (and relatedly expertise in) past performances activates the poem's semantic power. In this sense to search for discrete references to specific texts is to limit that power, where to hear a formulaic unit of utterance could bring to mind any number of referents, depending on the audience member's experience and expertise, with no single specific target text in mind.

The phrase "swift-footed Achilles" is a good example. We have already seen that its use in Book 1 of the *Iliad* runs counter to its ostensible meaning: on each occasion "swift-footed" introduces an immobile Achilles. Far from (re)enacting his epithet, this Achilles acts in a way that strikes an off-key note with it. Were there only the one instance, we might be tempted to think that it points to a specific moment in Achilles' epic career when he was swift-footed (as we discussed above); cumulatively, however, they suggest something rather different, namely that the Achilles of this poem is going to be different from his traditional portrait, and that the emphasis of this poem lies somewhere other than on his martial prowess: its target is the tradition as a whole, not any single other instantiation of it. In the opening scene Achilles is swift to anger (rather than of foot) and, digging in his heels, withdraws from battle. As a result, for the majority of his epic "swift-footed" Achilles is to be found kicking his heels in his tent, missing from the action, *still*. Each use of his epithet, then, reminds us how far his performance departs from his previous epic career. Contrast this usage with the case of Iris, the gods' messenger who is "swift-footed" (πόδας ὠκέα) only when she *is actually* swift of foot (i.e. in motion as a messenger). For Achilles, however, to whom this phrase is most often applied, the vast majority of cases introduce him *speaking*. In other words, the phrase is so clearly associated with Achilles that in the *Iliad* Homer can use it even when Achilles is not in motion.[77]

---

[77] πόδας ὠκὺς Ἀχιλλεύς is generally used to introduce speeches: 1.58, 84, 148, 215, 364; 9.196, 307, 606, 643 (i.e. it structures all his responses to the embassy); 11.112, 607; 16.48; 18.78, 97, 187; 19.55, 145, 198, 419; 21.222; 22.14, 229, 260, 344; 23.93, 776; 24.138, 559, 649, 751. The only exceptions are: 1.489; 11.112; 22.229, 23.776; 24.751. Otherwise, the phrase "swift-footed" (πόδας ὠκέα) applies to Iris, the gods' messenger: 2.790, 795; 3.129; 8.425; 11.199, 210; 18.202; 24.87, 188; cf. Hesiod *Theogony* 780.

According to Roger Dunkle, the traditional expectations that an audience might bring with them to a tale about Achilles here contrast with his present action to create what Foley describes a "gap of indeterminacy" in their understanding.[78] As Dunkle argues, this gap is later resolved when the plot summons "forth the traditional Achilles to pursue and kill Hektor" (Dunkle 1997:233). Yet, when finally roused, Achilles turns out to be not swift-footed enough: first he is diverted from Troy by the even fleeter of foot Apollo (21.509–611); then he races Hektor around the walls of Troy (22.136–166),[79] all the time unable to catch him. Homer captures the central paradox in a memorable simile that dwells on the inability of this swift-footed Achilles to outrun his prey: "as in a dream a man is unable to catch the one fleeing before him, / the one is unable to flee nor the other to catch, / so Achilles was not able to grab Hektor in his fleetness nor Hektor to escape" (ὡς δ' ἐν ὀνείρῳ οὐ δύναται φεύγοντα διώκειν· / οὔτ' ἄρ' ὃ τὸν δύναται ὑποφεύγειν οὔθ' ὃ διώκειν· / ὡς ὃ τὸν οὐ δύνατο μάρψαι ποσίν, οὐδ' ὃς ἀλύξαι, 22.199–201). Achilles' swift-footedness is of even less importance in the Funeral Games of Book 23, which again he sits out (and where, as we noted above, it is his epic rival, Odysseus, who wins the prize for being fleetest of foot: 23.758–783). It is also the least of his qualities to emerge during the ransoming of Hektor in Book 24: when he "springs up like a lion" (24.572), it is to see to the formalities for Hektor's return, not to strike down an opponent (though this line is prefaced by Achilles warning Priam not to anger him).

What we are describing here is Achilles' *immanent* swiftness, for it is only because we would normally associate Achilles with swiftness that we can make sense of all of these instances where his swiftness either has no impact or lies somewhere else (how he is quick to anger or will enjoy but a short life).[80] For this kind of dissonance to work in a performance context, the audience needs to know, or at least be aware, of other *Achilleis* who *were* swift-footed. Here we might follow Gregory Nagy (1979:45–49), who first observed that the conventional opposition between Homer's two protagonists, Odysseus and Achilles, emerges in part from a structural opposition in myth between the forces of *mētis* (intelligence) and *biē* (force), for which swiftness of foot often functions as a metonym.[81] Swiftness creates superheroes and Achilles' foot-speed is a

---

[78] See Dunkle 1997:227; Foley 1991:41.

[79] The two are brought together in their speed grammatically by Homer's use of the dual: "the two of them whirled around the city of Priam three times with swift feet" (ὡς τὼ τρὶς Πριάμοιο πόλιν πέρι δινηθήτην / καρπαλίμοισι πόδεσσι, *Iliad* 22.165–166).

[80] See Slatkin 1991:36–37; cf. Barker and Christensen 2008:9.

[81] For lameness bestowing upon a figure "the privilege of an uncommon man, of an exceptional qualification" see Vernant 1985:21. For the contrast between *biē* and *mētis*, see Nagy 1999 [1979] *passim*. For the operation of the *mētis* motif in the *Odyssey*, see Cook 1995. In Aesop's fables, feigned lameness is a characteristic of clever, devious animals, see Aesop *Fables* 198 and 214.

"determinative metonym for his conventional exceptionality" (Christensen 2015:23). When an audience hears the invocation of this phrase, it engages with more-or-less fixed ideas of Achilles known from other performances.

Yet, while the unit of utterance πόδας ὠκὺς Ἀχιλλεύς survives only in our *Iliad*, the motif or *idea* of Achilles' swift-footedness, if not this precise verbal quotation, is widespread and not limited to the world of early Greek hexameter epic. Arguably, our preference for thinking in terms of traditional referentiality rather than text-based theories of allusion or intertextuality is best demonstrated by two non-literary examples. Zeno's famous paradox explicitly uses Achilles as the paradigmatic fleet of foot man who is not able to overtake a tortoise (Aristotle, *Physics* VI 9 239b10 15).[82] From the world of material culture there survives an Attic black-figure kylix (drinking cup), circa 570–565 BCE, on which the ambush by Achilles of Polyxena and Troilus is depicted (see Illustrations 1a and 1b). We could read this scene as an illustration of the epic poem, the *Cypria*, where this episode is said to have taken place, though scholars are more wary now of assigning episodes on Greek pottery to textual sources or even thinking of them as illustrations. Indeed, even though this example presents a static image of Achilles—as determined by the medium, of course— nevertheless, the artist adeptly manages to capture his speed of foot with the placement of Achilles at one end of the frame and Troilus at the other, and by depicting the latter on horseback. As we turn the cup in our hands, so that we can see all the figures, the stationary Achilles becomes animated in our imagination as the "swift-footed Achilles" who can chase down even a galloping horse in order to slay Troilus.

These examples demonstrate the broad scope of traditional referentiality, which brings us to our second methodological claim: to read Homeric epic in terms of its intergeneric (and intertraditional) rivalry with other poetic forms. As we have discussed elsewhere (see Christensen and Barker 2006:15 and *passim*), we imagine that in the course of their lives, audiences of early Greek poetry would have been exposed to multiple performances of multiple genres that explored many of the same ideas and issues in many different forms and with many different outcomes. Moreover, these different performances of traditions and genres would have responded to and reformed each other. For an indication of how this might work, the motif of swift-footed Achilles is again useful to think with.

---

[82] The idea of swiftness of foot and its insufficiency can be found too in Aesop's fable of the tortoise and the hare. We thank Andreas Michaeopoulos for these references.

Illustrations 1a-1b. Attic black-figure kylix by the C Painter. Side A (top): Achilles, crouching, waits for Troilus. Side B (bottom): Troilus and Polyxena flee from Achilles' ambush. Paris, Musée du Louvre, CA6113. Photos, Wikimedia Commons user Bibi Saint-Pol.

In a fleeting fragment recorded by the later rhetorician Athenaeus, Xenophanes, one of the so-called pre-Socratic philosophers, uses language that strongly resonates with the fleet of foot Achilles of Homer (Xenophanes fr. 2, 16–19 = Athenaeus X 413f–414c):

οὐδὲ μὲν εἰ ταχυτῆτι ποδῶν, τόπερ ἐστὶ πρότιμον,
ῥώμης ὅσσ' ἀνδρῶν ἔργ' ἐν ἀγῶνι πέλει,
τούνεκεν ἂν δὴ μᾶλλον ἐν εὐνομίηι πόλις εἴη·

Swiftness of feet—the thing honored most
in all of man's acts of strength in the contest
—could never make a city governed well.

While the form ταχυτὴς ποδῶν does not occur in early Greek hexameter epic, the near-equivalent form ταχὺς ποδῶν does. Mostly it occurs in the *Iliad*'s scenes of battle, as if denoting that being swift of feet would (or should) normally describe an action in battle.[83] Without considering the broader referentiality of πόδας ὠκύς, nevertheless, the last instances of ταχὺς ποδῶν *all* relate to Achilles, suggesting again the association of swift feet with this specific hero.[84] In rejecting swiftness of foot as a sufficient value for governing a city, Xenophanes could be alluding to the conflict set up at the beginning of the *Iliad*, where the swift-footed hero contests the king's authority and precipitates a political crisis in the Achaean camp.[85] Or one might think too of the Phaiakian youths in the *Odyssey*, whose swift-footed ability in the games Odysseus questions as a signifier of heroic stature. Earlier in the poem Xenophanes asserts first that "our wisdom is better than the strength of men and horses" (οὐκ ἐὼν ἄξιος ὥσπερ ἐγώ. ῥώμης γὰρ ἀμείνων / ἀνδρῶν ἠδ' ἵππων ἡμετέρη σοφίη, fr. 2 14–15), and again that "it is not just to prefer strength to good wisdom" (ἀλλ' εἰκῇ μάλα τοῦτο νομίζεται, οὐδὲ δίκαιον / προκρίνειν ῥώμην τῆς ἀγαθῆς σοφίης, fr. 2 15–16). Here, then, Xenophanes frames his comments about the swift-footed hero within culturally-charged language about the importance of sympotic wisdom and intelligence over physical strength.[86] Indeed, the sympotic context for Xenophanes' poetry would both complement and replace the quasi-sympotic banqueting of the Phaiakians.

While offering, as we see it, a series of suggestive echoes, such readings assume, as we argued above, a one-to-one mapping from the source text (Xenophanes) to its target (either the *Iliad* or *Odyssey* or both), where the relationship goes one way, all the way back to Homer. However, such a view not only overlooks the likelihood that these sources belong to a much wider exploration of the value put on physical excellence (*biê*) or intelligence (*mêtis*)—a tension that runs deep in Greek culture from Pindar to Plato.[87] We suggest too that Homer is part of this debate, not separate from it. A non-hierarchical model, such as we have proposed above, turns on its head the idea that Xenophanes is alluding to Homer to suggest that the *Iliad* itself is (re)deploying the swift-footed hero to present a challenge to the political arena, where the issue of

---

[83] 5.885; 6.514; 8.339; 13.249, 348, 482; 17.676.

[84] 17.709; 18.2 (Antilochus as a messenger to Achilles), 354, 358; 20.189 (Achilles makes Aeneas run swiftly); and particularly his inability to catch Hektor (21.564; 22.8, 173, 230).

[85] See Chapter 5, "Enabling Strife, Founding Politics."

[86] Archilochus appears to draw on similar notions when he famously declares: "I don't love a tall leader, or one striding far / or one who takes pride in his hair or shaved beard..." (οὐ φιλέω μέγαν στρατηγὸν οὐδὲ διαπεπλιγμένον / οὐδὲ βοστρύχοισι γαῦρον οὐδ' ὑπεξυρημένον, fr. 114).

[87] Pindar similarly redeploys the phrase ταχυτὴς ποδῶν to celebrate the athletes at the games (*Olympian* 1.95; cf. *Isthmian* 5.10). In contrast, Plato's Socrates argues in his defense that he is of far greater service to the state than victors at the Panhellenic games (*Apology* 36d).

government lies at the heart of his striving with Agamemnon. In this understanding, the *Iliad* is both reimagining the values that Achilles supposedly represents in heroic epic *and* engaging in intergeneric rivalry of the kind that we see voiced by Xenophanes. For its part, the *Odyssey*'s depiction of the Phaiakians in a quasi-sympotic setting may well suggest this epic's direct engagement with the poetry and politics of the symposium.[88] Thus we see such moments of contact between different poems, traditions and genres (even media), as illustrated by the motif of "swift-footed Achilles," not as singular one-to-one matches or lines of direct influence that issue from the priority of Homer, but rather as a plural and dynamic set of responses to and representations of the idea of the hero and the relative importance of physical strength in an ever-shifting, competitive environment. For the tradition is always shifting to include new receptions and reconfigurations of what appears traditional.[89]

One final example may serve to illustrate the extent to which the themes, ideas, and very language of early Greek poetry were continually used and repurposed in the reception and rethinking of mythical material for present concerns. If Xenophanes' reuse of the "swift-footed" motif can be said to communicate anxiety about prizing physical excellence over moral worth—and in turn contribute to the debate on selecting appropriate leaders and an awareness of the dangers of big individuals (or "heroes")—a rather different slant is provided by one of the victory songs in praise of the tyrant slayers Harmodius and Aristogeiton, also preserved in Athenaeus (XV 695a = PMG 895):

φίλταθ' Ἁρμόδι', οὔ τί πω τέθνηκας,
νήσοις δ' ἐν μακάρων σέ φασιν εἶναι,
ἵνα περ ποδώκης Ἀχιλεὺς
Τυδεΐδην τέ †φασι τὸν ἐσθλόντ† Διομήδεα.

Dearest Harmodius, you have never died,
But they say you live in the isles of the blest
Where swift-footed Achilles
And Tydeus' fine son, Diomedes, are.

In this celebratory song the tyrant-killer is said to have joined "swift-footed" Achilles and Tydeus' son Diomedes in the Isles of the Blest.[90] The overlap of these

---

[88] See further Barker and Christensen 2006.

[89] Cf. Scodel 2002:32 who argues that "traditionality...is a cultural construct, the social memory of the past." On social memory in conjunction with Homer, see the discussion of Panhellenism in Chapter 6.

[90] ποδώκης...Ἀχιλεὺς is an alternative form of the more popular πόδας ὠκὺς Ἀχιλλεύς. It occurs at *Iliad* 18.324; 20.89; 23.792. Cf. Plato Com. fr.15.1.

two figures is interesting (for more on which see Chapter 3), but of immediate concern to us is the selection of the two heroes in the first place: why are they singled out, and not other heroes from myth? The answer lies, we suggest, in their role as heroes who are recognized for standing up to authority. In one way this would seem to be a pointed throwback, or *allusion*, to their role in the *Iliad*, where Achilles contests the authority of Agamemnon, and Diomedes equally pointedly recalls Achilles' challenge as a precedent for his own verbal sparring with the king—both acts which, importantly, are figured as laying down a new political framework for dealing with crises in the Achaean camp.[91] These later "popular" verses—lines from a drinking song—praise and elevate a figure from the more immediate past, the tyrant-slayer Harmodius, to the level of a culture hero of all time on par with an Achilles or Diomedes from the *Iliad*. In this move, the epic heroes themselves are transformed, from figures who stood up to authority to those who successfully slayed the king—as if Harmodius had made good on Achilles' initial impulse to strike down Agamemnon in *Iliad* Book 1.[92]

Yet this transformation should also alert us to how the mythologizing process, which we can observe taking place here, is drawing upon generations-old poetic contests, capitalizing upon resonances latent in these figures inherited from epic. The idea of challenging the king is also heard, albeit jumbled up (ἀμετροεπής, ἄκοσμα, *Iliad* 2.212, 213), in the Achillean-like complaints of Thersites in *Iliad* Book 2, whom Homer describes as continuously hurling abuse at Achilles and Odysseus (τῶ γὰρ νεικείεσκε, *Iliad* 2.221); in the *Aithiopis* he apparently reviled Achilles to such a degree that the latter struck him down—a different take again on dissent from authority and slaying the tyrant.[93] Meanwhile in the *Odyssey* Demodokos sings about the conflict between Achilles and Odysseus, with Agamemnon removed from the contest and a happy spectator (*Odyssey* 8.73–82). And these latencies were not a creation invented out of nothing by the Homeric poems; the *Iliad* and *Odyssey* themselves were manipulating and channeling them from other epics and epic traditions, as well as from other poetic forms and even other media.

---

[91] On Achilles as standing up to authority (in the form of Agamemnon), see Barker 2009; cf. Chapter 5 below.

[92] Of course, such tales are not always positively received: Plato's Socrates, for example, objects to tales that depict leaders pursuing personal enmity (*Republic* 378c1-d3).

[93] Thersites enjoys a lively afterlife for his epic dissent, which is configured as either (or both) comic (e.g. Lucian *How to Write History* 14) or (and) political (e.g. Libanius *Progymnasmata*, Encomium 4). In Plato he is of interest precisely for the kind of afterlife he might enjoy: in *Gorgias* (525e) he is an example of a soul that can be cured in the afterlife; and in *Republic* (620c) he chooses to be reborn as an ape. On Thersites as a "bona fide satirist," see Rosen 2003:123 (on the *Aithiopis*). Halliwell 1991:281 too draws attention to Thersites' role as a "habitual entertainer," and points to Plato's shrewd description of him as a γελωτοποιός (*Republic* X.620c3).

In sum, in this book we ply as eclectic an approach as possible, by drawing on the tools which traditional referentiality *and* neoanalysis afford us, with certain caveats in mind. We try to avoid, for example, the positivistic assumptions of neoanalysis, which sees signs in our textualized poems as relying on something specific that no longer exists. We also are reluctant to overly limit the range of meanings available in a text by relying solely on authorial intention or allusion between fixed moments. In addition, while many of those who use the range of approaches that fall under the term "intertextuality" will come to results similar to ours, we prefer to use a method of analysis that enables more complex and dynamic interactions. In our endeavor to model a method of reading that is less hierarchical and more reflective of a range of potential interpretive associations, we believe we offer an approach to the epics that can simultaneously embrace the responses of ancient and modern audiences alike.

Homer's Thebes: Overview

As we anticipated earlier, this book will proceed with a series of "case studies" that will function as a way both to examine how the Homeric poems use Theban material and to test, advance, and at times challenge our methods. Although we have already made it clear that our intention in this book is not to reconstruct Theban myth or lost epics, on occasion we will introduce and discuss material about Thebes in order to provide the necessary context for better appreciating and understanding the iconoclastic character of Homer's use of Theban myth. Rather than ordering these reflections in terms of the notional cosmic history of Theban myth (e.g. starting with Cadmus and then following in succession to Herakles, Oedipus, and the Seven) we organize the material thematically, which entails moving back and forth in mythic time and between the *Iliad* and the *Odyssey*. Our choice of themes—politics, time, form, strife, distribution, and Panhellenism—reflect what we consider to be the most pertinent, and certainly the most forceful, issues through which Homer's poems probe the ideas behind Thebes, and their limits.

Chapter 1 ("Troy: The Next Generation") explores the *Iliad*'s engagement with Thebes through the theme of politics. The Theban material that we focus on here is the story of the Seven and the exchanges among Agamemnon, Diomedes and Sthenelos in Book 4. One reason for beginning our investigations here is because this material is among that which is most explicitly flagged as being drawn from other sources. (Agamemnon frames his account of the Seven as a story that is well known and derivative—"they say.") In this example, it is clear that the *Iliad* is aware of the rival tradition of Thebes; as a result, this passage represents the ideal case for thinking through what Theban elements are referenced and how they are (re)deployed in the context of the *Iliad*'s narrative. What makes this example particularly interesting is the competitive frame in which Thebes is cited: it becomes, quite literally, the site of battle—yet not its own battle but rather a battle for what Thebes might mean in the *Iliad*. It occurs in the context of the continuing dissection of Agamemnon's leadership, as that hero initially retells the story of the Seven as a lesson for his own troops (namely Tydeus' son, Diomedes), only—again—to meet resistance and challenge. Through the different responses that Agamemnon's story provokes, the story of Thebes in—and its significance for—the world of the *Iliad* similarly becomes transformed. The tale about singular action becomes a means for stressing the importance of collective action, as the *Iliad* instrumentally projects antiquated values on to the heroic action at Thebes.

As well as the theme of a single, and *singular*, warrior, Chapter 1 also brings to light the *Iliad*'s positioning of Thebes as a world where the values of individual heroism hold sway: this world is now, from the perspective of the *Iliad*, a thing of the past; concurrently, Thebes as a paradigm is relegated to irrelevance. Chapter 2 ("The Labors of Herakles") explores this idea of being out of time in more detail through the figure of Herakles. Herakles is the hero of Greek myth par excellence, at once immortal and mortal, against whom all other mythological figures, including Homer's heroes, must be assessed and matched. Both Homeric poems, however, simultaneously appropriate and marginalize Herakles from a nebulous range of myths, and characterize—or, better, define or limit— him as a *Theban* hero; his greater Panhellenic potential is quietly but insistently suppressed. In particular, Herakles functions as a locus through which metaphysical questions such as the boundaries of human life and excellence are reframed. In this way Homer's heroes *use* Herakles to make sense of their world and to confront, and deal with, their own mortality. Herakles, as a result, becomes a strangely isolated, inimitable figure, neither a mere mortal like them, nor, however, the immortal demi-god of popular myth. Immortality in Homer's world is to be sought through other means, the power of epic song.

The question of poetics—how the Homeric epics compose and create using material extraneous to their particular tale—is central to the third chapter on form. This chapter ("Homer's Oedipus Complex") lingers on the scene where we leave Herakles, in the *Odyssey*'s Nekyia where the eponymous hero himself positions his story in and against particular (and peculiar) presentations of other heroic traditions. Using the fleeting reference to "Oedipus of many pains"—an epithet that explicitly aligns this Theban character with Homer's quintessential suffering hero—we trace the ways in which Odysseus promotes his fame, not only by virtue of the language that he uses to describe heroic endeavor, but also by the means through which he communicates it. Crucial to the success of his enterprise is the broader context in which Oedipus' not-so tragic tale is embedded: the catalogue of Theban women. By considering how the *Odyssey* integrates this alternative poetic form into its own narrative, we are provided with an opportunity to reflect on Homeric poetics more broadly and how epic fame can be (re)formed.

The final three chapters turn away from the pattern of focusing on specific tales or story traditions to consider larger movements in and around epic poetry, based on the idea of interpoetic rivalry. In Chapter 4 ("Doubling Down On Strife") we investigate the theme of strife (*Eris*) as a compositional and cultural feature of Homeric poetry. Before considering strife in Homer, we examine in some detail the ways in which Hesiod provides not one but two origin stories for strife in his cosmological epics. By recontextualizing strife within the Hesiodic framework of a "cosmic history," and using the ideas of interformularity and intertraditionality discussed above, we then explore how the Homeric epics are engaged in an interpoetic debate about rivalry not only with the Hesiodic epics but also, so far as we can judge, with the remnants of the Theban tradition. What is particularly interesting is the sense that this metacontest (striving about strife, as it were) is at once both highly competitive and significantly productive. The form and meaning of strife appear to shift and evolve through its varying representations.

One strong theme to emerge from this investigation is the "domestication of strife." Chapter 5 ("Theban Palimpsests") explores further the idea that strife can somehow (in some ways) be managed and negotiated for positive ends. Where the previous chapter takes a broad view of the general resonance of the theme of strife, Chapter 5 explores its representation and significance in the *Iliad* and the *Odyssey*. Here, Homer's tales reveal what we call a certain "secondariness" in positioning themselves both as temporally coming after and as final respondents in a discussion about strife. This idea relates to the positioning of the Homeric poems within the epic cosmos as foundational narratives—poems that not only narrate events that take place in a bygone age of heroes (cf. Hesiod) but also explain the death of the race of heroes and set out what comes in their wake. In the place of the exploits of an individual hero is collective action enabled by and structured through the foundation of institutions. In this way, one positive outcome of the strife that erupts at the beginning of the *Iliad* is the establishment of a political community based on the management and negotiation of dissent. The story we will tell is not, however, a wholly progressive one, as the *Odyssey* in particular returns insistently to probe the difficulties of and fissures within managing strife.

The proposal that the Homeric poems emerge successfully (with Hesiod's poems) to articulate a Panhellenic epic cosmos that stretches from the beginning of the cosmos to the present day brings us back to the question of *why Thebes?*—why Theban epics did not successfully make the critical transition to writing. In our final chapter ("Beyond Thebes") we reflect on the relationship between Theban and Trojan narratives through the frame of Panhellenism. Our investigations in Chapters 4 and 5 suggest that poetic agonism conditioned a culture of replacement and succession in epic narratives in part as an instrument of or function within the development of Panhellenic culture. We explore this idea more critically in Chapter 6 where we suggest that Homer's Thebes (the culmination of all the Theban narratives expropriated) is colored as a specifically *Boiotian* tradition. As part of poetic rivalry and the eventual preeminence of Homer, the *Iliad* and the *Odyssey* "re-localize" Theban tales even as they elevate their universalism. In developing this argument, we consider two alternative movements: first, how individual local Boiotian traditions were integrated within Hesiod and other tales; and, second, how repeated intersections between and negotiations of epichoric narratives and emerging Panhellenic tales helped in turn to condition the Homeric epics.

Our epilogue briefly reflects on Homer's Thebes. It suggests that the process in which and by which the Homeric poems became "victorious" continued well past their textualization. We also look ahead to some of the ways in which the contributions of this book might be tested or reconfigured. In particular, we consider some examples of heroic reburials as analogs for the process of reception. Such a process is at once an example of the discrete and countless steps that we consider part of the generation of the larger tapestry of Greek myth and a metaphor for the process of re-reading and "repatriation" in which we too are implicated.

1

Troy, The Next Generation: Politics[1]

HOMER'S ENGAGEMENT WITH THEBES comes to the fore as the two opposing forces prepare to do battle for the first time in the *Iliad* on the plain in front of Troy's citadel. Agamemnon's review of his troops (*Iliad* 4.223–421) continues both the examination of his leadership and the introduction to some of the main Achaean figures. While some heroes—Idomeneus, the Aiantes, and Nestor—are praised for their eagerness for war, others are chastised for holding back. Among this latter group (which includes Menestheus and Odysseus) is the son of Tydeus, Diomedes.[2]

In criticizing Diomedes, Agamemnon compares him to his father, Tydeus, a hero who belongs to the Theban mythscape of an epic siege. Agamemnon's story of Tydeus' escapades at Thebes is the first and most detailed scene in the *Iliad* that directly relates the events of its rival tradition. In it, Agamemnon recounts how Diomedes' father first visited Mycenae with Polyneikes, for the purpose of seeking allies for the assault on Thebes; later Tydeus went to Thebes alone, where he challenged and beat the Thebans in athletic contests; on his return, he single-handedly defeated an ambush of fifty picked men, leaving only two survivors (4.370–400).[3] If only his son, Diomedes, were such a man.

The example of Tydeus is cited on three further occasions, each time as Diomedes takes a leading role in the action. In the first, Athena appears to Diomedes in the midst of his *aristeia* (*Iliad* 5.800–813), in itself a highly visible manifestation of this hero's response to, and stirring riposte of, Agamemnon's earlier stinging criticism. Relating some of the same events that Agamemnon had told, Athena reveals that, though she had urged Tydeus to keep the peace at Thebes, he had nevertheless challenged the Thebans to athletic contests. Later, in the wake of the failed embassy to Achilles, as the Achaean leaders meet to

---

[1] Many sections of this chapter draw on work originally published in Barker and Christensen 2011.

[2] On the *Epipolesis* scene and Agamemnon's speech, see Austin 1975:5; Martin 1989:63–72; and Beck 2005:154–164. Cf. Nagy 1999 [1979]:162–164. For the structure of the scene: Kirk 1985:353–354.

[3] On the use of such *paradeigmata* in speeches, see especially Willcock 1964 and 1977. Cf. Braswell 1971; Combellack 1976; Held 1987; Andersen 1987; Edmunds 1997; and Nagy 1996a:113–146.

plan a daring night raid on the enemy camp, Diomedes mentions his father's Theban embassy and emphasizes Athena's support in repelling their ambush, as he offers his own prayer to the goddess for support (*Iliad* 10.284-294). Finally, in Book 14, with Agamemnon again despairing of his army, Diomedes at long last provides his version of his father's tale and, by taking ownership of his paternal inheritance, affirms his own heroic credentials.

With these different, but interrelated, examples, Homer's *Iliad* demonstrates its awareness of a rival tradition that pertains to the siege of a city. Significantly, however, only these events—the exploits of Tydeus—are preserved as storied elements within Homer's tale.[4] No other aspects of a Theban plot are articulated, even if other major heroes, like Herakles and Oedipus, do gain passing mentions (as we shall see in later chapters). Moreover, even the Theban story that *is* related—Tydeus' travel there and back again—is frustratingly brief, elusive and even oddly inconsequential. Nevertheless, some scholars have argued that Agamemnon's framing of his account as derivative ("they say," 4.375) "presupposes a knowledge of the events," as if these events were an acknowledged part of the tradition and the *Iliad* (through Agamemnon) were representing them accurately and in due order.[5] Whether or not this is true—and we have our doubts, as we explain below—it remains striking that the focus is not where one might expect it to be. That is to say, Agamemnon, as well as Athena and Diomedes after him, has nothing to say about the attack of the Seven against Thebes itself, which one might have supposed would have been the primary comparandum for the Trojan story. Rather he concentrates on a single episode in the epic career of one of the heroes, which belongs not to the decisive battle for the city but to obscure preliminary events.[6]

Using these episodes involving Diomedes and the tales about this father, in this chapter we test our hypothesis that the Theban material in Homer is put to the service of the narratives of the *Iliad* and *Odyssey*, rather than preserving a remnant of the original narrative focus of a Theban poem.[7] We propose that a close examination of Agamemnon's tale of Tydeus reveals a thematic

---

[4]   "All the substantial narrative allusions to the Theban Wars cluster around the hero Diomedes and have to do specifically with his father Tydeus" (Sammons 2014:297–298).

[5]   Ebbott 2010 and 2014; cf. Vergados 2014:438. Both scholars are right to point to the audience's deep familiarity with a Theban epic tradition, but they do not consider how Homer might be exploiting it for effect.

[6]   Sammons 2014:299–300.

[7]   Sammons (2014:300) puts the question in slightly different terms, asking: how can we be confident that a corresponding episode loomed large or even existed in some archaic poem, or even performance tradition, to which we could imagine him alluding? While he suggests that "the very structure of narrative allusions can reflect the influence of other poems on the *Iliad*," ultimately he remains "pessimistic that even this can constitute compelling evidence that Homer's allusions are based on an external source."

disharmony with certain strains within the *Iliad* at large. This incongruity, we suggest, not only reflects the *Iliad*'s own consumption and interrogation of competing views on warfare, heroism and human society; it also represents an invitation to weigh the consequences of those choices in relation to other story traditions. To set the stage, we give a brief account of the epic careers of the Seven against Thebes as preserved elsewhere in the archaic Greek poetic corpus. Next, we analyze the individual components of Agamemnon's tale to explore how he creates a legendary tale of Tydeus with themes rooted in the mythical past and an emphasis on an individual's exceptionality. Then, by examining the tension between Agamemnon's message and the responses that it elicits (both from the characters involved and in the subsequent narrative), we argue that the embedded tale contrasts to, and is corrected by, the *Iliad*'s own developing interest in collective action.

Our argument will be that the subordination of the Theban material, upon which Agamemnon draws to the main narrative of the *Iliad*, encourages reflection on the relationship between the Homeric epics and the pasts presented within them. Arguably the most striking aspect of this Thebes story is the fact that it is presented as the *past*, an example—and a negative one at that—to the heroes of the (always) present, the heroes of Homer's *Iliad*.

The Battle for Thebes

> The epic called *Thebais* was composed about this war. Kallinos, when he comes to mention this epic, says that Homer composed it. Many authors of considerable repute have believed the same thing. And I praise this poem especially, after the *Iliad* and *Odyssey* at any rate.
>
> Pausanias IX 5[8]

When it comes to thinking about the story of the Seven against Thebes in epic, it is difficult to avoid being drawn in to a discussion of *an epic* "Seven Against Thebes." While we made it clear in the introduction that we neither consider it fruitful to try to reconstruct the lost or fragmentary epic(s) that told this story nor are interested in examining whether or not our *Iliad* draws on specific passages in an analytic fashion,[9] in order to appreciate the Homeric

---

[8] ἐποιήθη δὲ ἐς τὸν πόλεμον τοῦτον καὶ ἔπη Θηβαΐς· τὰ δὲ ἔπη ταῦτα Καλλῖνος ἀφικόμενος αὐτῶν ἐς μνήμην ἔφησεν Ὅμηρον τὸν ποιήσαντα εἶναι, Καλλίνῳ δὲ πολλοί τε καὶ ἄξιοι λόγου κατὰ ταὐτὰ ἔγνωσαν· ἐγὼ δὲ τὴν ποίησιν ταύτην μετὰ γε Ἰλιάδα καὶ τὰ ἔπη τὰ ἐς Ὀδυσσέα ἐπαινῶ μάλιστα.

[9] For a discussion of earlier comments reconstructing a *Thebais*' contents for this purpose, see Davies 2014:34–38. He argues that the "basic presuppositions of the *Iliad* and the *Thebais*...are similar" (38). For neoanalysis as an approach, see the section "Neoanalysis" in the Introduction.

representation of this material we must first give a brief preliminary sketch on what a notional Theban epic on the siege of the city may have included.

In antiquity the poem known as the *Thebais* was attributed to Homer by authors as far apart temporally as Herodotus (V 67) and Pausanias (IX 9.1).[10] While scholarship of the last two centuries has largely followed the Aristotelian trend of ascribing only the *Iliad* and the *Odyssey* to Homer, many have nevertheless seen the appearance in the Homeric poems of details from stories assumed to be part of a lost *Thebais* as indicating an extant tradition with which "Homer" was familiar.[11] Such a notion is entirely plausible, though we are more cautious about positing a monumental *Thebais* about which we can assert anything positive. Indeed evidence from the *Iliad* would seem to suggest a narrow, specific, and rather idiosyncratic engagement with Theban themes, one which, furthermore, privileges one putative Theban tradition (the *Epigonoi*) over another (the *Thebais*). In all likelihood one reason for this is the narrative drive of the *Iliad*, which, as we shall see, is interested in both establishing and then interrogating the internal dynamics of the Achaean political community. In order to appropriately assess Homer's praise for the younger generation and emphasis on coalition politics set against individual heroic endeavor (as imagined taking place at Thebes), it will be useful to briefly summarize what we think might have been in the lost Theban poems.

The fragmentary remains of the *Thebais* scattered through a range of diverse sources provide at least some picture of what the epic might have included.[12] Though nothing can be said about the poem's structure or characterization, its plot is assumed to have covered the events that later constitute Aeschylus' *Seven Against Thebes* and is further detailed in the mythographer Apollodorus (III 6). Cursed by their father, the sons of Oedipus, Eteocles and Polyneikes, contest the leadership for the city. Gathering allies from around the Greek world, they precipitate a dreadful conflict that leads to the death of many great heroes—not least the two of them, killed by their own hands at city's seventh gate.[13] Strikingly, in what appears to be the remains of its opening invocation, the *Thebais* begins not with Thebes but with Argos from where the expedition departed: "Goddess, sing of very-thirsty Argos, from where the leaders [departed for Thebes]."[14] As with the other fragments, we will discuss this opening further in Chapter 4

---

[10] Davies 2014:28–32.
[11] For a discussion and bibliography, see Davies 2014:32–41.
[12] The evidence is helpfully brought together and discussed in Davies 2014, Chapter 2.
[13] For the fragments of the *Thebais* see Davies 1988:22–26; Bernabé 1987:22–28. For the Seven myth, see the general narrative in Apollodorus III 57–77; cf. Hyginus 68–70. Cf. the discussion by Gantz 1993:502–518, and our discussion of the Stesichorus Lille fragment below in Chapter 5. See also Fowler 2013:408–414 on the early mythographers more generally.
[14] Ἄργος ἄειδε, θεά, πολυδίψιον, ἔνθεν ἄνακτες (fr. 1.1).

below; for the time being it is worth noting that the headline theme anticipates a story about a group of heroes engaged in a collective act. Indeed, while two of the lengthiest fragments attest to familial conflicts (fr. 2 and 3), others point to a gathering of heroes that aligns the Theban tradition both to the framework of a cosmic history (outlined in the introduction) and to the idea of a coalition of Achaeans from the Trojan War tradition (as represented by the Homeric poems). The smattering of details that refer to the magical horse Arion (fr. 6), the denial of immortality to Tydeus (fr. 5), and the involvement of Amphiaraus, Parthenopaios and others, unsurprisingly fail to communicate the character of the whole epic, leaving us guessing as to what the (or a) poem might have looked like. But what is clear is that these fragments do not align easily with the information about Thebes recorded in the Homeric poems, specifically in the *Iliad*. Again we should stress that Homer's Theban story centers largely on Diomedes' father, Tydeus, and expressly a single episode that would have been but a small portion of any epic's larger plot structure. Tydeus, as we shall see, comes across as a very different kind of hero than his son.[15]

We believe that Homer capitalizes upon and subverts poetic traditions in Theban myth in two ways. First, he chooses one character out of the many on whom to focus, thereby downplaying the element of coalition or a cooperative dynamic at play in Theban narratives. Second, by focusing on Tydeus and his contrast with Diomedes, the *Iliad*'s tale also undermines a conventional theme of generational decline, marking out the sons, for once, as better than their fathers. This strategy, as we discussed in the Introduction, has metapoetic concerns as well. Even though the *Iliad* is situated as coming after Thebes—Thebes has already been sacked by the time that Homer's poem is staged, it projects itself as anything but—as the only siege story worth telling. To make matters more complex, Homer may well be exploiting tensions already latent in the Theban traditions.

---

[15] For a survey of the stories about Tydeus omitted by Diomedes, see Janko 1992:163–164. *Thebais* fr. 9 PEG 1 (*apud* Σ [D] *Iliad* 5.16) presents us with a different view of Tydeus' personality: there he is not the god-respecting champion of the *Iliad* but a brutish cannibal whose actions disgust even his protecting goddess, Athena. The question of human obedience to the gods could have been thematic for an archaic *Thebais*, since later poets repeatedly emphasize that the Seven marched "not according to a path of good-fated birds" (αἰσιᾶν οὐ κατ' ὀρνίχων ὁδόν, Pindar *Nemean* 9.18–19, see Sammons 2014). The scholion on ἄτερ πολέμου ("outside of war") presents the embassy to Mycenae by Polyneikes and Tydeus as part of a known narrative about the war against Thebes: Ebbott 2014. Far from drawing a distinction between the *Iliad*'s account and any nominal Theban poem, the scholion even provides a detail that harmonizes the two: Agamemnon only heard about the tale because it was Thyestes to whom they made their appeal for allies.

The Seven Sons

There is mention of the Hyperboreans in Hesiod and in Homer as well in the *Epigonoi*, if Homer actually was the one who composed that poem.

Herodotus IV 32.7[16]

In contrast with the *Thebais*, the story of the *second* Seven against Thebes is not well attested during the Archaic and Classical periods. At an early period the failed Theban sack had accrued more than one "sequel," the first being Theseus' siege of the city to force the burial of the war dead (see Apollodorus III 7). Even later mythographers leave little space for the deeds of the sons. In Apollodorus' breezy account, for example, the sons barely warrant a mention: he concentrates instead on the many tales surrounding the death of Teiresias and the follow-up story involving Alcmaeon. As such the story that is strongly fronted by the *Iliad* appears to have enjoyed a rather tenuous existence.

It comes as no surprise, then, that very little certain is known of the epic poem referred to in ancient testimonies as the *Epigonoi*. Although it is attributed to Homer as early as Herodotus (IV 32), the stories that appear to be at home in that narrative—the sacking of Thebes by the sons of the Seven—are not well attested until after the Classical period;[17] modern scholars agree on only a single fragment as being genuine.[18] Even in the context of an imagined cycle of Theban epics,[19] the *Epigonoi* seems to be derivative from and secondary to the main stage: that is, the tales of Oedipus and the original Seven against Thebes. In nearly every surviving mention of the sons who came after, it is their nature as successors—as stand-ins or understudies for an original line up—that is emphasized, more than their role as heirs or inheritors of an epic glory. Depending as they do on a preceding tale for context and meaning, the tales of the Epigonoi seem incompletely formed. Such a reception of the *Epigonoi* narrative may be

---

[16] Ἀλλ᾽ Ἡσιόδῳ μέν ἐστι περὶ Ὑπερβορέων εἰρημένα, ἔστι δὲ καὶ Ὁμήρῳ ἐν Ἐπιγόνοισι, εἰ δὴ τῷ ἐόντι γε Ὅμηρος ταῦτα τὰ ἔπεα ἐποίησε.

[17] For the Epigonoi myth, see the short summary at Apollodorus III 80, which has the events start ten years later. This narrative says relatively little about what the sons of the Seven do and focuses more on Teiresias. Cf. the similarly brief treatment at Hyginus 71. See also the discussion in Gantz 1993:522–524. For early references, see Pindar *Pythian* 8.39–55. Tragedies on the Epigonoi are ascribed to both Aeschylus and Euripides: Fowler 2013:414.

[18] For the fragments of the *Epigonoi* see Davies 1988:26–27; Bernabé 1996:30–31. Davies 1988 accepts only fr. 1 as genuine. For the Theban epics in general, the most recent overview is Davies 2014. While earlier scholars argued that the *Epigonoi* was most likely a part of the *Thebais*, Davies 2014:107–108 insists that they were separate poems with the *Epigonoi* functioning as a closely related "sequel."

[19] For a Theban cycle that might include the *Oidipodeia, Thebais, Epigonoi*, and perhaps even the *Alcmeonis*, see Burgess 2011:184; West 2013:2–4; Fantuzzi and Tsagalis 2014.

endemic to the kind of story it tells. The tale of sons returning to complete the deeds of their famous fathers certainly has an air of a sequel about it rather than the material for a primary plot. Moreover, because of its marginal place in epic cosmic history—between Thebes and Troy, as it were—it lacks the paradigmatic quality of either of the other expeditions. Rather, it represents a transitional tale, caught betwixt and between one amalgamated coalition story and the grander, Panhellenic opera.

As we have already noted briefly, the twin aspects of derivativeness and secondariness, which characterize the fragments of the *Epigonoi* tradition, are reflected too in the *Iliad*: the very reason why Agamemnon introduces a Theban tale is to chastise one of the Epigonoi for not living up to the exceptional deeds of his father. Central to its agonistic strategy, then, is the exploitation of latent themes underlying that earlier expedition. In exploiting these themes, the *Iliad* is also in part responsible for perpetuating them and ensuring their inclusion as part of the dominant narrative about Thebes. Yet, as we shall see, the *Iliad*'s handling of the Epigonoi is a good deal more complicated, not least because of its own positioning as a post-Thebes story.

Before turning to consider the Homeric reception of the *Epigonoi* in detail, to end this section it is worth drawing out a number of significant themes at which the remaining fragments appear to hint. The only widely accepted fragment comes from the *Certamen*, the *Contest between Homer and Hesiod*: "Now, Muses, let us sing in turn of the younger men" (Νῦν αὖθ' ὁπλοτέρων ἀνδρῶν ἀρχώμεθα, Μοῦσαι, fr. 1).[20] This fragment reflects an essential secondariness in several ways. As the first line in an epic poem it does not start out by establishing its own story-world in the manner of an *Iliad* or an *Odyssey*; instead, its opening adverbs "now, in turn" (Νῦν αὖθ') indicate that it is dependent upon something that has come before, as if a singer is picking up the story at a point that another has just left off. It requires an earlier story-frame for its own existence. Second, rather than invoking a single hero or even specific men in a specific time and

---

[20] Other fragments attributed to the *Epigonoi* are either too uncertain or too generic to add much to the foregoing analysis. Bernabé accepts fr. 4 from Clement of Alexandria as genuine ("Many evils come to men from gifts," ἐκ γὰρ δώρων πολλὰ κάκ' ἀνθρώποισι πέλονται) but its inclusion in the *Stromata*'s list of plagiarized ideas gives no original context, but merely attributes the line to Antimachus of Teos (not to the *Epigonoi* specifically) and collocates it with a line of similar sentiment from the Cyclic *Nostoi* ("Gifts deceive the minds and actions of men," δῶρα γὰρ ἀνθρώπων νόον ἤπαφεν ἠδὲ καὶ ἔργα, fr. 8.1). Bernabé lists two more dubious fragments. In fr. 6, "They feasted on the meat of cattle and they loosed the horses' sweating necks, since they were sated with war" (ὣς οἱ μὲν δαίνυντο βοῶν κρέα, καυχένας ἵππων / ἔκλυον ἱδρώοντας, ἐπεὶ πολέμοιο κορέσθην). Fr. 7 features "men who gird for war, and when they are done, some pour from towers and a war-cry arises" (θωρήσσοντ' ἄρ' ἔπειτα πεπαυμένοι / πύργων δ' ἐξεχέοντο, βοὴ δ' ἄσβεστος ὀρώρει). These two fragments are certainly suggestive of epic themes (as we discuss them in Chapters 5 and 6), but they lack context and specifics.

place (by ethnonym or toponym etc.), the players of this poem have only a derivative or comparative nature: they are the younger men, the next generation. The context of the fragment underlines its secondary status: it follows directly on from what is considered to be the opening line of the *Thebais* (Ἄργος ἄειδε θεὰ πολυδίψιον ἔνθεν ἄνακτες), as "Homer" is made to recite examples of his Theban material (i.e. "heroic epic", as distinct from Hesiod's own brand of epic). That prior poem provides a place, Argos, that acts as metonym for narrative: it is the location from where the heroic agents (the epic ἄνακτες, 'lords') departed for Thebes, while the epithet πολυδίψιον ('very thirsty') suggests a rich mythological source on which to draw. (A thirst for blood, perhaps?) In a way, the derivative status of the *Epigonoi* represents in part the general attitude from early Greek poetry that the present is degenerate and the past was more "heroic." As we know from Hesiod, it was in a bygone age that heroic men walked the earth.

It is this potential theme that the *Iliad* addresses most pointedly through its appropriation of the story of the *Epigonoi*. As we discuss in the Introduction and later in our discussion on epic themes (Chapter 4), the compositional tool of the anticipatory doublet—in which a theme or motif is repeated and expanded in a secondary mention—may indicate a general conceptual relationship between Homeric poetry and its precedents. In this regard, Homeric poetry doubles and echoes what came before, but not in a way that is derivative from or secondary to that material, but antagonistic to it; it works with and builds on (strips down and reuses) previous siege narratives in order to be the best (and only) show in town. The *Iliad*'s appropriation of the *Epigonoi* and its revision of the *Epigonoi*'s status vis-à-vis the earlier Theban cycle are thus both a fine indication of the way Homeric epic uses Theban themes and a test case for a broader poetic understanding of the anticipatory doublet.

In the rest of this chapter we examine the Theban story as presented to us in the *Iliad*. Our concern will be to consider the place of Thebes in Homer's epic poem. This means exploring to what ends Thebes is incorporated within the *Iliad*'s narrative, and asking what effect this has on our understanding of the two epic traditions of Troy and Thebes.

On Not Being Alone

Our proposal, based on the relatively little that survives from the *Thebais* and *Epigonoi* fragments outlined above, is that the *Iliad* selectively adopts and adapts motifs, themes, characters, and story patterns from their tradition in order to advance its own narrative concerns. Homer's agonistic appropriation of this other storyworld requires downplaying the collective character of a notional expedition against Thebes, in favor of promoting the *Iliad*'s vision of a Panhellenic coalition against Troy. At the same time, the *Iliad* challenges the common epic theme of generational degeneracy—archetypally represented by Hesiod's myth of the ages—by privileging a father over a son. Diomedes' father, Tydeus, is the figure designated for both of these tasks.

As the *Iliad* prepares for its first epic confrontation between Achaeans and Trojans, Agamemnon seeks to spur his leading men into action. The last of those on the receiving end of a tongue-lashing is Diomedes. He is presented with his father, Tydeus, who, it is said, successfully overcame all adversity on his Theban expedition, as a model to live up to. This section will set out how Agamemnon's story about Thebes evokes a story pattern of solitary excellence that comes under increasing scrutiny over the course of the *Iliad*. What is striking is that Agamemnon relates a story about a hero on his way to a major war, not the main event itself but an episode expressly peripheral to it, "outside of war" (ἄτερ πολέμου). Focusing on the constellation of phrases around which Agamemnon forms his tale (μοῦνος ἐὼν πολέσιν, ἐπίρροθος, πυκινὸν λόχον, ἀεικέα πότμον, and the like), we will argue that, from the perspective of their wider deployment, several elements of Agamemnon's focus—a singular hero alone among his enemies who, with the assistance of a divine helper, thwarts an ambush and unleashes vengeance on his assailants—sound out of place in a tale which will articulate the disastrous results of its protagonist's assertion of his individuality. This dissonance has several important implications beyond guiding the audience in reading one of the key elements of the *Iliad*'s plot: that is, Achilles' separation and exceptionalism. It also brings to the fore larger, *foundational* political themes, drawn from the wider cosmos of epic poetry, and makes them the special province of *this story* and this poem. Furthermore, in emphasizing the collective and privileging the later generation over the former, the *Iliad* also offers a metapoetic reflection on its relationship to other poetic traditions.

At the end of his review of the troops, Agamemnon turns his attention from Odysseus, whom he chastises for shirking battle, to Diomedes. Imagining the young hero to be similarly reluctant to fight, he issues a string of rebukes ("why do you cower, why do you look down on the bridges of war?", τί πτώσσεις, τί δ' ὀπιπεύεις πολέμοιο γεφύρας; *Iliad* 4.371), and reminds Diomedes of his father's exploits at Thebes (4.372-400).[21] That Diomedes is singled out as the target of Agamemnon's invective after Odysseus is significant. As one of the *Iliad*'s youngest heroes, Diomedes may be viewed as an index for the response of

---

[21] Kirk 1985:368 is unclear why Diomedes is chosen for rebuke and suggests that it is only for the opportunity to present a digression on Tydeus. Taplin 1992:145–146 contrasts Diomedes' refusal to engage in strife with Agamemnon to Achilles' quickness to anger. Willcock 1964:144–145 considers Agamemnon's account of Tydeus to be vastly exaggerated.

the epic's internal audiences to its presented past—and by extension, an object lesson in reception for that story's external audience.[22] It is important, therefore, that Diomedes is repeatedly enjoined to think about his father, even though, as he later admits to Glaukos in Book 6, he himself "does not remember Tydeus" (6.223–224). For Diomedes the past is an indeterminate, shifting construct, a text in the process of being stitched together, and whose significance as a model for the present is repeatedly contested. By looking more carefully at what Agamemnon says about this past, and how he uses it, we aim to tease out the combined significance of the utterances through which the Achaean leader selectively crafts his narrative and reflect on what extent his emphases are discordant with the context of *Iliad* 4.

As well as making a direct comparison between father and son, Agamemnon singles out Tydeus as a hero to emulate (4.370–400):

> "ὤ μοι Τυδέος υἱὲ δαΐφρονος ἱπποδάμοιο
> τί πτώσσεις, τί δ' ὀπιπεύεις πολέμοιο γεφύρας;
> οὐ μὲν Τυδέϊ γ' ὧδε φίλον πτωσκαζέμεν ἦεν,
> ἀλλὰ πολὺ πρὸ φίλων ἑτάρων δηΐοισι μάχεσθαι,
> ὡς φάσαν οἵ μιν ἴδοντο πονεύμενον· οὐ γὰρ ἔγωγε
> ἤντησ' οὐδὲ ἴδον· περὶ δ' ἄλλων φασὶ γενέσθαι.
> ἤτοι μὲν γὰρ <u>ἄτερ πολέμου</u> εἰσῆλθε Μυκήνας
> ξεῖνος ἅμ' ἀντιθέῳ Πολυνείκεϊ <u>λαὸν ἀγείρων·</u>
> οἳ δὲ τότ' ἐστρατόωνθ' ἱερὰ πρὸς τείχεα Θήβης,
> καί ῥα μάλα λίσσοντο δόμεν <u>κλειτοὺς ἐπικούρους·</u>
> οἳ δ' ἔθελον δόμεναι καὶ ἐπήνεον ὡς ἐκέλευον·
> ἀλλὰ Ζεὺς ἔτρεψε <u>παραίσια σήματα</u> φαίνων.
> οἳ δ' ἐπεὶ οὖν ᾤχοντο ἰδὲ πρὸ ὁδοῦ ἐγένοντο,
> Ἀσωπὸν δ' ἵκοντο βαθύσχοινον λεχεποίην,
> ἔνθ' αὖτ' ἀγγελίην ἐπὶ Τυδῆ στεῖλαν Ἀχαιοί.
> αὐτὰρ ὃ βῆ, πολέας δὲ κιχήσατο Καδμεΐωνας
> δαινυμένους κατὰ δῶμα βίης Ἐτεοκληείης.
> ἔνθ' οὐδὲ ξεῖνός περ ἐὼν ἱππηλάτα Τυδεὺς
> τάρβει, <u>μοῦνος ἐὼν πολέσιν</u> μετὰ Καδμείοισιν,
> ἀλλ' ὅ γ' ἀεθλεύειν προκαλίζετο, πάντα δ' ἐνίκα
> ῥηϊδίως· τοίη οἱ <u>ἐπίρροθος</u> ἦεν Ἀθήνη.
> οἳ δὲ χολωσάμενοι Καδμεῖοι κέντορες ἵππων
> ἂψ ἄρ' ἀνερχομένῳ <u>πυκινὸν λόχον</u> εἷσαν ἄγοντες

---

[22] For Diomedes' youth, see Nestor's comments (*Iliad* 9.57–58). Andersen 1978 suggests that Diomedes is a Homeric innovation; hence, the poet can manipulate his story as he wishes. On Diomedes' maturation in the *Iliad*, see: Martin 1989:54–56; Christensen 2009:151–153.

κούρους πεντήκοντα· δύω δ' ἡγήτορες ἦσαν,
Μαίων Αἱμονίδης ἐπιείκελος ἀθανάτοισιν,
υἱός τ' Αὐτοφόνοιο μενεπτόλεμος Πολυφόντης.
Τυδεὺς μὲν καὶ τοῖσιν <u>ἀεικέα πότμον</u> ἐφῆκε·
πάντας ἔπεφν', ἕνα δ' οἶον ἵει οἶκον δὲ νέεσθαι·
Μαίον' ἄρα προέηκε θεῶν τεράεσσι πιθήσας.
τοῖος ἔην Τυδεὺς Αἰτώλιος· ἀλλὰ τὸν υἱὸν
γείνατο εἶο χέρεια μάχῃ, ἀγορῇ δέ τ' ἀμείνω."

"Oh my, son of wise-minded Tydeus the horse-tamer,
Why are you lurking, why are you peeping over the bridges of war?
It wasn't dear to Tydeus, at least, to lurk like this,
But he fought with his enemies far in front of his dear companions—
That's what those who saw him toiling say. I never met the man
　　　　myself
Nor saw him. But they say he was better than the rest.
For, certainly, he went to Mycenae *outside of war*
As a guest *when he was gathering an army* with godly Polyneikes.
Then, they went on an expedition to the sacred walls of Thebes,
And they were begging these *famous allies* to join them.
And they were willing to go and consented to what these men asked
Until Zeus changed their minds by revealing *fateful signs*.
So then, after they left and were on the road,
They arrived at the Asopos, deep in reeds and grass
There, the Achaeans sent Tydeus forward on embassy.
And he went, and met the many Cadmeans.
Dining in the halls of mighty Eteocles.
There, stranger though he was, horse-driver Tydeus
was not frightened, *alone among many* Cadmeans.
But he challenged them to contests and won victory in all
easily. Such a *guardian* was Athena for your father!
But the Cadmeans, drivers of horses, were angered
and, as he departed from the city, they set up a *close ambush*
of fifty youths; there were two leaders,
Maion, son of Haimon, peer of the immortals,
and Autophonos' son, Polyphontes, staunch in fight.
But Tydeus let loose on them a *unseemly fate*:
he slew them all and only one man he sent to return home:
he sent Maion, trusting in the signs of the gods.

Such a man was Aitolian Tydeus; but he fathered a son
weaker than he in battle, but better in the assembly."

The story arc as presented by Agamemnon tells of a single, isolated hero, aided
by a god, who successfully defeats an ambush and metes out punishment
to his attackers. This type of discourse is *neikos*, blame speech, used here by
Agamemnon to prick Diomedes' pride.[23] His tale has a clear and simple aim: it
functions to shame Diomedes for (allegedly) shirking battle even though he
has the aid of his companions, when his father had successfully faced many
men *alone* in an ambush. Yet Agamemnon's intentions extend beyond merely
shaming the hero, since he is trying to shape Diomedes into a singular hero to
replace the one he has just contrived to lose, Achilles.

There are a number of phrases in this passage that resonate throughout the
rest of the *Iliad*, pointing to shared story motifs and patterns between the two
heroic endeavors, the events at Troy and the battle for Thebes. One of these is
the phrase that serves to frame Agamemnon's account, the formula "gathering
warriors" (λαὸν ἀγείρων, *Iliad* 4.377). The same formula is used of gathering
warriors at key points in the epic, as when Achilles likens Agamemnon's taking
of Briseis to Paris' abduction of Helen from Menelaos,[24] or when Nestor tries to
convince Patroklos to persuade Achilles to return to battle or to take his place
instead.[25] On both occasions the formula refers to the process of recruiting allies
for the war on Troy, suggesting some kind of correlation between Agamemnon's
inset narrative about Thebes and the current war at Troy. For Mary Ebbott,
Agamemnon's use of a phrase that resonates with his own situation might
suggest a pointed reinforcement of his own recruitment of Achaean warriors
for the struggle at Troy, after the shock of Achilles' challenge and withdrawal.[26]
After all he *has* managed to bring together a coalition, one so broad and diverse
that Agamemnon could be regarded as the ultimate people-gatherer in the epic
tradition.[27] Yet, while the formula resonates with the gathering of groups and
the mustering of armies, Agamemnon's redeployment of it sounds off key. In
the tale that he offers Patroklos, Nestor gives an indication of what the theme
of "gathering allies" might look like: the recruiters show up, find their intended

[23] For an extensive analysis of blame expressions in Homer, see Vodoklys 1992. Cf. also Nagy 1999 [1979]:211–275 and Martin 1989:30–35.

[24] "Why did Atreus' son gather the host and lead it here? (τί δὲ λαὸν ἀνήγαγεν ἐνθάδ' ἀγείρας Ἀτρεΐδης; *Iliad* 9.338–339). That is to say, the expression here relates to the gathering of warriors for the Trojan expedition. All examples are taken from Ebbott 2014.

[25] Having described Athena as the one who gathered the warriors for the Pylians' battle against the Epeians (*Iliad* 11.716), he goes on to remind Patroklos of the instructions his father Menoetius gave to him before he and Achilles left for Troy (11.769–770).

[26] Ebbott 2014.

[27] On the importance of people-gathering in epic, see Haubold 2000, Chapter 1, especially p. 33.

warriors (*Iliad* 11.771–777), and are greeted and shown proper hospitality (*Iliad* 11.777–779). Agamemnon hints at a similar reception for Tydeus and Polyneikes in his hometown of Mycenae, whose men initially were willing to go—but then Zeus changes their minds and they reject the alliance. Agamemnon's story instead privileges the victorious *single* hero, Tydeus. The framing device that Agamemnon chooses to deploy, then, resonates discordantly with his chosen subject.

Agamemnon's particular, unconventional use of this formulaic unit (and fundamental epic theme) is further underlined by the related formula, κλειτοὺς ἐπικούρους, to describe the "famous allies" in Mycenae whom Tydeus and Polyneikes attempt (and ultimately fail) to win over. Ebbott notes that, except for this use within Agamemnon's Theban story, the term ἐπίκουροι in the plural refers only ever to the Trojan allies in the *Iliad*.[28] Its resonant meaning—men who are "famous" because they fight for κλέος—seems to point to the role of allies. These are men who are not compelled to fight for the sake of their city but choose to fight.[29] One might think that the Achaean army is similar, but critically it is not an assemblage of foreign parts.[30] Indeed, within Agamemnon's opening frame there are hints that the Achaeans as a group represent a different kind of a collective, where the king relates that Tydeus fought "far in front of his dear companions" (πολὺ πρὸ φίλων ἑτάρων, 4.373). "Companions" (ἕταροι) is a description that in the *Odyssey* refers, in a highly charged way, to the group who accompany Odysseus on his way back from Troy, while the repetition of the adjective φίλος—it was not dear (φίλον, 4.372) to Tydeus to lurk, but he fought in front of his "dear companions" (φίλων ἑτάρων)—gestures towards the key idea of friendship (*philia*). Like Tydeus' companions, the Achaeans are friends, φίλοι, bound together by something more than a desire to win glory, as Ajax makes clear in his final appeal to Achilles to return (9.642).[31] The Trojans are *epikouroi* precisely because they are *not philoi*, unlike the Achaeans, and the same is apparently true of Tydeus' allies. Or, to put it differently, whereas Agamemnon seeks to imply a favorable image of his leadership by comparing his gathering

---

[28] Ebbott 2014 also notes that the Trojans are called their "allies in fame" (with κλειτοί at least six times, τηλεκλειτοί 'far-famed' at least four times, and ἀγακλειτοί 'very famous' at least once).

[29] The situation is more complex, as one of the most famous of these allies, Sarpedon, articulates in 12.310–328: because he and Glaukon are most honored in their community, they need to fight in the front line. However, this social obligation in the end is subordinated to the importance of winning fame, as Sarpedon concedes that, were he immortal, he wouldn't fight in the front line after all, but, since they are not, they should try to win glory.

[30] Iris describes the Trojans in such terms, as they gather for the first time in the epic: the "many allies of Priam" (πολλοὶ...Πριάμου ἐπίκουροι) among whom "tongue differs from tongue among widely-seeded mankind" (ἄλλη δ᾽ ἄλλων γλῶσσα πολυσπερέων ἀνθρώπων, *Iliad* 2.803–804).

[31] On *philia* as a critical cohesive force in the *Iliad*: Goldhill 1991:80–93.

of allies with the (failed) attempt by Tydeus and Polyneikes, the very language of epic upon which he draws opens up his words to an alternative hearing that is less pertinent to the situation at hand. In spite of what Agamemnon says, the closer social bond of *philia* underpins the Achaean coalition. But then, this is not the only misapprehension under which he acts. In his description of Tydeus as someone who fights "in front of his dear companions" (πρὸ φίλων ἑτάρων 4.374), he indicates a position reserved for a champion or hero now absent among the Achaeans since Achilles is gone. Even in his initial framing of the Theban story, Agamemnon's attempt to shore up his own coalition and, through that, his own prosecution of a siege sounds off key and off message. He clearly yearns for a different narrative and a different kind of hero to support it, on which basis he constructs Tydeus as a certain kind of model for Diomedes.

Other discordant echoes between the two traditions further unsettle Agamemnon's account. The Mycenaeans of his tale are in fact at first willing to join up, only to turn back after receiving foreboding portents ("They were willing to give [famous allies] in turn and were praising what they were suggesting / but Zeus turned them back by showing fateful signs." οἳ δ' ἔθελον δόμεναι καὶ ἐπήνεον ὡς ἐκέλευον· / ἀλλὰ Ζεὺς ἔτρεψε παραίσια σήματα φαίνων, 4.380–381). As we will see, Sthenelos, in his rebuttal of Agamemnon, attributes the success of the Epigonoi to their attention to such portents (4.406–408), which not only suggests "that such signs were significant in the Theban tradition"[32] but corrects Agamemnon's tale—it was the sons of the Seven who sacked Troy, not their fathers. Portents are also significant in the Trojan War tradition. In his own attempt at (re)gathering the Achaean coalition to fight against the Trojans, Odysseus recalls the signs that they had received at Aulis, at the launch of their expeditionary force (*Iliad* 2.301–332): portents from Zeus frame his account ("big sign," μέγα σῆμα; 2.308; "great portent," τέρας μέγα: 2.324).[33] He is swiftly backed up by Nestor, who recounts how "the greatly powerful son of Cronus nodded in assent on that day when the Argives were embarking on the swift-traversing ships bringing death and destruction to the Trojans in the assembly of Book 2, flashing lightning on the right side, revealing signs of good omen" (ἐναίσιμα σήματα, *Iliad* 2.350–353). While Odysseus' description of Zeus' "great portent" (τέρας μέγα) is picked up by Agamemnon's description of the "divine portents and help from Zeus" (τεράεσσι θεῶν καὶ Ζηνὸς ἀρωγῇ, 4.408), which the Epigonoi obeyed in their successful attack on Thebes, Nestor's description

---

[32] Ebbott 2014.

[33] Ebbott 2014. Odysseus introduces the portent as a μέγα σῆμα 'big sign' (2.308) before quoting Calchas' interpretation that the Achaeans will fight for nine years and be victorious in the tenth. The quotation of Calchas refers to the petrified snake as a τέρας μέγα: "so to us Zeus the deviser revealed this great portent" (ἡμῖν μὲν τόδ' ἔφηνε τέρας μέγα μητίετα Ζεὺς, *Iliad* 2.324).

of the good omens (ἐναίσιμα σήματα, 2.353) that the Achaeans at Troy have received contrast directly with the baleful omens (παραίσια σήματα, 4.381) received by the Mycenaeans. Indeed, it is because of these baleful signs that the Mycenaeans are deterred from joining the expedition against Thebes, and that Tydeus is sent on *another embassy*, this time to Thebes itself.[34] And, where the Mycenaeans had declined to join Polyneikes in obedience to divine signs (παραίσια σήματα, 4.381), so Tydeus spares Maion in obedience to divine signs (θεῶν τεράεσσι πιθήσας, 4.398).[35] A story ostensibly about a coalition turns out to be ambushed by a rather singular hero.

Further examples of interformularity with other Homeric passages reveal disharmonious tones in Agamemnon's main presentation of Tydeus' deeds. Arguably the most obvious disconnect with the *Iliad*'s narrative is Agamemnon's account of the ambush that surprises Tydeus on his way back from his embassy in Thebes. Generally more at home in the *Odyssey*'s narrative of epic labors and return, the ambush tends to be configured as incongruous with the Iliadic focus on, if not ideal of, face-to-face combat on the battlefield.[36] It may be true that even in the *Iliad* the ambush *can* be viewed as a venue for performing singular deeds, but examples tend to be restricted to speeches[37] or the Odyssean misadventures of Book 10 (on which, see further below).[38] More pointedly, Agamemnon's description of the ambush visited upon Tydeus as "close" (πυκινός) occurs on only two other occasions: at the end of the *Iliad* when Priam assures his fellow

[34] Thus it turns out that Tydeus' "embassy to Mycenae is not so much arbitrary as it is redundant; Agamemnon's narrative is fashioned so that Tydeus participates in two embassies" (Sammons 2014:301). Sammons describes this structure as conforming to Fenik's (1968) "anticipatory doublet." In the first embassy, Tydeus arrives in the company of another hero, he is treated with gracious hospitality, and his mission is nearly a success. In the second embassy, he goes alone to a hostile city, and the embassy ends not only unsuccessfully but with an outbreak of violence.

[35] Sammons 2014 notes a further doubling: Tydeus first challenges the Thebans to athletic contests and defeats them; later he is waylaid by a Theban ambush and defeats them in battle. Hence two challenges, two contests, and two victories. The doubling, which may be significant for thinking about Thebes as the other to the Homeric tradition of a siege and as the place where the family is horrendously doubled up, suggests an overdetermination on Agamemnon's part—an inability to exactly match the events at Thebes with his immediate concerns in this narrative.

[36] See *Iliad* 1.227, 6.189, 8.521, 11.379, 13.279, 18.519–21, 24.779; *Odyssey* 4.277, 388, 395, 441, 531, 463, 8.515, 11.526, 13.268, 13.425, 14.217, 14.469, 15.28, 16.369, 16.463, 20.49, 22.53. Cf. Pindar *Nemean* 4.59–61 and Hesiod *Theogony* 173–174.

[37] When Achilles criticizes Agamemnon for his unwarlike spirit, he pairs battle with ambush: "you have never dared in your heart to arm with the host to go to war nor to go into ambush with the best of the Achaeans" ("οὔτέ ἐς πόλεμον ἅμα θωρηχθῆναι / οὔτε λόχον δ' ἰέναι σὺν ἀριστήεσσιν Ἀχαιῶν / τέτληκας θυμῷ," *Iliad* 1.226–227). See Kirk 1985 *ad loc*.

[38] Dué and Ebbott 2009 argue against the prevailing view that the *Iliad* presents the ambush in a negative light, by suggesting that post-Homeric notions of honour and battle behaviour have prejudiced readers. Certainly, mining the epics for ideology is fraught with difficulty: see, for example, Thalmann 1988, 1998; Rose 1997; and Hammer 2004.

Trojans not to fear a "close ambush" (*Iliad* 24.779);[39] and in a contested line in the *Odyssey* where Odysseus recounts the command he gave inside the famous horse (ἠμὲν ἀνακλῖναι <u>πυκινὸν λόχον</u> ἠδ' ἐπιθεῖναι, *Odyssey* 11.525).[40] In Priam's reassurance we may read an implicit denial of the ambush and the Trojan horse tradition as an appropriate ending for the *Iliad*'s foundational narrative of political settlement. Priam's faith is based on Achilles' promise to him that he (Achilles) will hold the Achaeans back, while the Trojans mourn Hektor. The guarantee of an undisturbed burial for the hero of Troy not only goes some way to resolving the theme of ransom denied that Agamemnon had initiated at the beginning of the epic, but also gestures towards an uneasy settlement between the warring sides, however fragile or fleeting that truce might turn out to be.[41] In the second example, while the fate of Troy is made to rest on a πυκινὸς λόχος 'close ambush', Odysseus' order points to his role in the *Odyssey* as the ambusher of the suitors: Odysseus here is the leader of the ambuscade, at once both like Tydeus and not like him because he initiates the ambush to capture the city—and will ambush the suitors to recapture his own. Hence the invocation of πυκινὸς λόχος communicates the perspective each epic takes on its tradition: the *Iliad* forever postpones the threat of the ambush as a result of its impetus towards the generation of some kind of common understanding in the context of death and mourning; for the *Odyssey* the ambush becomes central to the hero's successful return home. In Agamemnon's tale it functions simultaneously in contradictory ways: as part of the internal argument advocated by Agamemnon, the phrase fleshes out Tydeus' heroism; on the other hand, its broader associations stand in tension with the *Iliad*'s limited presentation of the ambush. Tydeus' defeat of an ambush has the tone of epic acclaim, but as a direct lesson to his son Diomedes it is harder to discern its relevance to or indeed value for this epic.

---

[39] Periphrastically, there is one additional instance where a λόχος is referred to as πυκινός. During Glaukos' narrative of Bellerophon, the trap set for that hero is described as a πυκινὸν δόλον (6.187) only to be called an ambush three lines later (189). On the significance of πυκινός in *Iliad* 24, see Lynn-George 1988:230–233.

[40] Aristarchus omitted this line, but it existed in his notes: see Heubeck and Hoekstra 1989:108–109. Cf. Van der Valk 1963. The scholion reports that other manuscripts printed had "the wooden horse" (δούριον ἵππον).

[41] A resonance between Priam's use of πυκινὸς λόχος and Agamemnon's may indicate homology in the political situations. Tydeus, in Agamemnon's tale, has been ambushed *even though* he went as a messenger to the Cadmeans—their ceasefire lasts only long enough for the Cadmeans to enact sinister plans. Priam, it seems, forestalls anxiety about similarly underhanded plans. Here, then, we find a contrast between Tydeus' world and Priam's: by end of the *Iliad*, a truce *can be* trusted, however precarious and temporary—the Trojans subsequently post guards just in case. Cf. Lynn-George 1988:254.

In this light it is worth considering Agamemnon's description of the punishment that Tydeus metes out to his assailants as an "unseemly fate" (ἀεικέα πότμον). Aside from this instance, this phrase occurs *only* in the *Odyssey*.[42] While the suitor, Leocritus, is the first to employ this phrase, in his epic fantasy that Odysseus will meet an "unseemly fate,"[43] every other instance correlates to Odysseus' ultimately successful defeat of the suitors and the shame he inflicts on them. Important for Agamemnon's message, then, is the semantic charge of ἀεικέα πότμον that relates visiting an unseemly fate on one's enemies to taking retribution against acts of injustice.[44] Odysseus himself articulates such a moral: the suitors, condemned by the gods, as he puts it, for "reckless acts" (σχέτλια ἔργα, *Odyssey* 22.413), "suffer an unseemly fate because of their own recklessness" (τῷ καὶ ἀτασθαλίῃσιν ἀεικέα πότμον ἐπέσπον, *Odyssey* 22.416). When Agamemnon uses the phrase ἀεικέα πότμον he has in mind a starkly Odyssean message in which the suffering that Tydeus metes out to his Cadmean ambushers is regarded as divinely sanctioned retributive murder.

An Odyssean tonality can be heard in Agamemnon's description of that other venue in which Tydeus excels: the games. According to Agamemnon, Tydeus was able to conquer all easily because he had Athena as an ἐπίρροθος, a 'helper'. The word itself recurs only when Odysseus prays during the foot-race in honor of Patroklos (*Iliad* 23.770) and Athena hears him. Yet the association of the hero competing in games with Athena by his side resonates most strongly in the *Odyssey*, where Odysseus beats all the Phaiakians in a display of heroic bravado, just as Tydeus does here. Interestingly, Diomedes himself and Achilles after him will later echo Agamemnon's description, when they both threaten Hektor with the words "if any god is perhaps also my helper" (εἴ πού τις καὶ ἔμοιγε θεῶν ἐπιτάρροθός ἐστι, *Iliad* 11.365–366; 20.452–453).[45] But, where

---

[42] *Odyssey* 2.250, 4.339, 4.340, 17.130, 17.131, 19.550, 22.317, 22.416.

[43] "But he would meet an unseemly fate here if he should fight against many" (ἀλλά κεν αὐτοῦ ἀεικέα πότμον ἐπίσποι, / εἰ πλεόνεσσι μάχοιτο, *Odyssey* 2.250–251). Evidence gathered in Danek 1998 attests to other versions of Odysseus' tale, in which our hero defeats the suitors with the help of a small army he had gathered from the countryside, including shepherds, swineherds, and Laertes himself. Remarks such as those by Leocritus, therefore, also work to counteract the audience's familiarity with other versions in which Odysseus was pointedly not alone but enjoyed considerable support in his battle against the suitors.

[44] The combination of these two lexical items contributes to the resonance of retributive acts in this phrase. See, for example, Simonides fr. 26.1–3 and Pindar *Olympian* 2.35–37. ἀεικής is combined with clearly bad things like destruction (λοίγος, e.g. *Iliad* 9.495), slander (λώβη, e.g. 11.142), pay for work (μίσθος, e.g. 12.445), the brutal ἔργον of war (14.13; also Herakles' service at the hands of Eurystheos, 19.133). Cf. Ouranos' deeds as ἀεικέα (Hesiod *Theogony* 166). Solon uses this adjective provocatively to describe the situation of slavery suffered by Athens' poorer citizens (Solon fr. 4.23–25).

[45] Elsewhere the related ἐπιτάρροθος serves similarly to mark an individual hero's special relationship with the gods. For ἐπιτάρροθος see *Iliad* 5.808, 5.826, 11.366 (Diomedes), 12.180, 17.339

the presence—imagined or actual—of a divine helper helps facilitate the performance of exceptional deeds, by the same token the assistance that the individual receives menacingly elevates the hero to a god-like status.[46] Not only does the god-aided hero bring death for the myriad mortalshe encounters; relatedly at such points the individual figure can appear worryingly removed from the world of his fellow men that, for all of the scenes of individual conflict, remains the heart of the *Iliad*'s representation of heroic epic.[47]

To sum up our argument thus far: while Agamemnon presents a hero of some valor and note, phrases resonant with the rest of the Homeric corpus serve to destabilize his vision of Tydeus as a figure whom the son should emulate. Of all the phrases that contribute both to the general force of his Theban tale and yet also to its insufficient or even inapposite purchase on the Iliadic context, it is Agamemnon's description of Tydeus as "being alone among many" (μοῦνος ἐὼν πολέσιν) that stands out. A recurring motif in Homeric epic and archaic Greek poetry in celebration of the individual hero, the meaning of being alone varies depending upon the social frame—martial or familial, individual or political—of the story at hand.[48] As such, the Iliadic connotations of isolation bear heavily upon determining the thematic allegiances of Agamemnon's tale. Odysseus' notorious contemplation of retreat in Book 11, for example, echoes a fear of isolation—of being left alone on the battlefield—expressed by a number of warriors during the epic.[49] Nor is the vulnerability of the single hero restricted

---

(Aeneas), 20.453, 21.289 (Achilles) and *Odyssey* 24.182 (Odysseus). Only on one occasion is the help, both the subject and object of it, plural; that is when the narrator describes the pain of the gods helping the Danaans (*Iliad* 12.180). Note that the only occurrence in the *Odyssey* comes when a figure from the enemy group (the dead suitor Automedon) claims that Odysseus had a god as a helper, even though Athena's assistance of her favorite is a continuous, and conspicuous, feature of the narrative; the *Odyssey* seems consciously to avoid the term ἐπιτάρροθος. Outside Homer, this lexical item may mark divine helpers from a ritual perspective. See, for example, Sophocles. fr. 583. 7–10, *Papyri Graecae Magicae* 6.25.7 (where Apollo is called ἐπίρροθε), and Macedonius *Paean in Apollinem et Aesculapium = Inscriptiones Graecae* II² 4473.9 (where Asclepius is referred to as a helper against diseases). Cf. Orphic Hymn 61.10–12 and Aeschylus *Seven Against Thebes* 357–358.

[46] The *Iliad* emphasizes the double-edged nature of divine "assistance." In the case of Diomedes, his *aristeia* comes as a result of Athena's aid, but its force is attenuated by his wounding of Aphrodite (*Iliad* 5.336). Consider too: (1) Agamemnon and the false dream he receives from Zeus in Book 2; (2) the ultimate outcome of Achilles' plea to Zeus via his mother in Book 1 (his best friend will die); and (3) Hektor's death: at first, he believes that he is being aided by Deiphobus, but it is actually Athena sealing his doom (22.296–305). On some of the negative connotations underlying a hero's *aristeia*, see Nagy 1999 [1979]:30–32.

[47] For a recent articulation of the Homeric epics' increasing human focus, see Graziosi and Haubold 2005:68–99, 98–103, 121–149.

[48] For references to μοῦνος ἐὼν πολέσιν in archaic Greek poetry, including in the reconstructed new Archilochus fragment (Obbink 2006), see Barker and Christensen 2006:25n1.

[49] "It will be chilling if I am caught / alone..." τὸ δὲ ῥίγιον αἴ κεν ἀλώω / μοῦνος, 11.405–406. Cf. 11.467, 12.41, 17.94, 17.472, 20.188, 22.456. Zeus grants Hektor honor and glory "alone among

to scenes of battle. When Diomedes volunteers to spy in *Iliad* 10, he asks for a companion to go with him on the basis that two hold an advantage over one (10.224–226): Diomedes' forethought in this matter is borne out when the lone Dolon is outwitted, overcome and done in by his two Achaean counterparts.

The problem of being alone serves to emphasize a fundamental feature of the war at Troy as argued by several recent commentators such as Oliver Taplin and Dean Hammer: the *Iliad*'s Achaeans are essentially a *coalition*.[50] From its beginning, the *Iliad* shows an intense interest in the survival of the Achaean group; and, from what we can piece together from Achilles' statements, the Achaeans are fighting at Troy because of an agreement among the leaders, not because Agamemnon exercises any special authority over them.[51] Most importantly, however, it is the split in their polity in Book 1 that acts as a catalyst for the *Iliad*'s narrative, a substantial part of which explores how the multiple Achaean commanders can, or should, work together to preserve the expedition and consolidate the symbiotic relationship between the leader and the led. Unlike the Trojans, whose hopes rest almost entirely on Hektor and his management of their allies, Achaean strength comes from their *partnerships*, from pointedly *not being alone*. Indeed, the narrative takes pains to emphasize the importance of the army and the cooperation of its leaders after the departure of Achilles through the assembly, mustering, and catalogue of Book 2 and the rallying of the troops in Book 4—even as Agamemnon in his leadership role continues to flounder and throw that coalition into doubt.[52]

This burgeoning unity, however, is balanced by the isolation of the primary hero, Achilles. The language of singularity, in fact, features in the story of Achilles in several meaningful ways. Unlike his comrades, Achilles does not use the language of μοῦνος 'alone' to denote his vulnerability, since his semi-divine nature means that he need not fear isolation in battle even when fighting a god. Instead, significantly, when *he* talks about being alone, he emphasizes his *political* isolation: he bemoans how Agamemnon has taken a prize from him "alone of the Achaeans" (ἐμεῦ δ' ἀπὸ μούνου Ἀχαιῶν, 9.335), which had been the action

---

[50] many" (15.611)—but, fatally, only for a short period.

A number of scholars have recently drawn attention to the importance of the group in the *Iliad*, whether that is read in terms of epic's interest in the survival of the people (Haubold 2000:40–100) or as an incipient political framework of some kind (Detienne 1996:91–102; Donlan 2002, cf. 1979; Taplin 1992:57–66; Carlier 1996; Schofield 1999:21–30; Hammer 2002, cf. 1997; Barker 2009, cf. Barker 2004; Elmer 2013). It is certainly the case that the *Iliad* forcefully challenges Agamemnon's wilful assertion of authority: see especially Taplin 1990; cf. Haubold 2000:52–68. See further in Chapter 5.

[51] E.g. *Iliad* 1.152–60; 9.337–9.

[52] See Schofield 1986:28–30 on the importance of Nestor in the assembly and mustering of Book 2. Heiden 2008b reads the Catalogue of Ships as privileging group commemoration over the celebration of individual aristocratic leaders.

that precipitated his withdrawal from the Achaean community. Moreover, when Achilles draws a connection between Agamemnon's taking of his prize Briseis, and the cause of the war, the abduction of Helen, he wonders sarcastically whether the Atreidae "alone of mortals" love their women (ἦ μοῦνοι φιλέουσ' ἀλόχους μερόπων ἀνθρώπων, 9.340). Achilles' use of μοῦνος here suggestively points toward the *Iliad*'s intersection with (and departure from) its tradition, by virtue of which a slave girl stands in for Helen as the cause of strife, and conflict takes place as much among the Achaeans themselves as between the Achaeans and the Trojans.[53] Underlying all of these occurrences is Achilles' paradoxical status as a figure who both guarantees the Achaeans' victory over the Trojans and who sends myriad *Achaeans* (*Iliad* 1.2–3) to their doom.[54] Indeed, it should be remembered that Achilles himself initially shows great interest in the group's welfare and articulated their concerns in the opening assembly (*Iliad* 1.123–9; cf. 61, 87, 150, 162, 163–4), which *he* calls (1.54)—before his singular connections with the gods sever him from his community.[55] The rest of the narrative investigates whether, how, and to what extent Achilles can be brought back into the fold. When Agamemnon uses the μοῦνος formula to mark out Tydeus as exceptional and hold him up as exemplary, his message has to be heard through the interference of all these other examples in the epic.

Indeed, the phraseology here might again seem more appropriate to an Odyssean soundscape, where being alone amplifies the accomplishment of *nostos*. Events of that epic come to a head when Odysseus takes direct action by shooting Antinoos through the neck with an arrow as the latter sups from his wine cup, before turning his wrath on the rest of the suitors. At this point the narrator suggestively draws attention to the harsh juxtaposition between the two acts—drinking and fighting—by asking rhetorically who would have thought that "one man alone among many" (μοῦνος ἐνὶ πλεόνεσσι) could bring death to so many opponents (*Odyssey* 22.11–14). Where the *Iliad* plays against the inherited trope of a singular god-assisted hero on the battlefield, the *Odyssey*

---

[53] For Helen as the *cause célèbre* of the tradition, see Mayer 1996.

[54] Cook 1999: in the epic careers of heroes such as Achilles and Odysseus we see them both suffering and meting out suffering; indeed, it is written into their very names.

[55] In little over one hundred lines, Achilles goes from championing the public cause to swearing an oath promising the destruction of the group he had purported to support (1.241–244). See Haubold 2000:68–83, for whom all of the epic's leaders fail to save their people. On Achilles as speaking on behalf of the group, see Taplin 1992:61. Donlan 1979:58 argues that Achilles' "leadership authority" is grounded in his relationship to the group, but fails to account for Achilles' prayer for their destruction (*Iliad* 1.239–44). On Athena's decisive intervention in the assembly, see Barker 2009:49–52.

appropriates it and applies it to the new, and even more challenging, circumstances facing its single hero.[56]

That is true also of the alternative application of μοῦνος to denote single sons in both Homeric epics. Given the fact that the burden of preserving the family line depends on them entirely, they represent a group of particular fragility in the *Iliad*,[57] a point that is stressed (albeit in different ways) in the appeals made by Phoenix and Priam to Achilles, and that resonates here in Agamemnon's appeal to Diomedes through his father, Tydeus.[58] The most explicit statement of generational anxiety comes in the *Odyssey*, as Telemachus describes how Zeus made his family line "single" (μούνωσε Κρονίων), yielding a grandfather, a father, and a son, single sons all (μοῦνον Λαέρτην...μοῦνον δ᾽ αὖτ᾽ Ὀδυσῆα...μοῦνον, *Odyssey* 16.117-120).[59] Although Telemachus' plea captures something of the precariousness of a single male line extending over three generations, he utters it in the *presence* of his (disguised) father. This singular use of μοῦνος, repeated three times in the space of as many lines, then, marks the moment when Odysseus' single line begins to reassert its hegemony, initiating a process that culminates in the epic's triumphal end, as the three single sons fight together in glorious defeat of the suitors' relatives.[60] In contrast, it should be remembered that, while the single line of male descent may evoke doubt about a family's future, multiple sons risk something potentially even worse: internecine conflict within the family and division of the patrimony. Just such a scenario characterizes other family histories of those involved in Troy, such as, notoriously, the family of Agamemnon, though it is most prominent

[56] The *Odyssey* describes its eponymous hero as "being alone" repeatedly. See 3.217, 12.297, 15.386, 16.105, 20.30, 22.107, and 23.38.

[57] Dolon is also marked out as an *only* son among five sisters (*Iliad* 10.317). Cf. Ilioneus (14.492). Both only sons are killed: the single male issue adds poignancy to their death, since with them their line too perishes.

[58] Phoenix stresses that Peleus treated him like an only son (*Iliad* 9.482), while Priam misrepresents his situation to depict himself as a father to an only son, Hektor (24.242).

[59] Telemachus' expression of his family's exceptionality is remarkable: the unique verb μουνόω in hexameter epic is glossed by three successive lines with μοῦνος in the line-initial position. Goldhill 2010 investigates the use of μοῦνος, particularly in this passage, for marking out the exceptionality of Odysseus, his line, and this poem.

[60] Telemachus is described as a single son by Eurycleia (*Odyssey* 2.365). Connected to the single son motif is the epithet "late-born" (τηλύγετος) applied to Telemachus in a simile at *Odyssey* 16.19. Its occurrences in the *Iliad* suggest another highly charged term: Helen uses it of her daughter (*Iliad* 3.175), Agamemnon of his son (*Iliad* 9.143), and Phoenix of himself, loved by Peleus (482); cf. Homeric *Hymn to Demeter* 164–165 where Demophoon is described as "late-born" twice: τηλύγετος and ὀψίγονος. On its unclear etymology and meaning, see Heubeck, West, and Hainsworth 1988:194. For some audience members of the *Odyssey* the arrival of a "*telugetos* son" may provocatively recall *Telegonus*, a(nother) son of Odysseus (by Circe). For discussions of the *Telegony*, see Burgess 2001:143 and 153–154; and Marks 2008:87–90.

in the cycle of songs in rivalry with Homeric epic, *the tales about Thebes.*[61] As we shall see below, Diomedes, himself a single son, will have the last word on his singular father.

When Agamemnon deploys Tydeus as a lesson for his son, and describes him as a warrior-gatherer, alone among many, victorious over the Cadmeans both in the games and in the ambush, inflicting upon them shameful deeds, with a god as his helper, he triggers a number of meanings whose semantic reach far exceeds his sole focus on Diomedes. While being alone is something that *epic* heroes in particular experience, the meaning of isolation depends on the strategy of each narrative. The *Iliad* weighs general anxiety over being alone in battle or isolated from one's group against the destructive singularity of a hero like Achilles; the *Odyssey* inverts that anxiety and celebrates it without ever entirely abandoning the sense of fragility. The man alone in Agamemnon's tale, then, although at first glance perhaps fitting in well with the *Odyssey*'s revisiting of the exploits and return of the exceptional hero,[62] certainly seems at odds with the *Iliad*'s broader concern with coalition politics, all the more so when one considers that just such an exceptional man (Achilles) has *already* destabilized the alliance over which Agamemnon presides because of the leader's failure to keep the public good in mind.

Agamemnon's use of the discourse of *neikos* to spur Diomedes on will have its desired effect, when in the very next book Diomedes will stand out from the crowd by performing extraordinary deeds with Athena as his helper. Even then, however, the *Iliad* resists an exclusive focus on individual exploits, as Diomedes' *aristeia* is crucially limited by Apollo's intervention and interrupted by an elaborate scene of *xenia*—an institution critical for managing interpersonal relationships—played out on the battlefield, which makes the contrast to Agamemnon's tale all the starker.[63] We noted above how Agamemnon frames his lesson by describing Tydeus as coming to Mycenae "outside of war" (ἄτερ πολέμου, 4.377); moreover, Tydeus' heroic excellence is demonstrated by his individual performance in the games and in an ambush—a set of circumstances that differ markedly from the situation narrated in the *Iliad*. Indeed, the whole point of Agamemnon's Theban tale is to illustrate the hero's singularity: Tydeus was someone who, as Agamemnon puts it, "fought against enemies far in front of his dear companions" (ἀλλὰ πολὺ πρὸ φίλων ἑτάρων δηΐοισι μάχεσθαι,

---

[61] See PEG fr. 2 with n11 above.

[62] So Kirk 1985:369–370. While Agamemnon's language may sound "Odyssean," this label, we suggest, indicates more the paucity of extant epic narrative than it does any conscious allusion to our text of the *Odyssey*. If nothing else, the self-reflexive use of these motifs by the *Odyssey* demonstrates why it will not really do to describe Agamemnon's Theban tale as Odyssean: the *Odyssey* itself is reinventing the basic story pattern of the great exploits of the solitary hero.

[63] *Iliad* 6.119–236. See Taplin 1992:58–59. On Diomedes' troubling *aristeia*, see further below.

4.373). The context is important here: Homer is preparing his audience for the first engagement between the Achaean and Trojan *armies* in the narrative, an engagement that for the first time in the war—so we are led to believe—will be lacking Achilles (and his men). Having already conspired to lose his most outstanding warrior, Agamemnon tells a story of Thebes that emphasizes the exceptionality of an individual figure. Holding out for a hero, Agamemnon tries to replace the absent Achilles with Tydeus' son, whom he hopes will be a chip off the old block. Instead, he receives not one but *two* responses, as first Sthenelos and then Diomedes after him counter the lessons of this Theban story.

The Not-So-Magnificent Seven

We have argued so far that Agamemnon's use of Thebes to shame Diomedes has introduced a rivalry not just between father and son, but also between different poetic traditions, contexts for heroism, and, in concert, ways of evaluating epic glory. The dissonance between the account that Agamemnon provides and the story in which he is a participant, moreover, invites consideration of how the *Iliad* itself is unlike these other tales. As we discussed in the Introduction, there is nothing inherent in the stories set about Thebes that made them any less amenable to the admission of political themes than those set around Troy. Yet their selective (mis)representation limits the appeal and broader application of this material. In the case that we have just examined, the distortion and devaluing of Thebes as a paradigm is complex and multilayered; Agamemnon, after all, turns to Thebes for a positive representation of heroic behavior, though its focus on a singular hero turns out to be ill-suited to the *Iliad*'s story about a gathered army struggling both to successfully prosecute a siege and to maintain equilibrium in the coalition. Other examples are not so restrained. A case in point is the twin set of responses that Agamemnon's Theban tale provokes. In their engagement with the past, Sthenelos and Diomedes take on Theban traditions directly and more aggressively.[64]

Initially, however, Diomedes remains silent in the face of Agamemnon's rebuke (4.401–402). By its very nature, silence can be difficult to read. In Homer, silence generally implies deference to the political position of the speaker,

---

[64] Agamemnon stresses the second-hand nature of his tale (*Iliad* 4.374–375). In Homer tales may be confirmed (cf. Nestor's frequent eye-witness testimony) or simply related: the Tydeus narrative, then, receives special notice as a second-hand tale that cannot or may not need to be verified. If no confirmation is required, this may point to the well-known status of the tale whereby Agamemnon can rely upon the fame of the father to shame the son. Diomedes' later avowal, however, that he cannot remember his father may contribute to a distancing effect implicit in Agamemnon's phrase.

though it falls short of expressing full agreement.[65] Here, Diomedes' refusal to speak marks him out as different from Achilles, insomuch as he will not directly answer back to his commander-in-chief, even given due cause. At the same time, his silence means that we do not know what he thinks about Agamemnon's criticism, at least not directly and not now.

Instead, it is Diomedes' companion, Sthenelos, who springs to the defense of his slighted comrade (4.404–410):

"Ἀτρεΐδη, μὴ ψεύδε' ἐπιστάμενος σάφα εἰπεῖν·
ἡμεῖς τοι πατέρων μέγ' ἀμείνονες εὐχόμεθ' εἶναι·
ἡμεῖς καὶ Θήβης ἕδος εἵλομεν ἑπταπύλοιο
παυρότερον λαὸν ἀγαγόνθ' ὑπὸ τεῖχος ἄρειον,
πειθόμενοι τεράεσσι θεῶν καὶ Ζηνὸς ἀρωγῇ·
κεῖνοι δὲ σφετέρῃσιν ἀτασθαλίῃσιν ὄλοντο·
τῶ μή μοι πατέρας ποθ' ὁμοίῃ ἔνθεο τιμῇ."

"Son of Atreus, don't lie when you know how to *speak clearly*.
We claim to be better than our fathers:
we took the foundation of seven-gated Thebes
though we led a smaller army before better walls
because we were relying on the signs of the gods and Zeus' help.
Those men perished because of their own recklessness.
Don't put our fathers in the *same honor*."

Sthenelos frames his riposte to Agamemnon's Theban comparison by drawing a connection between speaking the truth and speaking clearly. To speak clearly (σάφα εἰπεῖν) on a subject is to speak knowledgeably about it, with the authority of a poet.[66] Knowledge is here connected to clarity of expression—an important consideration in the dynamics of oral performance, where the bard had to make sure that his audience was with him every step of the way in his recounting of events, even if the issues themselves were complex and would demand

---

[65] For a detailed analysis of replies to speech in the *Iliad*, see Elmer 2013. Diomedes' silence prompts a variety of responses: Scott 1980:17 suggests that Diomedes is silent because of the *aidos* he feels for Agamemnon; Nagy 1999 [1979]:161–164 argues that Agamemnon's taunt compels Diomedes to prove his worth in deeds; Martin 1989:71–72 suggests that Diomedes' silence is an assertion of social superiority. For the general import of silence in Homer, see Montiglio 1993.

[66] σάφα as an adverb occurs only here with a verb of speaking in the *Iliad*; on the other hand, σάφα εἰπεῖν occurs frequently in the *Odyssey*, such as when Telemachus admits to Nestor that no one can tell him clearly what has happened to his father (*Odyssey* 3.89); see: *Odyssey* 2.30, 43, 108; 17.106; 24.144. The interest in speaking σάφα befits the *Odyssey*, which is well known for its acute self-reflexive awareness of narration. See, for example, Goldhill 1991, Chapter 1.

(and repay) further thought.[67] In the brief interlude as Odysseus pauses from recounting his post-Iliadic wanderings, the Phaiakian king, Alkinoos, reckons him like a bard on the basis that his words have a shape and beauty, and that he *knows how* to catalogue the events appropriately.[68] Sthenelos' blunt rejoinder that Agamemnon has misspoken relates to this idea of providing a clear account: the king has failed either to provide a clear paradigm or to align his version of events at Thebes with the *Iliad*'s narrative of the Trojan tale. According to Sthenelos, Agamemnon's Theban tale is off message.

A principal aspect of that falsification, in Sthenelos' eyes, is Agamemnon's labored, and misplaced, construction of a Tydeus who can serve as a model for his son. There was a famous story, known at least as far back as the scholia on the *Iliad*, that told how Athena withdrew her favor from the hero, in disgust with him when he ate the brains of a defeated enemy. Whether that particular story about Tydeus was familiar to the *Iliad*'s audience is impossible to say. Evidence from tragedy, however, paints a picture of a hero well known for his boasting and transgressive action. It seems safe to assume, then, that the Theban tradition had characterized Tydeus with behavior that verged on the fringes of acceptability (like so many heroes), and that this reputation would have preceded him in Homer's *Iliad*. Agamemnon's encomium is flatly one-dimensional in comparison, devoid of any poetic nuance, insufficiently alert or attentive to the problems of singular action, let alone to the more gruesome aspects of Tydeus' epic career.[69] Indeed, one might suspect Agamemnon of having a blind spot to Tydeus' negative traits, given his own ethically transgressive behavior that has already manifested itself in the *Iliad* and that will lead ultimately to his downfall.[70]

---

[67] On the importance of clarity in Homer's poetic art: Richardson 1996.

[68] "Your words have a shape and within you is a noble mind, and you know how to narrate your story just like a bard" (σοὶ δ' ἔπι μὲν μορφὴ ἐπέων, ἔνι δὲ φρένες ἐσθλαί. / μῦθον δ' ὡς ὅτ' ἀοιδὸς ἐπισταμένως κατέλεξας, *Odyssey* 11.367–368). Cf. Graziosi and Haubold 2005: 47–48.

[69] Janko 1992:163–164 suggests that Homer "knew the story of this war but avoided telling how Tudeus, frenzied and dying, sucked out the brain of his foe" (163), which, for example, is referenced in Aeschylus *Seven Against Thebes*, where Tydeus is described as "the murderer, the corruptor of the city, the greatest teacher of evils for Argos, caller of Furies, servant of Murder, Adrastos' counselor of these evils" (τὸν ἀνδροφόντην, τὸν πόλεως ταράκτορα, / μέγιστον Ἄργει τῶν κακῶν διδάσκαλον, / Ἐρινύος κλητῆρα, πρόσπολον Φόνου, / κακῶν δ' Ἀδράστῳ τῶνδε βουλευτήριον, 572-575). In any case Tydeus' fall from favor seems sufficiently integrated into (but not explicitly described in) the Homeric frame to allow for rather wide knowledge of this motif.

[70] We owe the description of Agamemnon as "ethically transgressive" to one of the reviewers of Barker and Christensen 2011, on which this chapter is based. Agamemnon's actions in Book 1, in which he unilaterally takes back Achilles' prize, are acknowledged as transgressive by the gods: Athena calls the action hubristic (*Iliad* 1.214). Furthermore, in professing to rank Chryseis above his wife Clytemnestra (*Iliad* 1.113-4), Agamemnon ironically brings to mind his later fate, when his wife will murder him in part because he returns home in thrall to another slave girl, Cassandra.

The full force of Sthenelos' charge that Agamemnon has failed to speak clearly (and thus truthfully) relates to the very point of the comparison in the first place. It was not their fathers who triumphed at Thebes, Sthenelos points out; it was *they*, the sons of the seven, who "took the seat of seven-gated Thebes."[71] Sthenelos' retort marks an important recalibration of Agamemnon's exemplum and unmasks the conceit of a Theban tale that entirely omits any mention of the battle for the city or of Tydeus' singular deeds in that effort.[72] The Seven against Thebes had failed as an expedition, and fails again as a model against which to compare their sons, since it was those sons who had succeeded where they had failed.[73] No wonder Sthenelos' reply cuts to the quick: even on Agamemnon's own terms, where the Theban story is used as a stick with which to beat Diomedes, the exemplarity of Tydeus' heroic deeds fails the critical test—it was Diomedes and his comrades who sacked the city, not his father.

Sthenelos' assertion that the sons are better than their fathers is remarkable given the usual epic assertion of the superiority of the older generation.[74] And it is all the more remarkable given the fact that they have yet to take Troy. This moot point could have been seen to lessen the status of the sons now fighting at Troy, as if they were not strong or courageous enough; this is how Agamemnon takes it, for example, which had prompted him to offer the Theban tale in the first place. Yet in actual fact it goes to stress the magnitude of the current conflict and, of course, of the current poem in performance. After all, Sthenelos observes pointedly, they had taken Thebes, where their fathers had previously failed, "with a smaller army." The fact that they are still struggling at Troy in a Panhellenic coalition makes the stakes of the Trojan War even higher and the narrative of the *Iliad* even more worthy of note.

---

[71] Sthenelos' description of the city's fall echoes the account of the city's foundation in the *Odyssey* (with the verb "seize" (εἵλομεν, 4.406) replacing the *Odyssey*'s "build" (ἔκτισαν, *Odyssey* 11.263): Pache 2014. The narrative of Thebes' annihilation is ultimately and inextricably bound up with its foundation. Sammons 2014:311 points out that it is rare for the appropriateness of a mythological *paradeigma* to become a matter of explicit debate.

[72] Sammons 2014:313 is right to argue that "Homer, too, eschews any narrative of the war's ending...choosing rather to focus inwardly on a single narrative (the wrath of Achilles) slightly off-center from these 'main' events." The *Iliad*, however, does make it clear that: (1) Troy's fall is now inevitable; and (2) this outcome is a result of Achilles' actions in the narrative (his defeat of Hektor). Agamemnon's recollection of Tydeus' deeds fails even to address the relevance of his tale for this larger narrative, even were we to grant him license for not making the most salient point in comparing Troy and Thebes—that they are both cities under siege and destined to be sacked.

[73] On the failure of exemplarity, see Goldhill 1994. Even on the terms set by Agamemnon, Thebes simply does not measure up to the standards of the *Iliad*.

[74] The *Iliad* frequently points to the differences between epic heroes and the men of today, as when a hero picks up a stone that no one alive (in the audience's time) could lift (5.302–304, 12.380–383, 12.445–450, and 20.285–287). See Ford 1992.

In addition to failing on its own terms, Agamemnon's example is subtly corrected by the resonance of phrases deployed by Sthenelos in response. One of these is the phrase "by their own recklessness" (σφετέρῃσιν ἀτασθαλίῃσιν), by means of which Sthenelos establishes an explanation for why they—the sons—had succeeded where their fathers had failed: their fathers had brought ruin upon themselves. Self-caused destruction, as indicated by forms of the phrase σφετέρῃσιν ἀτασθαλίῃσιν, is a powerful notion in Homeric epic.[75] In its only other occurrence in the *Iliad*, Hektor resolves to meet Achilles on the basis that he has brought catastrophe on the Trojans because of his own reckless actions (making them camp out on the plain, even once Achilles has made his intention to return to the fray clear), and must face the consequences as a result.[76] In the *Odyssey* it is a recurring, almost obsessive, refrain, advertised prominently at the beginning of the poem to explain the doom of Odysseus' companions ("for they perished because of their own recklessness," αὐτῶν γὰρ σφετέρῃσιν ἀτασθαλίῃσιν ὄλοντο, *Odyssey* 1.7), and then later applied with insistent regularity to the misbehavior of the suitors.[77] Resonating strongly with this moralizing strain, Sthenelos' redeployment of Agamemnon's Theban tale realigns Thebes not with the *Iliad* (by virtue of it being a sack narrative) but with the *Odyssey*, drawing a connection between their fathers' failure to take Thebes and the archetypal case of deserved suffering preserved in extant epic: just as the suitors came to a bad end due to their own recklessness, so did the original magnificent Seven against Thebes. Far from being an example of how to behave,

---

[75] In the *Iliad* ἀτάσθαλος is associated with bad leadership and its ascription to an enemy is a typical strategy to claim right on one's own side: see Nestor on the Epeians (11.695); Menelaos on the Trojans (13.461); and Priam on Achilles (22.418). Hesiod draws an association between ἀτάσθαλος and ὕβρις to condemn the bad king (e.g., *Works and Days* 261); ὕβρις ἀτάσθαλος characterises the silver age of men (*Works and Days* 134). Deeds referred to as ἀτάσθαλα justify retribution: see Hesiod *Theogony* 164; 207–210; 992-996; cf. Hesiod fr. 30.15–20.

[76] "Now, since I lost the people *by my own recklessness*, I feel shame before the Trojans and Trojan women" (νῦν δ' ἐπεὶ ὤλεσα λαὸν <u>ἀτασθαλίῃσιν ἐμῇσιν</u>, / αἰδέομαι Τρῶας καὶ Τρῳάδας ἑλκεσιπέπλους, *Iliad* 22.106). Agamemnon does not admit the same, but does concede his blindness (19.134–137), a theme he anticipated at 2.111–115 and repeated in Book 9. The difference may be character-based, but it may also be contextual. Hektor accuses himself of ἀτασθαλία in private; Agamemnon admits to blindness in public.

[77] See Rutherford 1986:151n37; Cook 1995:24; and de Jong 2001:12, who notes that the root ἀτασθαλ- occurs only once—*Odyssey* 1.7—in narrator text, while of the twenty-eight occasions it is used in character text, the majority (fifteen) refer to the suitors. No less a figure than Zeus announces that men in general are to blame for their own suffering ("They have pains beyond their lot because of their own foolishness," οἱ δὲ καὶ αὐτοὶ / <u>σφῇσιν ἀτασθαλίῃσιν</u> ὑπὲρ μόρον ἄλγε' ἔχουσιν, 1.33–34), which, as Cook 1995:32–37 argues, suggests that the *Odyssey* establishes criminal acts rather than divine whim as the cause of human suffering. Nagler 1990:346 shows that the proem's myopic focus on Odysseus' companions betrays a broader anxiety regarding "the hero's outright violence" against the suitors, back home in the "'real' political world" of Ithaca.

the Seven are better seen as a case to avoid—a rebuke even more pointed if, as we suggested above, the audience would have been familiar with the stories about the ethically transgressive Tydeus.

A second phrase deployed by Sthenelos more directly challenges Agamemnon's description of a god-fearing Tydeus. Where Agamemnon describes Tydeus as trusting in the gods (θεῶν τεράεσσι πιθήσας), Sthelenos asserts that the sons succeeded where their fathers failed because it was *they* who "obeyed the signs of the gods and Zeus' aid" (πειθόμενοι τεράεσσι θεῶν καὶ Ζηνὸς ἀρωγῇ, 4.408). In the context of this previous usage, Sthenelos' formula both meets Agamemnon's claim, and trumps it: it is no longer the single hero who trusts in the gods, but the whole group, which is in and of itself more fitting for a narrative about a siege of a city; it is no longer nameless gods who are believed in but Zeus, the ultimate author of this epic and heroic narrative more generally.[78] In disputing Agamemnon's appeal to Tydeus' divine pedigree, Sthenelos draws the starkest distinction between the conduct of the two generations: the expeditions of the sons against both Thebes *and* Troy were, and *are*, divinely sanctioned, and overseen by Zeus.

Sthenelos ends his riposte with the assertion that the two generations should not be held in the same honor (τῶ μή μοι πατέρας ποθ' ὁμοίη ἔνθεο τιμῇ). Although Agamemnon means for his tale to compare one exceptional hero to another, the effect of introducing Tydeus into the *Iliad*'s world leads Sthenelos to make the necessary subsequent comparison and correction: Tydeus' deeds may have been extraordinary, but his expedition *failed*. The subsequent narrative bears out Sthenelos' defense of his friend's martial prowess. Agamemnon's description of Diomedes hesitating and "looking down at the bridges of war" (πολέμοιο γεφύρας, 4.371) is picked up by the narrator himself immediately once battle is joined, when he compares Diomedes to a river in flood, "who sweeps away bridges as he swiftly flows," (ὅς τ' ὦκα ῥέων ἐκέδασσε γεφύρας, *Iliad* 5.87–88), thereby in the process *sweeping aside* any lingering doubt over his fighting ability.[79] It is not only the fact, however, that Agamemnon is wrong about Diomedes' lack of martial prowess and is corrected by the narrative; in his formulation that ranks Diomedes as being "better in the assembly" than his father but, by implication, not in war, Agamemnon critically misreads the interests of this epic in debate and political formation. Indeed, he will learn soon

---

[78] For the association of the phrase, "and the will of Zeus was being accomplished," with the generation of heroic epic narrative, see Chapter 3, n39, below.

[79] In this way Diomedes prefigures Achilles, who chokes the waters of a real river in *Iliad* 22 and who also asserts that he will not shrink from "the bridges of war" (οὐδ' ἂν ἔτι δὴν / ἀλλήλους πτώσσοιμεν ἀνὰ πτολέμοιο γεφύρας, *Iliad* 20.426–427). For Diomedes as a second Achilles, see Lohmann 1970:221; Griffin 1980:74; and Schofield 1999:29 for a bibliography. Cf. Nagy 1999 [1979]:30–31

enough the extent to which his own poor performance as leader in the assembly will have catastrophic consequences on the battlefield for his efforts to take Troy. In the *Iliad* the hero has to be both a doer of deeds *and* a speaker of words.[80] As we shall see, Diomedes' later strength in the assembly points to his contribution to the Achaean coalition, and to the establishment of a new kind of political order.[81] His involvement in that process begins here with his reply to Sthenelos.

On Not Remembering Tydeus

Through Agamemnon's critique and Sthenelos' response Homer offers his audience the opportunity to compare heroic relatives and their poetic traditions. These embedded narratives naturally invite comparison to the compositional and poetic strategies of this poem vis-à-vis its tradition. Sthenelos' response to Agamemnon has highlighted the importance of omission, by means of which essential aspects of the Theban story—notably the sack of the city—are left out in the telling of this siege narrative, the *Iliad*. Where Agamemnon assumes an equivalence in the circumstances of the two comparanda in order to make his point, Sthenelos affirms important distinctions in both situation and outcome to expose the inaptness of Agamemnon's criticism of Diomedes.

Of particular importance in Sthenelos' pointed response is the insistence on collective responsibility: men enjoy success or come to a bad end as a group. Diomedes underlines this second theme when he addresses *Sthenelos* and not Agamemnon at all (4.411–418):

> <u>τὸν δ' ἄρ' ὑπόδρα ἰδὼν</u> προσέφη κρατερὸς Διομήδης·
> "τέττα, σιωπῇ ἧσο, ἐμῷ δ' ἐπιπείθεο μύθῳ·
> οὐ γὰρ ἐγὼ νεμεσῶ Ἀγαμέμνονι, ποιμένι λαῶν,
> ὀτρύνοντι μάχεσθαι ἐϋκνήμιδας Ἀχαιούς·
> τούτῳ μὲν γὰρ κῦδος ἅμ' ἕψεται, εἴ κεν Ἀχαιοὶ
> Τρῶας δῃώσωσιν ἕλωσί τε <u>Ἴλιον ἱρήν</u>,

---

[80] *Iliad* 9.443 (Phoenix). The collocation of battle and assembly (μάχη and ἀγορή) occurs at two critical junctures in the narrative. In the first, the narrator describes the end of the first Achaean assembly in terms of Agamemnon and Achilles fighting with opposing words ("the pair stood apart, fighting with words, and they ended the assembly," <u>μαχεσσαμένω</u> ἐπέεσσιν / ἀνστήτην, λῦσαν δ' <u>ἀγορὴν</u>, *Iliad* 1.304–305). Diomedes himself echoes this description when he announces that he will fight the king in his folly ("I will fight you first, son of Atreus, when you are acting like a fool," "Ἀτρεΐδη, σοὶ πρῶτα <u>μαχήσομαι</u> ἀφραδέοντι," *Iliad* 9.32). See further Chapter 5 below.

[81] Diomedes' power in words forestalls Agamemnon's retreats in Book 9 (31–49), reunites the Achaeans for war after the failed embassy (9.697–709), and provides a counter-plan to Agamemnon's flight in Book 14 (110–132). For an examination of Diomedes' contribution to the political order and bibliography, see Christensen 2009. On Diomedes as enacting—in a more socially constructive format—Achilles' initial dissent from Agamemnon, see Barker 2009:61–66.

τούτῳ δ' αὖ <u>μέγα πένθος</u> Ἀχαιῶν δηωθέντων.
ἀλλ' ἄγε δὴ καὶ νῶϊ μεδώμεθα θούριδος ἀλκῆς."

Then looking darkly at him mighty Diomedes replied:
"Sit in silence, obey my speech.
I will not criticize Agamemnon shepherd of the people,
since he is rallying the well-greaved Achaeans to fight.
Glory will attend to him if ever the Achaeans
Overcome the Trojans and take *holy Ilion*;
on the other hand, he'll have *great grief* should the Achaeans perish.
But come, let the two of us think about rushing valor."

The general referentiality of the introductory formula "looking darkly" (ὑπόδρα ἰδών) has already been established in the *Iliad*. Indicating the annoyance of the speaker with the previous speech, it characterizes Achilles' angry confrontation at the beginning of the *Iliad* with Agamemnon.[82] Given this association, it is all the more striking that this young hero pointedly does not confront the commander-in-chief face-to-face, but instead directs his verbal volley at his friend, Sthenelos. In contrast to Sthenelos, Diomedes remained silent in the face of Agamemnon's abuse, even though he himself had been the primary target of it. Now he clarifies the reasoning behind that silence: in criticizing him, Diomedes reasons, Agamemnon intends to rally the troops. This strategy, he recognizes, is appropriate behavior for the shepherd of the people. The king *ought* to be doing this kind of thing.

Yet Diomedes also adds an important gloss to how leadership should be conceived—and this comment suggests a further, albeit far subtler, correction of Agamemnon's Theban tale. Diomedes observes that the king enjoys a symbiotic relationship with his army, linking Agamemnon's fate closely to that of the Achaeans as a whole. Thus great glory would be the king's should the Achaeans take Troy; but, should they perish, he will instead experience "great suffering" (μέγα πένθος). μέγα πένθος is the unit of utterance with which Menelaos describes his intense emotional response to Patroklos' death (*Iliad* 17.139), while the *Odyssey* uses it only of its long-suffering fathers, twice of Laertes, once of

---

[82]   ὑπόδρα ἰδών first appears at *Iliad* 1.148 to introduce Achilles' verbal assault against Agamemnon, after which it is applied to: Achilles (*Iliad* 20.428; 22.260, 344; 24.559); Odysseus and Diomedes (*Iliad* 4.349 and 411; cf. 2.245; 5.251; 10.446; 14.82); Glaukos, in reaction to Hektor (*Iliad* 17.141); Hektor to silence Poulydamos (12.230; 18.284; cf. 17.169); Zeus, silencing Hera (*Iliad* 5.888; 15.13). In the *Odyssey*, the phrase primarily refers to Odysseus (*Odyssey* 8.165; 18.4; 337, 19.70; 22.34, 60, 320): both Antinoos (17.459) and Eurymachus (18.388) give themselves away by this reaction when teased by (the disguised) Odysseus. Holoka 1983 interprets this phrase as denoting the class status of the speaker.

Odysseus (*Odyssey* 11.95, 24.233; 17.489). In its only other occurrences in the *Iliad*, however, which serve to frame this episode, Nestor twice uses the expression to denote the "great suffering" that the Achaeans endure together, because their leaders are not leading (*Iliad* 1.254, 7.124). With this same turn of phrase, then, Diomedes further glosses Agamemnon's leadership and corrects his instruction. Where Agamemnon eulogizes the individual Tydeus, Diomedes economically, but decisively, observes the critical symbiosis between the leader and his group: *Agamemnon* will receive *kudos* should *the Achaeans* take Troy, but, were *they* to perish, *he* would receive acute pain. Agamemnon's heroic record—whether he gains great glory or succeeds only in bringing great pain to himself—depends on *the collective*.

Diomedes' observation that the leader's fate is inextricably connected with that of the group over which he presides strikes a chord with the narrative. From its beginning the *Iliad* has put Agamemnon's leadership under the spotlight and emphasized the importance of the people; in fact, before insults started flying in the assembly, Achilles himself had stressed the importance of the group in an articulation of *his* epic exploits.[83] There, Achilles had allowed personal recriminations to deflect him from his initial concern to speak for the community, and ultimately ends up cursing the very people he had spoken up to support.[84] Here, Diomedes shows a different way of handling Agamemnon's poor leadership: whatever else can be said, the group needs to be consolidated under a leader, perhaps even arguably in spite of him. We have already seen this point enacted in the very actions that Diomedes performs, when, in response to Agamemnon's abuse, he remains silent. That moment is made all the more significant by the narrator's word play: Diomedes did not answer "because he *respected* the *respected* king's reproach" (αἰδεσθεὶς βασιλῆος ἐνιπὴν αἰδοίοιο, *Iliad* 4.402). In both word and deed Diomedes shows the necessary esteem for his leader, as a leader, even if the king for the most part does not show himself worthy of it. At the same time, this respect for Agamemnon's office is tempered by a recognition that the success of the enterprise rests with the camaraderie shown by the Achaeans. The very structure of the scene bears this point out: even as Diomedes holds his tongue out of respect for the king, Sthenelos speaks up in defense of his friend; in turn Diomedes rebukes Sthenelos for criticizing the king. Their twin reactions not only show the importance of friendship and sociality to the *Iliad*; they are a *performance* of it.

In their responses to Agamemnon's praise of the singular hero, the two sons of the Seven against Thebes demonstrate an alertness to and interest in

---

[83] *Iliad* 1.123–129; cf. 54, 61, 87, 150, 162, 163–164. See nn. 25, 27, and 29 in the Introduction. Cf. Haubold 2000, Chapter 1.

[84] See Barker 2009:46–47.

collective strands of heroic action that chime with the *Iliad*'s narrative focus on relationships in the Achaean polity. Far from focusing on the exceptional individuality of its primary hero, what the situation at Troy demands, like that which we might imagine for Thebes as well, is a story of a coalition—a coalition of the willing in Achilles' earlier formulation.[85] In the broader context of the poem Diomedes' response serves an important additional purpose. It defuses the politically destabilizing strife latent in Sthenelos' speech and re-establishes a common will behind the king just in time for the poem's first martial engagement. When Diomedes goes into battle and assumes his father's mantle, he does so fighting with more than individual glory at stake; the hopes of Agamemnon's people are carried with him. Appropriately enough, it is in this context that he earns the epithet, previously used of Agamemnon (sarcastically by Achilles), "best of the Achaeans."[86]

Agamemnon's criticism of Diomedes for not being like his father in war is further countered and complicated by the events of Book 5, when the Achaeans and Trojans come to blows for the first time, during which Diomedes assumes a primary role in the fighting. Indeed, it is his performance of being the best in battle that, while ostensibly bearing out Agamemnon's call-to-arms, serves rather to highlight the ambiguous state of the exceptional hero, as one who, having no peers in battle, vanquishes all comers *and* threatens to surpass human bounds. During this comprehensive episode (which extends into the next book) the name of Tydeus punctuates the narrative at key moments to put Diomedes' actions into relief—first when the wounded Diomedes belatedly invokes his father's name and Athena's support for him in order to gain vengeance; then when Athena impels him on to fight with the gods; and finally, when acknowledgement of his bonds of hospitality to the Lycian Glaukos through their fathers brings his *aristeia* to an end.

Several features of Diomedes' *aristeia* betray an underlying ambivalence in, if not outright concern about, its value that complements the inappositeness of Agamemnon's Theban example and builds on its critical reception. First, it is significant that Diomedes claims his father in the way Agamemnon desires, but only under duress. Though we are told at the beginning of the episode that Athena has put "strength and daring" in him (μένος καὶ θάρσος, 5.2–3), it is not until *after* he has been wounded by Pandarus (5.95–100) that Diomedes claims a special relationship with the goddess by appealing to her for the care that she showed his father (5.115-117) so that he might kill the man who wounded him.

[85] As Achilles puts it, the Achaeans have followed Agamemnon to Troy to please him (*Iliad* 1.158), but how would any one of them willingly obey him (1.150) now that he is threatening to take away their prizes? On the importance of this expression, see Hammer 1997.

[86] See Nagy 1999 [1979], *passim* for the fateful resonance of this phrase.

Athena responds by placing the "fearless father's fury" in his breast, the "very stuff which shield-swinging Tydeus used to have" (ἐν γάρ τοι στήθεσσι μένος πατρώϊον ἧκα / ἄτρομον, οἷον ἔχεσκε σακέσπαλος ἱππότα Τυδεύς, 5.125–126). Additionally she gives Diomedes the ability to distinguish man from god with the specific command to wound Aphrodite (126–132).[87]

Thus it is in the context of martial rage that Diomedes asks Athena for help *as once she helped his father*, and only then when his own efforts have been insufficient to commit the very specific act of vengeance that he desires. In this way Diomedes' self-identification with his father is carefully defined and limited. This is important because the direct consequence of Athena's assistance is to make Diomedes superhuman. The flip side to him being made an irresistible force of nature, and directly stemming from it, is the fact that his humanity is put at risk; he even dares to do battle with the gods themselves. Such daring, when he wounds the goddess Aphrodite, earns him a stern rebuke from Dione, who compares him to Otus and Ephialtes and Herakles (other heroes who wounded gods, 5.382–405), behavior that, for the goddess, marks him out as foolish and short-lived (5.407–408), and in need of being reined in by Apollo (5.440–442). It is at this point, when he is already in danger of transgressing human limits, that Athena chides him for *not* being sufficiently *like his father*. Recounting her version of the episode that Agamemnon had previously narrated,[88] Athena spurs Diomedes to even greater fury and to even more extreme behavior, so that Ares, of all the gods, is cowed, complaining of this "arrogant son of Tydeus" (Τυδέος υἱὸν ὑπερφίαλον Διομήδεα, 5.881) whom Athena hurls (ἀνῆκεν, 882) like a weapon against the other gods. Athena's sponsorship of Diomedes encourages him to go *too far* in fighting even the gods, in a manner that recalls the excesses of his father. Diomedes' excesses here also anticipate the actions of the unbridled Achilles that the *Iliad* brings to the fore in Book 21, when the hero's very humanity seems to be at stake. Ironically it is when Diomedes is impelled to push the boundaries of what it means to be human that he appears most like his father.

The cumulative tone of Diomedes' *aristeia* in Book 5, then, becomes successively more difficult to read. While it is true that he performs deeds that no

---

[87] Stamatopoulou 2017 argues that the wounding of Aphrodite by Diomedes is a model for the depiction of Herakles in the Hesiodic *Sheild* (on which see Chapter 6, "Beyond Thebes" and "The Boiotian Hesiod").

[88] Athena's version of the story in *Iliad* 5 supplements Agamemnon's in various interesting ways, but especially by recounting events from the divine perspective. Not merely confirming Agamemnon's vague sense that Tydeus enjoyed the aid of the goddess, Athena gives more specifics about how she helped him and what advice she gave. But, besides this, she seems in general to place less emphasis on her own aid to the hero and more on Tydeus' inborn heroic temper: Sammons 2014:304–306.

other mortals could achieve (cf. "Tydeus' son [completed a great deed] which not even two men could carry off / such as men are today," Τυδεΐδης μέγα ἔργον ὃ οὐ δύο γ' ἄνδρε φέροιεν, / οἷοι νῦν βροτοί εἰσ', 5.303–304), his fame is one that makes him a pawn of the gods—he is pricked by Athena, only to be slowed by Apollo; Dione promises Aphrodite that he will not live for long; even the frenzied Ares takes issue with his behavior. In each of these moments, Diomedes' paternity is referenced. In this light, the *Iliad* credits Diomedes' inheritance for a martial prowess whose excesses must be policed by the gods. While his *aristeia* ultimately fulfills Agamemnon's aims when he criticized his lack of enthusiasm for battle, at the same time it raises concerns that issue from Agamemnon's articulation of that very wish—for a singular hero performing singular deeds for his own glory. As an example of what such an exceptional hero looks like, Diomedes well illustrates the problems of excessive martial valor and power, since he has the effrontery to fight the gods themselves. In losing his humanity, Diomedes has his name added to a catalogue of heroes whose arrogant assaults against the gods are not to be forgotten or indeed imitated. At these points the name of his father is prominent, suggesting that it is precisely when he risks being something other than human that he appears to perform the role Agamemnon so desperately desires of him, as his father's son.

The end of his *aristeia* is similarly marked by an appearance of his father, and it comes significantly hot on the heels of another narrative about a singular hero. Challenged by Diomedes to defend his paternity in the opening exchanges of their verbal sparring, Glaukos recounts the deeds of the hero Bellerophon, a story that is told, it seems, particularly for the benefit of his opponent. Like Tydeus, Bellerophon is described as "trusting in the gods"—the only other character in the Homeric poems to be described in this way.[89] Both, moreover, defeat a set of enemies (Tydeus in athletic contests, Bellerophon in battle) and are subsequently ambushed, only to prove victorious again. Finally, both are said to have been abandoned by the gods; for Bellerophon this is simply stated without any explanation (*Iliad* 6.200–202). The motif of the hero losing the trust of the gods seems especially pointed when it follows Diomedes' *aristeia*. As with Agamemnon's Theban tale above, the narrative serves the immediate purpose of persuading the targeted audience: in this case Glaukos, wisely,

---

[89] The combination πειθόμενοι τεράεσσι θεῶν καὶ Ζηνὸς ἀρωγῇ 'trusting in divine portents and Zeus' aid', which occurs only in Sthenelos' speech, appears to utilize two ideas. The first (τεράεσσι πιθ-) occurs twice in the *Iliad* in tales of heroes who accomplished great deeds because they trusted in the signs of the gods (Tydeus, 4.398; Bellerophon, 6.183). The second, involving the noun τέρας, occurs many times in the *Iliad* and the *Odyssey* to describe actual or potential *signs* from the gods (general or specific). The noun τέρας is used to refer to specific and concrete signs given for particular moments and actions; ἀρωγή, on the other hand, appears to be a reference to a god who is consistently on, and by, your side.

deflects Diomedes' martial provocation by using the story of Bellerophon to establish a common bond of *xenia*. Yet, also like the Theban tale, the story about Bellerophon resonates more broadly with the thematic dynamics of the *Iliad*.[90] His tale—a stranger in a strange land, without family or bonds of *xenia* to accompany him into old age—reflects on the epic as a whole, by underlining the importance of establishing divinely sanctioned social practices (like *xenia*) and of remembering and reconstituting the communities at home.[91]

In contrast to Agamemnon's Theban tale, this story gains acceptance.[92] Diomedes acknowledges the veracity of Glaukos' account and recognizes their ties of *xenia*. Even as he affirms their bond, however, he admits to not knowing his father. "I do not remember Tydeus," he concedes, "since he left me when I was still a child, at that time when the people of the Achaeans were destroyed at Thebes" (Τυδέα δ' οὐ μέμνημαι, ἐπεί μ' ἔτι τυτθὸν ἐόντα / κάλλιφ', ὅτ' ἐν Θήβῃσιν ἀπώλετο λαὸς Ἀχαιῶν, *Iliad* 6.223-224).[93] Above we noted that Diomedes, conscious perhaps of the uncertainty surrounding his paternal inheritance, or even anxious about what that might entail, represents an important test case for the *Iliad*'s positioning of itself in reference to other traditions. In Book 4 he accepts Agamemnon's insults and allows the comparison to his unknown father to stand. In Book 5 Diomedes shows that in military prowess (and in marginal behavior) he has the potential to be his father's son. Here in Book 6 he accepts the bonds of *xenia* with another hero through (a reminder of) the relationship forged by the father he doesn't remember. The one thing that he does know about his father is how his actions led to the destruction of the "people of the

---

[90] As Andersen 1987 argues, paradigms have an additional function in Homeric poetry: they facilitate the mirroring of the embedded tale to and from the outer narrative (the epic) and may also thus function to model for us or instruct us how to read epic.

[91] It is tempting to hear an echo of Agamemnon's pursuit of a foreign bride to the detriment of the communities before Troy and at home, or the privileging of *nostos* that is so central to the *Odyssey*.

[92] From a metapoetic perspective, we also believe that Glaukos' use of his ancestry gives us a peek at the Homeric strategy of instrumentalizing genealogy. Glaukos selectively presents a genealogical narrative to affect a present situation; his audience accepts the account and thus confirms the present relationships they share. Agamemnon similarly "re-reads" a genealogical tale in order to impact his current reality. His audience, however, contests his tale and de-authorizes the account, destabilizing the interpretation initially offered. Not only does Agamemnon's Theban story narrowly focus on a series of "off-center" moments in that other tradition; the story itself fails to gain audience sanction and thus this alternative story about a siege lacks authority.

[93] Even as Diomedes professes not to remember his father, he *does* recall the gift that Bellerophon gave to his *grandfather* Oeneus (6.223-224). Athena, who describes Diomedes as "little like" his father (ἢ ὀλίγον οἷ παῖδα ἐοικότα γείνατο Τυδεύς, 5.800), also seeks to goad him by invoking the name of Tydeus (5.124-132 and 800-813). This rather odd episode, reminiscent of Athena's testing of Odysseus in *Odyssey* 13, has attracted suspicion: see, for example, Apthorp 2000; Nagy 2004:36-37.

Achaeans" (ἀπώλετο λαὸς Ἀχαιῶν). As Johannes Haubold (2000) has shown, the *laos* is the epic group par excellence whose security is consistently under threat in the *Iliad* due to the poor judgment and ill-discipline of its leaders. Their salvation will only be secure (and secured) once the race of heroes is dust and institutions have been founded in its wake. Within this foundational framework, Thebes is consigned to a dim and distant past—a "time when" the people of the Achaeans were killed. Contrast the *Iliad*, which, in following the career of Diomedes, presents itself as the narrative that both explains the (necessary) disappearance of the race of heroes and establishes the social and political ties out of which formal institutions like *xenia* and the *agora* may become realized. The next time that we see Diomedes will be in the *agora*, first acting (in Book 7) as the Achaean spokesman in rejecting Priam's compromise proposal (to return the booty that Paris had escaped with, but not Helen), and then standing up to Agamemnon and ensuring that the Achaean coalition remain at Troy (Book 9).

Diomedes—and through him, the *Iliad*—performs a sophisticated set of poetic moves whereby a Tydeus is presented as a role model ill-suited to our *Iliad* (Book 4), whose martial strength, when imitated, has cosmic threatening implications (Book 5), and whose presence as an ally and example of *xenia* is emphasized instead (Book 6). Diomedes pointedly cannot recall the Tydeus everyone talks about; but he purposefully reminds us of the one this epic wants us to remember. It is not until a good deal later, in *Iliad* 14, that Diomedes himself finally breaks his silence in a way that challenges both the importance that Agamemnon had tried to claim for Tydeus and the rival tradition in which Tydeus would have played a prominent role.

A Hero Not of Our Time

As we have just anticipated, part of the story of Diomedes' reflections on his father is that he goes through stages of denial, imitation, re-vision, and finally qualified acceptance. The steps in this process can be viewed both discretely—as instances of Homeric heroes selecting the meaning required for the rhetorical challenge at hand—or cumulatively—as if the epic were bit-by-bit altering a Tydeus inherited from the tradition into someone better fit for this world. We certainly do not believe that these options are mutually exclusive; each also reflects poetic strategies and stances of the larger poem. In this light, it is worth considering the continuing arc of Tydeus' presence in the epic. On two separate occasions, Diomedes invokes his father again and claims something in addition from that story tradition. Although in *Iliad* 6 he claims not to remember his father, when he accepts Odysseus' invitation to go on a night adventure, he recalls how Athena had once supported Tydeus (*Iliad* 10.284-291); later, in the context of (again) contesting Agamemnon (14.110–132), he provides even more information about his father, in reconstituting him for a role in the *Iliad*.

In the wake of Achilles' rejection of the Achaean embassy (and explicitly Agamemnon's authority), it is Diomedes who speaks up and offers the necessary riposte to the grim news (9.696-712). In the very next book, when it is proposed that the Achaeans should conduct a night sortie into Trojan territory to gain information, it is Diomedes to whom Odysseus turns when looking for a companion. In answering Odysseus' call, Diomedes asks Athena to support him as she had once supported Tydeus (*Iliad* 10.284-291). Here the Theban material is recast in the form of a prayer, as the hero reminds Athena of her support to his father by recalling his embassy to Thebes and by allusively pointing to the mischief that he had worked there.[94] This scene continues a movement that began with Agamemnon's invocation of Tydeus as a hero beyond compare, whom Diomedes must try to emulate. In fact, Diomedes' prayer reaffirms Tydeus as the hero who fights alone and who enjoys a special relationship with Athena. Only, on this occasion, such a hero is needed. The adventure on which Diomedes and Odysseus are about to embark is a risky incursion behind enemy lines, where the usual rules of Iliadic warfare have no place. (It is not surprising that the whole book comprising of the "Doloneia" episode has been considered suspect: it is *so* very un-Iliadic.) Diomedes, too, needs to be a different kind of hero in this episode, more akin to the wily Odysseus (also a favorite of Athena's) or his singular father. The pair of them will go on to spy, to lie to an enemy combatant they capture, and to murder men in their sleep.

Even here, however, the narrative that unfolds does not match Agamemnon's construction of an epic Tydeus and reimagining of Thebes. It is of critical importance that Diomedes and Odysseus work in tandem, not alone—they will overcome the single Trojan spy, Dolon, as a result of their partnership. Moreover, their actions should be seen—and are framed—as performed in the service of the Achaean collective, even if in this instance they act apart from it. Indeed, this episode follows immediately after two public meetings that bookend Book 9—the assembly at the beginning that Agamemnon convokes in order to announce the failure of the expedition, and the equally hastily reconvened council at its end that considers Achilles' rejection of the embassy. In both meetings, it is Diomedes who reaffirms the collective will to continue to prosecute the siege of Troy. He forcefully rejects the untraditional alternatives—Agamemnon's decision to give up on Troy in the former, and in the latter, Achilles' unwillingness to relinquish his anger and fight. Diomedes' singular deeds are performed in conjunction with a comrade for the benefit of the group at large, who are in

---

[94] Vergados 2014:442.

desperate need of some respite from the dire straits in which they find themselves due to the unilateral action of another singular hero.

In an important way Diomedes' night mission marks the beginning of his recuperation of his father. Like Tydeus, he engages with the enemy outside the main arena of war and alone, save for a like-minded comrade; unlike his father, he risks himself in order to establish an advantage for his own coalition that contributes to the larger narrative at hand—the siege of the city. In this complex mirroring we can read both a reinterpretation of the Tydeus scene and an appropriation of it. Where the earlier scene presents a Tydeus whose characterization is ill-fitted to the *Iliad*'s world of collective action, the nighttime adventure—which would seem equally at odds with this picture—redeploys Tydeus' qualities in a way that complements and builds on the poem's dynamics, largely thanks to the actions of Diomedes, who helps construct and carry out the ambush.

The figure of Tydeus makes one last appearance in the *Iliad*, in the assembly scene of Book 14. When the Achaeans' two best counselors, Odysseus and Nestor, counter another one of their leader's disastrous propositions, Agamemnon desperately looks around for advice (*Iliad* 14.107–108). After his critical interventions in scenes of debate in Book 9, it is again Diomedes who speaks up (14.110–132):

> ἐγγὺς ἀνήρ· οὐ δηθὰ ματεύσομεν· αἴ κ' ἐθέλητε
> πείθεσθαι, καὶ μή τι κότῳ ἀγάσησθε ἕκαστος
> οὕνεκα δὴ γενεῆφι νεώτατός εἰμι μεθ' ὑμῖν·
> <u>πατρὸς δ' ἐξ ἀγαθοῦ καὶ ἐγὼ γένος εὔχομαι εἶναι</u>
> <u>Τυδέος, ὃν Θήβῃσι χυτὴ κατὰ γαῖα καλύπτε</u>
> πορθεῖ γὰρ τρεῖς παῖδες ἀμύμονες ἐξεγένοντο,
> οἴκεον δ' ἐν Πλευρῶνι καὶ αἰπεινῇ Καλυδῶνι
> Ἄγριος ἠδὲ Μέλας, τρίτατος δ' ἦν ἱππότα Οἰνεύς
> πατρὸς ἐμοῖο πατήρ· ἀρετῇ δ' ἦν ἔξοχος αὐτῶν.
> ἀλλ' ὃ μὲν αὐτόθι μεῖνε, πατὴρ δ' ἐμὸς Ἄργεϊ νάσθη
> <u>πλαγχθείς· ὡς γάρ που Ζεὺς ἤθελε καὶ θεοὶ ἄλλοι.</u>
> Ἀδρήστοιο δ' ἔγημε θυγατρῶν, ναῖε δὲ δῶμα
> ἀφνειὸν βιότοιο, ἅλις δέ οἱ ἦσαν ἄρουραι
> πυροφόροι, πολλοὶ δὲ φυτῶν ἔσαν ὄρχατοι ἀμφίς,
> πολλὰ δέ οἱ πρόβατ' ἔσκε· κέκαστο δὲ πάντας Ἀχαιοὺς
> ἐγχείῃ· τὰ δὲ μέλλετ' ἀκουέμεν, εἰ ἐτεόν περ.
> τῶ οὐκ ἄν με γένος γε κακὸν καὶ ἀνάλκιδα φάντες
> μῦθον ἀτιμήσαιτε πεφασμένον ὅν κ' ἐῢ εἴπω.
> δεῦτ' ἴομεν πόλεμον δὲ καὶ οὐτάμενοί περ ἀνάγκῃ.

ἔνθα δ' ἔπειτ' αὐτοὶ μὲν ἐχώμεθα δηϊοτῆτος
ἐκ βελέων, μή πού τις ἐφ' ἕλκεϊ ἕλκος ἄρηται·
ἄλλους δ' ὀτρύνοντες ἐνήσομεν, οἳ τὸ πάρος περ
θυμῷ ἦρα φέροντες ἀφεστᾶσ' οὐδὲ μάχονται.

"The man is nearby—we will not look long for him. If you are willing
To consent and each of you does not get troubled by anger
Because I am the youngest among you by birth.
I also claim to be from a noble father by birth,
Tydeus, whom a heap of earth covers in Thebes.
Three blameless children were born to Portheus
And they used to live in Pleuron and steep Kalydon:
Agrios, Melas, and the third was the horseman Oeneus,
The father of my father. He was exceptional for his excellence.
But while he remained there, my father left for Argos,
Driven out. This was, I guess, how Zeus and the other gods wanted it.
He married one of the daughters of Adrastos and lived in a home
Wealthy for life: he had enough wheat-bearing fields,
And there were many orchards on all sides;
And he had many flocks. He also surpassed all the Achaeans
With a spear. You all have heard these things, if they are true.
Thus, you cannot claim that I come from low birth or I am a coward
And disregard the speech I set forth if I speak it well.
Now, let us go to war by necessity, even though we are wounded.
There, let us keep ourselves out of the strife of the missiles,
Lest someone add a wound to a wound.
But we shall send forth and encourage others, even those who before
Stood apart and did not fight, pleasing their hearts."

In order to underline his capacity to speak authoritatively on matters of public concern in spite of his youth ("youngest by birth," γενεῆφι νεώτατος, 112), Diomedes claims his inheritance as the son of a noble father, Tydeus (113–114).

This is the second time that Diomedes has insisted upon his nobility and capability in war before the Achaeans (cf. 9.34–36), only now he broadens his scope to include his father's nobility as well. This move is all the more striking given that he previously denied any memory of his father, when responding to Glaukos' detailed genealogical narrative back in Book 6; here, Diomedes provides an account of his ancestral line, starting with his father. He identifies several important details, including his grandfather's excellence (ἀρετῇ δ' ἦν ἔξοχος αὐτῶν, 118), the material wealth of his *maternal* family (δῶμα /

ἀφνειόν, 121–122), his father's death and exile (πλαγχθείς, 120), and Tydeus' excellence with the spear (124–125).[95] This last detail is particularly pointed, for Agamemnon had earlier criticized him for not living up to the martial standards of his father. Here, we see Diomedes responding to that insult, that he is inferior to his father in war, as he acts on Agamemnon's second slight, that he is better than his father in public speech (εἶο χέρεια μάχῃ, ἀγορῇ δέ τ᾽ ἀμείνω, 4.400).[96] By this time, the king has belatedly come to appreciate the value of a hero who can perform great deeds both in battle and in the assembly.

In this way Diomedes' genealogical narrative can be understood within the framework of his prior encounters with Agamemnon. His mobilization of his genealogy is limited and follows the pattern observed earlier. *This* Tydeus is not the god-assisted victor of Agamemnon's story.[97] Instead of recounting Tydeus' heroic exploits, Diomedes describes him as an exile rejected by Zeus and the other gods (120)—as Bellerophon before him had been, according to the story that Glaukos tells Diomedes. This loss of divine favor is notable in light of Agamemnon's earlier insistence on Athena's support—and indeed of Athena's and Diomedes' own rendering of that special relationship. Moreover, after (finally) claiming Tydeus as his father ("I claim to be the offspring of a noble father, Tydeus," πατρὸς δ᾽ ἐξ ἀγαθοῦ καὶ ἐγὼ γένος εὔχομαι εἶναι / Τυδέος, 113–114), Diomedes straightaway notes his passing: "whom now the heaped up earth covers in Thebes" (ὃν Θήβῃσι χυτὴ κατὰ γαῖα καλύπτει, 114). This is very unlike other patrilineal claims, such as Odysseus', which serves to headline his account of his epic fame (*Odyssey* 9.19). On the contrary, Diomedes appears to undercut his father's fame by passing over any mention of famous deeds in favor of burying him at Thebes.

When Diomedes does elaborate on Tydeus' life, he does so in a way that again markedly contrasts with previous configurations of the hero's career. Where Agamemnon's Theban story had isolated Tydeus as a singular hero to whom the son will struggle to live up, Diomedes places him instead in the context of his ancestral line (117) and imagines him living profitably off the fat of the land given to him by his father-in-law (121–124). Just such a scenario had been put to Achilles in Book 9, as Odysseus offers Achilles recompense in the form of Agamemnon's largesse—lands, titles and the hand of his daughter included. There the singular hero had forcefully rejected the proposal, in the *Iliad*'s most overt statement of the choices facing him: he could either live a

---

[95] For the structure of this speech, see Lohmann 1970:140–146; and Janko 1992:162–163.

[96] See Elmer 2013: 189–191, who argues that Diomedes may have a genealogical connection to socially constructive speech.

[97] Janko 1992:163–164 suggests that behind Diomedes' mention of his father's wandering is his exile for kin-murder—a story meant to make his fate "more pitiable" (164).

long life of peaceful existence at home without fame *or* embrace an early death with the prospect of ensuring everlasting glory in compensation. In the terms established by Achilles, and in pointed contrast to what turns out to be this hero's fate, Diomedes pictures his father living a life of ease, the very antithesis of a story worthy of fame. Indeed, the one mention that Diomedes makes of his father's military prowess comes almost as an afterthought: "he excelled all others with the spear" (κέκαστο δὲ πάντας Ἀχαιοὺς / ἐγχείῃ, 124–125). This is hearsay that Diomedes is not able, or willing, to corroborate—an accomplishment in *games* perhaps even anticipating Agamemnon's own problematic victory with the javelin in Book 23 (884–895).[98]

The members of each epic generation, for whom authority derives from their predecessors, depend for their future fame on their capacity to reinvent that tradition. Here, Diomedes, and through him Homer, furnish the new by reworking and re-interpreting the old.[99] The four moves that Diomedes makes— burying his father, tracing his own lineage to his forebears, replacing his father's heroic deeds with a scene of peace and prosperity, and casting doubt on the process of memorialization—all contribute to an act of double erasure performed on Tydeus *and* his story at Thebes. First, by tracing his nobility *not* to his exiled father but instead to his grandfather Oeneus and Kalydon, Diomedes emphasizes the derivative and evolving nature of the epic tradition. Then, by undermining his father's fame, he implies that the story that is important is the story that can be verified, that is to say, the tale unfolding before our very ears, the *Iliad*, guaranteed by the muse herself. Finally, just as the fame of Tydeus' deeds is obscured, so Thebes itself is diminished in status—simply a burial ground for an unknown warrior. The rhetorical power of this speech simultaneously represents and reproduces Diomedes' different form of heroism from his father. Yes, he is (or can be) ferocious in battle (sometimes overly so), but he's also politically astute and a speaker of words. A hero, in other words, of and for *this* epic.

Agamemnon's renewed suggestion (carried over from Book 9) is to abandon the war and sail from Troy secretly at night. After Nestor and Odysseus' strong rebuttal, this time it is left to Diomedes to offer the advice: all the Achaeans should rejoin battle; even those who have been wounded can encourage the others to fight (*Iliad* 14.110–132). Diomedes introduces this short and direct proposition, which consists of only five verses, by a full eighteen-line account

---

[98] Achilles awards Agamemnon a prize before the latter even casts his spear, thereby depriving the king of the opportunity to show his worth, even as Achilles shows respect (it seems) for him. On the ambiguities latent in this scene, see Postlethwaite 1998.

[99] As Telemachus puts it in the *Odyssey*, an audience is always eager to hear the newest song (*Odyssey* 1.351–352).

of his epic genealogy. The story of Thebes is fully subordinated to keep the Achaeans at Troy and the *Iliad* on track, in the fullest expression yet of group dynamics. Earlier Diomedes had rebutted Agamemnon's despair by claiming that he and Sthenelos will stay at Troy and fight (9.48–49), even should everyone else depart, affirming the comradeship that the pair demonstrate in response to Agamemnon's Theban tale. Here Diomedes speaks on behalf of the whole Achaean contingent at Troy to reaffirm their shared commitment to this siege story. His purpose thus served, we don't hear of Diomedes again, apart from at Patroklos' funeral games, where he wins the first, and foremost, of the contests: the chariot race. The focus turns instead to two other comrades, Patroklos and the very singular Achilles, whose story the *Iliad* tells.[100]

Conclusion

In the Introduction we suggested that it is more fruitful to analyze individual components of hexameter epic verse as common inheritances from an ever-evolving and expanding tradition, which are then deployed contrastively to help define and articulate the particular features of the poem in question. In this chapter we have discussed how Agamemnon's tale of Tydeus as a primal hero chimes dissonantly with the *Iliad*'s broader and more nuanced articulation of collective political activity. Such disharmony is addressed directly by Sthenelos' response, while Diomedes, conscious of avoiding (further) political strife with the king, reveals an acute understanding of the critical symbiotic relationship between the shepherd and his people, even as he seeks to maintain group solidarity behind the king. Following up his genealogy somewhat later, Diomedes subsequently reaffirms that the situation in their world is significantly different from that of their fathers and subtly asserts the pre-eminence of his tale, our *Iliad*, over the stories about Thebes.

There is also an important metapoetic connection made between the Theban and Trojan traditions through the participation of Sthenelos and Diomedes in both. As agents in the destruction of Thebes, the two sons attest to the pre-eminence of their generation over their fathers'; but as subsequent witnesses to and participants in the *siege* of Troy they function to mark the comparative difficulty of the later campaign. In addition, the presence of these same warriors in both conflicts projects a temporal frame upon the narratives that makes Thebes Troy's antecedent. Thus, thematically, the *Iliad* effectively makes Thebes *anticipatory* to its own denouement. While Thebes occupies the prior position, Troy

---

[100] Slatkin 2011:116–117 notes that as soon as Patroklos "rises up—Diomedes disappears, and with him the traces of Thebes;" cf. Pache 2014:282. See also Nagy 1999 [1979]:162–163.

gains value and magnitude by coming after. It did not have to be this way. As we learn elsewhere in the *Iliad*, Troy has been sacked before. The single and singular warrior responsible for having already sacked Troy, moreover, is none other than the Theban hero par excellence—Herakles. This much-storied hero is the subject of our second chapter.[101]

---

[101] See Sammons 2014:315–316, particularly for the storied relationship between Herakles and Tydeus.

2

The Labors of Herakles: Time[1]

IN THE LAST CHAPTER we saw Tydeus, one of the original Seven against Thebes, being held up as a model for his son, Diomedes, to emulate. At key points in Diomedes' maturation in the epic the name of his father is invoked, first before he proves himself in battle and later when he shows himself a man of politics who greatly surpasses his father in the arena of debate. In fact, it is in no small part due to his interventions in Book 9 and Book 14 that the Achaeans stay at Troy in the absence of their greatest warrior, Achilles; it is Diomedes who keeps the poem of the siege on message. The kind of singular heroics that Tydeus represents—at least in Agamemnon's characterization—is out of step in the *Iliad*'s movement towards the foundation of a political community, where the Achaean heroes fight for a political voice as much as for the sack of Troy. After all, Tydeus lies dead and buried with the rest of his generation at Thebes; Thebes is already *past*. It is left to the sons of the Seven, along with comrades-in-arms from all around the Greek world, to lay down the institutions and social practices in this new siege story that will remain with us long after the race of heroes has turned to dust.

As a son of a Theban War veteran, Diomedes enjoys prominence in the *Iliad* until the moment when Patroklos takes an active role and roundly criticizes his friend, the even more singular hero Achilles, for sitting out the fight. At this point the poem's focus shifts to Achilles, where it will remain for the rest of the epic. After Patroklos is killed, Achilles resolves to seek vengeance for his friend against Hektor. Recognizing that to stay at Troy seals his own fate, Achilles offers his mother a consolation (*Iliad* 18. 117–119):

> "οὐδὲ γὰρ οὐδὲ βίη Ἡρακλῆος φύγε κῆρα
> ὅς περ φίλτατος ἔσκε Διὶ Κρονίωνι ἄνακτι,
> ἀλλά ἑ μοῖρα δάμασσε καὶ ἀργαλέος χόλος Ἥρης."

---

[1] Many sections of this chapter draw on work originally published in Barker and Christensen 2014.

"For not even violent Herakles escaped his fate,
though he was most dear to lord Zeus, son of Kronos,
but fate tamed him and the anger of Hera, hard to endure."

If even the mighty Herakles could not escape his fate, then what use is there for Achilles to bewail his? In this final reckoning, heroes are only *semi* divine; like us, they are fated to die.

While many of Homer's heroes turn to well-known myths to make sense of their situations, Achilles' use of Herakles here seems off-beat and at the same time particularly charged. It is anomalous because until this point Achilles has not referred to any other figure from myth by name (even though he is famously recorded as singing the "famous stories of men" when the embassy meets him in Book 9: ἄειδε δ' ἄρα κλέα ἀνδρῶν, 9.189). As we have seen in the previous chapter, however, references to other non-Trojan War heroes are liberally scattered throughout the speeches of Agamemnon, Sthenelos, Glaukos, and Diomedes, thereby providing indications, if fleeting and obscure, of the *Iliad*'s agonistic relationship with the broader heroic epic tradition. The lack of such references by Achilles *until this point* is no less telling, since it both marks him out as exceptional (as if there were no figure to whom he should appeal or could be compared) and serves to highlight the importance of Herakles (now that Achilles turns to him). There is good reason why it is Herakles whom Achilles should cite. Not only is Herakles arguably *the* foremost heroic figure of Greek myth, if one takes into consideration his various representations in media from across the Greek world (and beyond);[2] according to some of these other sources he also famously survived death and lived on with the Olympians. To insist on his death, as Achilles does here, would seem to indicate some emendation—or, at least, repurposing—of his tale by Homer's protagonist. More broadly, it provides a tantalizing glimpse into the rivalry between Homer's poem and a Herakles tradition, played out over the critical issue of immortality.

As we have already discussed in this book, the presence of Theban elements in the *Iliad* and *Odyssey* can be viewed in terms of a dynamic rivalry through which the Homeric poems shape Thebes and its tradition for their own narrative strategies. In this light it is worth considering that among other things Herakles is a *Theban* hero. On the one hand, Herakles is a hero to rank alongside any to be found in Homer, a superhuman son of Zeus who has many adventures. On the other, he barely figures in surviving epic, with only hints of his heroic endeavors in Homer and Hesiod, supplemented by fragments of purportedly contemporary epics.

---

[2] For the wide circulation of stories about Herakles, see Malkin 1998:156–209; 2011:119–142.

In this chapter we begin by sketching out the antiquity of Herakles in myth and assessing its resonance in the fragmentary and extant poetry from the Archaic period. After exploring Herakles' independent existence outside Homer, we explore how speakers in the *Iliad* relate, and *relate to*, the accomplishments of this hero, in trying to make sense of or influence their situations. By focusing on Herakles' appearances in the *Iliad* through the lens of the poem's sustained engagement with and manipulation of formulaic language, we will be able to reconsider Achilles' curious statement as part an agonistic process by which the *Iliad* appropriates *and* marginalizes a hero ill fit to its tale. Our final section reflects on Herakles' appearances in the *Odyssey*, which if anything present a figure even more out of time with this epic's new world of human toil and labor. Extreme in both action and fate, Herakles is a figure from whom Odysseus—that other great traveling, *suffering* hero—is studiously careful to distance himself.

The Epic Herakles

There can be little doubt that Herakles was one of the most popular and enduring figures in Greek mythical representations of varying kinds.[3] In iconography Herakles adorns temple friezes and drinking vessels in equal measure.[4] In cult he ranks alongside the heroes of the Trojan War saga and others associated with protecting communities.[5] But he also exceeds other *heroes*: in Athenian dedications and prayers we find the formula "to the twelve gods and Herakles" (e.g. IG II 1.57).[6] Quintessentially, Herakles bestrides the human and divine worlds. As Herodotus notes, he was the only figure to receive sacrifices as both hero and god.[7]

While iconography alone attests to Herakles' popularity throughout the Greek world, early literary material provides broad (if shallow) evidence of his importance and the elements of his basic *fabula*.[8] For Pindar, Herakles represents a paradigmatic figure for competing athletes, dedicating his life to completing tasks and upholding the Olympian order.[9] Part of this athletic portrayal depicts him living a life of leisure with divine company in an idealized representation

---

[3] Herakles in the Mycenaean period: Fowler 2013:261. Cf. Galinsky 1972; Gantz 1993:374–381.

[4] For Herakles imagery in Athens, see Boardman 1975; for images of his apotheosis, see Holt 1992.

[5] Cf. Farnell 1921:95–98. For a recent discussion of Heraklean ritual as reflected in Euripides' play, see Papadopoulou 2005:9–57. For a broader overview of scholarship on Heraklean ritual and cult since Farnell, see Stafford 2010.

[6] Herakles' divinity problematic for the Greeks: Shapiro 1983:9; rare from an Indo-European perspective: Davidson 1980:198; distorted by the literary record: Verbanck-Pierard 1989.

[7] Herodotus II 44. On Pausanias: Ekroth 1999:150.

[8] On this use of *fabula*: Burgess 2009.

[9] Herakles was of course associated with the foundation of the Olympic Games and invoked as such at Pindar *Olympian* 2.8, 3.11, 6.68, and 10.10. Cf. Apollodorus II 141; Hyginus 273.5.

of the acclaim and festive celebration that each victor could expect from his community upon returning home.[10] Typical of tragedy, Herakles' super-human, uber-masculine characteristics come tinged with darker overtones.[11] In Euripides' *Herakles*, at the zenith of his glory he is visited by the goddess Madness and slaughters his entire family; in Sophocles' *Trachiniae*, he is the returning hero who perishes at the hands of a jealous wife. In both of these cases, the hero's antisocial threat is emphasized and his apotheosis downplayed, notably in Sophocles' play, even as it depicts his final moments.[12] His antiso-cial behavior also features in Euripides' *Alcestis*, where he turns up drunk and expecting hospitality at a household in mourning; that (in shame) he subse-quently ambushes Death to return Alcestis to his friend, Admetus, only further marks out the hero's abnormality, as well as the play's uncomfortable tonal shifts between tragedy and comedy. It is his merrymaking, voracious appetite and general boorishness that make him a frequent target of humor and abuse in comedy.[13]

The further back we go, the murkier Herakles' appearances become; still, it is possible to detect the extent to which the language and motifs characteristic of Herakles in extant archaic Greek poetry intersect with elements from our epics.[14] Ancient biographical accounts even associated stories about Herakles with Homer's epic output;[15] though now considered unreliable, these witnesses

---

[10] *Isthmian* 4.54–60 depicts Herakles' afterlife among the gods, married to Hebe and reconciled with Hera, as a reward for his righteous deeds and support of the divine order. Cf. *Nemean* 1.67–79. Isocrates also claims that Herakles was more honored in Thebes than all of the other deities (*Philip* 88) and that Pindar marks out his special significance with the phrase ἥρως θεός (*Nemean* 3.22).

[11] Herakles' problematic masculinity is a feature of Victoria Wohl's 1998 study of gender in tragedy.

[12] On Euripides' *Herakles*: Papadopoulou 2005. On Herakles in Sophocles' *Trachiniae*: Liapis 2006.

[13] The "hungry Herakles" was a stock gag in comedy: see, e.g. Aristophanes *Peace* 741; *Wasps* 60.

[14] In addition to the early Greek hexameter poems that we discuss below, there may have been a poem from Eleusis about his descent into Hades, the fragmentary *Meropis* features Herakles, and he is prominent in the archaic poetry of Steisichorus (*Geryon, Kyknos, Kerberos*): Fowler 2013:260–261.

[15] Ancient testimonia link Homer with composers of Herakles epics, counting Panyasis, Peisander, and Homer among the five best poets: Proclus *Life of Homer* 1.2; Tzetzes *Prolegomena to Hesiod's Works and Days*: Bernabé 1996:166–167, 171–174; cf. Davies 1988:129–131. Homer is also linked with Creophylus as teacher and student (Photius), in-laws (scholion to Plato *Republic* 600b) or as guest-friends whose relationship was sealed by the gifting of the *Sack of Oechalia*: Strabo XIV 1.18; Proclus *Life of Homer* 5.30: Bernabé 1996:157–160. Creophylus as a "more laughable companion of Homer": Plato *Republic* 600b; cf. Davies 1989:113–129. The dating and geographical range of these poets also echoes the broad dates and shifting locations for Homer. Creophylus and Peisander are conventionally dated to the seventh century at Samos and Rhodes respectively, whereas Panyasis is dated to the sixth century in Halicarnassus: Davies 1989:114, 129, and 149–153. West 2003:21–23 dates Peisander also to the sixth century based on his representation of Herakles with a club and lion-skin.

provide evidence for the strong similarity of the different compositions with respect to shared language, motifs, and story patterns, and suggest that any poems circulating about Herakles may have been similar in style and content to the Homeric epics that survived.[16] In all likelihood, the early epics helped in part to establish Herakles' character, his traits, and the basic outline of his story in a Panhellenic context.[17] Equally, his mutable nature as hero or god (and sometimes both) necessarily positions him as an exception to the Homeric epics' emphasis on human mortality and the correlative importance of fame.[18]

In the absence of any extant early Greek hexameter poem devoted to Herakles, we have to rely on fragments of possible poems, a single Homeric Hymn, and glimpses of the hero in the *Theogony* to put flesh on the bones of the epic Herakles.[19] The longest of our sources is the Hesiodic *Shield*, and it provides a good example of the kinds of interformularity and intertraditionality that we will see operating within the *Iliad*.[20] As we discussed in the Introduction, Bakker's "scale of...interformularity" assists in describing levels of engagement with motifs and diction within the same tradition, while intertraditionality has to do with repetitions of and reflections on motifs and diction among different

---

[16] On the use of the ancient biographical tradition for thinking about the reception of poetry: Graziosi 2002. West 2013:17 imagines "no comprehensive *Heracleia* covering his whole career" but instead a "Herakles cycle" similar to a set of poems dedicated to a particular figure in the Near-Eastern traditions (e.g. Gilgamesh). Davies 1989 excludes Herakles epics from his consideration.

[17] According to the *Suda* (s.v *Peisandros*), the Rhodian Peisander, who flourished in the seventh century, wrote about the "deeds of Herakles" in two books (and was the first to give him a club!). Two extant fragments of Panyasis (4 and 5 Bernabé) bestow a lion skin upon the hero.

[18] Herakles' excessive violence and antisocial individualism precluded him from participation in communal warfare and reciprocal honor: Galinsky 1972:9–10. For the "non-Homeric" nature of apotheosis and immortality for mortals: Griffin 1977. While it is true that the Homeric epics largely suppress narratives that grant immortality to mortals, such notions are not unknown to archaic Greek hexameter poetry. Ariadne becomes immortal at Hesiod *Theogony* 947–949; in the Hesiodic *Catalogue of Women* Artemis makes Iphimedes (Iphigeneia) immortal when she is sacrificed (fr. 23.24); Ino (Leukothea), a sea nymph, is said to have once been mortal (Burkert 1985:172). Ganymede and Tithonos achieve problematic forms of immortality in the *Hymn to Aphrodite*, as we shall see below (see n39 below).

[19] See Gantz 1993:374–460 for an extensive summary of the early evidence for Herakles' myths. According to Proclus, before going to war, Nestor tried to dissuade Menelaos by offering him tales about men ruined by women. In this list, he included the madness of Herakles as a negative example (*Chrestomathia* 114–7). Cf. *Commentary on Plato's Alcibiades* 214.3–6. See also Hainsworth 1993:285; Lardinois 2000:649. Heath 1987:187 suggests that all the tales are of love-madness (cf. Scaife 1995:167). Herakles' madness was popular at an early period and mentioned in the work of Steisichorus and even Pindar: Fowler 2013:269. The epic *Sack of Oechalia* apparently told of Herakles' madness and abduction of Iole: Hesiod fr. 26.31–3; cf. Eusthathius on *Iliad* 300.43. Cf. West 2013:276.

[20] For these terms, see Bakker 2013 and the Introduction. For a recent overview of the Hesiodic *Shield* that focuses on its engagement with the *Iliad*, particularly its "consciously post-Homeric" depiction of a *theomachos*, see Stamatopoulou 2017:11–16. On the *Shield*, see further Chapter 6, "Beyond Thebes" and "The Boiotian Hesiod."

traditions. The narrative of the *Shield*, like that of the *Iliad*, is motivated by a divine plan and culminates in one-on-one combat between the hero and his antagonist, in this case between Herakles and Kyknos.[21] Its Herakles even talks like a Homeric hero, articulating the arduous tasks he must perform while anticipating his own *kleos* (94 and 106–107). More striking still, a significant portion of the poem (139–317) is occupied by an arming sequence that involves the ekphrasis of the poem's eponymous shield. Betraying compositional similarities to the shield of Achilles in the *Iliad*, Herakles' shield presents a hero who looks decidedly Achaean, armed with sword, helmet, and shield rather than his customary iconographic lion-skin and club.

Where there is a difference is in the concern to plot the hero's life story, from his conception through to his performance of great deeds. Following a plot that recalls the pattern of murder, exile, and reintegration used in stories of displaced heroes in the *Iliad*, Herakles' parents migrate to Thebes,[22] where Zeus "was planning in his thoughts *wondrous deeds*" (ἔνθα καθεζόμενος φρεσὶ μήδετο θέσκελα ἔργα, *Shield* 34). This language has broad purchase in surviving early hexameter epic poetry. In the *Iliad* Homer uses θέσκελα ἔργα 'wondrous deeds' to describe the combat between Paris and Menelaos (3.130); in the *Odyssey*, in response to Alkinoos' request for information about his ex-Trojan War comrades, Odysseus glosses his news as θέσκελα ἔργα (11.374).[23] In the two Homeric poems, then, the "wondrous deeds" relate to the actions of the heroes of the epics. Here in the *Shield*, however, "wondrous deeds" has a divine dimension, in that it denotes Zeus' plan to impregnate Amphitryon's wife. This usage more closely matches a Hesiodic fragment in which Zeus contemplates θέσκελα ἔργα, as strife among the gods is set in motion by Helen's marriage ("for then, indeed, he was devising *wondrous* deeds," δὴ γὰρ τότε μήδετο θέσκελα ἔργα, Hesiod fr. 204.96). In this case, as in the *Shield*, the phrase marks a close equivalent of "the plan of Zeus," suggesting, as with that famous formula, a heroic narrative (full of "wondrous deeds") to follow. In the *Shield*, Zeus' contemplation of "wondrous deeds" conceives of Herakles as a "guardian against ruin (ἀρῆς ἀλκτῆρα) for both gods and men" (29), a role that this poem sets about demonstrating. It is particularly notable that this phrase occurs on only two other occasions in extant early Greek hexameter poetry outside the *Shield*—in the *Iliad*, when Achilles bemoans how he *failed* to be a "guardian against ruin"

---

[21] *Shield* 58–60. As in the *Iliad*, the primary conflict is moved by a combination of Apollo and Zeus, while Athena spearheads actual intervention.

[22] *Shield* 1–28. The pattern recalls the plight of Bellerophon (*Iliad* 6.155–195) and Phoinix's tale of his own life (9.457–484).

[23] In its only other occurrence in extant early Greek hexameter poetry, θέσκελα ἔργα describes the baldric Herakles wears in Hades (11.610): see 176 (and note 317) below. On the popularity of this scene in sixth-century BCE art: Shapiro 1984:524–525.

for his comrade, Patroklos, and when the Trojan warrior Akamas, having taken revenge for his brother, declares, "Therefore a man prays to leave behind him in his house a brother as ἀρῆς ἀλκτῆρα."[24] Thus the *Shield* not only draws on motifs and language shared with the Trojan War tradition; it also ranks Herakles' birth and purpose as an act equivalent to the events of that war and Herakles himself as—naturally—the superior guardian-like figure, against whom even Homer's Achilles fails to measure up.[25]

Such shared points of language and theme pervade arguably earlier and more fragmentary epic remains of Herakles. Though the *Sack of Oechalia* leaves barely three lines of hexameter, one names Nestor as the sole survivor of Herakles' attack, an incident that Nestor himself reflects on in *Iliad* 11, as we shall see.[26] The fragments of Peisander's *Herakleia*, also three lines in length, use language recognizable from other extant early Greek hexameter poems alongside motifs—such as Athena helping the hero and etiological wordplay—familiar to any modern reader of Homer and Hesiod.[27] The more extensive fragments of Panyasis' *Herakleia* (over sixty hexameter lines)[28] include a catalogue of gods who endured at his hands, not dissimilar to Dione's consolation to Aphrodite in *Iliad* 5.385–395.[29] Although the content of some of the longest passages seems un-Homeric to us, the phrases and imagery certainly draw on the same language from which our examples of early Greek hexameter epic derive.[30] The one complete surviving archaic Greek hexameter poem dedicated

[24] Cf. *Shield* 128 (Herakles' arms described as ἀρῆς ἀλκτῆρα); *Iliad* 18.100, 14.485.

[25] See Stamatopoulou 2017:17 for a nuanced reading of the *Shield*'s depiction of Herakles as "an agent of justice aligned with the will of Zeus."

[26] Cf. frr. 1, 4 and 8 Bernabé, See Bernabé 1996:161–164. On Nestor's story, see the section "Out of Time" below.

[27] Fr. 7: "for him [Herakles] at Thermopylae grey-eyed Athena / made hot baths along the strand of the sea," τῶι δ' ἐν Θερμοπύληισι θεὰ γλαυκῶπις Ἀθήνη / ποίει θερμὰ λοετρὰ παρὰ ῥηγμῖνι θαλάσσης. Fr. 8: "There is no criticism even to tell a lie on behalf of one's life," οὐ νέμεσις καὶ ψεῦδος ὑπὲρ ψυχῆς ἀγορεύειν. Add to this two partial lines (frr. 9 and 10 Bernabé): "there's no sense with Centaurs" and "of the most just murderer," νοῦς οὐ παρὰ Κενταύροισι· δικαιοτάτου δὲ φονῆος. According to Athenaeus XI 783c, Peisander's epic indicated that Telamon (Ajax's father) was a favorite of Herakles; cf. Bernabé 1996:170.

[28] Dionysius of Halicarnassus *On Imitation* II 2 and Quintilian X 1 52–54 compare Panyasis to Hesiod and Antimachus, praising Hesiod for his language but giving Panyasis some attention for his judgment; cf. Bernabé 1996:173–174.

[29] "Demeter endured; the famous Lame-god endured; Poseidon endured; and silver-bowed Apollo endured / to serve a mortal for one year / and even Ares stronghearted endured under his father's compulsion," τλῆ μὲν Δημήτηρ, τλῆ δὲ κλυτὸς Ἀμφιγυήεις, / τλῆ δὲ Ποσειδῶν, τλῆ δ' ἀργυρότοξος Ἀπόλλων / ἀνδρὶ παρὰ θνητῷ θητευσέμεν εἰς ἐνιαυτόν, / τλῆ δὲ καὶ ὀβριμόθυμος Ἄρης ὑπὸ πατρὸς ἀνάγκη (Panyasis *Herakleia* fr. 3 Benarbé = 16 K).

[30] Fr. 16 Bernabé = 12 K discusses at length the virtues of wine and even goes so far as to grant equal fame to the man who delights in the feast as to one who leads an army into battle (8–9). Subsequent fragments moralizing about drinking (17 and 19 Bernabé) may function to create

to Herakles is the Homeric *Hymn to Herakles*. The hymn is one of the shortest of the collection, but even its mere presence in the corpus is enough to demonstrate Herakles' unique status as a hero to be honored like a god. Though brief, the *Hymn* serves to establish two key ideas. The first relates to a familiar trope from Homeric epic: Herakles is a son of Zeus and the "best" of those born on earth (1–3) "who both performed and suffered many terrible things" (πολλὰ μὲν αὐτὸς ἔρεξεν ἀτάσθαλα, πολλὰ δ' ἀνέτλη, 6–7). In these lines Erwin Cook observes that "the very qualities that make the hero useful to the community leave him an inherently ambiguous figure."[31] Homeric epic shares this ambivalence about the figure of the hero, since both Achilles and Odysseus are marked out in their respective epics for suffering, both their own and that which they cause to others.[32] Herakles too, then, "can serve as a vehicle for exploring the social consequences of an individual's physical pre-eminence,"[33] particularly as a figure who represents a locus of contradictions.[34]

More fundamentally, however, Herakles is an even more problematic figure—and this relates to his praiseworthy status as an *immortal* hero. The *Hymn* presents Herakles as enjoying life on Olympus with Hebe as his wife and identifies his specific sphere of influence: he is asked to bestow excellence and happiness.[35] By virtue of living a blessed afterlife, Herakles is very different from the heroes in Homeric epic, with one exception. In the *Odyssey* we learn that Menelaos similarly receives special dispensation in death thanks to his marriage with Zeus-born Helen: he will live on forevermore and after in the Isles of the Blest (*Odyssey* 4.563–569). At the same time, in Homer's depiction of their current married life, the blessed couple seem anything but, with Menelaos telling the story of how Helen tried to entice the Achaeans out of the wooden horse by imitating the voices of their wives, while for her part Helen drugs the wine to help them all forget their miseries.[36] In a similar way to Herakles, who suffered in mortal marriage(s) only to win immortality through union with a

---

tension between the eventual madness or loss of control by Herakles and his heroic resolve. Of course, bereft of the larger context, the actual tone and purpose of the passage is difficult to resolve. Moreover, the fact that these two longest fragments are preserved in quotation by Athenaeus should give some pause about the contrast between *his* use of these lines and their original context(s).

[31] Cook 1999:112.

[32] Cf. Nagy 1999 [1979]:83–93; Haubold 2000, Chapter 2

[33] Cook 1999:112.

[34] Herakles as vacillating between civilized and bestial, serious and burlesque, sane and insane, savior and destroyer, free and slave, divine and human, male and female: Loraux 1990:24; cf. Kirk 1973:16.

[35] Cf. *Odyssey* 11.603: Galinsky 1972:15.

[36] On the *Odyssey*'s problematic representation of this troubled marriage, see Bergren 1981; Olson 1989.

divine female, Menelaos has had to suffer in marriage, but now with his divine wife safely returned to him he can look forward to a life everlasting.[37]

Suffering more than both heroes is Odysseus, who remains resolutely fixed on returning home to his wife, despite the enticement of immortality offered to him by Calypso before his final journey home even begins.[38] The quasi-magical formula with which the goddess offers Odysseus the chance to become immortal—"to be deathless and ageless for all days" (θήσειν ἀθάνατον καὶ ἀγήραον ἤματα πάντα, 5.136)—resonates through the epic cosmos. We hear it when Demeter tries to make Demophoon immortal in the Homeric *Hymn to Demeter* or when Eos succeeds in making Tithonus deathless but not ageless in the *Hymn to Aphrodite*.[39] Significantly, it resonates too with Herakles' situation in a way that marks out his unique status. In his *Theogony*, Hesiod describes Herakles as the husband of Hebe who lives "painless and ageless all of his days" (ναίει ἀπήμαντος καὶ ἀγήραος ἤματα πάντα, 950–956).[40] Replacing "deathless" (ἀθάνατον) with "painless" (ἀπήμαντος), Hesiod draws attention to Herakles' status as immortal, while his agelessness—the other critical component of immortality as we note from the counter example of Tithonus—is assured by his marriage to Hebe, the instantiation of undying youthfulness. Thus the three marriage pairs—Herakles/Hebe, Menelaos/Helen, Odysseus/Penelope—all appear as variations on a theme whose progression helps both to index cosmic history and to communicate a particular story's relationship to its poetic traditions. In this arch-narrative structure Herakles represents the ultimate fantasy

---

[37] A fate Nestor warns him about in the mythical tradition: see n19 above.

[38] Calypso mentions the possibility *after* Zeus has commanded her to release Odysseus, *Odyssey* 5.135-6; cf. 7.251, 336.

[39] For Zeus and Ariadne, see *Theogony* 947 (τὴν δέ οἱ ἀθάνατον καὶ ἀγήρων θῆκε Κρονίων); see also the reconstruction of Hesiod fr. 23a, (θῆκ[εν δ᾽ ἀθάνατον καὶ ἀγήραον ἤ]ματα πάντ[α, 12); *Hymn to Demeter* 242 (καί κέν μιν ποίησεν ἀγήρων τ᾽ ἀθάνατόν τε) and 260 (ἀθάνατόν κέν τοι καὶ ἀγήραον ἤματα πάντα); *Hymn to Aphrodite* 5.214 (where Ganymede becomes immortal; ὡς ἔοι ἀθάνατος καὶ ἀγήρως ἶσα θεοῖσιν); and 218–224 (where Eos asks for Tithonus "to be immortal and live for all days," ἀθάνατόν τ᾽ εἶναι καὶ ζώειν ἤματα πάντα) but forgets to ask for "youth" and to "wipe away ruinous old age" (ἥβην αἰτῆσαι, ξῦσαί τ᾽ ἄπο γήρας ὀλοιόν). For an analysis of the *Hymn to Aphrodite*, see Van Eck 1978; Falkner 1995:121–123; Segal 1974; and Faulkner 2011. For the development of the formula, see Janko 1981. This formula generally seems to indicate that for the Greeks immortality was bipartite, but it specifically marks figures—apart from Herakles—who are not Olympian gods, e.g., Medusa's head on the Aegis (*Iliad* 2.447); Achilles' horses (17.444); Calypso's and Alkinoos' guard dogs; Medusa (277) and Echidna (304) in the *Theogony*. Things thus described are typically marginal to other divinities or in some way *fabricated*.

[40] Two reconstructed Hesiodic fragments also connect Herakles' divinity to his marriage. In one (fr. 25) he dies and then ends up living with the other gods "deathless and ageless because he has fine-ankled Hebe as his wife" (ἀθάνατος καὶ ἄγηρος, ἔχων καλλ[ίσ]φυρον Ἥβην, 29); in the other, the hero lives "griefless and without care for all time, ageless and immortal because he has great Hebe" (ναίει ἀπήμαντος] καὶ ἀκηδὴς ἤ[ματα πάντα / ἀθάνατος καὶ ἄγη]ρος ἔχων μεγαλ[Ἥβην, fr. 229.8–9).

of a hero who achieves a godlike status, and takes the divine Hebe as his wife; Menelaos, by virtue of his marriage to Helen, succeeds in gaining entry to the mysterious Isles of the Blest, where, if not strictly an immortal, he may reside for eternity (with Helen?); Odysseus expressly resists the offer of immortality, in order to return to his mortal wife. Moreover, in contrast to the epic *fabula* of Herakles, the Homeric poems are at pains to show that immortality cannot be achieved unambiguously. For Homer's heroes, there is only ever the *wish* to be ageless and deathless, as expressed by Hektor (*Iliad* 8.539) and Sarpedon (*Iliad* 12.323). Indeed, such miraculous transformation is explicitly denied to the heroes of the Trojan War in the *Iliad*, as Zeus is warned of the destabilizing consequences of extending the life of his son Sarpedon—a critical moment in the epic, as we shall see.[41] Instead, immortality for the heroes is conceived of differently, as being achieved through the poetic performance itself. By rejecting an immortal life with Calypso, the "One who covers" or the "Hider," Odysseus escapes being hidden from view and is able subsequently to reveal and enact famous deeds that will lead to his immortalization in epic song.

This brief survey shows that—from what we know of the epic tradition *about* Herakles—he occupied a complex, somewhat ambiguous place in narrative myth. He comes to exemplify the best (and worst) of Greek heroes in different poetic traditions, changing form according to each new poetic incarnation— now a mortal hero fighting a dangerous brigand (the *Shield*), now a drunk hedonist (Panyasis), now a god (the *Hymn*), now Zeus' instrument in bringing order to the cosmos (*Theogony*).[42] It is easy to imagine an epic Herakles performing like the brief glimpse of him we get in Hesiod's *Theogony*, where the hero suffers and metes out suffering in equal measure, before being rewarded in the end for his fidelity to a divine mission. For our purposes, however, it is enough to note that the complexity that pervades his archaic *fabula*, such as the tension between his identities as hero and god, and in particular the interformular means of expressing that complexity, mark him out as a significant figure for the Homeric poems in their agonistic engagement with rival traditions. In describing the

---

[41]   In one of the Hesiodic fragments that alludes to his apotheosis through his marriage to Hebe, Herakles dies in a very mortal—even a rather Homeric—way as a "city sacker" poisoned by his wife before he achieves agelessness and immortality ("death's end came quickly for Herakles the city-sacker, the son of Amphitryon, once he accepted it," Ἀμφιτρυωνιά[δ]ηι Ἡ[ρακλῆϊ πτολιπό] ρθωι / δ[εξ]αμένωι δέ ο[ἱ αἶψα τέλος θανάτοι]ο παρέστη, fr. 25.23–4). This, in combination with some of our testimonia and the fragments discussed earlier in this chapter, provides some evidence for an epic and more mortal Herakles.

[42]   In Hesiod's *Theogony* the hero slays order-threatening monsters and rescues Prometheus: *Theogony* 287 (Geryon), 314 (Lernean Hydra), 332 (Nemean Lion), and 526 (the liver-eating eagle). Another one of Herakles' cult-names is Beast-slayer (e.g. Euripides *Iphigeneia at Aulis* 1570: Ὦ παῖ Ζηνός, ὦ θηροκτόνε, "Oh child of Zeus, oh Beast-killer": see IG V 2.91).

Theogonic Herakles warding off evil sickness (κακὴν δ' ἀπὸ νοῦσον ἄλαλκεν, *Theogony* 527), Hesiod recalls the hero's cult-title *alexikakos* and its attendant connections.[43] Yet this formula also powerfully brings to mind a scene near the end of the *Iliad* when Achilles—at his most Heraklean—wrestles with the river Scamander. How Herakles is used in Homer, and what repercussions follow for our understanding of the epics, is the subject of the rest of this chapter.

A Son of God

Given the varied representations of Herakles in the archaic and classical Greek popular imagination, we can confidently posit that Herakles was already a hero of some pedigree prior to the formation of our Homeric epics, and that he enjoyed a well-known epic tradition. We have identified several key aspects of this, including, on the one hand, his mighty strength, his many labors, and his role in establishing (Zeus') order; and, on the other, an emphasis on his suffering and hints of his excessive violence. The balance is encapsulated by his ultimate fate—as a man, who suffers and dies, and as the son of Zeus, who survives death to live a blessed afterlife with his divine consort. Yet, while Herakles makes several appearances in Homer, both in the narrative[44] and in speeches by characters,[45] Homer never treats Herakles at any length or in any detail. This reticence is an indication of the Homeric poems' antagonistic rivalry with the

---

[43] For inscriptions with this cult name see IG VII 3416.1–2 ('Ηρακλεῖ / 'Απαλεξικάκῳ); SEG XXVIII 232. *Inscriptiones Creticae* II xix 7.2 gives this cult name to Zeus when coupled with Herakles (Ζῆνά τ' ἀλεξίκακον καὶ 'Ηρακλέα πτολίπορθο[ν]). See Farnell 1920:147–149. For the wide range of this cult name especially in Attica, see Fowler 2013:313n180. The rescue of Prometheus signals a reconciliation with Zeus that earns the "strong son of Alkmênê...the Theban-born Herakles, *kleos*"—again, a rather Iliadic series of events.

[44] The narrator includes his son (and grandsons) in the roll call of the Achaean army in the Catalogue of Ships (2.653–670, 679); upon regaining his supremacy in battle, Hektor kills the go-between for Eurystheus and Herakles (15.638–640); the gods gather on the battlefield at the site where Herakles built a wall (20.144–148). Cf. the *Odyssey*: Herakles killed the son of Eurytos in defiance of all rules of hospitality (21.14–41).

[45] Dione consoles Aphrodite for the wound that she receives from Diomedes, by complaining about the injuries that the gods suffered from Herakles (5.392–404); Herakles is a point of contention as his son Tlepolemus clashes with Sarpedon (5.628–654); Athena recalls the help that she once gave to Herakles (8.362–369); Nestor tells how Herakles killed all of his brothers (11.689–693); Sleep reminds Hera of how Zeus was greatly angered when she made Herakles suffer greatly (14.249–266). After he recounts his lovers and his offspring with them, Herakles included (14.323–325), Zeus recalls the pain he felt for his son (15.18–30); Achilles faces up to his own death by recalling that even Herakles had to die (18.117–119); Agamemnon relates how Zeus too was deceived, which meant that Herakles suffered long at the hands of Eurystheus (19.95–133). Cf. the *Odyssey*: along with Eurytos, Herakles could rival the gods with the bow (*Odyssey* 8.224–226); He now enjoys a life of pleasure with his consort Hebe among the gods while his shade (*eidolon*) ranges furiously in Hades, bow in hand, remembering his suffering and the unenviable task of entering Hades (11.601–627).

Heraklean *fabula*, and follows on from our discussion in the previous chapter about Homer's silence on (and silencing of) the siege of Thebes.[46]

While reticent on the details, the Homeric epics nevertheless show an awareness of something of these details, which we have sketched out above. A survey of the hero's appearances indicates a consistent portrayal, which largely aligns with evidence outside Homer.[47] Herakles is born of both mortal and immortal fathers (*Iliad* 14.324–325; *Odyssey* 11.267–269); he must accomplish many labors (*Iliad* 15. 133–135) and is long-suffering (*Odyssey* 11.620–622) at the service of Eurystheus (*Iliad* 15.635–640 and 19.74–140). He is helped by Athena (*Iliad* 8.362–369) and Hermes (*Odyssey* 21.14–40); loved by Zeus (*Iliad* 15.24–32) but hated by Hera (*Iliad* 14.242–265); and has done battle with the gods themselves (*Iliad* 5.381–400). He has sacked many cities, including Troy (*Iliad* 14.266, 20.145),[48] commited violent acts, even against a host (*Iliad* 5.381–400; *Odyssey* 21.14–41).[49] He dies but lives on with the Olympian gods (*Odyssey* 11.603). Even so, as we shall see in this section, Homeric reference to these events establishes a dynamic engagement with the Herakles tale on the level of both language and traditional themes that functions almost exclusively to raise the profile of Homer's heroes and themes.

Citations of Herakles are not only more frequent in the mouths of Homer's characters (eleven out of a total of sixteen occasions across both Homeric poems); they also enjoy a different status than instances in the narrative. While the Homeric narrator is figured as a reliable conduit for the tradition with full control over the material, his characters lack the same degree of authority. Their use of traditional material is often represented as sitting uneasily with the

---

[46] This noticeable reticence about an alternative heroic tradition is typical of the Homeric poems. Citations of Thebes in the *Iliad*'s version of a siege are similarly restrained and indirect, and the *Odyssey* is almost completely silent on the tradition of the Argonauts: Circe mentions the Argo as the one ship to survive the Symplegades (12.69–72). The story of the Argo, however, was likely of great importance to the *Odyssey*: West 2005. In itself, this silence can be regarded as a sign of the Homeric poems' agonism. A similar pattern can be detected in later literature: the Athenian tragedians rarely depict material from the *Iliad* and *Odyssey* though they fed at Homer's table; Thucydides steers clear of Persian War material (at least directly), given its close association with Herodotus.

[47] For a similar summary of Herakles in Homer: Mackie 2008:1–11.

[48] While the epics clearly reflect some details, they may not reflect others such as Zeus' Amphitryon disguise: Fowler 2013:260. Other references to the Sack of Troy by Herakles among early mythographers (especially Hellanicus' rather full account): Fowler 2013:311–315; Gantz 1993:400–402.

[49] Herakles is often cited in the formulaic epithet βίη Ἡρακληείη, unusual because unlike with other instances, such as "swift-footed Achilles" or "Odysseus of many turns," here it is the hero's characteristic that is the noun while his name assumes an adjectival form): *Iliad* 2.658, 672, 5.628, 11.689, 15.640, 18.117 and 19.98; cf. *Odyssey* 11.601. The idea of a violent, unmanageable Herakles is the essence of his traditional role in epic: Nagy 1999 [1979]:318.

surrounding narrative,[50] which makes their strategies more readily transparent and analyzable. At the same time, the complex engagement between their (mis) use of the material and its context is, as we discussed in Chapter 1 with the stories of Bellerophon and Tydeus, highly revealing of each epic's own poetic strategies. A good example is when Athena, prevented by Zeus from helping the Achaeans, complains to a third party about how she once did Zeus a favor by helping Herakles complete his labors (*Iliad* 8.362–369). Given, however, the fact that she recounts this story to *Hera*, Herakles' avowed enemy, the choice of example is an odd one. Though Hera "does not fail to obey" (8.381), the reference to Herakles sounds somehow out of place, if Athena is trying to persuade Hera to do her bidding.[51] In fact, precisely because the example seems to have no effect, we might posit that Herakles is no longer a concern for Hera—the Trojans have replaced him as the cause of her ire, and the heroic narrative resulting from her redirected anger is this poem. Examining other cases where Herakles is (re) deployed as a *paradeigma* by gods and men allows us both to identify moments of cross-poetic rivalry and to reflect on the specific forms and consequences of Homer's agonistic engagement with the tradition.

In part, Homer allows Herakles to be appropriated by his speakers as a negative *paradigm*. After a passing mention in the Catalogue of Ships as the father and grandfather of two contingents of troops, Herakles appears next when Dione consoles Aphrodite after her wounding by the Tydean Diomedes. We discussed this passage in the previous chapter from the perspective of showing how the example of Tydeus spurs Diomedes on to a battle frenzy that renders him invincible, to the point where he challenges the gods themselves— a potentially dangerous transgression. Dione offers Aphrodite the consolation that other Olympians have suffered at the hands of men (*Iliad* 5.384).[52] Two men, Otus and Ephialtes, assaulted Ares. Worse still was Herakles, who, though he fought alone, wounded not only Hera but even Hades.[53]

Dione's description of Herakles is significant in various ways. First, she does not refer to Herakles by name, but instead via a series of periphrastic constructions: initially as "the strong son of Amphitryon" (κρατερὸς πάϊς Ἀμφιτρύωνος, *Iliad* 5.392) or "the man, the son of Zeus" (εὖτέ μιν ὠὗτὸς ἀνὴρ υἱὸς Διὸς

---

[50] "Examples...where a character deploys a story in order to make a rhetorical point indicate the difference from the narrator, since, unlike the Homeric poet, characters deploy stories without full cognizance or control over the relationship between traditional story and narrative context" (Kelly 2010:275).

[51] Kelly 2010:274–275.

[52] An indication of the insult here—that *men* have pained the gods—comes in the description of pains as "difficult," a collocation that is elsewhere only used by Odysseus, who looks forward to punishing his traitorous servant Melanthius (22.177).

[53] For Herakles' wounding of Ares as represented in the Hesiodic *Shield*, see Stamatopoulou 2017.

αἰγιόχοιο , *Iliad* 5.396), then later (and more pointedly) as "the hateful man" and "worker of violence" (σχέτλιος ὀβριμοεργὸς, *Iliad* 5.403). As we learn in the *Odyssey*, providing or withholding a name is of critical importance. Odysseus is able to engineer the escape from Cyclops' cave by providing no name ("Nobody," *Odyssey* 9.366); yet he ends up incurring Poseidon's wrath by revealing his name to Cyclops (*Odyssey* 9.504–506). This fateful epic boast draws attention to the importance of naming—one cannot have fame and renown if no one knows about your deeds—and the paradox in the *Odyssey* whereby Odysseus wins fame and renown precisely by maintaining disguise.[54] In this case, Dione's reluctance to name Herakles underlines her point that the actions of this hero are not to be commended or emulated. In addition, the striking, and unique, collocation of man and son of Zeus in one complete hexameter line, εὖτέ μιν <u>ωὑτὸς ἀνὴρ υἱὸς Διὸς</u> αἰγιόχοιο ("this same man the son of aegis-bearing Zeus"), points to what is at stake in Dione's description—the portrait of a man who dares to fight the gods.[55] At one level, Dione is making a rhetorical point, comforting Aphrodite for a wound that Diomedes has just given her.[56] At another, however, the violence that Dione describes is colored in a particular way. Her accounts both of the assault on Ares by Otus and Ephialtes and of Herakles rivaling the gods describe a world where gods and men are in regular and direct conflict with each other.

Dione caps her account of the "worker of violence" (ὀβριμοεργός) by observing that, as his arrows continued to trouble the gods, he did not take heed of his "unseemly deeds" (ὃς οὐκ ὄθετ' αἴσυλα ῥέζων, *Iliad* 5.403). It is not only his striving against the gods that is to be condemned; it is the fact that Herakles does not consider his actions to be problematic that is the problem—indeed, this is one reason why his "doing" is deemed "unseemly." Significantly, this description of Herakles performing unseemly deeds (αἴσυλα ῥέζων) is picked up later in the epic in a highly charged context, when the river god Scamander similarly complains to Achilles about the shamefulness of his assault (21.214).[57]

---

[54] See especially Odysseus' concern to conceal the suitors' dying groans with the sound of music (*Odyssey* 23.135–137): paradoxically "the hiding of the immediate fame of the deed broadcasts the canniness of Odysseus": Goldhill 1991:94–95.

[55] The image of Herakles taking on the gods with his bow implicitly complements the *Odyssey*, where Odysseus tempers his claims about being able to handle a bow by expressly refusing to rival the gods, unlike Eurytos and Herakles (*Odyssey* 8.224); cf. the picture of the image (*eidolon*) of Herakles raging in Hades with his bow (*Odyssey* 11.601–630).

[56] Indeed, Dione's description of the treatment that Hades receives for his wound (τῷ δ' ἐπὶ Παιήων ὀδυνήφατα φάρμακα πάσσων / ἤκέσατ'· οὐ μὲν γάρ τι καταθνητός γε τέτυκτο) is repeated soon after, when Diomedes wounds Ares (5.900) and the god of war is forced to leave the field of battle. The repeated τλῆ μὲν / τλῆ δ' (x2) resonates with the same structure in Panyasis' *Herakleia* fr. 3 Bernabé = 16 K.

[57] It is used too by both Mentor and Athena, who proclaim that Odysseus should be allowed to act harshly as a king, if his people are going to treat him so shabbily (*Odyssey* 2.232; 5.10). The

We will return to discuss this example in more detail shortly; for the moment it is sufficient to note that, according to Dione (as we saw in the last chapter), Diomedes has been acting *like a Herakles* by doing violence to the gods. But there is a critical qualification to make: Diomedes' actions *are here being* marked out as excessive in the extreme. Soon after—in fact, immediately once Diomedes has fulfilled Dione's warning and been the latest hero to wound Ares—the *Iliad* makes it clear that performing such unseemly deeds will no longer be possible, let alone acceptable: Apollo intervenes to police the boundary between men and the divine and explicitly rule out men competing with gods.[58] In this process Herakles' own actions become consigned to a period before the *Iliad*. Unrestrained violence of this kind is not, and *cannot* be, part of the world inhabited by Homer's heroes.

Notably, Herakles is most frequently cited in the *Iliad* when, the gods take center stage. When the Achaeans are hemmed in behind their walls, Hera sets out to disrupt Zeus' plan by enlisting Sleep in her plan of seduction. Sleep is wary, however, because of what happened the last time he helped Hera when she was working against Herakles. Once again, details are kept to a minimum: Sleep also withholds Herakles' name (he is again "that man": κεῖνος, 14.250) and presents an abbreviated narrative of Herakles' deeds—just one hexameter line for Herakles to sack Troy and start his return home, like an Odysseus (ἔπλεεν Ἰλιόθεν Τρώων πόλιν ἐξαλαπάξας).[59] Instead, Sleep focuses on Hera's machinations, as a result of which Herakles is carried over the sea as far from his friends (νόσφι φίλων) as Achilles is from his father (19.422).[60] The interformular moments here suggest Herakles' capacity to be a hero on a par with the Homeric Achilles and Odysseus. Or rather, the introduction of Herakles as a city-sacker who is apart from his friends invites us to think about him in the way we think about Achilles and Odysseus, and ponder the ways in which they differ. Crucially, the *story* of Herakles' greatness is never narrated in the *Iliad*. Homer is interested in the deeds of Herakles only insofar as they function within this epic and help set into relief the actions and thoughts of his heroes.[61]

---

point here is clearly a provocative one, with the implication being precisely that kings should not commit shameless deeds, since ideally they are part of a symbiotic relationship with their people.

[58] *Iliad* 5.433. Cf. Nagy 1999 [1979]:318: the flexibility of the adjective-noun combination implies that the "Herakles figure and <u>bie</u> are traditionally linked on the level of theme."

[59] In the *Odyssey*, when Telemachus uses this line to ask for information about his father (*Odyssey* 3.85), we are witness to Odysseus' *kleos* in action, as Nestor gives a lengthy report about Odysseus and his heroic qualities.

[60] This idea also engages with the motif "though I have come from afar": Sarpedon (5.471–492).

[61] Hera reassures Sleep that, while Zeus may have cared about his son, he won't help the Trojans (Τρώεσσιν ἀρηξέμεν, 14.265). Ironically, while seeming to confirm Herakles' unique status as Zeus' favorite, she's also wrong. Zeus aids the Trojans throughout the poem in order to grant

The same is true when Zeus regains his senses and expands on Sleep's allusive narrative. His focus is less on his suffering son (15.30), than on the pain he himself feels (15. 34–35) and Hera's agency in opposing him (15.36–38).[62] Once again Herakles' endeavors are held up as an implicit comparison to the *Iliad*'s narrative: just as Hera interfered then and caused Zeus grief, so is she now. But there is also a crucial difference. Hera's betrayal of Zeus barely sets his plan back at all: in fact, it prompts Zeus to provide his most explicit and fullest enunciation of it yet (15.49–77).

The time for such cosmic infighting has passed. That much is implied a little before when Zeus, full of desire for Hera, catalogued his long list of female conquests (14.315–328). For, while undoubtedly not the most tactful line for seduction, a catalogue of women can, *should*, be deadly serious on the basis that Zeus' powerful seed will produce male heirs. So Zeus enumerates the sons who were born from these unions—Minos, Radamanthus, Perseus, Perithoos, and, of course, Herakles, his "violence-minded" son (14.324). From an intertraditional perspective, a divine union and catalogue of women resonates powerfully with Hesiod's *Theogony*, where we see Zeus fathering heroes who clear the world of monsters and evildoers. More generally, the coalescence of themes around divine conflict, deception, and reproduction reveals the latent danger in the coming together of the father of gods and men and his divine consort: Hera's deception of Zeus could herald *another* Theogony. Here, however, no son rises from this union to challenge the father; Herakles' birth in fact marks the end of Zeus' issue. The succession narrative, after all, belongs to a world prior to Homeric epic.[63] Instead, though this section recalls the genesis of *heroes*, the poignant irony that unfolds is that the *Iliad* is an epic of *dying* heroes, not the birth of new ones.[64] The motif transference from such primeval struggles between Zeus and Hera as well as the triple invocation of Herakles results in an oddly underwhelming take on one of *the* central motifs of the Herakles myths.[65] But it also anticipates the problems caused by the sons of mortals in human

---

[62] Achilles' plea for his honor to be respected (*Iliad* 1.408). Elsewhere Zeus makes his assistance explicit as a warning to the gods (8.11), and turns his eyes from battle safe in that knowledge (13.9). Ares defends the Trojans (5.507). Hera manages to trick Aphrodite into helping her by using this line (14.192).

[62] For the especially forceful use of language in this speech: Christensen 2010:558–559.

[63] The potential overthrow of Zeus has already been circumvented: Thetis, prophesied to give birth to a son greater than the father, has already been married off—to a mortal: Slatkin 1991.

[64] No children are born to gods anymore. Zeus and Hera have non-procreative sex. This is another way in which the content of Homer's tale differs from those prior to it.

[65] As if to illustrate the point, after Zeus announces that his plan is back on track, Hektor regains his primacy in the field. The fact that he kills only one man should not diminish its significance, since that man is the son of the intermediary between Herakles and Eurystheus (15. 639–640). It represents another act of severance.

worlds and the Iliadic motif that the gods only derive pain from involvement in mortal affairs.

By invoking him in *paradeigmata*, the *Iliad* appropriates and subordinates Herakles to its own needs in several ways. Primarily, Herakles, appearing in the speeches of the poem's characters, does not enjoy the narrative spotlight but is relegated to the fringes of the tale, repurposed as either a model or a memory of heroic action, rather than depicted as an agent of heroic deeds himself. Still, given the gods' interest in Herakles in the episodes that we have discussed, we may have expected that model or memory to be privileged. If anything, the opposite is true: though the gods' stories do not directly contest the son of Amphitryon's godhood, they do provocatively fail to mention his position as a god. Moreover, in the recasting of Herakles as simply one of many actors in the tales told by this poem's agents, as a counterpoint to the heroes of this tale he does not fare well: his type of heroism belongs to the distant past, a past from which the *Iliad* is moving. Indeed, it is precisely his status as both a mortal *and* son of god, who can rival the immortals and disrupt the Olympian order, that Herakles appears out of step with the transformation taking place in (and being represented by) the *Iliad*. Even though he and Achilles share such a divided nature, Herakles' tale functions to set him apart from the time and place of the *Iliad*'s participants, as we shall see in greater detail in the next section.

Out of Time

So far we have seen how Homer's divine speakers characterize Herakles as mighty and violent, while at the same time marginalizing him as a figure from the epic cosmos' distant (and perhaps even less human?) past. This picture of an out-of-place and out-of-time Herakles also emerges through a study of the speeches of the *Iliad*'s mortal characters.

One Homeric figure who himself represents a connection to the (differently configured) heroic past is Nestor, whom Homer introduces on his first appearance in the epic in terms that make this link to the past explicit. This hero has been witness to two previous generations of heroic men; this—the heroes of the Trojan War—was the third (*Iliad* 1.250–252). In his capacity as the link to the past (or voice of the tradition), Nestor frequently recalls the character of earlier heroes or their previous heroic action at important moments as comparanda for the events and heroes of the *Iliad*. At arguably the most critical moment, when Patroklos is gathering information for Achilles about how their comrades are faring, Nestor delivers his longest speech in the poem. In it, he mentions Herakles. This Herakles is depicted as assaulting the city of Pylos. Of his many brothers, only Nestor survived (τῶν <u>οἶος</u> λιπόμην, 11.690).

As we have seen from previous examples both in this chapter and the last, while the minimal detail may imply that the whole story was well known, it is also important to examine how the reference works in context. Here, Nestor uses Herakles' violence against his city and family to put the focus on his own heroic deeds. He does so by redeploying the idea of the lone hero in provocative ways. First, Nestor pictures Herakles violently assaulting the city all by himself (ἐκάκωσε), as if he were still singly, and *singularly*, performing epic labors—a world away from the depiction of a city's siege that we get in the *Iliad*, with the massed ranks of armies on both sides. At the same time, Nestor goes on to identify himself as the single figure, alone of all his brothers, to have survived Herakles' onslaught, as if he were an equivalent figure, a solitary hero bereft of a community, or, even more pointedly, the "lonely" Nestor mentioned in the cast of the Heraklean *Sack of Oechalia.*[66] Indeed, by transferring the single motif from Herakles' assault to his singular survival, Nestor prepares the way for his own heroic performance. And, yet, Nestor's epic deeds differ radically from Herakles', in that they form part of a narrative of collective action, not dissimilar to the battle that is taking place before Troy. For Nestor's story pertains to the situation at hand, if paradoxically reached through the idea of his lone survival. When Nestor reaches the climax of his story, describing how all glorified him among men (11.761), he turns suddenly to the case at hand and adds: "But Achilles will enjoy his own valor *alone*" (αὐτὰρ Ἀχιλλεὺς / οἶος τῆς ἀρετῆς ἀπονήσεται, 762–763). Nestor, we recall, is relating this story to Patroklos, in the hope of attracting him back into battle. At present, one man, Achilles, is refusing to fight: Nestor's proposal, implicit in this story, is for Patroklos to fight in his place. Therefore, while the Herakles story would seem to put emphasis on the lone fighter, the very dynamics of this tale depend on the *associations between* the heroes. And it works. Patroklos is motivated to fight for the Achaeans. After him, belatedly Achilles too will return, not for his individual glory, but rather to avenge his fallen comrade.

There is one further observation. Nestor frames his fleeting reference to Herakles as being set in "the time before" (τῶν προτέρων ἐτέων, 11.691). As the poem has already determined, Nestor knows a thing or two about previous generations (cf. *Iliad* 1.250–252). A consistent pattern begins to emerge. A speaker raises the example of Herakles in order to make the point about (excessive) violence. It's not that the *Iliad* condemns violent acts per se; rather, such

---

[66] Nestor's use of the "individual" (οἶος) motif recalls his presence in one of the few surviving fragments of Herakles' epic, the *Sack of Oechalia* ("Nestor alone survived in flowery Gerênos." Νέστωρ <δ'> οἶος ἄλυξεν ἐν ἀνθεμόεντι Γερήνωι, fr. 8.1), whose Iliadic resonance we mentioned above. While we do not know how that epic played out, here Nestor moves swiftly to recounting a battle between the Pylians and Epeians, in which he stars.

individual acts of brutality and daring are generally consigned to a past world. The extreme acts of Herakles—those which made it possible for him to succeed as a solitary champion—are, as Nestor implies, actions that destroy communities and leave the survivors *alone*. For communities to thrive, they must be able to control and withstand violence and fight *together*. In the *Iliad* Herakles' actions are relegated to a violent past in order to separate them from the present; where similar acts are integrated into the poem's present, they are characterized as threatening to the emerging social order.

If anything, the disjunction between citations of Herakles and the narrative of the *Iliad* is at its most pronounced in the confrontation between his son, Tlepolemus, and Sarpedon. Tlepolemus, previously introduced in the Achaean catalogue, is the only one of Herakles' sons fighting in this current war for Troy.[67] Facing him is Sarpedon, king of Lydia, whose entry brings to a close the Trojan catalogue; his credentials in this poem, moreover, have just been established by his stern, but fair, rebuke of Hektor earlier in the book.[68] But more is at stake than a battle between individual heroes; their meeting reflects upon traditions associated with Herakles and this story of Troy.[69]

The terms of engagement are established in the narrator's opening verses. Elsewhere, the line that describes their advance ("When they came near to one another," οἳ δ᾽ ὅτε δὴ σχεδὸν ἦσαν ἐπ᾽ ἀλλήλοισιν ἰόντες, 5.630) usually heralds an immediate coming to blows. Here, as Adrian Kelly has observed, however, "the poet surprises us with an 'extra' verse (631)."[70] This additional line, "son and grandson of Zeus the cloud-gatherer" (υἱός θ᾽ υἱωνός τε Διὸς νεφεληγερέταο), not only identifies the two men as related to Zeus but also sets up the dominant theme of the two speeches. This clash will be about genealogy. Whose connection to Zeus is better?

The power of this contrast draws on its interformularity. Tlepolemus, whose description here recalls his introduction in the Catalogue (as "the big and noble son of Herakles" (Τληπόλεμον δ᾽ Ἡρακλεΐδην ἠΰν τε μέγαν τε, 5.628; cf. 2.653), immediately identifies genealogy as the decisive factor in this confrontation.

---

[67] As the leader of the nine ships from Rhodes (2.653–654), he is set apart from the other Herakleidai as a kin-slayer who had to flee his relatives into exile (2.653–670). One might fairly wonder if this is the best of the Herakleidai Homer could choose as a representative, or if this choice is strategic.

[68] *Iliad* 5.471–492.

[69] This scene is similar in tone to the objections made by Sthenelos to Agamemnon about the differences between the Seven against Thebes and the Epigonoi in Book 4 (387–400 and 404–418), on which see Chapter 2 above; cf. Mackie 2008:34–40 for both passages. For other discussions of this exchange, see Kelly 2010:264 for a bibliography; Lohmann 1970:27; Martin 1989:127; Mackie 1996:77–78; and Alden 2000:157–161.

[70] Kelly 2010:263–264.

"They are liars," he says to Sarpedon, "who say that you are the son of Zeus, holder of the aegis" (ψευδόμενοι δέ σέ φασι Διὸς γόνον αἰγιόχοιο / εἶναι, 5.635–636). It is he, through his own father Herakles, who can truly claim a bond of kinship with Zeus.[71] But Homer's additional introductory verse highlighted above implicitly undercuts Tlepolemus' charge. Back when Tlepolemus is first introduced, Homer uses the phrase "*sons and grandsons* of the violent Herakles" (υἱέες υἱωνοί τε βίης Ἡρακληείης, 2.666). Here, we have the near echo "*son and grandson* of Zeus the cloud-gatherer" (υἱός θ᾽ υἱωνός τε Διὸς νεφεληγερέταο).[72] Plurality gives way to singularity; Herakles gives way to Zeus. The audience hears an echo of Tlepolemus' paternity even in the very description of Sarpedon's: the former is one of many sons of Herakles, the son of Zeus; the latter *is* the son of Zeus. Tlepolemus already comes across as inferior, even before he speaks.

The critical importance of this displacement is evident from Tlepolemus' basic argument where he denigrates the core subject of *this* narrative—the sack of the city. In a manner similar to how we might imagine Heraklean traditions responding to the Troy story, Tlepolemus boasts that his father, Herakles, has *already* sacked Troy.[73] Such a claim could, and *should*, be a threat to Homer's *Iliad*. If Troy has already been besieged and taken by another hero from another tradition, what need is there to listen to or take account of this version? A similar anxiety emerged in our discussion in the last chapter regarding the siege of the *other* city, Thebes. There we argue that the *Iliad*'s response was twofold: to deauthorize the story by putting it into the mouth of a speaker with a case to make (who remains silent on the events of the siege itself), and to position it as prior to *this* siege story. One reason why this second move was probably so important was the likelihood that Theban traditions had used the same strategy, by representing its city hero, Herakles, sacking Troy before the real business of besieging Thebes could be undertaken. In this case too the *Iliad* deploys a twin assault: news of the other sack is provided by a none-too-impartial observer, whose argument is predicated on the precedence that other sack provides: since he is the son of Herakles, the hero who has already taken Troy, then he—Tlepolemus—is far superior to the Trojan ally whom he is about to fight.

While Tlepolemus uses Herakles as a paradigm for the present situation, and as a means of determining the outcome, the intertraditional resonance is far from so easy to control. In order to magnify his father's prestige (and by association his own), Tlepolemus claims that Herakles sacked Troy with only

---

[71] "Such men as, they say, was the great strength of Herakles" were begotten of Zeus (637–638).

[72] The only other occurrence of "son and grandson" (υἱός θ᾽ υἱωνός τε) comes from Laertes at the end of the *Odyssey* (24.515), which certainly would blunt Tlepolemus' attack: Kelly 2010:264n18.

[73] See Chapter 6 on the material from Erginos, where we see this strategy of Theban traditions "punching back" and claiming their superiority over the stories of the Achaean-Trojan conflict.

six ships and not many more men. One unintended consequence that follows, however, is the suggestion that Tlepolemus—who has a vast supporting cast of Achaean heroes after all—is a considerably lesser hero, if, now in the tenth year of fighting, Troy has still yet to fall (again).[74] But it is not only the case that Tlepolemus' choice to link his reputation to his father's sack of the city runs the risk of diminishing his own heroic credentials; that prior sack also loses stature by being passed over so presumptuously and briefly—as we saw happen with Thebes in the previous chapter. Tlepolemus' boast that Herakles needed only six ships and a few men could open the way to a very different interpretation—that the whole enterprise did not really amount to all that much.[75] What is made explicit in the *Odyssey* (1.352–353) with Telemachus' claim that audiences like to hear the latest song is equally pertinent to thinking about the *Iliad*'s performance, as it deprioritizes those events conceived of as prior to it. The fact that Herakles has already sacked Troy ought to be an important counterpoint for, or even challenge to, this tale of a war at Troy.[76] And yet, while the *Iliad* demonstrates interest in the subject of the city's survival,[77] it does not represent the sacking itself; mention of Troy's ultimate downfall is instead left to the *Odyssey*, when Demodokos sings of the fall of Troy at Odysseus' behest (*Odyssey* 8.495). In the *Iliad* Troy's sack is infinitely deferred or, in the case under examination here, part of a character's recollection of a dim and distant event. Displaced from the authority of the narrative voice and relegated to the era of a "past generation of men,"[78] Herakles' prior sacking of Troy will have little relevance to or impact on this poem.

---

[74] "By linking his own story with the hypertext of Herakles and the previous sack of Troy, Tlepolemus sets up an unrealistic—in fact, unflattering—model for himself." To bring up Herakles in this context, even if he is Tlepolemus' father, is "just not a good link to make": Kelly 2010:269. Cf. Sammons 2014:300, who calls the one place where Herakles' conquest of Troy is mentioned "something of a rhetorical failure."

[75] Just such a strategy is used by Thucydides to magnify his war in contrast to the Trojan War, which only lasted so long because, he deduces, the Achaeans lacked sufficient supplies and continually had to forage (I 11).

[76] Tlepolemus uses the Trojan past "as an informative paradigm for the present, indeed future, of the city" (Kelly 2010:266).

[77] The phrase Ἰλίου ἐξαλάπαξε/ἐξαλαπάξαι πόλιν/πτολίεθρον, referring to the sack of Troy, has already been used by Zeus in shock at Hera's apparent vindictiveness (she wants Troy's sack, *Iliad* 4.33), as it is used by Agamemnon, who wishes that Zeus grant him Troy's sack (8.288).

[78] Tlepolemus identifies "past generations of men" (ἐπεὶ πολλὸν κείνων ἐπιδεύεαι ἀνδρῶν / οἳ Διὸς ἐξεγένοντο ἐπὶ προτέρων ἀνθρώπων, 5.636–637), of which his father was a part. The expression προτέρων ἀνθρώπων occurs twice elsewhere. Hesiod uses it to describe a poet (*aoidos*) who sings of the glorious deeds (κλεῖα) of former men and the gods who hold Olympus (*Theogony* 100). In the *Iliad*, Nestor instructs Antilochus for the chariot race by pointing to the turning post, either a grave marker of someone who died long ago or a racing goal made by earlier men (23.331–332). For Nestor, this difficult symbol (σῆμα) has lost its meaning. From the *Iliad*'s perspective, the

Sarpedon's pithy response, dismissive not only of Tlepolemus' posturing but also of his father's epic career, gives articulation to Herakles' irrelevance. His initial move is to undercut the magnitude of Herakles' deeds by attaching blame to the founder of the city: Troy fell because of Laomedon's folly (ἀφραδία, 5.649),[79] a state of mind associated with people or creatures like the Cyclops who bring evil upon themselves.[80] Sarpedon's reference to "sacred Troy" (Ἴλιον ἱρήν, 648) economically re-establishes the sanctity of city in contrast to the actions of its founder.[81] More pointedly, Sarpedon robs Herakles of his name, labeling him simply "that man" (ἤτοι κεῖνος, 648). As we observed above, the withholding of a name runs counter to the impulse of epic poetry to record *kleos*. Once again, Herakles is being denied fame by being pointedly not named. Moreover, the combination of κεῖνος with the intensifier ἤτοι tends to be used by speakers in an aggressively dismissive manner.[82] Indeed, as many have noted for the *Odyssey*, the demonstrative κεῖνος can function to stand in place of the hero's name, delaying the granting of fame and occluding the meaning of the reference.[83] Deliberate in his response, Sarpedon downplays the glory of that man's previous deeds and, at the same time, denies the relevance of Herakles to this sack of Troy.

The payoff is both immediate and unambiguous, and at the same time more complex and meaningful than it might first appear. The two heroes simultaneously cast their spears; Tlepolemus is killed instantly. The implication is emphatic: Herakles and his progeny have no role to play in this epic tale of Troy's sack. Yet the scene is more multifaceted and fraught than that, since Sarpedon *too* almost dies. The reasons why he does not perish here shed important light on the *Iliad*'s (re)deployment of Heraklean themes. At first, Sarpedon is rescued

---

generation of former men (προτέρων ἀνθρώπων) marks an age before, whose symbolism is now lost in the mists of time.

[79] The idea of ἀφραδία (foolishness) has obvious associations with *atasthalia* discussed in the last chapter (see Chapter 1, nn75–77).

[80] *Iliad* 2.368; 5.649; 10.122, 350; 16.354; *Odyssey* 9.361; 10.27; 17.233; 19.523; 22.288. Cf. *Works and Days* 134, 330. While Trojan actions in the *Iliad* can be interpreted as acts of folly (Pandarus breaking the truce; Paris refusing to give up Helen), for the most part Homer is remarkably even-handed in his treatment of both sides.

[81] *Iliad* 4.46, 164, 416; 5.648; 6.96, 277, 448; 7.82, 413, 429; 8.551; 11.196; 13.657; 15.169; 17.193; 18.270; 20.216; 21.128, 515; 24.27, 143, 383; *Odyssey* 11.86; 17.293.

[82] For example, when Diomedes dismisses Achilles' rejection of the embassy (*Iliad* 9.701), when Nestor recalls the evil deeds of Aegisthus (*Odyssey* 3.195), and when various authoritative speakers anticipate the suitors' doom (Zeus at *Odyssey* 5.24 and 24.480; Teiresias at 11.118). There appear to be two exceptions, one in either epic. Priam uses ἤτοι κεῖνος to denote Peleus (*Iliad* 24.490), while Eumaios uses it of Telemachus, when talking with the disguised Odysseus at *Odyssey* 14.183.

[83] For the use of κεῖνος as typical with Odysseus in the *Odyssey*, see de Jong 2001:73; for the concomitant delayed naming of Odysseus, see Peradotto 1990.

from the battle and protected by the swift actions of his comrades (663, 692). The action of our *Iliad* differs markedly from the action of a singular hero who could sack a city with only six ships. Ultimately, however, it is Zeus who saves Sarpedon. Capping his description of the spear's path through Sarpedon's thigh, Homer changes tack and adds: his *father* warded off ruin (πατὴρ δ' ἔτι λοιγὸν ἄμυνεν, 5.662). Here, then, is the final riposte to Tlepolemus' taunts about his genealogy. Zeus *as* Sarpedon's father intervenes on his behalf to save him.

Even now the dynamic engagement between the traditions is not yet complete, since the epic leaves Sarpedon's fate literally hanging by a breath. This "son of Zeus" (Διὸς υἱός) is at first protected by Athena (who wards off her favorite, Odysseus, from coming any closer), before he finally musters the strength to call out to Hektor for help.[84] This appeal, though, looks as if it is his last. In a sophisticated manipulation of epic formulae, Homer implies that Sarpedon is on the brink of death: as his companions leave Sarpedon by a great oak, "his spirit left him, and dark mist fell on his eyes" (τὸν δ' ἔλιπε ψυχή, κατὰ δ' ὀφθαλμῶν κέχυτ' ἀχλύς, 5.696). At this notable moment, Homer has combined two formulae τὸν δ' ἔλιπε ψυχή and κατὰ δ' ὀφθαλμῶν κέχυτ' ἀχλύς that else-where denote death.[85] From the perspective of traditional language, Sarpedon *should* die here; instead, remarkably, he breathes again (αὖτις δ' ἀμπνύνθη, 597).

This sophisticated, and pointed, manipulation of formulae confirms Sarpedon as a hero of special note in the *Iliad*.[86] Again, the comparison to Tlepolemus' father is telling. Unlike the storied Herakles, Sarpedon's destruc-tion is not being warded off permanently; he is saved here only to die another day, at the hands of Achilles' comrade, Patroklos (16.502). Just before Sarpedon and Patroklos meet, Zeus ponders whether to save his son (16.433–438). Hera intercedes and strongly takes issue, not because Zeus couldn't save his son—he *could*—only he *should not*. It would set a dangerous precedent: after all, all the

---

[84] Odysseus, who doesn't miss much, notices Sarpedon's plight and ponders in his mind whether to go after "the son of Zeus" (Διὸς υἱόν, 672). Athena wards him off, since it was not his destiny (μόρσιμον) for him to kill "the son of Zeus" (Διὸς υἱόν, 675). If these signs were not proof enough, Homer again names him as "the son of Zeus" (Διὸς υἱός, 683), in the same position in the line, when Sarpedon pleads for Hektor to protect him.

[85] ...δ' ἔλιπε ψυχή (*Iliad* 16.452; *Odyssey* 14.426); κατὰ δ' ὀφθαλμῶν κέχυτ' ἀχλύς (*Iliad* 16.344). For the argument here and below, see Barker 2011.

[86] "Homer's sophisticated comment on the partiality of their perspectives is surely not uncon-nected with the progress of the subsequent combat itself...for it eventuates in Tlepolemus' death and Sarpedon's wounding and removal from battle, something that happens in no other major duel in the *Iliad*. Given the fact that Sarpedon needs to be kept healthy for his combat with Patroklos...Homer was not constrained to construct the scene in this way" (Kelly 2010:273–274). Indeed not. Kelly, however, fails to explain *why* Homer would construct the scene in this way.

gods would then want to save their favorites. Thus she persuades Zeus to accept fate and instead focus on saving Sarpedon's *body* for burial.[87]

This, then, is the critical difference between a hero like Sarpedon in the *Iliad* and the Herakles of the tradition, who continues to live with his consort Hebe among the immortals, forever blessed. Sarpedon, a son of Zeus to rank alongside Herakles, *could* have received the same treatment from his father—but Homer has the gods expressly deny this as an option. Behavior like this, when gods and men fought with each other, and when men *could* become like gods and live forever, is typical of a prior world, where heroes and gods were not yet that distinct, where Zeus' authority was not quite so unassailable, and where a *Theogony* was still in the making.

This exchange—on the surface a battlefield clash of arms between two heroes of famous fathers—is in effect the meeting, weighing, and resolution of competing epic traditions and ways of conceptualizing, and valorizing, heroic activity. In reply to Tlepolemus' bluster about his famous father who had sacked Troy, Sarpedon offers an incisive interpretation that both minimizes that alternative version and amplifies *this* current account: Herakles was successful because his opponent was dishonest and stupid; the battle had been fought over horses by a handful of men. The real stakes, however, are higher still. This scene sets the tone of the *Iliad* as a world in which even the great (and seemingly singular) Achilles must die and where Zeus heeds Hera's advice to let Sarpedon die lest it cause divine discord (*Iliad* 16.439–458). Sarpedon *could* be another Herakles, but on this occasion Zeus *chooses not* to save his son. In the *Iliad*'s new world order, heroes are represented as all-too-human men, struggling to come to terms with their (newly found?) reciprocal roles within their communities— most explicitly articulated, it should be remembered, by *Sarpedon* (*Iliad* 12.310– 328)—and especially with their mortality.

The selective presentation of Herakles has its basis in two interrelated poetic strategies that have emerged in our discussion of Homer's Thebes. One is poetic rivalry: Homer's agonistic engagement with his tradition is here manifest in the *Iliad*'s expropriation from and downgrading of the rival siege story of Thebes as an adequate vehicle for the expression of epic deeds and character. The other is thematic: in a movement that traces the history of myth from the creation of the cosmos to the everyday lives of Homer's audiences, Herakles occupies an important place. Betwixt and between two eras—the creation of the gods and the extinction of the race of heroes—he is the one figure who still has a foot in both worlds. In these terms the *Iliad*'s re-conception of time is highly

---

[87] Tlepolemus comes into conflict with Sarpedon, being roused by "overpowering fate" (μοῖρα κραταιή, 5.629). This phrase occurs only in the *Iliad*: 5.83; 16.334, 853; 19.410; 20.477; 21.110; 24.132, 209.

charged. By locating its own events *after* Thebes and *after* the labors of Herakles, the *Iliad* separates both Herakles' life events and his heroic qualities from the world of its story. Herakles remains a necessary model figure in the epic cosmos, but only insofar as he represents a bygone era of singular heroes. How the *Iliad*'s singular hero, Achilles, matches up to, and surpasses, Herakles, is the subject of our next section.

Even Herakles Had to Die

In the previous section we discussed how references to Herakles in the *Iliad*, though sporadic, brief, and largely communicated via different characters with their own agendas, deliver a consistent message. While certain actions (sacking cities, labors under Eurystheus, fighting the gods) or themes (suffering and doing violence in equal measure) relate to traditional Heraklean tales, so far as we can tell from the available evidence, the positioning of the hero as "out of time," we suggest, derives from the *Iliad*'s posture as the epic that tells the heroic story of the separation of the worlds of gods and men. In this section we consider the consequences for thinking about Achilles if Herakles represents a bygone world. In continuing our investigation of characters' (mis)use of Herakles as a paradigm, we turn the spotlight on to those moments in the narrative where Achilles and Herakles are brought into some kind of comparison with each other. In these cases both Achilles' differences from and *similarities* to Herakles are significant in ways that goes beyond their shared possession of the epithet "lion-hearted" (θυμολέοντα).[88] While Achilles is comparable to Herakles in might and singularity, ultimately it is through his non-Heraklean social relationships that he achieves continuing relevance in this stage of transition to a world of men.

When Achilles calls the assembly in Book 19 to announce his intention to return and rouse the troops for war, Agamemnon intercedes to lay the ground for formal reconciliation. Substantively this means finally offering Achilles the compensation for the insult done to him at the beginning of the epic; but Agamemnon takes the opportunity to have one final say to explain (away) his slighting of Achilles. Another story about Herakles forms the basis of this

---

[88] It is used of Herakles at 5.639 by his son, Tlepolemus, and at *Odyssey* 11.267, where Odysseus describes his birth. At *Iliad* 7.228, Ajax refers to Achilles as "man-breaker, lion-hearted" (ῥηξήνορα θυμολέοντα). As the only hero in the *Iliad* who receives Herakles' traditional epithet, Achilles is implicitly compared to this other great hero: Nagy 1999 [1979]:137. It should be noted, however, that Hesiod also interestingly uses the epithet for Achilles, to describe Thetis giving birth to the hero (*Theogony* 1007). A similar case can be found in the *Odyssey*, where Penelope describes her husband in "Heraklean" terms (*Odyssey* 4.724). For the use of this epithet in each epic to align Achilles and Odysseus respectively with Herakles, see Wilson 2002b.

apology. He was, Agamemnon explains, temporarily blinded by the goddess Atê (19.78–145), just as Zeus had once been when Herakles was about to emerge into this world.[89] According to Agamemnon, Zeus, in excitement at Herakles' impending delivery, gathers the gods to announce the birth of a man who will be lord over the Argives.[90] Seeing an opportunity for mischief, Hera elicits an oath from Zeus that whoever is born that day will lord it over all; subsequently, she delays Herakles' birth and induces Eurytheus', thereby making the former subservient to the latter. And so it came to pass that Herakles suffered long at the hands of Eurystheus, and all the time Zeus suffered watching him.[91]

There are a number of observations that build on our analysis thus far. First, this story is explicitly set in a time before (ποτε 'then', 95; ἤματι τῷ ὅτ' "on that day when," 98). In fact, Agamemnon's conclusion—that Atê now makes mischief among men—underlines the point that she no longer operates on Olympus, since Zeus has long since thrown her out. That is to say, Olympus is no longer subject to the kind of intense rivalry and dissension among the gods that we hear about in this story; Zeus' power and authority are inevitable, as much as Hera and others may rail against them at times. Instead, the focus of the *Iliad* is on conflict among men, which bubbles to the surface again here: insofar as the story about Herakles represents an apology of sorts, it is also a(nother) performance of eristics on the part of the king.[92] By recalling Zeus' blindness as a precursor for his own, Agamemnon exalts himself to the position of king of kings,[93] and once again betrays his dominating, and domineering, concern to exercise authority over Achilles, even as ostensibly he concedes the injustice he has done him.[94] Once again, however, a character's paradigmatic story defies an unequivocal reading; indeed, it is quite typical that a directive by Agamemnon

---

[89] On the use and meaning of *Atê* in archaic Greek thought: Sommerstein 2012; cf. Dodds 1957:1–27. On this final Achaean assembly: Barker 2009; Elmer 2013.

[90] The speech introduction used by Agamemnon (19.101), appears twice elsewhere. In the Homeric *Hymn to Apollo*, Hera uses it to press her claim that Zeus has slighted her by giving birth to Athena (3.311). Earlier in the *Iliad*, Zeus warns the other gods not to get involved in the warring between the Trojans and Achaeans (*Iliad* 8.5). Thus it seems to indicate moments of critical importance on Olympus.

[91] Just as Zeus "used to always groan" (αἰεὶ στενάχεσχ', 132) at seeing his dear son labor on behalf of another by doing slave work (ἔργον ἀεικές: *Iliad* 14.13; 19.133; 24.733; *Odyssey* 3.265; 11.429; 15.236; 23.222), so Priam laments Hektor's death (24.639).

[92] We explore in more detail the theme of conflict (*eris*) in Chapters 4 and 5.

[93] The scholia extend this connection to the rest of the poem: "and he compares him [Agamemnon] to Zeus in other places: his eyes and head (2.478); father of men and gods (22.167); and shepherd of the host (2.243). His scepter is from Zeus (2.101–108); his shield is similar to the aegis (11.36; cf. 5.742, 17.593, and 21.400); his thoughts [are compared to] whenever [Zeus] makes thunder and lightning (10.5)" (Scholia bT to *Iliad* 11.36b *ex.* 1–7).

[94] For Agamemnon's opening comments as an attempt to assert his authority: Barker 2009:80–82. The formal elements of the *paradeigma*: Lohmann 1970:75–80; cf. Edwards 1991:245.

should escape his full control. In Agamemnon's story Achilles comes across not so much as a Hera-like subordinate in the council of gods but as a hero like Herakles, forced to complete tasks at the behest of a far inferior superior (Eurystheus/Agamemnon).[95]

This multifaceted example marks social and cosmic relationships as well as to advance Iliadic concerns, particularly with regard to the poem's central hero. Agamemnon may be using the exemplar of Herakles to explain a hierarchy that makes a more valiant warrior subordinate, if he is looking beyond his self-comparison to Zeus at all; ironically, however, his account also anticipates Achilles' role-playing as Herakles, at the very point when the poem's protagonist is finally about to rejoin battle and perform his own heroic endeavors. Embracing this Heraklean guise in the rest of the assembly, Achilles remains uninterested in talk and social contracts, eager instead for the blood, tears, and sweat of battle.[96] Yet Achilles ends up frustrated in his desire to play this role straightaway, as first Agamemnon and then Odysseus insist on making formal reparations. This disjunction between the hero's Heraklean desire for combat and the *Iliad*'s more complex narrative of social affiliations relates to our discussion in Chapter 1, and to this epic's construction of a political community. Achilles has been flirting with performing a Heraklean role ever since he first withdrew from the Achaean coalition in Book 1, when he had called the rest of the Achaeans nonentities for their (silent) support for Agamemnon and condemned them to suffering without his support in battle. His unilateral action, moreover, won Zeus' (albeit grudging) endorsement against Hera's will, as if this were a narrative about the son of Zeus carrying out important labors in the face of divine opposition. But even in this self-assertive opening act Achilles cannot completely remove himself from social ties. His withdrawal from battle *also* means removing his men along with him (*Iliad* 2.773–779); though he no longer fights, he keeps a keen eye on the action, alert to the suffering of the Achaeans, even as he rejects Odysseus' delivery of Agamemnon's offer (*Iliad* 9.349–353); even after the embassy, we find him waiting in anticipation of further communication (*Iliad* 11.599–601), and dispatching his friend for further news.. It was Achilles too who initially established the assembly and spoke on behalf of the suffering group, even underlying their role in the equitable distribution of goods, which he attempts to defend against Agamemnon's grasping command.

---

[95] "The fact that Agamemnon admits his own *ate* by citing this Herakles story ironically establishes him as a parallel to Eurystheus and Achilles as a parallel to Herakles": Davidson 1980:200. This passage also shows beyond a doubt that the Homeric epics were aware of the basic outline of Herakles' story: Fowler 2013:260–261.

[96] A rather ironic turn of events given how instrumental he was in establishing the assembly as a place for dissent from the king at the beginning of the *Iliad*: Barker 2009:40–66.

Later on, he dismisses Agamemnon's reparations, in terms that appear a rejection of a code of behavior, but that turn out to be a restatement of social obligations, obligations which end up committing him to staying at Troy, even as the embassy departs having failed to re-enlist him in the fighting.

His lack of interest in those very social obligations in Book 19, which appears to us almost Heraklean in its emphasis on immediate action and almighty power, stems, moreover, from a very personal cause: the loss of his friend, Patroklos. At key points in the epic, then, Homer invites his audience to see Achilles as a hero from a previous era, with a special connection to the gods and set apart from the world of men in terms of his superhuman power, a Herakles in the making. And yet, Achilles never quite cuts that figure; he is only briefly a hero acting at his own behest. This is why the threat of Heraklean violence looms large over the thoughts and actions of the *Iliad*'s hero, the always present potential turn that the epic might take, were it not for the social relationships in which Achilles finds himself entangled and the institutions which he has helped to establish and activate.[97]

This struggle between heroic definitions (and missions) has been a feature of the poem from the very first mention of Herakles in the Catalogue of Ships. Immediately after the Dodecanese contingent, in which Tlepolemus plays the major role as the leader of Rhodes, comes Achilles, who, Homer reminds us, was presently sitting out the war (2.685). The way in which Homer describes Achilles pointedly resonates with Herakles' epic characterization, while at the same time marking the difference between them. As we have seen above, Herakles is closely associated with enduring and completing tasks. Here, Homer describes Achilles as "having labored much" (πολλὰ μογήσας, 2.690), a phrase that is cognate with Herakles' own labors, even as it is also used to denote Odysseus' heroic activity. In fact, each Homeric protagonist engages with the theme of laboring in ways significantly different from Herakles. In the *Odyssey* the formula resonates strongly with the idea of *nostos* through the labors that Odysseus must endure.[98] In its first occurrence in the *Iliad* in the opening assembly, Achilles uses it to assert the toils that he has undertaken and suffered in war for the collective

---

[97] See further Chapter 5 below.

[98] In the *Odyssey* the phrase relates most often to Odysseus: 2.343; 4.170; 5.223, 449; 6.175; 7.147; 8.155; 19.483; 21.207; 23.101, 169, 338. It also extends, however, to his family and retainers: Athena (as Mentor) to Telemachus, 3.232; Odysseus to Eumaios, 15.489; the narrator about Eumaios welcoming Telemachus, 16.19; the narrator about Laertes, 24.207. On this aspect of the *Odyssey*, see Chapter 3 below. In the phrase's only occurrence in Hesiod, the hero it describes is Jason (*Theogony* 997). The traditional referentiality of πολλὰ μογήσας, then, encompasses the major Achaean heroes of collective action, even as its meaning recalls Herakles' laboring.

good (*Iliad* 1.162).[99] As Hesiod's *Theogony* demonstrates, Herakles' labors too had a social end connected with them, as part of Zeus' ordering of the cosmos. Still, the emphasis that Achilles puts on his hard work in battle and his commitment to the common cause suggests a somewhat different picture from that of a lone hero enduring all manner of tasks set for him in a (still) supernatural world full of gods and monsters.

This repositioning of the hero through a cognate, yet subtly different, motif (interformularity) can also be read as an appropriation of an alternative tradition (intertraditionality). Here in the Catalogue, Homer expands upon those labors by associating them specifically with the sack of Lyrnessos and the "destruction of the walls of Thebes" (διαπορθήσας καὶ τείχεα Θήβης, 2.691). As we have already been at pains to point out in the Introduction, Homer is here describing Achilles' sack of a minor settlement in the Troad. Yet the audience could be forgiven for also thinking of the far more famous *Boiotian* Thebes, from which Herakles hails (as Homer knows: *Iliad* 14.323–324) and which also has an epic tradition of a siege associated with it.[100] In place of the labors of the Theban Herakles Homer presents us with the labors of the *Iliad*'s Achilles over (not that) Thebes. Indeed, this Thebes has a tangentially critical role for the plot of the poem, since it is from this city and through these toils that Agamemnon had won Chryseis as a spoil of war—according to Achilles, when he recounts the events of the opening of the epic to his mother (1.366). It is when Agamemnon has to return her, and he demands another prize in return, that he provokes Achilles' wrath. Thebes (but not that one) lies behind what turns out to be the catalyst for this epic tale about the fall of Troy.

As the *Iliad* gears up towards its final movements and the return of Achilles to battle, Homer marks the moment by having Zeus invite all the gods to enter the battle. In this controlled competitive environment, the *Iliad*'s agonism with its epic rivals comes to the fore—not only the *Theogony* (again) but other now lost traditions, like those associated with the one Trojan hero to escape the city's sack, Aeneas.[101] As the gods agree to put an end to their (Theogonic) direct conflict with each other, and as the prelude to the (metapoetic) confrontation between Aeneas and Achilles, the narrator describes a scene of cosmic magnitude. The gods gather at the "high earth-piled wall of divine Herakles, which Pallas Athena and the Trojans made him so that he might get away from and

---

[99] In the embassy Phoenix appeals to Achilles through this phrase (9.492). In Patroklos' funeral games, Menelaos praises Antilochus, who at this point comes across as Achillean, for his efforts (23.607).

[100] Significantly, the only other occurrence of this phrase is at 4.378, where it does indeed denote Boiotian Thebes.

[101] On Aeneas' confrontation with Achilles as an intertraditional exchange (mediated through the intervention of the gods), see Nagy 1999 [1979]:274–275.

escape the sea-monster whenever it chased him from the beach to the plain" (τεῖχος ἐς ἀμφίχυτον Ἡρακλῆος θείοιο / ὑψηλόν, τό ῥά οἱ Τρῶες καὶ Παλλὰς Ἀθήνη / ποίεον, ὄφρα τὸ κῆτος ὑπεκπροφυγὼν ἀλέαιτο, / ὁππότε μιν σεύαιτο ἀπ᾽ ἠιόνος πεδίον δέ, 20.145–147).[102] Again Herakles is firmly located in a bygone age, when walls were needed to ward off monsters from the sea, not the world of the *Iliad*, where it has been the Achaeans and Trojans who have been fighting from the beach to the plain and whom walls—both those longstanding and those built in the course of this epic—have been holding back. It is somewhat paradoxical that Herakles is associated with the construction of this particularly high section of the walls, when, as we have seen, he is famous elsewhere for having breached them. Indeed, soon afterwards Poseidon bitterly complains about the original construction of Troy's walls (*Iliad* 21.441–457), reminding Apollo both of their suffering in their cause ("so that the city might be unbroken," 447) and of the deception of Laomedon that still rankles him. Here too the poem remains silent on Troy's former destruction and the hero responsible—Herakles. In this version Laomedon's original sin has gone unpunished, Herakles' sack has been forgotten, and the Achaean cause is made all the greater. Nor will the *Iliad* narrate their fall, save for the brief telescoping of time halfway through the epic when Homer takes us beyond this poem and beyond the heroic world itself to witness the gods' final destruction of the city (*Iliad* 12.13–33). Nor, even, does the action of the epic take place around these walls, save here, as a rampaging Achilles puts the Trojans to flight, leaving Hector alone outside the city, from whose walls his parents watch with horror, as Achilles chases their son round and round them.

Instead Homer builds other walls, which form the intense focus of the action, and which are equally an affront to the gods—the walls hastily erected by the Achaeans to protect their ships. In their haste, the Achaeans forget to offer due prayers and offerings to the gods, who, as a result, condemn the walls to oblivion even as they are being built—the complainant is again Poseidon, and the precedent to which he appeals is again Troy and Laomedon's deception (7.451–453). Thus these non-traditional Achaean walls, constructed in and by this poem, stand in for and replace the Trojan walls of myth.[103] But that is not all. They also represent the appropriation of a core element from the Theban tradition. As we mentioned in the Introduction, in Homer's epic, the Achaeans, the besiegers of Troy, become themselves besieged, hemmed in behind the walls that they have built without the gods' blessing. What is more, these walls have

---

[102] Again the information about Herakles is minimal, carefully limiting his role and impact in the narrative.

[103] These Achaean walls become the focus of the most intense fighting in the central section of the war narrative, from Book 12 to Book 16 (12.12, 64, 223, 257, 261, 352, 458; 14.15; 15.361; 16.558).

seven gates, as if Thebes en bloc has been relocated to the Troad.[104] And in a way it has. The description of the Herakles-built walls of Troy as "lofty" recalls the common formula "lofty-gated," which is used in the *Iliad* only—aptly enough in the current example—of Troy—and—less aptly—of Troadic Thebes.[105] As an epithet that resonates with Troy and that paradoxically suggests its vulnerability as a city, its use in describing a minor city in the Troad with the famous name of another city under siege arguably constitutes the greatest act of erasure of the famous-gated Thebes from the epic record.

As we have seen, the fleeting mention of Herakles' walls recalls a previous era of divine construction on the one hand and marauding monsters on the other. Moreover, it serves to bring to an end a passage unlike any other in the *Iliad*, as the gods battle it out among each other for ascendancy. The strife on Olympus that has been threatening to break out ever since the end of *Iliad* 1 finally comes to pass: though it is not ultimately a *Theogony*—Zeus is above it all, unassailable—the Theogonic resonances help to lend the necessary aura of an end of days for Homer's heroes. On the other side of this wall, as it were, is the metapoetic confrontation between the hero of this epic and the one Trojan War hero to survive it. From the vantage point afforded by Herakles' Trojan wall, then, we can observe a telescoping of time, from the epic conflagration of gods battling it for themselves (and the narratives that tell of this early period of cosmic history), through a period when heroes like Herakles built human structures to protect men from monsters (and the narratives associated with this post-cosmological pre-heroic conflict world), to the present war that is threatening to destroy, and will succeed in destroying, the race of heroes—the *Iliad*. And on this other, heroic, side of this wall enters Achilles, who, once his (non) conflict with Aeneas has been put to one side, slaughters all in his wake, battles with a river god, and threatens to sack Troy's citadel singlehandedly, as if a hero from another world—a would-be Herakles.

The Heraklean tonality of the *Iliad*'s final scenes of battle extends to a complex case of interformularity. As mentioned in passing above, Herakles appears in cult-language as a "protector from evils" (*alexikakos*)—a title that is echoed in hexameter poetry when the Hesiodic Herakles "wards evil disease" from Prometheus (κακὴν δ' ἀπὸ νοῦσον ἄλαλκεν, Hesiod *Theogony* 527)[106] and Theognis asks Artemis to "ward away the evil fates" (κακὰς δ' ἀπὸ κῆρας

---

[104] Cf. Tsagalis 2014.

[105] τεῖχος ὑψηλόν: *Iliad* 12.388; 16.397, 512, 702; 21.540. The epithet ὑψίπυλος, is used only of Troadic Thebes (6.414) and Troy (16.698; 21.544). Cf. the new Archilochus fragment 19 (...ὑψίπυλον Τρώων πόλιν...): Barker and Christensen 2006.

[106] Cf. Hesiod's *Shield* when Zeus conceives Herakles to be "a defender against ruin for the gods and mortal men" (ὥς ῥα θεοῖσιν / ἀνδράσι τ' ἀλφηστῇσιν ἀρῆς ἀλκτῆρα φυτεύσαι, 28–29). Cf. Hesiod fr. 195.29.7.

ἄλαλκε, 13).[107] In the *Iliad* the verb ἀλέξω is deployed in highly specific places where a stronger party defends a weaker.[108] As powerful as this language seems to be, however, it shares formulaic elements with the verb ἀμύνω, most clearly evident in the formula *λοιγὸν ἀμυν-.[109] This formula is introduced at the very beginning of the epic, as Achilles looks for someone to ward off the danger resulting from Apollo's anger (βούλεται ἀντιάσας ἡμῖν ἀπὸ <u>λοιγὸν ἀμῦναι</u>, *Iliad* 1.67), and becomes especially marked when Achilles points out that his withdrawal will deprive his people of someone who can "ward off danger" for them (1.341 and 398).[110] One of the many elements of the embassy negotiations during Book 9 centers on this theme, as first Odysseus and then Phoenix try to reestablish Achilles as the defender of the Achaeans.[111] At the end of his speech, Phoenix even replaces Odysseus' traditional formula (which uses the more *traditionally* restricted ἀλέξω) with Achilles' alternative variation (applying the more contextually marked ἀμύνω), taken from the beginning of the epic,[112] engaging in the type of dynamic manipulation of conventional language that, we suggest, characterizes the formation of the Homeric epics in general.

At the point when the *Iliad* slips into its Theogonic reckoning as Achilles (re)enters battle, he appears no longer as the hero who wards off danger, but as the one who must be warded off. Here, for the only time in the epic, Homer

---

[107] From a diachronic perspective forms of ἀμύνω replace ἀλέξω: Christensen 2013:268–272. Hesiod calls the golden race "spirits" (δαίμονες) who are "warders against evil" (ἀλεξίκακοι): *Works and Days* 123. Asklepios wards off disease ('Ασκληπιὸ[ν ε]ἴσατο Δηοῖ / νοῦσον ἀλεξή[σ]αντ', IG II² 4781.1–2); the compound *Alexikakos* appears with Apollo (e.g. 'Α[πόλλωνι τῶι 'Α]λεξικάκωι, SEG XXI 469 C.54 and ἀλεξικάκου 'Απόλλωνος, MAMA IV 275A.3), Herakles ("Herakles, blood of Zeus, slayer of beasts, you were not born the only warder against evil in earlier years," 'Ηρακλες, αἷμα Διός, θηροκτόνε, οὔ νυ τι μοῦνος/ ἐν προτέροις ἐτέεσσιν ἀλεξίκακός τις ἐτέχθης, Clara Rhodos 2 (1932) 208,45.1–2), and Zeus (Ζῆνά τ' ἀλεξίκακον καὶ 'Ηρακλέα πτολίπορθο[ν], *Inscriptiones Creticae* II xix 7.2).

[108] Christensen 2013: 271. Some of this is prefigured by the poetics of ἀλκή as described by Collins 1998.

[109] This formula is particularly Iliadic: Christensen 2013:266 and 273–274. For special associations for the formula: Nagy 1999 [1979]:72–76; Slatkin 1991:87–88.

[110] Much of this argument is summarized from Christensen 2013:271–279.

[111] Odysseus uses ἀλέξω ("consider how you will ward off the ruinous day for the Danaans," φράζευ ὅπως Δαναοῖσιν ἀλεξήσεις κακὸν ἦμαρ, 9.251), only to be countered by Achilles, who for the first time uses a form of ἀλέξω himself ("Let him consider how to ward the ruinous fire from the ships," φραζέσθω νήεσσιν ἀλεξέμεναι δήϊον πῦρ, 9.347). In turn, Phoenix appropriates Achilles' earlier language, as he criticizes Achilles for withholding his protection out of anger (οὐδέ τι πάμπαν ἀμύνειν..., 9.435), and makes the protection both personal ("I made you my child, so that you might ward unseemly ruin away from me," ἀλλά σὲ παῖδα... / ποιεύμην, ἵνα μοί ποτ' ἀεικέα λοιγὸν ἀμύνης, 9.494–495) and political (9.517–518).

[112] "So he was warding the evil day away from the Aitolians" ὡς ὃ μὲν Αἰτωλοῖσιν ἀπήμυνεν κακὸν ἦμαρ, 9.597; cf. 9.251. Lest Achilles or anyone else miss the rhetorical point, Phoenix deploys the reduplicated aorist participle of ἀλέξω to warn that Achilles will lose honor, should he delay warding off war (9.605).

substitutes the combination *λοιγὸν ἀμυν- with the phrase λοιγὸν ἀλάλκοι (21.138, 250, 539). This substitution occurs at the moment when the river Scamander rises up in offense at Achilles' indiscriminate massacre of Trojans and denotes the god's attempt to shield his people from their destruction.[113] At his most Heraklean in appearance, wrestling gods and slaughtering men in their myriads, Achilles is described in language that inverts the relationship between Herakles the protector and the audience, and that in turn highlights the dangerous nature of such heroes.[114] At once, through the adaptation of traditional imagery and the inversion of conventional language, Homeric epic invokes the nature and name of Herakles but indicates the problematic ambiguity of these bygone heroes in its world.[115]

Thus, when Achilles cites Herakles as the example of a hero who could not escape his fate, "though he was most dear to lord Zeus, son of Cronos, / but fate tamed him and the grievous anger of Hera" (οὐδὲ γὰ οὐδὲ βίη Ἡρακλῆος φύγε κῆρα / ὅς περ φίλτατος ἔσκε Διὶ Κρονίωνι ἄνακτι, / ἀλλά ἑ μοῖρα δάμασσε καὶ ἀργαλέος χόλος Ἥρης, 18.117–119),[116] he activates a latent theme that runs through the *Iliad*. The way that Herakles is treated should now be familiar: the brevity of the citation perpetuates the de-emphasis on Herakles; the attribution of Herakles' death to "fate" and "Hera" (119) casts the former hero as collateral damage in the conflict of the gods. He is neither an agent nor really a god at this point, but just another mortal who suffered because of the gods.[117] In this case Herakles is even denied explicitly the one thing that signified his unique importance in the whole of the tradition—survival beyond death.

The collocation of the death of Zeus' dearest son and the inescapability of fate (as represented by Hera) recalls Sarpedon. As noted above, Zeus' love and care extends only so far as to secure Sarpedon's *body*, not to keep him alive, precisely because of the issue of fate. We are now firmly in a world where men

---

[113] Christensen 2013:277–278.

[114] For Herakles imagery in the characterization of Achilles: Nagy 1999 [1979]:318; Schein 1984:134–136.

[115] The epic further marks the strangeness of this tale with his invocation of the Heraklean walls and the gathering gods. The divine audience of Achilles' *aristeia* contrasts powerfully for the poem's external audience with the divine council and "trial" at the beginning of Book 24. At this later point the gods pass judgment on Achilles' mistreatment of Hektor's corpse: while they are not unanimous (Hera attempts to hold on to the prior distinction between Achilles the divine-born hero and Hektor the man), they do signal that Achilles' behavior is no longer acceptable. See further below in Chapter 5, "Enabling Strife, Founding Politics."

[116] In this passage Achilles imagines a Herakles who eventually submitted to the *keres*. This is strange because, as a cult-hero, Herakles was specifically invoked as an averter of the *keres*: Galinsky 1972:14.

[117] This idea of not being able to escape one's fate returns near the end of the *Odyssey*, where Athena ensures that even the most considerate suitor, Amphimedon, does not escape his fate (*Odyssey* 18.155). Similarly, Odysseus observes that the gods and fate tamed the suitors (*Odyssey* 22.413).

are not rescued from death like Herakles in myth. Accordingly, Achilles looks forward to a future life not with the blessed gods but on the lips of men. He will win *kleos* (18.121), bringing wretched mourning upon Trojan women (18.122–125). By embracing the heroic paradigm of a short life with eternal renown, with the suffering it entails, Achilles willingly performs his story as a Heraklean tale. He accepts that he has caused destruction to his own and is resolved to turn this force against his enemies. On the other hand, while Achilles uses the paradigm to explain that this type of suffering is necessarily a component of his mortality, implicitly he is *not* Herakles, who died to be reborn. Rather, he will die and be reborn in the tale he is now part of, equally uniquely as himself, swift-fated Achilles.[118]

Ultimately, Achilles' epic frustrates his attempt to be a Herakles, even as he dismisses his social obligations (Book 19), fights a river god (Book 21), denies a fallen hero right of burial (Book 22), and is nourished by the ambrosia of the gods dispensed by Athena. For we see him first establish funeral games for his fallen comrade, which allow his community to mourn and honor that man, and, ultimately, respect the supplication of the father of his friend's killer, to allow even that man burial.[119] It is this love for his fallen comrade, Patroklos, whose death is the very stimulus behind his thinking here, that marks Achilles out as different from a hero like Herakles. Even as Achilles is at his most singular and extreme—his most Heraklean, as it were[120]—we see the effect of his ties of friendship (18.98, 103). Ultimately, Herakles represents a marginalized hero, projected into the past, and separated from what is most important to people in the world of today—(acceptance of) death and (guarantee of) burial.

[118] There may be engagement as well with external traditions on the afterlife and worship of Achilles: see Hooker 1988 for Achilles-cults and Hommel 1980 for Achilles worship in the Black Sea basin. Hedreen 1992 presents an updated discussion drawing on archaeological, epigraphic, and literary evidence. Tension between ritual and poetic traditions are significant to epic meaning, see Nagy 1999 [1979]:67–174.

[119] Herakles of course was famous for founding the Olympic games, while "games of Oedipus" are mentioned in passing in Patroklos' games (*Iliad* 23.679). In accordance with the poetic agonistics that we have been tracing in this book, Achilles' establishment of games (*agon*) in honor of his fallen friend, and in particular their depiction of a new politics of mediation (cf. Hammer 2002) in their judging, could represent another assault on Heraklean and Theban traditions: see further Chapter 5, "Enabling Strife, Founding Politics."

[120] At least according to the *Iliad*. Elsewhere we see Herakles engaged in the kind of companionship that could make him a suitable paradigm for the Achilles-Patroklos relationship: consider his nephew Iolaus or his lover Hylas. The fact that the Homeric poems *only* show Herakles in isolation seems significant.

Conclusion: A Wish Never to See the Like Again

In this chapter we have seen how the *Iliad*'s careful engagement with and management of Heraklean *fabula*—avoiding naming the hero, never giving away too many details—reveals its antagonistic relationship with the tradition even as it draws on language and themes from it. As the Theban hero par excellence, Herakles is modified to (not) fit the world of Homer's *Iliad*. Through the use of his genealogy, the downgrading of the importance of his expedition, and the selection of details whereby he becomes rather less Theban (or, at any rate, his Theban identity is not celebrated), he is positioned primarily as a counter-model to the collective affairs of the *Iliad*'s heroes—even Achilles, whose mortality and comradeship come into focus when he cites Herakles as a heroic precedent. Taken together, Herakles' appearances in the *Iliad* point to a hero out of time, a semi-god from a prior generation uninterested in, and incapable of, forming the kinds of social bonds that motivate and structure the behavior of Homer's heroes. Correspondingly, the *Iliad* and its heroes represent a world a step further on in terms of cosmological development from the world of the *Theogony* and its depiction of warring gods and individual culture heroes beginning to lay down Zeus' will. In fact, in part due to its appropriation of Herakles, the *Iliad* both represents and *reproduces* the separation of the race of heroes from the Olympian gods and the establishment of a world of men in its wake. As further proof of this argument, we finish this chapter by turning to the *Odyssey*, whose treatment of Herakles is even briefer, even starker, and even more clearly indicative of a hero ill-equipped either to survive the transition to the world of men or measure up to *the* man, Odysseus.

So much is clear from the first of the *Odyssey*'s triptych of Heraklean references. This initial example occurs when Odysseus moderates his boast to the Phaiakians by specifically declaring that he is *not* going to strive with the men of the past. The two heroes that he singles out are Herakles and Eurytos of Oechalia. Ironically, according to Odysseus, these men had themselves overreached their station by having continually endeavored to strive with the gods (8.222–225).[121] In the *Iliad*, as discussed above, Herakles is frequently mentioned in implicit comparison to Achilles, and Achilles himself even cites Herakles as a precedent. In contrast, Odysseus expressly asks *not* to be compared to Herakles. Such figures belong very much to a past whose relevance or indeed continued value is now very much in question.

---

[121] Odysseus is consistent in this regard: in *Iliad* 10 he also rules himself out of any comparison with great heroes.

The stakes of Odysseus' refusal are clearly seen in the final reference to Herakles, as the narrator sets the scene for the climactic and critical bow contest. The bow, Homer tells us, was a guest-gift given to him by Iphitus.[122] This man is long since dead, for Herakles had "killed him in his house, even though he was a guest, respecting neither that hospitality nor the gods' regard, the hard man" (ὅς μιν ξεῖνον ἐόντα κατέκτανεν ᾧ ἐνὶ οἴκῳ, / σχέτλιος, οὐδὲ θεῶν ὄπιν ᾐδέσατ' οὐδὲ τράπεζαν, *Odyssey* 21.27–28). The point of Odysseus' rejection of Herakles as a comparison should now be clear.[123] Such behavior as Herakles displays here— killing a guest and disrespecting the gods—evokes Polyphemos the Cyclops, who memorably denies interest in Zeus as god of hospitality, just before he grabs two of Odysseus' men to eat—according to Odysseus, that is.[124] The significant point is that the reference to Herakles' daring deeds (μεγάλων ἐπιίστορα ἔργων) occurs directly before Odysseus performs daring deeds of his own, deeds would be, under any other (normal) circumstance, be considered equally violent and questionable, particularly for the transgression of *xenia*: Odysseus slaughters all of the suitors who have been feasting in his home. Another name for this act would be the murder of *guests*, the very same act of which Herakles stands accused, were it not for the fact that the *Odyssey*, through its depiction of Athena's support for the hero and the suitors' many instances of disrespect, has carefully framed Odysseus' actions as legitimate and not disproportionate. Herakles could be a paradigm for Odysseus, were it not for the *Odyssey* expressly instructing us otherwise.

This brings us to Herakles' only other appearance in the *Odyssey*: in Odysseus' shadowy meeting with the souls of the dead. Even in its conceptualization this episode has strong Heraklean resonances. Herakles was famous as the hero who descended into Hades (to capture Cerberus) and returned back alive. By enduring his own Hades adventure, Odysseus sets himself on par with Herakles, and sets the standard for heroic deeds in epics to come. Yet, at the same time, in Odysseus' reversioning of the hero's descent into the underworld, Hades

---

[122] Iphitus is the son of Eurytos, the hero paired with Herakles in that initial reference, and whose demise was narrated.

[123] How appropriate is a hero who is essentially homeless and a mad-murderer of his wife and children for Odysseus' tale? It is interesting, on the other hand, that Herakles is not used as a model or comparison for Agamemnon: both men are killed by their wives after they come home with a new woman as war-booty. As David Sider has pointed out to us, this similarity between Agamemnon and Herakles is manipulated by Sophocles in his use of Aeschylus' *Agamemnon* as a literary model.

[124] Commenting on the Herakles passage in the *Odyssey*, Galinsky 1972:12 writes, "This is one of the most devastating indictments of Herakles in literature, exceeded only by Sophocles and the shrill bias of the church fathers, and most subsequent writers took care to make him a more civil fellow. Whereas earlier in the *Odyssey* Homer had relegated Herakles to a mythological past, he now propels him into Odysseus' own time without softening his stone-age behavior."

appears to be not so much a physical location as a place that is accessed through ritual, as the spilling of blood summons or conjures up the dead. Odysseus does not so much descend into Hades as the shades of Hades rise up to greet him. Here is another deed where Odysseus' daring is both Heraklean (in that he confronts the dead) and crucially non-Heraklean (in that he does not go into Hades himself).

At the very end of his encounters with the dead, Odysseus spies Herakles (11.601–629).[125] Or, rather, as Homer carefully articulates, it was Herakles' "image" (*eidolon*) that Odysseus saw, since his actual self (*autos*) "among the immortal gods / delights himself at the feast and has fine-ankled Hebe as a wife" (τὸν δὲ μετ' εἰσενόησα βίην Ἡρακληείην, / εἴδωλον· αὐτὸς δὲ μετ' ἀθανάτοισι θεοῖσι / τέρπεται ἐν θαλίῃς καὶ ἔχει καλλίσφυρον Ἥβην, / παῖδα Διὸς μεγάλοιο καὶ Ἥρης χρυσοπεδίλου, 11.601–603). In what follows, this Herakles (the *eidolon*) tries to draw an affiliation with Odysseus by stressing the similarity of their plights: they have both suffered greatly ("*you also* have undergone a terrible fate," καὶ σὺ κακὸν μόρον ἡγηλάζεις); like Odysseus he too has had difficult tasks to accomplish ("and he assigned me difficult labors," ὁ δέ μοι χαλεποὺς ἐπετέλλετ' ἀέθλους). Again, the two heroes are affiliated, this time directly by Herakles himself; in framing the episode, Odysseus resists too close a comparison. Odysseus has *already* drawn attention to the otherworldliness of this Herakles. "About him rose a clamor from the dead," Odysseus narrates, "as if birds were flying everywhere in terror" (οἰωνῶν ὥς, / πάντοσ' ἀτυζομένων, 11.605–606), while he "like the dark night" (ὁ δ' ἐρεμνῇ νυκτὶ ἐοικώς, 11.606) gripped his bow in readiness to shoot, "glaring terribly" (δεινὸν παπταίνων, 11.608). Worse still is his baldric, "fearful" (σμερδαλέος, 11.609) to look at, all the worse, it seems, for bearing images that bring to mind the description of his shield in the Hesiodic poem of that name.[126] Odysseus comments that so fierce were these images that he wishes never to see the like of them ever again (11.610–614).[127]

We noted in the paragraph above the remarkable description of a dual Herakles—or, rather, a duality whereby Herakles is both *the hero* who survives

---

[125] There is a brief reference to his birth (the "bold and lion-hearted") and a passing mention of Megara ("her, whom the always untiring fury of the son of Amphityron had held," 266–70), which may well have evoked her murder and the death of their children (the story told by Euripides' *Herakles*).

[126] Wondrous things (θέσκελα ἔργα): *Iliad* 3.130; *Odyssey* 11.374, 610; *Shield* 34; boars and lions (σύες χαροποί τε λέοντες): cf. only *Sheild* 177; battles (ὑσμῖναί τε μάχαι τε φόνοι τ' ἀνδροκτασίαι τε): cf. only *Theogony* 228; cf. *Hymn to Aphrodite* 5.11; *Shield* 155; hard labors (χαλεποὺς ἐπετέλλετ' ἀέθλους): cf. only *Shield* 94.

[127] Cf. Anderson 2012:139 and 149. This description has prompted some to see a representation of eighth-century BCE or earlier Mycenaean ornamentation.

death and a hero who, like many others, flits through a shadowy existence in Hades.[128] Nevertheless, the *Odyssey*'s categorical distinction between the hero's self (*autos*) and his image (*eidolon*) is remarkable. Outside the Odyssean underworld, *eidolon* is used in Homer to denote the phantom of Aeneas that Apollo produces in order to rescue the hero from Diomedes, and the image of Penelope's sister that Athena fashions to comfort her in her grief.[129] That is to say, the *eidolon* functions as a metapoetic signifier, which, by distinguishing its truthful fiction from the fictional truth of *autos*, draws attention to the act of artistic creation. In his play *Helen*, Euripides deploys the term *eidolon* to denote a phantom Helen at Troy over whom so many heroes fought and died, as opposed to the real Helen who for all this time has been holed up in Egypt.[130] More is at stake here than whether Helen really went to Troy or not. As Victoria Wohl has written (2015:114), "The Helen we see onstage is repeatedly taken for a *mimēsis*, a fictional double for the real Helen... [as] Euripides reminds us again and again that the world of the play is just a dramatic fiction."[131] We suggest that Odysseus' striking formulation indicates a similarly metadramatic encounter.

At one level, the distinction between the real and the mirror Herakles is raised only to be passed over, as Odysseus dwells on the terrifying properties of the latter, with which he goes on to engage. One reason for this must be, again, to diminish Herakles' standing. Odysseus pays lip service to the idea that Herakles lived on in a blissful afterlife, but the interest and focus of this episode is on the Herakles whom Odysseus encounters. At the same time, however, the difference pointedly raises the problem of Herakles in Homeric epic. In Odysseus' stark distinction between the mirror image (*eidolon*) and the self (*autos*), we find a unique and explicit separation between a hero and his story. And again it works to the detriment of Herakles. It is his *eidolon* that, by virtue of its epic-like description, is associated with his legendary deeds, to which Odysseus is currently contributing in his tall tale to the Phaiakians; the *autos* Herakles is nowhere to be seen. The shadowy eidolon thus masquerades as, and substitutes in for, the *autos* (divine) Herakles whose story is marginalized from Homer's world and whose outcomes—an immortal life with a goddess—are explicitly rejected by the *Odyssey*'s hero in the epic's opening movement.

There is one further point to make. When Odysseus attempts to embrace the *eidolon* of his mother's soul, "three times if flitted through his arms like a shadow or a dream" (τρὶς δέ μοι ἐκ χειρῶν σκιῇ εἴκελον ἢ καὶ ὀνείρῳ / ἔπτατ',

---

[128] For the picture of the hero who survives death, see the Homeric *Hymn to Herakles*, esp. 15.8.

[129] *Iliad* 5.449 and 451; *Odyssey* 4.796. For denoting the souls of the dead: e.g. *Odyssey* 11.84, 213.

[130] At, e.g., Euripides *Helen* 34 and 582.

[131] We thank Sophie Raudnitz for this reference. On metatheater in Euripides' *Helen*, see especially Downing 1990.

Odyssey 11.207–208). If a shadow can function as a metaphor for reflecting on the impermanence of human life, it can also call to mind the idea of the person living on after death in *stories.*[132] Fragment B145 of Democritus preserves the proverbial-sounding assertion that "a story is a shadow of the deed" (λόγος ἔργου σκιή), as if the shade were a metaphor for the continuing afterlife of an object granted through the means of storytelling. The tension is highly charged between the pitiful existence of the soul, which assumes the image of the person as if it were a shadow, and the claims of epic in general to confer *kleos* and life after death. When Odysseus returns to the world of the living, the *Odyssey* countermands the glory of a short life exchanged for *kleos aphthiton* by granting its hero both fame and continued life.

No less than his wall in the *Iliad*, Herakles' *eidolon* functions as a kind of metonym for how the Homeric poems exploit their epic past. The epics present an "eidolon" of the past, but reframe it, and adjust its meaning for a new world. Thus, the *eidolon* of Herakles resembles the very shadow of past tales of heroes that permeates the superstructure of both epics. But, in the end, it is not the thing itself. The *Iliad* and the *Odyssey* are new forms of their own making. In the next chapter we will turn to consider this heroic superstructure again, lingering a while longer with the shades of the Odyssean underworld to question the depiction of Oedipus and reflect on the form of Odysseus' representation.

---

[132] The idea that the shadow is like the image of a person in the afterlife is expanded on in Pindar, who reflects that "man is a dream of a shadow" (σκιᾶς ὄναρ, *Pythian* 8.95), while a fragment of Sophocles declares that "man is only breath and shadow" (ἄνθρωπός ἐστι πνεῦμα καὶ σκιὰ μόνον, fr. 13).

3

Homer's Oedipus Complex: Form[1]

IN THE LAST CHAPTER we saw how Herakles, while rarely mentioned explicitly in the *Iliad*, nevertheless casts a long shadow over the events of the epic. Haunting Achilles' every move, Herakles stands as the hero from a bygone age. His singular actions had not only brought Zeus' order to the world of men, but also had brought about Troy's first downfall for the slight against the gods who had built its sacred walls. At key points in the poem, when Achilles asserts his singularity over his comrades, his actions take on a Heraklean hue. Yet the poem never allows him to act alone or without consequence for those dearest to him; correspondingly it also never allows those Heraklean elements to become normalized. Instead, in the world of the *Iliad*, the kind of heroic deeds that resemble those of Herakles appear outdated and excessive. This is not to say that Heraklean tales did not also probe the anxieties of, or the fault lines within, the hero's make-up; from the surviving evidence it seems clear that Herakles was popularly conceived of as *also* a hero who both suffered greatly and brought suffering to his people. But in the *Iliad* and *Odyssey* the problems are both intensified and magnified, owing to the poems' interest and concern to explore the hero's relations to his fellow men. Positioning themselves at, and to a certain extent participating in the construction of, the transition from the heroic age to the world of men, the Homeric poems relegate Herakles to a period prior to the foundation of institutions of the kind that Achilles establishes in the *Iliad*, and that Odysseus polices in the *Odyssey*.

Our first two chapters have explored the ways in which the nexus of politics and time as it is configured through two Theban figures, Tydeus and Herakles, marginalizes the Theban tradition and promotes the *Iliad* as the epic that, through the story of a siege, heralds the coming of a new age, after the demise of the race of heroes. In this third chapter we take a closer look at another broad theme—this time poetic *form* itself—through a third Theban hero, Oedipus. In Book 11 of the *Odyssey*, Odysseus entertains his Phaiakian hosts by narrating his

---

[1] Many sections of this chapter draw on work originally published in Barker and Christensen 2008.

experiences in the underworld. After conversing with his mother's soul—and before interviewing those of his fallen comrades from Troy—he sees a parade of women, which he goes on to catalogue for his audience. It includes the mother of Oedipus, Epikastê (*Odyssey* 11.271-280):

"μητέρα τ' Οἰδιπόδοα ἴδον, καλὴν Ἐπικάστην,
ἣ μέγα ἔργον ἔρεξεν ἀϊδρείῃσι νόοιο
γημαμένη ᾧ υἷϊ· ὁ δ' ὃν πατέρ' ἐξεναρίξας
γῆμεν· ἄφαρ δ' ἀνάπυστα θεοὶ θέσαν ἀνθρώποισιν.
ἀλλ' ὁ μὲν ἐν Θήβῃ πολυηράτῳ ἄλγεα πάσχων
Καδμείων ἤνασσε θεῶν ὀλοὰς διὰ βουλάς·
ἡ δ' ἔβη εἰς Ἀΐδαο πυλάρταο κρατεροῖο,
ἀψαμένη βρόχον αἰπὺν ἀφ' ὑψηλοῖο μελάθρου
ᾧ ἄχει σχομένη· τῷ δ' ἄλγεα κάλλιπ' ὀπίσσω
πολλὰ μάλ', ὅσσα τε μητρὸς ἐρινύες ἐκτελέουσ."

"And I saw the mother of Oedipus, fair Epikastê,
who in the ignorance of her mind did a great deed
by marrying her own son; he, after killing his own father,
married her. The gods soon made it known among men.
But though he suffered pains in much-loved Thebes
he continued to rule the Cadmeans through the god's baleful plans.
She descended to the house of the powerful gate-fastener Hades,
lashing a noose to a steep rafter,
subdued by all her anguish. And she left her son pains,
as many as a mother's Furies bring to fulfillment."

Here Odysseus offers such a strikingly compressed and oblique account of Oedipus' "many pains" (ἄλγεα...πολλά) that an ancient scholion commenting on this passage glosses it by turning to Sophocles' canonical version of *Oedipus Tyrannos* to fill in the background to the story.[2] It is a trend that continues to the present day. The absence of characteristic details, such as Oedipus' blinding, children, or exile, has led some critics to suppose that Homer did not know of

---

[2] See Scholia V to *Odyssey* 11.271 *ex.* 1-20. For brief comments on Homer's use of this scene, see Fowler 2013:404-405.

these events.[3] Alternatively, others have regarded the Homeric account as the original version of the myth, from which later representations departed.[4]

Neither approach, however, focuses on how this story functions in its context or plays a role within the wider narrative. As we have been exploring in this book, stories from the mythical past can have very different functions in the Homeric poems. When the content of these stories run counter to versions of the same myth which as we glimpse it elsewhere, interpretations tend to focus overmuch on whether Homer's account innovates on, deviates from, or represents some primordial original. We have tried instead to refocus attention to *what* stories are told, *how* those should be understood, and *why* they are told *where* they are. In this chapter we continue our interrogation of Homer's use of Theban myth by examining the description of Oedipus and the catalogue form in which he appears. Following the structure of our previous chapters, we will first sketch out and discuss Oedipus' heroic career outside of Homeric epic, such as it can be reconstructed. Then we identify and explore examples of traditional formularity in the passage cited above—the only time Oedipus' story is narrated in the entire Homeric corpus, save for a passing reference in the *Iliad*. Focusing on the thematics of the hero "of many pains," which aligns Oedipus with the master-sufferer Odysseus, we show how—again—Homer's poem both radically limits the history of the figure from Thebes and, within those strict parameters, makes Oedipus' story serve the interests of this narrative.

In our final section we dwell on the broader context in which this passage occurs—Odysseus' catalogue of women (presented to his Phaiakian audience). Where Homer draws on stories of the Seven against Thebes to emphasize Iliadic themes of politics, and on Herakles myths to redefine and complicate conceptions of the hero, his treatment of Oedipus brings into relief rivalry with other poetic forms. The Oedipus passage, while only fleeting, is significant for providing an insight into how the *Odyssey* integrates and redeploys the catalogue form, chiefly used elsewhere in epic for communicating genealogy. Here, not only does the *Odyssey* relegate rival heroic narratives to the status of catalogue entries within its own master tale—and, more severely, as part of an embedded narrative (Odysseus'); it also instrumentalizes them to his own purpose. By virtue of integrating them into his own tale, Odysseus transforms

---

[3]   See Eustathius *Commentary on Homer's Odyssey* I 413.12–414.29. Wyatt 1996 too suggests that Oedipus' blinding was unknown to Homer and originated in a misreading of the account in the *Odyssey*. See also Davies 2014.

[4]   E.g. Heubeck and Hoekstra 1989:93–94: "The description of Epikastê, wife of Laius, and mother of Oedipus, is the oldest identifiable version of the Oedipus legend, and contains all the central elements of the story..." Then they discuss the self-blinding, children between the two, and voluntary exile—all famous from myth but absent from this version.

them from potential narratives in their own right into mere indices that mark the turning point of his story and enable his return home.

Oedipus in Epic Fragments

Of all the myths from classical Greece, the story of Oedipus and his family is arguably among the most famous.[5] On the basis of the plays that have survived, the Oedipus family drama appears to have been one of the most popular sources for tragic performances, complementing the broader vision of Thebes that looms large over the Athenian stage as the "other" city where bad stuff happens.[6] Given the long cast list, the varied themes (both political and familial), and the complexity of these tragic representations, we can assume with some confidence that stories of Oedipus were also once prominent in epic poetry as well, perhaps even rivaling those of the Trojan War heroes, Achilles and Odysseus, as part of a Theban epic cycle.

Nevertheless, Oedipus' story is mentioned in only one place in Homeric poetry, in Homer's *Odyssey* 11.271–280 (the passage quoted above), while the hero is passingly name-checked during the funeral games held in honor of Patroklos, which take place near the end of the *Iliad* (*Iliad* 23.679).[7] Furthermore, evidence for an epic poem dedicated to Oedipus is rather limited.[8] By way of contrast, the episode for which Oedipus was later most renowned and which is assumed to have played a major role in his epic—his defeat of the Sphinx—is widely evidenced in extant visual representations.[9]

Frustrated by the lack of comparable literary material from the period, scholars turn to later sources to reconstruct an Oedipus epic. One of the most extensive is the scholion to Euripides *Phoenician Women* 1760 (= *FGrHist* 16 F 10), itself based on an account by the mythographer Peisander, which Alberto

---

[5] For overviews of the Oedipus myth, see Apollodorus III 49–56; cf. Hyginus 66–67. For how most mythographers follow Sophocles and Euripides, and the other variants: Gantz 1993:491–500. On the early mythographers: Fowler 2013:402–408.

[6] For Oedipus myth on the Athenian stage: Zeitlin 1986.

[7] See Cingano 1992 for an attempt to harmonize the accounts of Hesiod (*Works and Days* 161–165), Homer (*Iliad* 23.677–680), and Pherecydes regarding the death of Oedipus. Whereas Cingano is concerned with differences in accounts, our methodology points to the relevance, as a feature of poetic rivalry, of the Homeric narrative's reference to Oedipus' games. The imagery could not be clearer, as if the past represented by Oedipus' games is not up to the task of being compared to Patroklos'.

[8] See Bernabé 1996:19–20 and Davies 1988:20–21 for the single testimonium and fragment.

[9] The encounter between Oedipus and the Sphinx becomes a popular motif in art in the mid-fifth century BCE: LIMC s.v. Oidipous IV.10–88. An earlier version (c. 530 BCE) may show the confrontation: Gantz 1993:495. Oedipus' struggle with the Sphinx does not definitively appear prior to Aeschylus' *Seven Against Thebes* and the lost satyr-play *Sphinx* associated with it, although Hesiod lists the Sphinx as a danger to Thebes (*Theogony* 326–327): Gantz 1993:494–495.

Bernabé uses to provide the basic outline of the poem's plot.[10] The details are as follows: because of Laius' rape of Chrysippos,[11] Hera sends the Sphinx to punish the Thebans; Laius himself is killed by Oedipus, who in turn solves the riddle and marries his mother; upon discovering the truth, she kills herself while he blinds himself; afterwards he remarries and has four children with Euryganeia.[12] The fact that this summary appears to tell the *whole story* from the curse through the birth of Oedipus' children makes it highly suspect as the outline of any nominal poem. It is more probable that Peisander's account, as reported by the scholia, represents an attempt to record a general outline of the story surrounding Oedipus rather than the specific contents of an epic poem. Indeed, it seems equally likely that many of these details have in themselves been imported from later traditions, notably the tragic versions by Sophocles.[13] Suspicion falls on those motifs that emphasize Oedipus' incest, his intellectual ability, or his later exile to Athens, if only because of their prominence in Sophocles' material. In any case, the speedy ascension of his plays to canonical status makes disentangling later innovation from earlier epic representation highly problematic.

What we are left with are remains even more fragmentary than for the other Theban stories discussed in Chapters 1 and 2. The one fragment that is generally accepted as coming from an Oedipus epic seems to refer to the death of Haimon.[14] Another fragment purports to provide the Sphinx's riddle, appearing in two near identical versions, one in the scholia to Euripides' *Phoenician Women* 46, the other in Athenaeus' *Deipnosophists* X 83 (attributed to the Greek historian Asclepiades).[15] This fragment, however, is almost universally considered not to be part of an original *Oedipodea*. From our perspective, while these fragments and the motifs identified above are suggestive of what ancient Oedipus epics might have contained, the evidence remains entirely inconclusive. Altogether, the remnants of an epic Oedipus give us relatively little to go on, unless we follow the lead of many scholars and assume that the stories dramatized in tragedy were also known to the poets weaving epic song. While this is hypothetically interesting—and may in fact be crucial in imagining a fifth-century BCE

---

[10] For a discussion of the inadequacy of doing so: Davies 2014:4–7. For the contents of this epic: Cingano 2014.

[11] For the Chrysippos tradition, see Gantz 1993:488–489: the earliest sure appearance was in Euripides' *Chrysippos* (which Gantz is willing to entertain as a Euripidean invention); cf. the alternate tradition of Atreus and Thyestes killing their half-brother. For the two different tales: Fowler 2013:432–433.

[12] For Oedipus' four wives (Epikastê, Iokasta, Asymedousa, and Euryganeia) see Fowler 2013:403–404.

[13] See Davies 2014:7–17 for this summary and an extensive discussion of the scholarship.

[14] "But still, the most noble and loveliest of all / The dear child of blameless Kreion, shining Haimon" (ἀλλ' ἔτι κάλλιστόν τε καὶ ἱμεροέστατον ἄλλων / παῖδα φίλον Κρείοντος ἀμύμονος, Αἵμονα δῖον, fr. 1).

[15] See Davies 2014:10–12; Edmunds 1981:32. For a discussion of the riddle: Gantz 1993:496.

Athenian reception of an epic Oedipus—it does not provide us with a firm basis for interpreting *Homer's* selection of detail. For that we need to turn to what is happening in the *Odyssey* and explore what Oedipus appears in the first place, how he is represented, and what potential ramifications there are for thinking about his story.

Oedipus of Many Pains

> Nestor digresses and tells Menelaos how Epopeus was destroyed after debauching Lykourgos' daughter along with the stories of Oedipus, the insanity of Herakles, and the tales concerning Theseus and Ariadne.
>
> Proclus, *Chrestomathia*[16]

In his book on the Epic Cycle, Martin West considers this summary from Proclus' *Chrestomathia* to be a likely scene from the lost *Cypria* (West 2013:99–100.). In making this point, he notes that Wilamowitz (1884:149) first recognized that the women alluded to in this passage were also those who appear in Odysseus' description of the women in the underworld. West strains to find a connection between Oedipus' story and that of Menelaos, but the general sense is clear: both accounts deliver warning of the dangers that can come from women, especially when journeys are involved.[17]

Nestor's use of a list of women from myth to make a persuasive case to his addressee is interesting for a number of reasons. In general terms it offers a glimpse into how myth can be adapted to fit the aims of the speaker. It also features a list of relationships between women and men. More specifically pertinent to our inquiry, the example both illustrates a poetic strategy of appropriating and instrumentalizing prior tales for the purpose of the present, and features an attempt to make a connection between the stories of the Trojan War and those of Thebes. Oedipus, admittedly, does not seem an obvious or desirable comparandum for Odysseus if we take the former's primary dramatic role on the Athenian tragic stage in isolation. His status as a hero of Thebes, however—perhaps, even, as a *returning* hero—along with his various relationships with women, actually make him an important counterpoint to the *Odyssey*'s Odysseus.

The story of Oedipus represents, as we mentioned above, a story within a story, in that it appears in the account that one character is delivering to another. As such, it provides for a particularly useful, albeit complex, exploration of the

---

[16] Νέστωρ δὲ ἐν παρεκβάσει διηγεῖται αὐτῷ ὡς Ἐπωπεὺς φθείρας τὴν Λυκούργου θυγατέρα ἐξεπορθήθη, καὶ τὰ περὶ Οἰδίπουν καὶ τὴν Ἡρακλέους μανίαν καὶ τὰ περὶ Θησέα καὶ Ἀριάδνην.

[17] Proclus *Chrestomathia* 114–117 and *Commentary on Plato's Alcibiades* 214.3–6. See also Hainsworth 1993:285 and Lardinois 2000:649. For these tales, see Chapter 2, n19, above.

redeployment of mythical material within a poem especially interested in the power of storytelling.[18] Its interpretation is all the more challenging given the fact that the character narrating the tale is Odysseus, the man "of many wiles" (*polumêtis*, *Odyssey* 2.173; cf. 9.1), whose trickery and intelligence has already been headlined when he first takes the reins of his story (*Odyssey* 9.19). The reference to Oedipus, then, must be read with Odysseus' broader rhetorical strategy in mind,[19] a strategy that has a very specific and immediate aim—to accomplish his homecoming.[20]

In fact, this Theban tale has the specific function of appealing to his Phaiakian hosts, as he takes a break from recounting how he arrived on Phaiakia having lost all of his men. This intermission takes the form of a tour of the dead, a scenario that already seems to have been an epic staple, if visual evidence is anything to go by. Indeed, the hero most famously associated with descending into, and successfully returning from, Hades is no other than Herakles, the one hero who, as we have seen, lives on after death. As we saw in the previous chapter, Odysseus is even recognized by Herakles (or, rather, by his *eidolon*), who not only "pities" Odysseus (ὀλυφυρόμενος), but expressly empathizes with him on the basis that their toils are similar (*Odyssey* 11.618–619). Coming from the hero whose underworld exploits represent the model for trips to Hades, this is praise indeed.[21]

If the recollection of Herakles' arguably most famous labor, along with the sly nod towards the other hero, is suggestive of interpoetic agonistics, the *Odyssey*'s interview with the dead raises the stakes by being put in the mouth of its wily hero. By allowing his protagonist to take over the telling of the tale, Homer offers us a glimpse into the construction of poetic narrative. This becomes all the more charged when Odysseus responds to audience requests, as when the Phaiakian king, Alkinoos asks him to recount his meeting with the dead Trojan War heroes

---

[18] See Stewart 1976:146–195 for an extensive treatment of the epic's interest in poetic creation. Cf. Pucci 1987:209–213; Segal 1994:113–141; Saïd 2011:125–132.

[19] On Odysseus' "apologia", see: Frame 1978:34–73; Most 1989; Parry 1994; Olson 1995:43–64; Richardson 1996; de Jong 2001:149–51.

[20] Odysseus' ability as a storyteller is especially prodigious. The fact that he can interrupt his own tales implies a command over his audience: Rabel 2002. For differences between storytelling in the *Iliad* and the *Odyssey*: Minchin 2001:205–206.

[21] Currie 2006:22n102 reads this interaction in terms of allusion between texts: "The *Odyssey* confronts an earlier lost **Herakleïs* at *Odyssey* 11.601–26, and an earlier lost **Catalogue of Women* at *Odyssey* 11.225–332." See also Danek 1998:231: "Odysseus shows himself...as a hero who could potentially be brought into contact with every heroic story known to the listener, and our *Odyssey* presents itself as an epic which could potentially take up the material of all known epics and thus ultimately replace all other epics" (Currie's translation).

(*Odyssey* 11.370–376), and he duly obliges.[22] With the audience thus primed by the trailer to catch up on his former comrades-in-arms, Odysseus provides an account that reflects in various ways on his continuing epic endeavor and the story still under construction. Agamemnon's appearance, for example, allows Odysseus to present an archetypical bad homecoming as a counter-model for his as yet unaccomplished *nostos* (*Odyssey* 11.406–464), and invites the audience to ask how he will avoid Agamemnon's fate.[23] Meanwhile, his erstwhile epic rival, Achilles, turns out in the end to reject undying fame in favor of still being alive, his thoughts turned towards his father and son (*Odyssey* 11.474–538)—all concerns that very much match Odysseus', all in stark opposition to the glorious Achilles of the *Iliad*.[24] Even the picture of a silent Ajax bearing his grudge to the grave serves to magnify Odysseus' achievement, by demonstrating the magnanimity of the hero to let bygones be bygones (*Odyssey* 11.541–567). Odysseus' choice of characters to catalogue and the way he represents them intimately reflects the concerns of *his* narrative.

Returning now to Odysseus' Oedipus story (*Odyssey* 11.271–280, quoted and translated at the beginning of this chapter), we can observe the ways in which it engages in interpoetic agonistics through its manipulation of referential formulae, notably homing in on the idea of the suffering hero.

As we discussed in Chapter 2 on Herakles, pain and destruction are commonly associated with heroes in early Greek poetry and myth, who have the capacity to experience and dole out both in like measure. Where Achilles may be considered to be a hero who causes pain more than he suffers it, and Odysseus the reverse, both heroes are marked out for and to a certain extent defined by

---

[22] We should not overlook Alkinoos' praise in this section. Alkinoos notes that, while there are many men on the earth who fashion lies (ψεύδεά τ᾽ ἀρτύνοντας, 11.366), Odysseus is graced by the "shape of *epea*": themselves (σοὶ δ᾽ ἔπι μὲν μορφὴ ἐπέων, 367) and records a tale as skillfully as a bard (μῦθον δ᾽ ὡς ὅτ᾽ ἀοιδὸς ἐπισταμένως κατέλεξας, 368). The narrator of the *Odyssey*, however, provides a caveat for such compliments: not only does Odysseus lie elsewhere in the epic; after he has told one of his Cretan lies to Penelope, the narrator declares that "he knew many lies similar to the truth" (ἴσκε ψεύδεα πολλὰ λέγων ἐτύμοισιν ὁμοῖα, 19.203). Odysseus as *aoidos* walks the same line as Hesiod's Muses from the *Theogony* who "know how to speak many things that are similar to the truth, and know how to utter true things when [they] want to: (ἴδμεν ψεύδεα πολλὰ λέγειν ἐτύμοισιν ὁμοῖα / ἴδμεν δ᾽ εὖτ᾽ ἐθέλωμεν ἀληθέα γηρύσασθαι, 27–8). For Odysseus' lies: Haft 1984; Emlyn-Jones 1986; Minchin 2007:269–270; and most recently Newton 2015. For the accord between Hesiod and Odysseus: Nagy 1992:36–82.

[23] On Agamemnon's *nostos* as a counter-model, see Olson 1990; Katz 1991:29–53; Felson-Rubin 1994:95–107.

[24] To a point. When contemplating his fateful choice—whether to live a long life without glory or else a short one with it—he opts for the former, only first to remain at Troy, compelled by his comrades' appeals, and then to fight, because of his best friend's death. Once resigned to death, Achilles thinks of his father in his own old age: *Iliad* 34.507, 534–542. On the Iliadic Achilles being ambushed by the *Odyssey*: A. Edwards 1985.

suffering. It should come as no surprise, then, that Oedipus should be related to Odysseus through this theme. But it is the traditional referentiality of the resonant phrases describing Oedipus as "suffering many pains" (ἄλγεα πάσχων, 11.275; ἄλγεα...πολλά, 11.279–280) that is noteworthy.

The motif of "suffering pains" is anticipated in the very opening lines of the poem (*Odyssey* 1.1–5):

> ἄνδρα μοι ἔννεπε, Μοῦσα, πολύτροπον, ὃς μάλα πολλὰ
> πλάγχθη, ἐπεὶ Τροίης ἱερὸν πτολίεθρον ἔπερσε·
> πολλῶν δ' ἀνθρώπων ἴδεν ἄστεα καὶ νόον ἔγνω,
> <u>πολλὰ</u> δ' ὅ γ' ἐν πόντῳ <u>πάθεν ἄλγεα</u> ὃν κατὰ θυμόν,
> ἀρνύμενος ἥν τε ψυχὴν καὶ νόστον ἑταίρων.

> Tell me, Muse, of the man of many ways, who many times
> was driven back, after he had sacked the holy citadel of Troy.
> He saw cities and knew the mind of many men,
> and *suffered many pains* on the sea in his heart,
> struggling for his life and the nostos of his companions.

This programmatic statement immediately establishes a matrix of associations between *algea*, the hero and the story to be told in the announcement (but not full disclosure) of this epic's subject matter.[25] The narrator advertises Odysseus' suffering of many pains in terms of the hero's struggle for his life and for the homecoming of his companions. Significantly, the *Iliad*'s proem also puts a similar stress on "many pains," centering this particular theme as a feature of epic narrative.[26] But important differences remain between the two epics. In the *Iliad* it is the hero's destructive wrath that causes "*countless* pains" for the Achaeans (<u>μυρί'</u> Ἀχαιοῖς <u>ἄλγε'</u> ἔθηκε, *Iliad* 1.2), and sends *many* strong souls of heroes to their death (<u>πολλὰς</u> δ' ἰφθίμους ψυχὰς Ἄϊδι προΐαψεν / ἡρώων, *Iliad* 1.3–4).[27] In this other poem, *algea* belong not to the hero as in the *Odyssey*, but to other men, and to death, not, as in the example of Odysseus, to *surviving*.[28]

---

[25] The historical semantics of *algea* indicates suffering inflicted on others: Meissner 2006:117–118.

[26] In examining wounds in the *Iliad*, Holmes 2007 comments upon the thematic importance of *algea*: a "complex, multi-layered engagement with suffering also inaugurates a tradition of questioning whether those twin pleasantries, undying *kleos* and Helen, justified their costs" (81).

[27] For the theme of Achilles' wrath in the *Iliad* and in archaic Greek poetry in general: Muellner 1996.

[28] Who suffers and how they suffer is not as we might have imagined: Achaeans, not Trojans, suffer many pains as the result of Achilles' rage; they do not receive glory in recompense for their suffering, rather their souls are sent to Hades. This dynamic is part of the double-edged nature of the hero who suffers and causes suffering: Cook 1999.

The attribution of these "pains," via Achilles' wrath, to the will of Zeus (*Iliad* 1.5) provides an interpretative framework for thinking about the theme in the *Iliad*, which in turn helps to inform Odysseus' decision to attribute *algea* to Oedipus. In the *Iliad*'s opening movement, Apollo sends a plague on the Achaean host, for the disrespect that Agamemnon showed his priest, a plague the narrator identifies as *algea* (*Iliad* 1.96 and 110). At the beginning of Book 2, as Zeus ponders how best to put his plan to honor Achilles into action, the false dream that he sends Agamemnon (which will have the ultimate effect of propelling the Achaeans into battle) is described as providing *algea* (*Iliad* 2.39). Later on in that battle Zeus, together with Poseidon, wreaks "bitter pains" on the fighting warriors, since he (Zeus) willed victory for the Trojans in honor of Achilles (*Iliad* 13.346). From these divine perspectives *algea* relate to destruction of the race of heroes who fought and died at Troy.[29] Relatedly, while both Achilles and Agamemnon recognize the pains that their striving has brought them,[30] underlying their quarrel are *algea* that go to the heart of the conflict itself. As we are introduced to Helen for the first time, the Trojan elders comment: "There's no nemesis for *suffering pains* for such a length of time over someone so beautiful" (οὐ νέμεσις Τρῶας καὶ ἐϋκνήμιδας Ἀχαιοὺς / τοιῇδ' ἀμφὶ γυναικὶ πολὺν χρόνον ἄλγεα πάσχειν, *Iliad* 3.156–157). The judgment by the Trojan elders of the pain brought to both sides has echoes of the *Iliad*'s proem. By relating this telling of the Troy story—with its focus on Achilles' wrath—to the broader tradition, which presents Helen as a heaven-sent bane, they gesture towards the overarching cosmic framework, where the Trojan War serves to rid the earth of the race of heroes.[31]

The *algea* that issue from Achilles' wrath, then, express an ever-shifting and ever-expanding web of connections, to which the characters themselves seem to be alert.[32] Menelaos, for example describes how grief comes to him since both

---

[29] Similarly, when Agamemnon attempts a binding oath, he begs *algea* from the gods if he breaks it (19.264). For the gods assigning pains, cf. Hesiod *Works and Days* 741 and Theognis 1187–90. Rijksbaron 1992 notes that *didômi* is used frequently for gods bestowing *algea* on mortals whereas the verb *tithêmi* is used when humans impose them. Cf. Holmes 2007:50.

[30] Forced to reconsider his position by the turbulent events of the second assembly, Agamemnon acknowledges that Zeus "has given him pains" (ἀλλά μοι αἰγίοχος Κρονίδης Ζεὺς ἄλγε' ἔδωκεν, *Iliad* 2.375) by making him fight with Achilles. Achilles himself, when later describing the conflict from his perspective, uses the same language of pain: his loss of Briseis causes him *algea* (*Iliad* 16.55).

[31] The proem of the *Cypria* explicitly connects its narrative to the annihilation of heroes through the resonant phrase "and the will of Zeus was being accomplished." See n39 below. On Helen and the *dios boulê*: Mayer 1996.

[32] Gods suffer *algea* too: Hera suffers thanks to Herakles (*Iliad* 5.394); Zeus intervenes to put a stop to Ares' pains (5.895). Achilles' horses feel *algea* at *Iliad* 18.224. Hephaestus suffered because of Hera but was rescued by Athena (18.395–397); Thetis claims her share of suffering on account of her mortal son (18.429–430).

sides have suffered on account of the quarrel between him and Paris (μάλιστα γὰρ ἄλγος ἱκάνει θυμὸν ἐμὸν, *Iliad* 3.97–98). More strikingly, in his rejection of the embassy in Book 9, Achilles returns to the theme of many pains introduced in the proem, but with an important gloss: he too has suffered many pains, by always risking his life in battle (ἐπεὶ πάθον ἄλγεα θυμῷ / αἰεὶ ἐμὴν ψυχὴν παραβαλλόμενος πολεμίζειν, *Iliad* 9.318–322). In providing this additional scope for "many pains" in the *Iliad*, Achilles is making a rhetorical claim of outstanding performance on the battlefield: he stresses the effort that he has made in order to magnify the insult Agamemnon showed him by taking his prize.[33] Nevertheless, the recurrence of *algea* here marks a striking reversal, even *correction*, of the proem, in which pains were identified as the *object* of his wrath: now, Achilles insists, it is *he* who suffers.[34] This is more in keeping with the suffering hero of the *Odyssey*'s proem than the *Iliad*'s depiction of a people suffering at the hands of Achilles[35] and, along with the comments by the other heroes, shows the increasing human focus of the *Iliad*'s narrative in contrast to the cosmic scope of its beginning.[36]

A final word on the subject belongs to the wife of the man whom Achilles slays. In her lament over Hektor's body, Andromache makes it clear that her husband's death "leaves behind grievous pains" (λελείψεται ἄλγεα λυγρά, 24.742) not only for her, but also for her family and city.[37] With these words Andromache extends the concept of *algea* from the painful striving of the hero to the suffering fate of those who are left behind and dependent on their men—the

---

[33] For other correlations between *algea*, martial toil and death, see *Iliad* 13.670, 17.375, and 21.585.

[34] The *Iliad*'s narrative also dismisses rival claimants for the title of most suffering hero. In the Catalogue of Ships the phrase "suffering pains" (ἄλγεα πάσχων) occurs twice in the same end-line position as in our example of Oedipus' pains—the only two examples of this formula in the *Iliad*, where it serves to mark out two rival heroes, Tlepolemus (*Iliad* 2.667) and Philoctetes (2.721). The formula occurs a further six times in the *Odyssey* (including its use in relation to Oedipus): on each occasion it occurs in character-text (*Odyssey* 4.372; 5.13, 362; 15.232; 19.170), with the exception of a metaphor at *Odyssey* 5.295.

[35] The names of both Achilles and Odysseus may have thematic connection with grief. Achilles, whose name has been etymologized as "woe for the host" may have an essential connection to causing pain: Nagy 1999 [1979]:69–71. Odysseus, whose name has been related to *odusasthai* may be "hated" because of his tricks or he may be hated by the gods and thus suffer, depending on the interpretation of his name: Stanford 1952; Kanavou 2015: 90–101. For wordplay on Odysseus' name, including grief and *dus*-compounds: Louden 1995: 34–37. For etymology and inscriptional evidence: Wachter 2001:265–268.

[36] Cf. Graziosi and Haubold 2005.

[37] Andromache's lament is similar to a partial line from Hesiod's *Works and Days* (τὰ δὲ λείψεται ἄλγεα λυγρὰ / θνητοῖς ἀνθρώποισι, 200–201), where it is Shame and Nemesis (Αἰδὼς καὶ Νέμεσις, 200) who bring pains to the Race of Iron for their misdemeanours. Penelope also notes that pains have been left behind for her (*Odyssey* 19.330).

family unit and the wider political community more broadly.[38] This extension to include the family unit is, as we shall see, critical for the *Odyssey*'s repurposing of "many pains." Furthermore, the idea of leaving behind pains to a loved one is explicitly picked up in our passage, but inverted: it is the wife, Epikastê, who leaves behind pains for the hero, Oedipus.

From this survey of the evidence for the phrase "many pains" in the *Iliad*, two broad conclusions may be reached. First, it appears that the phrase advertises epic subject matter par excellence: "suffering many pains" may be considered a defining feature of epic narrative insofar as it relates to Zeus' plan to rid the world of the race of heroes and the human responses to that.[39] In its instrumentalized form, grief plays a critical role in that plan and is interwoven into the fabric of the story from beginning to end; but it also becomes a dominant theme of the characters' reflections on the conduct of the war. Our second point follows from this last observation: the *Iliad* reveals an ever-broadening range of associations related to an ever-increasing human focus. Its narrative conceives of *algea* not only as pains for the heroes in war, as Zeus' plan determines, and as many heroes, notably Achilles, articulate; it also presents *algea* as a disruption to both family and civic life. All three associations come together over the course of the *Odyssey* with a particular emphasis on those left behind and the survival of the hero.

Suffering pains is central to Odysseus' characterization throughout his poem. In the mouth of the gods, it demonstrates once more the close association between the narrative's subject matter and its structure. After the narrative's opening salvo (*Odyssey* 1.4), Zeus puts pains on the agenda, associating them explicitly with men's responsibility: by their own recklessness men win grief beyond what is fated (1.34). Athena, however, immediately qualifies Zeus' complaints against men, by pointing out that Odysseus suffers grief unjustifiably (*Odyssey* 1.49–50). Five books later, Athena again raises the issue of Odysseus' pains, using an exact replica of the line used of Philoctetes in the

---

[38] Cf. Priam's plea for Hektor to avoid Achilles (*Iliad* 22.53–54). Also of importance is the exchange on *algea* between Achilles and Priam in Book 24. Before he arrives at Achilles' dwelling, Priam ascribes his pains to Zeus (*Iliad* 24.241); Achilles asks Priam to set his grief aside (24.522) and warns him not to cause him more pains (24.568).

[39] In the *Iliad* Zeus' plan is explicitly connected to causing pain for the Achaeans (and Trojans) in the wake of Achilles' absence from battle, through the god's lying dream to Agamemnon, which has the result of intensifying the conflict (*Iliad* 2.39). Even so, the presence in line 1.7 of the formulaic line "and the will of Zeus was being accomplished" means that Zeus' plan also potentially encompasses the entire narrative of the *Iliad*, including the initial quarrel that provokes Achilles' wrath in the first place. For an analysis of the polysemy of Zeus' will, see Clay 1999. For the imperfect tense as emphasizing the incompletion of the plan, see Lynn-George 1988:38. On the *dios boulê* in the wider tradition, in particular the proem of the *Cypria* and the annihilation of the race of Heroes: Mayer 1996 (esp. for Helen); Murnaghan 1997; Marks 2002; Barker 2008.

Iliad (2.721)—another rival suffering hero left behind (and forgotten) on a desert island (5.13). Its occurrence in the *Odyssey*, however, marks the *end* of Odysseus' isolation and the start of his reintegration into the society of men. It marks too the start of the poem's incorporation of his suffering into its narrative.[40]

Algea feature prominently at another crucial juncture later. When Odysseus first arrives back on Ithaca and meets with his guardian goddess, her words to him contain the following advice (*Odyssey* 13.307–310):

> "...σὺ δὲ τετλάμεναι καὶ ἀνάγκη,
> μηδέ τῳ ἐκφάσθαι μήτ' ἀνδρῶν μήτε γυναικῶν,
> πάντων, οὕνεκ' ἄρ' ἦλθες ἀλώμενος, ἀλλὰ σιωπῇ
> <u>πάσχειν ἄλγεα πολλά</u> βίας ὑποδέγμενος ἀνδρῶν."

> "You must by necessity endure,
> and tell no one of all men and women
> that you have come back wandering, but in silence
> *suffer many pains*, accept the violence of men."

Here, Athena instructs Odysseus not to let it be known that he has returned after his wanderings, but rather to suffer his pain in silence. By intimately, yet quite explicitly, connecting Odysseus' many pains to his wandering, Athena recalls the opening lines, which had drawn the same association. In case we had thought that, because his wandering was at an end, so too was his suffering, this restatement of the *Odyssey*'s narrative purpose, roughly midway through the epic, draws attention to the importance of the one remaining obstacle facing Odysseus: that is, to the retaking of his home and household. Only then will our hero truly have achieved his *nostos*. Moreover, it indicates the manner in which the hero will make his *nostos* successful—by suffering in silence and biding his time. The same association is made when husband and wife first meet each other again, as Odysseus relates to Penelope the story of how he has wandered the cities of men suffering pains (19.170).[41] The fact that he tells this story in disguise demonstrates his willing implementation of Athena's plan, even as his account of the stranger's suffering ironically matches the narrator's description

---

[40] *Odyssey* 17.142. For other narrative assessments of Odysseus' suffering, see *Odyssey* 2.343, 5.83, 5.157. 5.336, 5.395, 13.90, 14.32, and 16.19. On the *Odyssey*'s re-start: Segal 1994:124.

[41] The arrival home after suffering grief becomes a dominant trope throughout the epic: Athena figures herself in such a fashion (*Odyssey* 3.232); Peisistratus gnomically reflects on the suffering a son of an absent father experiences (*Odyssey* 4.164). Suffering remains paramount in descriptions of tales that precede the story-time of the *Odyssey*: Nestor describes the continued suffering of the Achaeans (3.220); cf. Achilles' comments at 24.27, or Menelaos' description of his own (4.373).

of his many pains. Even (especially) in disguise Odysseus remains the suffering hero par excellence. In fact Odysseus is a master of testifying to his own suffering, both real and fabricated. In one of his first speeches he predicts that he will suffer greatly before his return home will be complete (5.302),[42] while his story to the Phaiakians, the very frame for his Oedipus story, is dominated by references to his suffering.[43] In many ways Odysseus' story is defined by his willingness and capacity to endure pain.

Yet *algea* do not belong exclusively to Odysseus, and their growing inclusiveness becomes an important part of the story. When he finds out that Athena has let Telemachus go abroad, Odysseus asks whether she did so in order that his son too "would *suffer pains* while wandering over the barren sea" (ἢ ἵνα που καὶ κεῖνος ἀλώμενος ἄλγεα πάσχῃ / πόντον ἐπ' ἀτρύγετον, 13.418–419). In the imagination of his father, Telemachus will return to Ithaca as a comparable example of the suffering hero.[44] Just as going out in search of his father's *kleos* plays an essential part of Telemachus' epic maturation, so his experience of grief ensures his status as his father's son. It is not only Telemachus who shares Odysseus' pain. Earlier, when Odysseus first arrives back in human society and encounters a model, and rival, *oikos*, he has words of advice for its marriageable maiden, Nausikaa. He wishes not only that the gods may grant her a man and a house, but also that she may enjoy *homophrosunê* with her husband.[45] (The *oikos* itself is not sufficient.) He continues (*Odyssey* 6.182–185):

> "οὐ μὲν γὰρ τοῦ γε κρεῖσσον καὶ ἄρειον,
> ἢ ὅθ' ὁμοφρονέοντε νοήμασιν οἶκον ἔχητον
> ἀνὴρ ἠδὲ γυνή· πόλλ' ἄλγεα δυσμενέεσσι,
> χάρματα δ' εὐμενέτῃσι· μάλιστα δέ τ' ἔκλυον αὐτοί."

> "For nothing is better or stronger than this:
> when two people who are likeminded in ideas keep a house,
> a man and woman; *many pains* for their enemies,
> a delight for their friends; but they are especially famous."

---

[42] Cf. *Odyssey* 5.362, 7.212, 8.182, and 19.483.

[43] See *Odyssey* 9.75, 9.121, 10.142, 10.458, 12.427. Odysseus headlines suffering as the dominant theme of his lying tales (see 13.263, 14.310, 15.345, 15.487, and 19.170). Figures whom Odysseus sees in the underworld are ordered by their suffering: both Tantalus and Sisyphus are defined by their eternal torment (11.582 and 593).

[44] The same line is used later when Odysseus finally meets his son (16.189 = 13.310). These are truly the father and son who have both suffered many pains.

[45] Bolmarcich 2001 suggests that Odysseus' words here point to a Penelope who closely resembles him.

Again, in Odysseus' terms of reference, the proper "like-thinking" (*homophrosunê*) that a man and wife share means that in tandem they can give *algea* to others, rather than merely experience it themselves: critically, too, their fame derives from this ability.[46] The sentiment expressed here strikingly foreshadows the end of the *Odyssey*, where the like-mindedness of husband and wife allows Odysseus to be the agent of pains rather than just a victim.

Thus far we have seen not only that *algea* feature prominently in the *Odyssey*'s opening frame and narrative structure; they also has special resonance with Odysseus and his homecoming, particularly in Odysseus' narrative about himself. One consequence of the depth and scope of Odysseus' suffering is the possibility that the poem is positioning itself against the *Iliad*, or, at least, an Iliadic tradition focused on the fight for Troy. In this way, the *Odyssey* appropriates the language of suffering in war and particularizes it within the single example of Odysseus' successful homecoming. In addition, by virtue of this move, the *Odyssey* presents a network of relations that appears to run deeper than that in the *Iliad,* where *algea* are largely connected with the Trojan War and the Achaeans' suffering (especially Achilles'). By way of contrast, in the *Odyssey* the thematization of suffering is extended to the family beyond the individual hero.[47]

An additional point has particular significance for thinking about Odysseus' Theban story. Suffering in the *Odyssey* also relates to rival families and broken homes. On this issue the interplay of *algea* resonates with the *Odyssey*'s focus on generational continuity, in which Odysseus' family excels—a single male inheritance line extends from Laertes through Odysseus to Telemachus.[48] Over the course of its narrative, the *Odyssey* juxtaposes the success of Odysseus' line with that of his fellow warriors at Troy, whether Agamemnon, Achilles or even Nestor.[49] The brief comparison to the House of Laius serves a similar purpose. In

---

[46] Odysseus also shares his *algea* with his family. His continued absence and suffering yields grief that becomes definitive for his wife Penelope (see *Odyssey* 4.722) and his son Telemachus (see 2.41, 2.193, 17.13). When he meets Telemachus for the first time and announces his identity, Odysseus triangulates his identity with his son's suffering: he is the father on whose account Telemachus has suffered greatly (16.189). This shared trait extends to members of his household: Eumaios requests that both of them take a break from their sorrows (15.400–401); at 19.471 Odysseus' nurse experiences grief; the cowherd Philoitios describes his grief at 20.203 and 221. Not surprisingly, it is in part the refusal to accept grief as important that sets the suitors apart from Odysseus and his family: Antinoos trivializes the grief of the cowherd (21.88).

[47] It should be noted, however, that Andromache's pain, articulated at the end of the *Iliad*, goes some way to anticipating this association, and arguably marks the *Iliad*'s response to its rival tradition.

[48] See Goldhill 2010, who discusses the fragility of Odysseus' genealogical line through the use of *mounos* in the speech of Telemachus in *Odyssey* 16. Cf. Chapter 1 n59 above.

[49] Nestor also provides a counter-example to the success of Odysseus' line: his thoughts are still fixed on the son he lost at Troy, Antilochus (*Odyssey* 3.111–112).

contrast to the perfect House of Laertes (grandfather-father-son) is the twisted House of Laius, where generational continuity and patrilineal inheritance have become all confused.[50]

By attributing many pains to Oedipus, therefore, Odysseus draws upon the same type of thematic rivalry through the manipulation and (re)deployment of traditional referentiality that *his* narrator uses to define the *Odyssey*'s world against the *Iliad*'s. By granting Oedipus "many pains," Odysseus marks him out as a potential rival in suffering to his own claim for epic greatness. Of course it comes as no surprise to say that Oedipus' claim hardly stands up to scrutiny; even the structure of the passage, which separates of the adjective πολλά from its noun, ἄλγεα—a separation emphasized by enjambment (τῷ δ᾽ ἄλγεα κάλλιπ᾽ ὀπίσσω / πολλὰ μάλ᾽)—suggests that the attribution of "many" to "pains" comes almost as an afterthought. More telling is the implicit thematic comparison. In the *Odyssey* *algea* resonates with a network of associations with Odysseus and his family, where the comparison to Oedipus could be felt to be particularly charged: Oedipus, the hero who notably does *not* enjoy sound relations with his nearest and dearest, experiences pains *because* of his wife/mother and not *during* an attempt to reunite his family. In this way Odysseus comes off best in their match-up: both figures suffer, but it is Odysseus who suffers (more) for all the right reasons. In addition, by mobilizing his suffering in song and inserting himself for comparison into the canon of heroes, Odysseus will secure passage home and thereby complete his besting of Oedipus. Hence, it is paramount that Oedipus is introduced through his wife and mother, Epikastê, whose "great deed" begins the tale. To better understand her role in the passage, we must first take a more detailed look at Odysseus' catalogue of women and reflect on the importance of form.

A Theban Catalogue of Women

The *Odyssey*'s underworld scene, which depicts the shadowy afterlife of a long cast list and includes cameo appearances by the other Achaean heroes from Troy, is already enough to suggest the poem's rumination on fame and fortune, as well as its capacity to immortalize through epic song. In these terms, Odysseus' narration of the underworld furnishes him with the opportunity to confer his own fame and determine the place of his story in relation to other poetic traditions. Through his interview of former comrades, Odysseus positions his epic tale

---

[50] Slatkin 2005:323 suggests that the other poetic traditions (e.g. "*Telegony*") showed Odysseus pursuing his other options and, crucially, having offspring. While Odysseus' only rival in stringing the bow emerges as his own son, the *Odyssey* "does not pursue the implications of such a rivalry" (326).

in and against the Iliadic tradition (if not our *Iliad*); his reference to the Oedipus story has a similar aim with regard to the traditions surrounding Thebes. But his assault on Thebes is more sustained and more deep-seated than a fleeting mention of a single hero. Odysseus also provides a list of women famous for being the wives or mothers of a range of heroes. Odysseus' continued marginalization of Thebes is not only configured to diminish the content of the Theban traditions; it also represents that content in a *form* particularly associated with Homer's epic rival Hesiod, the poet from Theban Boeotia: the catalogue.

In our introduction we discussed the essential complementarity of Homer and Hesiod.[51] There we explained how these two poets and their poems were enshrined as part of a Panhellenic tradition that was reinforced through performance at public festivals and private symposia, as well as more explicit pedagogic instruction of various kinds.[52] One likely reason for their widespread dissemination, we suggested, relates to how together they chart the history of the cosmos from its origins (a world of gods) to the present day (a world of men), a history in which the *Iliad* and *Odyssey* tell the story (however allusively) of the death of the race of heroes. Another aspect of this movement, which is of critical importance here, is the foundation of a *political* structure embedded within and reliant upon institutions where previously genealogy had held sway. For example, where Zeus achieves cosmic order in the *Theogony* by using his seed to populate the world with heroes, in the Homeric poems order becomes associated with the foundation and realization of institutional practices, which are not only manifest in public forms like the assembly and council or in social bonds like *philia*, *xenia*, and supplication, but also, importantly, are not dependent on individual heroes.[53] Indeed, one key idea of the Homeric poems is the foundation of institutions and practices that will survive long after the race of heroes has been annihilated from the earth, which will provide the people with the security that the heroes promise (in epic formulae like "shepherd of the

---

[51] See Koning 2010 for the association between Homer and Hesiod in modern scholarship (35–39) and in antiquity (41–55). On the complementarity of the pairing in the *Contest of Homer and Hesiod*: Koning 2010:42, 256; cf. Graziosi and Haubold 2005:31. There are frequent attempts to date the two. Janko 2012 argues that cases of archaism diminish from Homer to Hesiod: from the *Iliad* and *Odyssey* to the *Catalogue of Women, Theogony,* and *Works and Days*. West 2012:240 has the following order: Hesiod (*Theogony, Works and Days*) c. 670; *Iliad,* c. 650; *Hymn to Aphrodite,* c. 625; *Odyssey,* c. 610; *Hymn to Demeter,* c. 580; *Catalogue,* c. 540. On the dating of the catalogue to the mid-sixth century: Ormand 2014:3–4. West 1985:130–137 argues for between 580 and 520; Janko 1982:87 suggests sometime as early as the ninth or eighth centuries BCE.

[52] See Graziosi 2010:111–113; Koning 2010 *passim*. Cf. Plato, *Republic* 377c.

[53] Slatkin 2011:161: "Much as the idea of succession linked with cosmic order is not spelled out in the *Iliad* but fundamentally underlies it, similarly, I suggest, the answer to the question of Odyssean δίκη is to be found in reading the *Odyssey* in light of the concept of δίκη as presented in the *Works and Days*."

people") but consistently fail to deliver.[54] In the *Works and Days*, Hesiod reproduces one of those institutional practices—the pursuit of justice—*in the very
structure* of his poem, by representing a case to an addressee (his brother Perses)
with an audience of kings as judges.

On the subject of *poetic form*: despite the extent to which the Hesiodic
and Homeric traditions appear to form a constructive symbiotic relationship
in mapping out the history of the cosmos, there are also critical distinctions
between them, most clearly in respect to this idea of structure. Where Hesiodic
narrative is macrocosmic in scale, Homeric epic operates on the microcosmic;
similarly, where Hesiodic narrative is diegetic, Homeric tends more to the
mimetic.[55] There are also differences in performative persona: the Hesiodic
voice is often more personal and uses biography as part of its authoritative
stance.[56] Significantly, this difference in poetic form is intimately bound up
with the evolution in political form that we sketched out above. As the heroic
epic poem that marks the decisive destruction of the race of heroes (in that
it depicts a "world war"), the *Iliad* is intensely interested in the foundation of
institutions—institutions like the assembly (*agora*) and council (*boulê*), which
will be left behind in their wake. Of particular significance, here, is the *Iliad's*
mimetic representation of these institutions. The assembly (especially) and (to
a lesser extent) the council are constructed in an agonistic form that structures
debate and emphasizes dissent from authority. Responding to these scenes—
trying to interpret and understand them, to find a position between the positions articulated—is similarly open-ended.[57] To put it directly: representations
of the assembly reproduce debate; or: *poetic form* is critical for the realization
of the *political structure*. In contrast a cosmogonic poem like the *Theogony* uses a
different poetic form to capture the political structures so important to its organization of action (and of the cosmos). This is the *genealogical catalogue*.

Just as Homer's representation of the assembly is agonistic, so the catalogue is at once both poetic and political in form. In the emerging Greek poli-
ties, genealogical catalogues were important vehicles for aristocratic groups to

---

[54] See Chapter 5 below. Cf. Haubold 2000, Chapter 1.

[55] See the Introduction ("Why Thebes?") for Hesiod as macrocosmic and Homer as microcosmic;
cf. Slatkin 2011. Koning 2010:116–117 discusses ancient distinctions between: Homer as dramatic
and mimetic, Hesiod as diegetic; Homer as tragic, Hesiod as not; and so on.

[56] Specificity of biography is part of the Hesiodic tradition: Koning 2010:130–132. See Edwards
2004:1–7 for a bibliographical survey and discussion of the historical circumstances reflected in
Hesiod's *Works and Days*, and pp. 19–25 for a discussion of the relationship between the poet, the
poetic persona, literary verisimilitude, and the historicity (or "familiar reality," 25) of the *Works
and Days*.

[57] Barker 2004; Barker 2009, Chapter 1. See also Chapter 5 below. On the intimate, and productive,
dynamic between poetic form (in a text) and political structures (outside it), see now Levine
2005.

communicate and (re)assert their dominance, while also establishing relationships between individual regions and their Panhellenic identities.[58] At the same time, the use of such poetic forms to express and enforce power runs contrary to the growing importance of the city in helping to shape political participation among the population at large.[59] The interplay between local authoritative genealogies and larger Panhellenic identities was complex and moved in multiple directions (as we will discuss in Chapter 6), but one eventual outcome was the limitation of individual claims to preeminence in favor of city-ethnic and larger Greek identities.[60] Even in a local context, then, genealogies were essentially conceived of as backward looking, deriving their force and authority in the present precisely by evoking and reproducing associations with (and in) the past.

A good example of an early Greek poem that occupies a somewhat ambiguous middle ground between these two kinds of poetic traditions and political structures is the *Catalogue of Women*. From what we can tell from its fragmentary remains this Hesiodic poem functioned alongside (and along with) Homeric epic to represent the end of the race of heroes.[61] It also exhibits elements and themes that are familiar from the *Iliad*, in particular the idea of strife (which we will discuss in the following two chapters below).[62] Yet in both orientation and form this poem is very different from the *Iliad*. It interweaves the grand Panhellenic Trojan War narrative with more local, epichoric features, structured along lines of familial and ethnic descent. Moreover, it does so through a complex form that uses a regular formula—*ehoiai* "or such as"—to introduce a new heroine (and the next story) within a broader genealogical superstructure, which brings a degree of order to these individual stories.[63]

---

[58] Fowler 1998:1–5 argues that genealogies are used by those in power to communicate and assert their dominance. According to Ormand 2014:36–37, Hesiod resides on both sides of the ideological divide. Rose 2012:180–186 considers the *Works and Days* to be anti-aristocratic. Clay 2003 prefers to see the two Hesiodic poems as providing complementary perspectives on the world from the Olympian and mortal vantage points.

[59] Ormand 2014:15: early political-poetic discourse shows a progression towards the authority of the *polis* over individual wealthy men.

[60] For political aims of the *Catalogue* see the lengthy discussion by Irwin 2005; more uncertain is D'Alessio 2005:217.

[61] On the *Catalogue* and the destruction of the race of heroes: Koenen 1994. Mayer 1996:2 discusses similarities between the destruction of the Trojan War in the *Cypria* and *Catalogue* fr. 204. Cf. Nagy 1999 [1979]:220; Koenen 1994:27–29. For the *Catalogue* as presenting Helen as a "next-generation Pandora": Ormand 2014:205–210 (quotation from p. 214).

[62] Ormand 2014:79: Competition in bride-gifts (*hedna*) is not about how much a woman is worth but how much a man is capable of paying. On women as a trope in social discourse for instability: Ormand 2014:85; cf. Bergren 1983.

[63] On the tension between the *ehoiai* formula and the genealogical catalogue form: Rutherford 2001. For the term "genealogical superstructure": Irwin 2005:36.

The most famous of these women is Helen, whose entry within the broader genealogical frame introduces another (kind of) catalogue: this additional catalogue within her catalogue entry lists the Achaean heroes who vied with each other to win her hand in marriage.[64] One of these heroes is no other than Odysseus. Even though Odysseus is most famous to us—because of Homer—as the father who returns home to his son and the husband who resists the charms of various women for his wife, the Hesiodic Catalogue nevertheless identifies him as one of Helen's suitors (fr. 198 MW = 154C Most, 2–9):

ἐκ δ᾽ Ἰθάκης ἐμνᾶτο Ὀδυσσῆος ἱερὴ ἴς,
υἱὸς Λαέρταο πολύκροτα μήδεα εἰδώς.
δῶρα μὲν οὔ ποτ᾽ ἔπεμπε τανισφύρου εἵνεκα κούρης·
ἤιδεε γὰρ κατὰ θυμὸν ὅτι ξανθὸς Μενέλαος
νικήσει, κτήνωι γὰρ Ἀχαιῶν φέρτατος ἦεν·
ἀγγελίην δ᾽ αἰεὶ Λακεδαίμονάδε προΐαλλεν
Κάστορί θ᾽ ἱπποδάμωι καὶ ἀεθλοφόρωι Πολυδεύκει.

From Ithaca the sacred force of Odysseus came to woo,
The son of Laertes who knows manifold-made plans.
He did not ever send any gifts for the thin-ankled girl,
For he knew in his heart that fair Menelaos would conquer,
For he was the mightiest of Achaeans in wealth.
But he sent messages to Sparta, always,
To horse-taming Kastor and prize-winning Polydeukes.

There are features of these lines consistent with what we might consider a Homeric Odysseus: this is a clever man, described with a *poly*-compound (πολύκροτα μήδεα), who understands that the nature of the competition for Helen is rigged in another's favor (Menelaos' wealth), and so contrives another way to appeal to the girl (by corresponding with her brothers). The periphrasis used to describe him ("sacred force of Odysseus", Ὀδυσσῆος ἱερὴ ἴς) may also recall the repeated formula for his son Telemachus (e.g "sacred force of Telemachus," ἱερὴ ἲς Τηλεμάχοιο, *Odyssey* 16.476), just as the formula for Menalaos, the "mightiest of the Achaeans" (Ἀχαιῶν φέρτατος) echoes the description of his brother in the *Iliad* (7.289). But this is a wholly Hesiodic setting in which Odysseus, the son of Laertes, is immediately marked out as being a suitor of Helen, whereas in the Homeric tradition Odysseus is famed for being Telemachus' father and the hero who returns home to slaughter the suitors of

---

[64] On this catalogue within a catalogue: Cingano 2005.

his wife.[65] The periphrasis "sacred force of Odysseus" (Ὀδυσσῆος ἱερὴ ἴς) may even hint at the special fecundity of his loins, on which, of course, the *Odyssey* is silent (if knowing, in its depiction of Odysseus' extra-marital affairs) though other narratives were apparently less circumspect. The rest of the *Catalogue* of Helen's suitors serves as a roll call for the Achaeans who went to fight at Troy, and provides the reason for that war: they swore oaths of fealty to whosoever would win Helen's hand.[66]

The story of this catalogued Odysseus, then, is severely limited, an entry within a larger narrative frame and one looking back to his genealogy. As Benjamin Sammons has argued, the catalogue is a device well suited to developing a "historical background to the epic world in which the narrative plays out."[67] Returning to the *Odyssey*'s catalogue of women, we can observe Odysseus participating in this process, doing the work of a poet in selecting, organizing, and presenting the souls of all the women he saw.[68] These women, moreover, are all mentioned in relation to a celebrated hero known to us from tradition, a legendary father, husband, or son. If, as Sammons puts it, the Hesiodic *Catalogue of Women* attempts to create a "comprehensive vision of mythological history,"[69] Homer's Odysseus edits that history down and updates it to include himself. But—and this is not a point that should be lost—his *self* is not yet in the underworld where the other metonyms for these traditions reside. He is very much still in the land of the living, in the guise of the poet telling the tale.

While Odysseus' narrative is a showpiece of the very malleability of myth and narrative,[70] it also engages in intertraditional rivalry not only through its content, which we will explore shortly, but also in its catalogue structure. We have just seen the extent to which Hesiod is associated with catalogue poetry: indeed, one reason why the *Ehoiai* has traditionally been assigned to Hesiod is precisely because of the long series of women who form the basis of the poem. Furthermore, as we noted, the *Ehoiai* uses a genealogical superstructure, which provides the poem with its teleological drive for explaining, and justifying, the current social organization, even if the use of the "or such as" formula at the same time suggests an uncomfortable multiplicity of directions that the story or genealogy might take.[71] In these terms Odysseus' use of the catalogue form

---

[65] For a discussion of Odysseus' importance in this passage, see Cingano 2005:127–135, who notes the tradition that Odysseus came up with the plan of the oath. Cf. Ormand 2014:188–192.
[66] See Tsagalis 2009:174; cf. Ormand 2014:191–192.
[67] Sammons 2010:76.
[68] Sammons 2010:76–78.
[69] Sammons 2010:79.
[70] Slatkin 1996:230; cf. Sammons 2010:85.
[71] Cf. Rutherford 2000:93.

represents something of a Hesiodic poetic stance.[72] That appropriation can be felt more strongly if one considers the fact that nearly all the women he catalogues are of Theban or Minyan ancestry.[73] At the same time, while this catalogue is, again, essentially genealogical—in the sense that Odysseus identifies the heroes born to these women—the lemmata themselves are not genealogically linked: only Tyro and Chloris are related, and even then only indirectly. That is to say, where genealogy provides the *Ehoiai* with a teleological structure (even if it is disrupted by the "or such as" formula), Odysseus' catalogue lacks a genealogical structure of any kind. With genealogy not providing a structure to the catalogue, it leaves open the question what is the principle of selection at stake. Why *these* women, why *this* order, remains something of a conundrum.[74]

Arguably, it is Odysseus himself who provides one answer, in the sense that it is through his eyewitness testimony ("I saw," ἴδον) that he orders the women. While not really resolving the issue—it does not explain the order in which Odysseus sees the women; that remains seemingly arbitrary or, at least, Odysseus' audience is not privy to it—this answer does have the virtue of drawing attention to the importance of Odysseus as a poet in the role of a Hesiod or, even better, an anti-Hesiod. As the poet-hero, he inserts himself into the catalogue, indeed in the two prime positions: he recounts his heartfelt meeting with his mother (or rather her shade) before we even know that he will be recounting a catalogue; directly after the catalogue, Herakles, renowned for his survival after death, compares Odysseus' suffering to his own (as we saw above). Thus Odysseus starts this genealogical history and brings it to a conclusion. His second move is to relegate the catalogue to the world of the dead. As we noted above, catalogues function by drawing a link between present and past. Indeed, they derive their present power precisely from their past associations.[75] In this case, however, there are no such associations: the figures whom Odysseus cites are all (long since) dead and buried; their influence on even the present day of

---

[72] On the *Odyssey*'s catalogue of women: Northrup 1980; Pade 1983; Doherty 1995:66–68; de Jong 2001:281–284. For a recent examination of the Nekyia see Sammons 2006:113–142, who argues that Odysseus' use of the catalogue differs from the narrator's. Our argument here has benefitted greatly from discussion with Irini Kyriakou.

[73] The exceptions are Leda (11.298) and Phaedra, Procris and Ariadne (11.321). The Minyans are presented as Boiotian rivals for the ruling family of Thebes, so this usage here may be part of a larger Odyssean approach; see further in Chapter 6 below.

[74] For suggestions, see Doherty 1995 and Larson 2014. Sammons 2010: 83 is less optimistic: "It remains unclear what kind of selection Odysseus offers (...) if the women of the catalogue do represent a selection, it is unclear what the principle of selection is."

[75] Cf. the introduction by Hunter 2005:3 to the *Ehoiai*: "this poem is one more illustration of the banal truth that social groups explain the present through stories about the past. In this case, the key fact about the present is identity: 'ethnic genealogies were the instrument by which whole social collectives could situate themselves in space and time'" (citing Hall 1997:41).

the *Odyssey* is crucially limited and marginal. There is only one hero whose past still links to the present: that is Odysseus himself, the hero currently singing about his past to help shape and prepare for his future (on Ithaca). Odysseus stands alone as the hero with a genealogy to be sung.[76] Odysseus: first and last and always.

The direct appeal of Odysseus' genealogical catalogue relates to the immediate performance context of the Phaiakian court, in which he is singing for his *nostos*. While his interpoetic agonistics are perhaps most evident in his staged bonhomie with his fellow Trojan War veterans, through the use of the catalogue of women Odysseus seems to have his sights firmly on the queen, Arete.[77] Indeed, we can imagine that Alkinoos' insistence on hearing about Odysseus' Trojan War colleagues is a result of his frustration at having to sit through a list of women whose relevance seems only tangential to the present story[78]—a judgment that in itself continues the *Odyssey*'s marginalization of these other mythical figures and stories. The reason for targeting Arete relates to the instructions with which both Nausikaa and Athena have coached the hero: both identify the queen as being critical to his success in expediting a homecoming (*Odyssey* 6.304–315). Odysseus' choice of a genealogical narrative may even relate specifically to Arete, who herself was introduced by means of a genealogical catalogue. Either way, Odysseus' tactic works and the payoff is immediate. After delivering his catalogue of women, Arete calls for the leading Phaiakian men to give him gifts (*Odyssey* 11.335–341). The Phaiakian queen, at any rate, has been entirely won over by Odysseus' account of famous women.[79]

There remains the question: why does Odysseus list *these women in these ways*?[80] If his goal is solely to win the support of the Phaiakians, we might expect his stories to privilege Poseidon, or at the very least not to conclude

---

[76] On the Hesiodic *Catalogue*'s relationship to the *Odyssey*'s catalogue of women: West 1985:32n7; Barker and Christensen 2008:10n42; Doherty 1995:66n4; Osborne 2005:17; Irwin 2005:49; Tsagarakis 2000:11–12. See Tsagalis 2010:326–328 on the structures.

[77] Before Odysseus arrives at the palace, Athena states quite clearly that if he pleases Arete then he will get to go home (*Odyssey* 7.75–77). Following this, Doherty 1992:168 makes the catalogue's explicit goal the pleasing of Arete. Cf. Wyatt 1989; Doherty 1991. Arft 2014:402 contrasts the catalogue with the martial, androcentric elements of the Nekyia's latter half directed toward Alkinoos. On Arete as audience to the catalogue: Doherty 1995:65–86, 90, 96–99; Slatkin 1996:228–230; Wyatt 1989:239; Tsagarakis 2000:83; Sammons 2010:83–84; Skempis and Ziogas 2009:239; Barker and Christensen 2008:10n43.

[78] Slatkin 1996:230 suggests that Alkinoos requests a different song because he objects to the material; according to Slatkin, Alkinoos expects a "*kleos*-song" which would include different subject matter, and which would be narrative rather than catalogic. Cf. Sammons 2006:125–126.

[79] On similarities between Arete and Penelope as ideal female members of Odysseus' internal audience: Doherty 1995:22, 65–69, 82–83, 92–121, and 76–86 (cf. Doherty 1991 and 1992). Cf. Minchin 2007:20–21; Larson 2014:414.

[80] Vergados 2014:447.

with the story of Eriphyle, who was responsible for the death of her husband, Amphiaraus.[81] Instead, the significance of the women seems to relate to their role as mothers, daughters, wives and mistresses. That is to say, the catalogue has an explicit genealogical focus, where what matters is to draw clear lines of filiation by which a *male* audience would have asserted its traditions, heritage, and even territorial claims. Yet there may be more to it than that. Given the immanent agonistic poetics of a dialogue with the dead and of the catalogue form itself, it is perhaps no surprise that Odysseus' catalogue of women is the episode most densely populated with Theban references in the entire Homeric corpus,[82] as Odysseus appropriates both form and content from the genealogical traditions early audiences would likely have associated with Hesiod. In addition to the high percentage of Theban women (Antiope, Alkmênê, Megare, Epikastê, Eriphyle), the catalogue also incorporates women and material from other major areas of the early Greek world—Thessaly, Pylos, Sparta, Crete, and Athens.[83] In this way Odysseus sets about creating an authorized Panhellenic narrative,[84] exerting control over local content in the manner of a Hesiodic poet to establish the hero as the necessary conclusion of the historical past expressed within the catalogue.

The Theban material, moreover, seems to have an additional charge. Among the heroines of the past Odysseus meets in Hades is Antiope, the mother of Amphion and Zethus, the founders of Thebes (*Odyssey* 11.260–265):

---

[81] A story that is reported at *Odyssey* 15.247.

[82] See Larson 2007 for an outline of Theban-Boiotian associations with the women of the catalogue, especially for an external audience. We are especially indebted to the discussion of Arft 2014.

[83] The catalogue includes thirteen heroines tied to: south-central Thessaly and the Aeolids (Tyro, Iphimedeia); Sparta, the Aeolids, and Athens (Leda); southern Thessaly, Boeotia, and the Aeolids (Chloris); Thebes and Boeotia (Antiope, Alkmênê, Megara, Epikastê, Eriphyle); Boeotia, Thessaly, and Athens (Klymênê); and Athens (Phaedra, Procris, Ariadne). See Vergados 2014:446, cf. 419–420, 426; Larson 2014. The full catalogue (*Odyssey* 11.225–327) reads: Tyro, the daughter of Salmoneus and wife of Kretheus (11.235–259); Antiope, daughter of Asopos, who bore Amphion and Zethus to Zeus (11.260–265); Alkmênê, wife of Amphitryon, and mother of Herakles from Zeus (11.266–268); Megare, daughter of Kreon, wife of Herakles (11.269–270); Epikastê, mother of Oedipus (11.271–280); Chloris, daughter of Amphion and wife of Neleus, mother of Nestor, Chromius, Periclymenus, and Pero who is linked to the Melampus narrative (11.281–297); Leda, wife of Tyndareus, mother of Castor and Pollux (11.298–304); Iphimedeia, mother of Otus and Ephialtes, the two Aloades (11.305–319); Phaedra and Procris (11.320); Ariadne, daughter of Minus (11.320–325); Maera and Klymênê (11.326); Eriphyle, the wife of Amphiaraus for whose death she was responsible (11.326–327).

[84] These regions emphasize areas around Attica and Boeotia specifically, perhaps communicating a positive relationship among these regions and reflecting the historical context of the *Odyssey*'s formation in Athens. On the other hand, it seems just as likely that Homer has Odysseus narrowing down a Panhellenic focus, restricting the range of the genealogy, as he creates more pointed contrasts.

τὴν δὲ μέτ' Ἀντιόπην ἴδον, Ἀσωποῖο θύγατρα,
ἥ δὴ καὶ Διὸς εὔχετ' ἐν ἀγκοίνῃσιν ἰαῦσαι,
καί ῥ' ἔτεκεν δύο παῖδ', Ἀμφίονά τε Ζῆθόν τε,
οἳ πρῶτοι Θήβης ἕδος ἔκτισαν ἑπταπύλοιο
πύργωσάν τ', ἐπεὶ οὐ μὲν ἀπύργωτόν γ' ἐδύναντο
ναιέμεν εὐρύχορον Θήβην, κρατερώ περ ἐόντε.

After her I saw Antiope, who was the daughter
of Asopos, who claimed she had also lain in the embraces
of Zeus, and borne two sons to him, Amphion and Zethus.
These first established the foundations of seven-gated
Thebes, and built the towers, since without towers they could not
     have lived,
for all their strength, in Thebes of the wide spaces. (trans. after
     Lattimore)

The foundation of Thebes was a particularly vexed issue for ancient mythographers.[85] As well as Amphion and Zethus, who are here presented as the first figures to found (ἔκτισαν) Thebes, there is Cadmus, who apparently founded the city on the basis of an oracle from Delphi. While Homeric epic acknowledges the importance of Cadmus in the *Iliad*'s naming of the Thebans as Cadmeans (Καδμεῖοι) and in the presentation of his daughter Ino-Leucothea in the *Odyssey* as a goddess, Odysseus here privileges the Amphion-Zethus narrative as the foundation story, implicitly placing the story of Cadmus later. The reason comes down to walls (again) and the implicit comparison between Thebes and Troy (again). Odysseus presents Amphion and Zethus as the founders of Thebes on the basis that they encircled the city with walls and towers (πύργωσαν),[86] where city foundation is equated with wall building.[87] The same correspondence between wall building and city founding is also found in the *Iliad*, where Poseidon describes how he and Apollo built the Trojan wall and thus made Troy

---

[85] The focus of the episode is on building walls as an act of foundation (11.262–265). To mythographers and scholars, Thebes was notorious for its double foundation myth and the chronological puzzle it creates. Cadmus is responsible for the other act of foundation, having obeyed the Delphic oracle to follow a cow to the site of his future city. The scholia to *Iliad* 13.302 refer to Pherecydes, who states that Amphion and Zethus first built the walls of the city, which was subsequently deserted and refounded by Cadmus (Gantz 1993, no. 41a); cf. the scholia to *Odyssey* 11.262. On the other hand Apollodorus III 5.5, Pausanias IX 5.6, and Diodorus Siculus XIX 53.4–5 all have Cadmus establishing the city first, while the latter two also draw a distinction between Cadmus founding the old city and Amphion and Zethus fortifying the lower city.

[86] Cf. "Hesiod" *Catalogue of Women* fr. 182 M-W. Pindar characterizes his Thebes as the city of Zethus (fr. 52k.44 S-M).

[87] Pache 2014:279–280.

into a *polis* (πολίσσαμεν, *Iliad* 7.453). The differences between these walls are powerful, as we discussed in the Introduction: those of Amphion and Zethus are replaced, while Troy's walls become a vehicle for the generation of *kleos* for the gods who founded them, the men who died around them, and the hero who found a way to get through them—no other, of course, than Odysseus the "city-sacker."

Clearly, then, the *Odyssey* interacts with the Theban material in a different way than the *Iliad*.[88] In the *Iliad* the references to the story of Tydeus were intricately linked to the immediate context. Agamemnon and Athena used a Theban story as a way to chide Diomedes on to performing greater (individual) deeds in battle. Diomedes himself later refers to his father in a prayer to Athena (using her past with Tydeus to win her support), and recalled his father's life when arguing that he too can give good advice in the assembly. In the *Odyssey*, on the other hand, the Theban tales are one tradition among the many that make up Odysseus' *Apologoi*. That is to say, the Theban material does not hold a special position in the broad spectrum of traditions that have been embedded in this epic. Unlike Tydeus' story in the *Iliad* it is neither repeated nor does it have the same (explicit) rhetorical, paradigmatic function. By weaving this colorful tapestry of epic stories Odysseus shows to his audience that he is in command of the entire oeuvre of oral epic. His knowledge is not limited to one kind of story but ranges over, and rummages through, traditions of varying geographic provenance and scope.

Odysseus stands as a performer on his own, appropriating stories from rival traditions and instrumentalizing them to serve his own ends. The hero-cum-poet is not just challenging Hesiodic and Theban themes in order to achieve his *nostos*; he is also reworking those themes to construct the world of home. The geographical references to Thebes and other epic centers of the past (including Athens) create a Hellenic fulcrum around which Homer uses Odysseus to create a new master narrative that places his hero and his universe at its epicenter. Specifically, he uses both Hesiodic form and Theban content to create a catalogue that helps pave the way for the one journey that is still ongoing and not yet complete, his own *nostos* (story). In doing so, he establishes a personal poetic voice that places itself as the necessary conclusion of the historical past expressed within the catalogue. Consigned to the past are heroes like Oedipus, introduced and framed via his Epikastê; how her role as both mother and wife of Oedipus functions within a genealogical catalogue is the subject of our penultimate section.

---

[88] Vergados 2014:448.

A Great Deed

In our analysis of the traditional referentiality of Oedipus' "many pains," we highlighted a meaningful connection between Homeric poetry's conceptualization of the kind of story that is worthy of epic song and the theme of suffering which the protagonist both inflicts and experiences in equal measure. The scope and meaning of the formula subtly changes according to the story-at-large. In Achilles' tale, *algea* are at once the motivation behind his behavior and the consequence of his rage: as his story unwinds, he cannot escape the pains that he has inflicted on his people and he comes to acknowledge his responsibility even for the suffering of an enemy. In the *Odyssey*, *algea* relate to the obstacles to a homecoming (suffering, wandering etc.), on the one hand, and yet, on the other, these are also the very means by which homecoming will be achieved and be worthy of epic song.

There is, then, a changing emphasis in the traditional referentiality of the phrase "many pains" depending upon the interests of the story-frame. Another formulaic unit from Odysseus' Oedipus tale that exhibits a similar pattern of slippage and transformation in early Greek poetry is Epikastê's "great deed" (11.271–274):

> "μητέρα τ' Οἰδιπόδαο ἴδον, καλὴν Ἐπικάστην,
> <u>ἣ μέγα ἔργον</u> ἔρεξεν ἀϊδρείῃσι νόοιο
> γημαμένη ᾧ υἷϊ· ὁ δ' ὃν πατέρ' ἐξεναρίξας
> γῆμεν."

> "And I saw the mother of Oedipus, fair Epikastê,
> who unwittingly did a *great deed*
> by marrying her own son; he, after killing his own father, married her."

In this section we explore how Odysseus' deployment of the phrase "a great deed" markedly differs from its usage elsewhere in Homeric poetry, which in turn sheds light on what Odysseus is *doing* with his Oedipus tale.

The first and most obvious usage of *mega ergon* in Homeric poetry is to denote some kind of exceptional deed. This meaning accounts for the vast majority of cases in the *Iliad*, though only once is it used in this positive sense in the *Odyssey*—and then in the Iliadic battle narrative of *Odyssey* Book 22.[89]

---

[89] See *Iliad* 11.734 (Nestor as narrator), 12.416, 13.366; *Odyssey* 22.408. This pattern seems to continue at Hesiod *Theogony* 954 and *Shield* 22 and 38. Cf. Hesiod frr. 195.22 and 38. On the Iliadic resonances of *Odyssey* Book 22, see Pucci 1987.

A survey of the *Iliad* supplies three further categories, all of which relate to the idea of exceptionality. At *Iliad* 7.444 the phrase explains why the gods are watching the war, because men are performing deeds worthy of note.[90] Twice *mega ergon* describes a deed that can no longer be performed by anyone nowadays (*Iliad* 5.303 and 20.286), as if denoting its specific province as the generation of the past, the race of heroes. Examples in character-speech preserve this sense: combatants use *mega ergon* to denote martial accomplishments of an outstanding nature, which are viewed by the characters themselves in positive light.[91] Hektor, for example, ultimately stands to face Achilles in the hope that he might accomplish "some great deed" (*mega ti*) and achieve eternal fame (*Iliad* 22.304–305.). In the *Iliad*'s world the exceptional deed is almost unambiguously positive as the subject and guarantor of eternal fame, and worthy of epic song.

In the *Odyssey*, with the exception of its occurrence in that Iliadic battle-scene which we have already noted, a less positive meaning accrues to the phrase. Its first instance sets the tone for the "big deed" in the *Odyssey*. Nestor, relating Agamemnon's disastrous homecoming to Telemachus, twice uses the phrase to characterize Aegisthus' plot against Agamemnon, and in particular his seduction of Clytemnestra (*Odyssey* 3.261 and 275). From this point on it becomes a description not only from which the characters distance themselves, but also over which the supporters and enemies of Odysseus do battle. Most conspicuous is Odysseus' use of the phrase to describe his companions' slaughter of the cattle of the Sun (*Odyssey* 12.373), or when he sees the suitors arming with the help of Melanthius (*Odyssey* 22.149); Penelope also uses it of the suitors, because of their behavior towards the beggar (Odysseus: *Odyssey* 18.221). In turn the suitors deploy the phrase when bemoaning Telemachus' odyssey (*Odyssey* 4.663; 16.346). The battle-lines are clearly drawn over the "big deed" in the last pairing in the epic. Eupeithes straight-out accuses Odysseus of having devised a μέγα ἔργον (here: "a monstrous act," 24.426) against the Achaeans, whom Odysseus either led to Troy and destroyed (ἀπὸ δ' ὤλεσε λαούς, 428) or else killed on his return. In response Halitherses condemns the suitors of having wrought a μέγα ἔργον by acting with "evil recklessness" (ἀτασθαλίῃσι κακῇσι, 24.458). Halitherses' condemnation of the suitors in these terms resonates with the poem's opening statement, which frames Odysseus' companions as having lost their homecoming "by their own recklessness" (σφετέρῃσιν ἀτασθαλίῃσιν, 1.7). A "big deed" is nothing to celebrate in this poem.[92]

---

[90] Cf. Hesiod fr. 195.20, where the gods are sitting as witnesses to Amphitryon's "big deed."

[91] *Iliad* 10.282, 16.208, and 19.150.

[92] Cf. *Theogony* 209. Additionally relevant may be the "wondrous deeds" (*theskela erga*) contemplated by Zeus in Herakles' conception, discussed above in Chapter 2, "The Epic Herakles."

Acting as an index for a change of values in heroic poetry, μέγα ἔργον marks the transition as the *Iliad*'s world of heroes gives way to the *Odyssey*'s world of mortals. In the *Iliad* it performs the role of commemorating extraordinary deeds in battle (however much those deeds may themselves be tinged with loss and regret). In the *Odyssey*, whose narrative eschews uncomplicated confrontations in war, it becomes clear that the *mega ergon* has the potential to threaten homecoming, if not deny it altogether. For the *Odyssey*, *mega ergon* means big trouble: it implies that such striving after doing a "big thing," rather than helping men to achieve fame, amounts to overreaching, what early Greek poetry elsewhere would call *hubris*.[93] Such big acts were for a time before; they should now be viewed with suspicion.[94]

Therefore, when Odysseus attributes a *mega ergon* to Epikastê, this is no cause for praise. In fact he goes on to gloss it as having been committed "in the ignorance of her mind" (ἀϊδρείῃσι νόοιο). The phrase is a hapax in Homer, which makes us pause to reflect on how we are to understand Epikastê's "big deed." Elsewhere the root *aïdr-* indicates an ethical judgment, specifically the idea that an action has been foolish. Significantly, forms of ἀϊδρείη occur on three further occasions in Odysseus' song to the Phaiakians. Odysseus has his most alert companion, Eurylochus, twice use it to describe how all the other men follow Circe "in their ignorance."[95] Odysseus also uses it to reflect on the consequences of unwittingly falling into the clutches of the Sirens: he who in ignorance sails his ship too close to them and hears their song does not get home to his wife and child.[96] Again, in the context of post-martial epic poetry, such foolishness may have a direct link to overreaching. In the *Works and Days* Hesiod criticizes men who go to sea in the spring as foolish: their love of money leads directly to evil and death.[97]

---

[93] Although Herakles certainly achieved great deeds, in the *Odyssey*'s narrative these great deeds are subordinated to his unexplained and explicitly unjustified murder of Iphitus.

[94] Solon fr. 4.5–8 draws a similar connection between foolishness, hubristic behavior, and *algea*. He criticizes the community's leaders for their foolishness (ἀφραδίησιν, 5) and arrogance (ὕβριος, 8): this lack of just thinking (ἄδικος νόος, 7) results in great suffering (ἄλγεα πολλά, 8). For a discussion of this passage see Irwin 2005:94–95, and 166–169 for its resonance with Hesiod. The phrase μέγα ἔργον does not occur anywhere else in early Greek poetry, apart from in Pindar *Nemean* 10.64. Its absence from Hesiod's *Works and Days* is most telling: in this poem which makes work a central theme, *erga* describe actions that are not worthy of fame but are everyday, tough, and boring, the necessary hard work that separates the good man from the bad (*Works and Days* 311, 316, 382, 554, 779). Here *erga* simply represent the daily toil that every man must face and suffer, but the performance of which can help men better themselves and achieve a higher ethical standing.

[95] οἱ δ᾽ ἅμα πάντες ἀϊδρείῃσιν ἕποντο (*Odyssey* 10.231, 257).

[96] ὅς τις ἀϊδρείῃ πελάσῃ καὶ φθόγγον ἀκούσῃ / Σειρῆνας, τῷ δ᾽ οὔ τι γυνὴ καὶ νήπια τέκνα / οἴκαδε νοστήσαντι παρίσταται οὐδὲ γάνυνται, *Odyssey* 12.41–43.

[97] Hesiod *Works and Days* 685.

Implicit in the ascription of ignorance to Epikastê, the companions, and the man who sails too close to the Sirens, is the contrast to the teller of the tales, Odysseus. This man is wily, clever, and pointedly *not* unknowing: he is the "man who *knew* the minds of men" (πολλῶν δ' ἀνθρώπων ἴδεν ἄστεα καὶ νόον ἔγνω, *Odyssey* 1.3). In the *Iliad* Odysseus is described as a man who seemed to know nothing (ἀΐδρεϊ φωτὶ ἐοικώς, *Iliad* 3.219), until he spoke, that is.[98] The criterion of knowledge is, in fact, one element that distinguishes Odysseus absolutely from Oedipus, at least in Homer. On the one hand, the ignorance is not even Oedipus' to own (and correct): he remains secondary in this curtailed account, a far cry from the tragic hero who rigorously prosecutes the investigation into his ignorance to its bitter end.[99] On the other, this concern about knowledge—specifically *knowing* one's parents—points to an immanent theme of the *Odyssey*, headlined from the start and a constant source of anxiety throughout. At the beginning of the *Odyssey* Telemachus famously declares that "no one ever *knows* his own father" (οὐ γάρ πώ τις ἑὸν γόνον αὐτὸς ἀνέγνω, *Odyssey* 1.216). A major symbol of his maturation is to be recognized as his father's son, which is what happens in his interviews with Nestor, Menelaos, and Helen (*Odyssey* Books 3 and 4). At the critical moment when he comes face to face with his father, he fails to recognize him and receives a stern paternal rebuke—no other father will return for him, Odysseus announces (*Odyssey* 16.204). Finally, at the point when he—of all the pretenders to his father's throne—is about to string the bow, he desists at the behest of his father's nod (*Odyssey* 21.124–129). In Chapter 2 we suggested that in the *Iliad* the shadow of Herakles haunts Achilles at every turn; in the *Odyssey* it is Telemachus who is stalked by the figure of Oedipus, the single son who didn't know his father and ends up killing him. It is perhaps no coincidence that evidence from one of the fragmentary alternative Odysseus *nostos* stories duly presents a Telemachus who kills his returning father in ignorance of who he was, in the fulfillment of the Odyssean Oedipal nightmare.[100]

It is not only Odysseus who is wily and clever: his wife, Penelope, is too, and she also figures significantly in this Oedipus complex. We have already discussed in the previous section the importance of Odysseus' focus on women in this part of his storytelling endeavor, as he directs his appeal specifically to the Phaiakian queen, Arete. At the same time, the emphasis on female characters also has resonance for the external audience, who at various times are

---

[98] Antenor's description. It is through *speech* that Odysseus sets himself apart and wherein "no other man could rival him" (οὐκ ἂν ἔπειτ' Ὀδυσῆϊ γ' ἐρίσσειε βροτὸς ἄλλος, *Iliad* 3.223).

[99] The vibrancy of Sophocles' *Oedipus Tyrannos* comes from playing on the fact that he is one and the same man, a man with great knowledge who is also ignorant of the most basic facts: his origins.

[100] See n50 above.

subject to Agamemnon's misogynistic rants against his wife, Clytemnestra, Helen's strange (and dangerously seductive) stories about her role in the fall of Troy, and, during the Apologoi, the strong presence of the Phaiakian queen and various other powerful females (from the witch Circe to the monstrous pair, Scylla and Charybdis). In a curious way the *Odyssey* presents its *own* catalogue of women as part of its narrative arc, starting with the goddess Kalypso, who promises Odysseus immortality, and ending with his wife, Penelope, for whom Odysseus rejects Kalypso's offer and to whom he returns home. Each entry in this list along the way contributes to the epic's depiction of women, concerns about familial relationships between the genders, the proper organization of home and household, and, above all, *genealogical continuity.*[101]

In the brief description of Epikastê, several themes are deployed that resonate with the characterization of Penelope. Both are ignorant of their husbands' whereabouts; both have a maturing, and suffering, son; both perform a "great deed." Penelope's is her weaving and unweaving of the death shroud for Laertes, narrated for the first time by Antinoos (2.93–106):

> ἡ δὲ δόλον τόνδ' ἄλλον ἐνὶ φρεσὶ μερμήριξε·
> στησαμένη μέγαν ἱστὸν ἐνὶ μεγάροισιν ὕφαινε,
> λεπτὸν καὶ περίμετρον· ἄφαρ δ' ἡμῖν μετέειπε·
> κοῦροι, ἐμοὶ μνηστῆρες, ἐπεὶ θάνε δῖος Ὀδυσσεύς,
> μίμνετ' ἐπειγόμενοι <u>τὸν ἐμὸν γάμον</u>, εἰς ὅ κε φᾶρος
> ἐκτελέσω, μή μοι μεταμώνια νήματ' ὄληται,
> Λαέρτῃ ἥρωϊ ταφήϊον, εἰς ὅτε κέν μιν
> μοῖρ' ὀλοὴ καθέλῃσι τανηλεγέος θανάτοιο,
> μή τίς μοι κατὰ δῆμον Ἀχαιϊάδων νεμεσήσῃ,
> αἴ κεν ἄτερ σπείρου κεῖται πολλὰ κτεατίσσας.
> ὣς ἔφαθ', ἡμῖν δ' αὖτ' ἐπεπείθετο θυμὸς ἀγήνωρ.
> ἔνθα καὶ ἠματίη μὲν ὑφαίνεσκεν <u>μέγαν ἱστόν</u>,
> νύκτας δ' ἀλλύεσκεν, ἐπὴν δαΐδας παραθεῖτο.
> ὣς τρίετες μὲν ἔληθε δόλῳ καὶ ἔπειθεν Ἀχαιούς·
> ἀλλ' ὅτε τέτρατον ἦλθεν ἔτος καὶ ἐπήλυθον ὧραι,
> καὶ τότε δή τις ἔειπε γυναικῶν, ἣ σάφα ᾔδη,
> καὶ τήν γ' ἀλλύουσαν ἐφεύρομεν <u>ἀγλαὸν ἱστόν</u>.
> ὣς τὸ μὲν ἐξετέλεσσε καὶ οὐκ ἐθέλουσ', ὑπ' ἀνάγκης·

---

[101] The *Odyssey* is intimately concerned with generational continuity, specifically the triple-generation of grandfather, father, and son: Goldhill 1991, Chapter 1; Felson 2002. The dissonance between Odysseus' claim that the gods made Oedipus' tale known among men and his own reluctance to elaborate on it may be a feature of the *Odyssey*'s general privileging of Odysseus' unbroken family line above all others.

"And she was devising this different trick in her thoughts:
She was weaving on the great loom she set up in her home,
A work of fine and very long threads. Then she announced to us:
"Young men, my suitors, since shining Odysseus has died
Wait here pursuing my hand in marriage until I complete
This garment, that my weaving might not be pointless,
A shroud for the hero Laertes, for when the ruinous fate
Of dreadful death comes over him,
And then no one of the Achaean women among the people
May criticize me if this man of great wealth lies without covering."
So she spoke and each of our proud hearts was persuaded.
And thereafter she was weaving on the great loom each day
But by night she set out torches and took it apart.
She tricked us this way for three years—she persuaded the Achaeans!
But when the fourth year came and the seasons were passing by,
One of the women who knew the matter clearly, informed us.
Then we discovered her unweaving the shining cloth by night.
So we made her, even though she was unwilling, finish it, under
    force."

The importance of this moment is underlined by the fact that it is recounted a further two times, each time from a different perspective.[102] We have already noted that Homer avoids calling Penelope's great deed by its name; yet there remains a tantalizing thread that ties Penelope's weaving to the deed of Oedipus' mother/wife. When Odysseus describes Epikastê's "great deed" (μέγα ἔργον), he first correlates it with her ignorance (ἀϊδρείῃσι νόοιο) and then hints darkly at the deed itself using the chiastic repetition of two verbal forms for the term "to marry": she did a great deed in the ignorance of her mind "by *marrying* her son; for, after slaying his father, he *married* her" (γημαμένη ᾧ υἷϊ ὁ δ' ὃν πατέρ' ἐξεναρίξας / γῆμεν). In this earlier episode, while Antinoos does not use the phrase "great deed" (μέγα ἔργον), he does use the metrically equivalent (and similar sounding) μέγαν ἱστόν, meaning the "great work" of the web the means by which Penelope accomplishes her great deed. Given their familiarity with

---

[102] Penelope narrates the tale to a disguised Odysseus (19.137–161); the suitor Amphimedon retells the story to the assembled souls in Hades (24.125–155). For a discussion of the scenes and their differences: Lowenstam 2000. For the suggestion that the shroud actually becomes the robe Penelope gives to Odysseus' in disguise: Whallon 2000. On weaving and female fame: Mueller 2010. For Penelope as a weaver of plots: Murnaghan 1987:95–96. On weaving in the *Odyssey* and *mêtis*: Slatkin 1996:234–237; Clayton 2004 *passim*. For the possibility that in other traditions of Odysseus' return home Laertes and Penelope were colluding: Haller 2013.

the widespread use and traditional referentiality of the phrase "great deed" in the Homeric corpus, an audience might hear a distant echo of Penelope's μέγαν ἱστόν in Epikastê's μέγα ἔργον. In addition, while Epikastê (precipitously) entered into marriage with her son (her μέγα ἔργον) in ignorance, by means of her μέγαν ἱστόν Penelope has been successfully deferring her own marriage to a suitor for years. The fact that she has achieved this deferral by means of her intelligence—an intelligence that, moreover, mirrors her "like-minded" husband's—also shows her difference from the unknowing Epikastê. Effectively cast as a figure far surpassing Epikastê, Penelope knows who her son is; commits a great deed through intelligence rather than without it; and acts, even if briefly, as an agent winning positive fame of her own.

Thus Odysseus' description of Oedipus and Epikastê has resonance in the poem far beyond his own self-aggrandizement, and importantly so. For Odysseus to achieve a proper homecoming, not only does he need to get home to his family; they—his wife and son—need to be part of it. Telemachus and Penelope have critical roles to play. In his fleeting representation of an Oedipus story, Odysseus provides a glimpse of the counter-model from the tradition, where the roles of father, son, and mother are hopelessly, and horrendously, mixed up.

Much-loved Thebes

We learn very little about Oedipus and his pains in the *Odyssey*, and what we do learn contrasts negatively with the example provided by Odysseus. Unlike Odysseus, whose wandering is implicit in the narrative and explicit in his own statements,[103] Oedipus' suffering comes not from wandering but from his over-determined familial relations with his mother/wife. Such a relationship represents an inversion of what happens in Odysseus' tales, where suffering precedes *nostos* and punishment is for those who prevent it. In spite of the resonant phrase "he suffered many pains," Oedipus does not turn out to be *that* much of a suffering hero—at least not in comparison to Odysseus (or, for that matter, the suffering Achaeans of the Iliadic tradition). From the perspective of Epikastê's "big deed," too, Oedipus does not display the same exceptionality in action that other heroes achieve elsewhere in the Homeric corpus. Instead his heroic career is framed indefinitely by the actions of his wife/mother. Upon learning of her "big deed"—taking her son as her husband—Epikastê takes her own life and descends into Hades, leaving Oedipus to live out his suffering alone and yet also to continue to rule over Thebes (*Odyssey* 11.276).

---

[103] E.g. *Odyssey* 19.168–170.

Being left to rule on in Thebes is indicative of Oedipus' passivity in this episode and again suggests a careful delineation of his suffering, as if the death of Epikastê had no impact on his subsequent life or leadership of the city. Interestingly, the basis for Oedipus ruling on is ascribed to the "the baleful plans of the gods" (θεῶν ὀλοὰς διὰ βουλάς, *Odyssey* 11.276). Elsewhere in early Greek hexameter poetry the planning of the gods is connected to the generation of epic narrative. This process is most transparent when the poet invokes the muse at the beginning of the *Iliad* and *Odyssey*; but Zeus' planning—or, better, *plotting*—is also prominent at the beginning of both Homeric epics, implicit in the phrase "and the will/plan of Zeus was being accomplished" (which fr. 1 of the *Cypria* also headlines) and explicit in the *Odyssey* where Zeus himself sets the agenda for the epic (with Athena's help).[104] In response to the actions of another rival figure, the hero Aegisthus, Zeus straightaway pronounces that mortals are always blaming the gods for their ills "when in fact they themselves suffer pain beyond their lot because of their own recklessness!" (*Odyssey* 1.32-34).[105] Athena, however, immediately contests the extent to which this opening declaration applies to Odysseus, and Zeus readily demurs. With this divine support, and in particular through the planning of Athena, Odysseus will bring destruction to his enemies. Thus it comes to pass that Odysseus is presently recounting a narrative of his suffering—a clear indication if there ever was one that he now enjoys the gods' full, if not unanimous, support. Here Odysseus' ascription of plans to unnamed gods may reflect his status as a human narrator (without privileged access to Olympus), or else a plurality that suggests no single narrative line. Either way, the description of their plans as baleful, *destructive*, critically defines Oedipus' rule in Thebes: whatever we might think about the detail that he continues to lead the city, in spite of everything, it is not to be considered a good thing. Where Odysseus suffers for his epic, there is no positive gloss to be put on the (vastly inferior) suffering of Oedipus.

While Oedipus rules on indefinitely, Epikastê's "great deed" of marrying her son is made known to men immediately (ἄφαρ δ; ἀνάπυστα θεοὶ θέσαν ἀνθρώποισιν, 11.274). Again, we are invited to draw a comparison with Odysseus'

---

[104] *Iliad* 1.5-6; *Cypria* fr. 1. Both epics too are sporadically punctuated with the further plotting of the action by certain gods. At *Iliad* 15.71, when Zeus delivers his most detailed articulation of his plan yet, he ascribes it to "the plans of Athena" (Ἀθηναίης διὰ βουλάς). At *Odyssey* 8.82 Demodokos' song about the Trojan War has the similar phrase Διὸς μεγάλου διὰ βουλάς, where the plotting is again assigned to Zeus. Cf. Hesiod *Theogony* 465 and 572. In what appears to be an arresting modification of the formula, Odysseus commiserates with Agamemnon over his fate by blaming "feminine plans" (γυναικείας διὰ βουλάς, 11.437).

[105] As Olson 1995:214 puts it, "The *Odyssey* is thus above all else a story of the troubles human beings bring upon themselves." For Zeus' view as more advanced moral thought: Finkelberg 1995; cf. Russo 1968: 288-295; Gill 1996:46n59.

own situation and narrative. The adverb "immediately" (ἄφαρ) contrasts with the gradual unwinding of (this) epic narrative, a process that is exemplified by the *Odyssey*'s concealment of the "man" of the story for a full five books and by Odysseus' deferred disclosure of his name in the Phaiakian narrative.[106] The use of the adjective "notorious" (ἀνάπυστα) with the unspecified divine agency further underlines the disjunction between the two scenarios. Odysseus is not only the subject of epic fame, in these books he is actively performing it. Even as he refers to Oedipus' story, by describing Epikastê's deed as notorious, he deprives his rival of the kind of vocabulary that would endow him with the fame worthy of a hero.[107] Still more striking is the identity of the group to whom the gods make known Oedipus' calamity. Where one may have expected a name for Oedipus' immediate group, such as his "people" (*laos*) or "townspeople" (*astoi*), both of whom, one might think, the gods ought to have told about Oedipus, Odysseus uses the word "humankind" (*anthrōpoi*). As this translation suggests, the nomenclature of *anthrōpoi* frequently occurs in generalized expressions: for our purposes two instances are particularly telling. In the *Iliad* Helen uses this label as she comments on her place within the poetic tradition (*Iliad* 6.388). Odysseus himself uses the term at the beginning of his tale to the Phaiakians to assert that he is the subject of song among all folk because of his trickery (ὃς πᾶσι δόλοισιν / ἀνθρώποισι μέλω, *Odyssey* 9.19–20). Odysseus' identification of this group as the recipients of the gods' revelation, then, slyly gestures towards the broadcast of his rival's narrative tradition, even as the *Odyssey* silences it.

Throughout this chapter we have been tracing the traditional referentiality of the language that Odysseus uses to describe Oedipus' suffering and Epikastê's infamous deed, with the aim of teasing out the implications for thinking about Odysseus' self-representation as the hero whose song is in performance. In this last section we turned to consider Odysseus' broader description of Oedipus' story in the framework of divine plotting and revelation. We close by reflecting on Odysseus' description of Thebes itself as πολυήρατος ("much-loved").

[106] Slatkin 2005:315–316. On Odysseus' disguise and gradual self-disclosure: Murnaghan 1987.

[107] Other uses of *anapusta* may support this assertion. The scholion (B 11.274.1) glosses it as meaning "spoken of and learned about through the mouths of everyone; or, manifest." Herodotus uses it where facts become known without any specifically noted agent (with some negative connotation): in Book 6 *anapusta* refers to the Spartan king Demaratus' suspect paternity (VI 64.3) and to the debasement of the Delphic oracle through Cleomenes' bribery (VI 66.10–12). In Book 9 of the *Histories* it describes Xerxes' domestic strife: his lust for the daughter of his own brother, Masistes, leads him to kill his brother, while his wife takes revenge on Masistes' wife. In all three of these cases, Herodotus uses the adjective to describe the revelation of unseemly information. Pausanias (IX 5.11) takes issue with Homer's account that Oedipus' marriage to his mother was *anapusta*: he does not see how Epikastê could have then given birth to four children with Oedipus. His own version assigns these four children to Oedipus' second wife Euryganeia. Cf. Pherecydes fr. 48 (= scholion to Euripides *Phoenician Women* 53).

Elsewhere in the *Odyssey* (it has no occurrences in the *Iliad*) πολυήρατος is best translated as "much-loved" or "very lovely." Helen gives Telemachus a gift for his "much-loved" wedding (*Odyssey* 15.126); Eumaios talks about arriving at "much-loved" youth (*Odyssey* 15.366); Odysseus looks forward with Penelope to going to their "much-loved" bed (*Odyssey* 23.354).[108] In the present context, however, the epithet "much-loved" or "very lovely" hardly seems appropriate to denote the Thebes of Oedipus and Epikastê.[109] In describing Thebes as πολυήρατος Odysseus is, at face value, possibly toying with what is conventionally known of Thebes as the place where bad stuff happens.

Odysseus' choice of words caused a scholiast to the *Odyssey* so much anxiety that he sought to clarify the sense of the word and find an alternative etymology (Σ *Odyssey* 11.275 Dindorf):

πολυηράτῳ] πολλὰς ἀρὰς καὶ βλάβας ὑπομεινάσῃ παρὰ θεῶν. B. Q. V. οὐ γὰρ ἐρασμίῳ· ὅπως ἂν ᾖ τῷ ὑποκειμένῳ ἀκόλουθον. V.

much-cursed] in that Thebes experienced many injuries and curses from the gods. In whatever way it is consistent with its subject [Thebes], it does not mean "lovely."

According to the scholiast, πολυήρατος is better understood to mean "much cursed."[110] While the scholiast would appear to be importing knowledge of the Theban tradition into his explanation, the adjective is, as Justin Arft has explained, "morphologically ambiguous enough to suggest forms of ἀράομαι and ἐράω."[111] Moreover, the apparent contradiction potentially "alerts us to a clever, layered association exploited by Odysseus," where the hero utilizes precisely the ambiguity in the epithet.[112] Given Epikastê's "great deed" of sleeping with her son, Thebes may indeed deserve an epithet that indicates its *loveliness*: its ruling family *is* much loved, excessively so, as the son marries his mother and begets his own brothers and sisters.[113] The "associations of both *eros*-heavy and

---

[108] Cf. Hesiod *Theogony* 404.

[109] There is only one "lovely" city in the *Iliad*, and this is the city depicted on Achilles' shield as being under siege (*Iliad* 18.509–512). As Pache 2014:286–287 notes, the epithet ἐπήρατος is unusual and echoes the Odyssean passage about πολυήρατος Thebes. Along with this epithet, the themes of a city under siege and a division of spoils resonates with the Theban tradition. See Chapter 5 below.

[110] Cf. ἡρᾶτο, *Thebais* fr. 2.8.

[111] Arft 2014:404.

[112] Arft 2014:404–405.

[113] Cf. the theme of Telemachus not becoming his father. The briefly unburied status of the suitors and the split judgment of their families over how to respond to their deaths in Book 24 recall themes from Theban myth. See Chapter 5 below.

cursed"[114] within the epithet πολυηράτος points to a family that could not be further removed from the perfect single male-line genealogy of the *Odyssey*. Moreover, as Odysseus puts it, while Oedipus ruled on in "much-loved Thebes," his mother/wife descended into Hades (ἀλλ ὁ μὲν ἐν Θήβῃ <u>πολυηράτῳ</u>... / ἡ δ' ἔβη εἰς Ἀΐδαο <u>πυλάρταο</u>, 11.227–228).[115] The metrical and syntactical correspondence between the two lines and two epithets <u>πολυηράτῳ</u> and <u>πυλάρταο</u> creates a jingling effect that underlines the *relations* between the two events. Epikastê has to die because her son-husband rules on. (Or does Oedipus have to continue to rule Thebes because his mother-wife is dead?) In contrast, Penelope and Telemachus wait in Ithaca for their husband and father (respectively) to return from his meeting with the souls of the dead.

The explosive charge of πολυήρατος as vacillating between much-loved and much-cursed creates aftershocks through the entire catalogue.[116] As Justin Arft has shown, the adjective πολυήρατος also aligns with an intratextual network of curse-associations. Odysseus himself occupies this ambiguous space as the one who is πολυάρητος, "much *prayed for*." Nausikaa introduces Odysseus in these terms at the beginning of the episode on Phaiakia (*Odyssey* 6.280). Later, in the famous digression on Odysseus' scar, he is described in the exact same terms by Autolykos (*Odyssey* 19.404). Yet, as the name given to him by his maternal grandfather suggests—Odysseus as the one who both suffers and causes suffering—he is also "much cursed" (*Odyssey* 19.407–409). The same suggestion is borne by the name *Arete*, which is not only associated with beseeching, praying, or even silence, but also implies *being* "accursed."[117]

With this in mind it is worthwhile reconsidering Odysseus' special appeal to Arete, for whose benefit the catalogue of women, and this Oedipal story, is being narrated. Take, for example, the final woman in the catalogue, who also comes from Thebes: "hateful Eriphyle" (στυγερήν τ' Ἐριφύλην, *Odyssey*

---

[114] Arft 2014:404

[115] This expression, εἰς Ἀΐδαο πυλάρταο, resonates exactly with two episodes in the *Iliad*. According to Athena, when Herakles was sent into Hades, she had to come to his aid (*Iliad* 8.367). Deiphobus boasts that he will send his opponent to accompany their dead comrade to Hades (*Iliad* 13.415). More broadly, the image of going to Hades recalls the *Iliad*'s proem (*Iliad* 1.3–4).

[116] Within this performance arena, the individual words are "explosively connotative" (cf. Foley 1999:xii, 305) with traditional associations, retaining aspects of their history, but shaped anew in each recurrence.

[117] For the most detailed etymology of the name Arete, see Skempis and Ziogas 200:215–228 with attendant bibliography. For an objection to a derivation from *araomai*, see Peradotto 1990:108. Other etymologies include "unspoken" (*ar(r)êton*) and a derivation from *arariskô*: see Kanavou 2015:124–125. Special thanks to Justin Arft for this note.

11.326).[118] As the heroine with the only negative epithet in the catalogue,[119] the appearance of Eriphyle both contrasts to the previous entries (e.g. καλήν τ' Ἀριάδνην, *Odyssey* 11.321), and prompts scrutiny of what it is that she has done which might warrant such a description. This appears to be her betrayal of Amphiaraus and her matricide at the hands of Alcmaon. While the theme of the treacherous wife resonates broadly with the actions of Clytemnestra, the adjective στυγερήν phraseologically aligns the heroine more specifically with Clytemnestra's "baneful song" (στυγερὴ δέ τ' ἀοιδή, *Odyssey* 24.200) and recalls that woman's description as a "baneful mother" (μητρός τε στυγερῆς, *Odyssey* 3.310), even if the poem remains silent on the matricide itself.[120] In fact, the suppression of Clytemnestra's matricide represents an important recalibration of the specific *nostos* theme of the threat of the deceitful wife at home waiting for the returning hero. The omission not only, of course, renders Orestes a more suitable model for Telemachus, as a dutiful son who resists his father's usurper(s) (and not the son who kills his mother); it limits Clytemnestra's role to that of husband-destroyer, a destroyer of *nostos*, and not as a victim of matricide.[121] Heard against this background, Odysseus' parting shot at the "hateful Eriphyle," the matricide, threatens to expose the logic of his catalogue—which has been precisely about *ordering* women—and (re)open up the fissures within this *nostos* narrative, where there is an uncertainty, even anxiety, about what kind of a woman Arete (and Penelope?) will turn out to be.

The critical moment is marked by the silence that greets Odysseus' account, that very special kind of audience response that signifies the withholding of consent, familiar from scenes in the *Iliad*.[122] But, where in the *Iliad* stunned silence represents a breakdown in communication, here it signifies its inverse, a kind of excess of communication where the audience are held in awe of—or spellbound by—what they have heard. Or, at least, this is how Arete interprets

---

[118] Arft 2014: 406–409

[119] A feature that differentiates this catalogue from the more universally positive Hesiodic *Catalogue*. Consistent with *ehoie*-poetry, Epikastê is introduced as καλήν: Arft 2014:403.

[120] Commenting on this striking omission, the scholia to *Odyssey* 3.309–310 and 3.310 draw an even more direct, extratextual connection between Eriphyle and Clytemnestra. These heroines seem to be something of a multiform pairing, at least by the time of the scholiast. Cf. Aristotle (*Poetics* 1453b22–25): "[The poet] should not break up traditional tales; for example, the story where Clytemnestra is killed by Orestes and Eriphyle by Alcmaon." Aristotle not only pairs Eriphyle and Clytemnestra, but also suggests that each mother-son unit represents a similar, coherent story pattern consisting of "traditional" elements (παρειλημμένους) that deserved preservation and were subject to artistic variation.

[121] Arft 2014:409.

[122] For example, the silence that greets Achilles' rejection of Odysseus' offer of recompense: "so he spoke, and all were in silence for a long time" (ὣς ἔφαθ', οἱ δ' ἄρα πάντες ἀκὴν ἐγένοντο σιωπῇ, *Iliad* 9.430).

it, as she describes how Odysseus' song has held them in thrall.[123] Regarding this woman, then, Odysseus need have no concerns: addressing the assembly Arete quashes any lingering doubts that the hero will not make it back home and urges her fellow Phaiakians to shower him with the guest-gifts appropriate for a returning Trojan War hero.

And yet, at the same time, precisely by playing the role of Odysseus' "hoped-for prayer" she brings down a great *curse* on her city and people. It will be as a direct result of the help that the Phaiakians give Odysseus that Poseidon will hide them away forevermore and after. Odysseus himself is entangled in the very language of this curse. Upon his arrival on Skheria, he is likened to a firebrand (δαλόν, *Odyssey* 5.488), as he buries himself (καλύψατο, *Odyssey* 5.491) in the ground, and covers his head (ἀμφικαλύψας, *Odyssey* 5.493). This passage resonates strongly not only with the prophesied destruction of the city (μέγα δ' ἡμῖν ὅρος πόλει <u>ἀμφικαλύψειν</u>, *Odyssey* 8.571), but also with Demodokos' song about the Trojan horse—wherein the city was fated to be destroyed "whenever it concealed" the horse (αἶσα γὰρ ἦν ἀπολέσθαι, ἐπὴν πόλις <u>ἀμφικαλύψῃ</u> δουράτεον μέγαν ἵππον..., *Odyssey* 8.510–511)—a story not only requested by and featuring Odysseus, but one that serves to introduce him to his Phaiakian guests. Arete's connection to the destruction of the city and her eventual gift-giving aligns her with elements of Eriphyle's tale. These associations reinforce the danger both Odysseus and Arete represent for the Phaiakians.

Conclusion

Thus far in this book we have been working with the hypothesis that Thebes and Troy may have been equally important mythscapes for archaic Greek poetry. While we have lost much of the Theban tradition, a multitude of instances where Homer appears to be including details from Theban tales in his poems remains. Rather than viewing such moments as faithful representations out of which one can reconstruct a Theban epic, we have tried to show the value of examining such intersections through the prism of poetic rivalry to shed light

---

[123] As well as the "enchanted" reaction of the Phaiakians (*Odyssey* 11.333–334=13.1–2), see also Alkinoos' positive evaluations of Odysseus' tales (*Odyssey* 11.363–376 and 13.4–15). The diction of Odysseus' "enchantment" is intriguing: κηληθμός occurs only in these two passages in the *Odyssey*. The BV scholion to *Odyssey* 11.334 glosses the noun as granting pleasure (*hêdonê*) and delight (*terpsis*). Cf. Eusthathius *Commentary on Homer's Odyssey* I 422.28-34 for etymological speculations. The lexical item itself is rare in Archaic and Classical Greek, appearing in Plato's *Republic* to describe snake-charming (358b3) and the type of pleasure that misleads men to change their opinions (413c2). On varieties of enchantment in the *Odyssey*: Walsh 1984. On the assessment that Homeric poetry enchants, see the result of the *Contest of Homer and Hesiod* (205), with Graziosi 2002:172–182.

on the narrative strategies of the Homeric poems. This work has been grounded in oral-formulaic theory, which, we have suggested, is better attuned to listening out for the deployment of resonant themes and issues than our more familiar literary paradigms.

In this chapter we have used such an approach to explore the ways in which Odysseus constructs a version of Oedipus as a comparandum for his own epic deeds. By focusing on the poetics of suffering, we have shown that not only is the accumulation of pain a significant feature of a hero's story, but that suffering acquires context-specific value. In the *Iliad* it is connected to martial achievement and the tragedy of Achilles' fame. In the *Odyssey* it becomes the very thing that makes Odysseus' *nostos* possible (as well as worth remembering). An analysis of Epikastê's *mega ergon* confirms the extent to which Odysseus manipulates both the details of the Oedipal tale and the diction of epic poetry itself to magnify his own status. In Odysseus' tale his suffering becomes the very standard against which all songs should be measured: suffering takes on moral meaning and functions as part of the ethical thrust of the *Odyssey* as a whole. This final analysis, we believe, is valuable because it points to Odysseus' attempts to suppress, edit, or otherwise manipulate other poetic traditions in the service of his tale. Such a strategy, we believe, is akin to that which heroic epic poets would have taken when struggling in their effort to make their song of many pains the most bewitching and orderly.

At the level of narrative structure, the *Odyssey* tradition seems to be trivializing the Oedipus tale by subordinating it within the account of Odysseus' greater sufferings. At the microcosmic level of narrative dynamics, we see Odysseus manipulating the tale to match his: he appropriates a traditional tale (and narrative device—the catalogue form) and tells it in a persuasive way to convince Arete and Alkinoos to help bring an end to his *algea*. At this point Odysseus is also suffering many pains, but, by getting home, he will ultimately endure and inflict suffering on others—namely the suitors currently eating him out of house and home. Indeed, this very story will help him achieve that end.[124] Furthermore, the Oedipus story carries with it the implicit counter-model of an imperfect homecoming, as Odysseus articulates the fear that Penelope will sleep with a stranger—as she does, apparently, in alternative traditions. In the *Odyssey*'s very carefully delineated storyworld the lesson is clear: look what happens when you do. Yes, Odysseus *will* come back as a stranger; but beneath the disguise lies the legitimate king and—more importantly—the legitimate

---

[124] Not that Odysseus' pains are to end even with the end of the *Odyssey*: Teiresias foretells of still more wandering (and suffering) to come (*Odyssey* 11.121-37). See Chapter 5, "Enduring Strife, Surviving Epic."

husband who will reclaim both his throne and his wife and be reunited with his son.

Singers in traditional situations do not slavishly repeat the songs they have heard; they manipulate the tensions inherent in a system of repetition and iteration to perform new songs that *sound old*. From the use of a single word to the abridgment or alteration of other tales, the oral poet challenges himself and his audience by reinterpreting their collective inheritance. We are reasonably confident that this is what Odysseus is doing when he sings of Oedipus' pains. What the passage of time *and* the poetic strategies themselves have obscured for us, however, is how deeply Homer has done the same.

The rest of this book turns to ponder this question more fully. Whereas these first three chapters of our book have concentrated on episodes in the two Homeric epics where Theban heroes are referenced, and explored how they are represented to serve the needs of the poem in performance, the next two chapters turn the analysis back to what seem to have been the dominant themes of a Theban tradition—the idea of strife and the unequal distribution of spoils. Using a close reading of both the Hesiodic poems and the Theban epic fragments, we show how the Homeric poems appropriate major thematic ideas from their rival traditions and redeploy them in the telling of their Troy stories—the anger of godlike Achilles and the return home of the man Odysseus.

4

Doubling Down On Strife[1]

IN THE FIRST THREE CHAPTERS of this book, we have avoided attempts to reconstruct lost Theban epics in favor of identifying where Theban material occurs in Homer and exploring the ways in which Homer re-presents that material by putting it at the service of his narratives. In Chapter 1 we examined Homer's most explicit engagement with Thebes, via a series of scenes in which Diomedes is compared to his father, Tydeus, one of the original Seven against Thebes. Our analysis brought to the fore a political focus that valorized coalition-building over individual action. In Chapter 2 we investigated Herakles as the hero who has already sacked Troy, but whose influence on the current war narrative is carefully delineated (and limited). Instead of being a model for the current generation of heroes at Troy, Herakles emerges as a figure from a previous age, when heroes could labor alone and be made immortal. In Chapter 3 we focused on a third Theban figure, Oedipus, to unpack some of the generic complexities underpinning Homeric epic. Relegated to a fleeting appearance in the *Odyssey*'s catalogue of women, Oedipus represents a hero stripped of the narrative elements through which he would have resonated through an epic cosmos. In these last three chapters we take a slightly different tack by refocusing on the Theban story and scrutinizing possible interpoetic rivalry with the Homeric poems. While this work will necessarily be more speculative—given the paucity of our source material—we hope nevertheless to reveal interesting dynamics that shed light on Homeric poetics. Again resisting the common pull towards reconstructing a putative Theban tradition, we attempt to identify those themes and motifs that seem in all likelihood less germane to a Trojan War tradition and to use these, together with the fragmentary remains, to rethink how the two traditions emerged from the same pool of epic language, themes, and story-worlds.

In this chapter we consider what is arguably the epic theme par excellence: strife. Strife is clearly important to the war narrative that the *Iliad* recounts; but

---

[1]   Sections of this chapter draw heavily on Christensen 2018a.

it is equally central to the tale of the homecoming of Odysseus, who is constantly striving to return home and then, once home, must overcome his opponents on Ithaca. Moreover, while the strife between the Achaeans and Trojans is the *raison d'être* of the *Iliad*'s story, the poem's starting point and primary focus is on strife *within* the Achaean camp; for its part, the *Odyssey* makes competition with other narratives a key feature of its composition. As a key example of the traditional referentiality of early Greek hexameter poetry, strife is most explicitly addressed and anatomized by Hesiod, whose account of its double origins goes some way to shedding light on its manifestations and uses in Homeric poetics. It is Hesiod's evidence to which we first turn.

Strife and the Age of Heroes

As we observed in the Introduction, when Hesiod mentions Troy and Thebes together, it is in the context of the destruction of the "divine race of heroes, called the demigods" (ἀνδρῶν ἡρώων θεῖον γένος, οἳ καλέονται / ἡμίθεοι, *Works and Days* 160–161), killed in action either around "seven-gated Thebes" (ὑφ' ἑπταπύλῳ Θήβῃ, 163) or at Troy (ἐς Τροίην, 166).[2] Significantly, this is not the only epic reference to the destruction of the race of heroes. According to a fragment of the *Cypria*, believed to be its proem, Zeus, in pity for an Earth overburdened with men, "fanned the flames of the great strife of the Iliakos War / to lighten her [Earth's] weight with death" (ῥιπίσσας πολέμου μεγάλην ἔριν Ἰλιακοῖο, / ὄφρα κενώσειεν θανάτωι βάρος, fr. 1.5–6). In both cases, Zeus lies behind the destruction (implicitly in Hesiod, explicitly in the *Cypria*),[3] and destruction takes the form of war ("evil war and dread battle [killed] them," τοὺς μὲν πόλεμός τε κακὸς καὶ φύλοπις αἰνή, *Works and Days* 162). The *Cypria* fragment provides the additional detail that war is the manifestation of, or defines, Zeus' "great strife" (πολέμου μεγάλην ἔριν). The importance of strife is identified in another Hesiodic fragment, where she divides the gods at the birth of Helen's daughter, Hermione: this provides Zeus with another opportunity to hasten the destruction of the heroes and annihilate the offspring of the gods.[4] As well as explaining the disappearance of the race of heroes, strife prominently appears elsewhere in the Hesiodic cosmos to account for where we come from (*Theogony*), and why we still need to continue to strive (*Works and Days*).[5]

---

[2] For a discussion of this passage, see the Introduction 5–10.

[3] For Zeus' plan in the *Iliad*'s proem, see Chapter 3, n39, above.

[4] "All the gods were divided in heart / because of strife," πάντες δὲ θεοὶ δίχα θυμὸν ἔθεντο / ἐξ ἔριδος (203-204)..

[5] As we shall see, *eris* also occurs prominently in both the *Iliad* (its proem) and the Theban epic fragments. One manifestation of its creative aspect (see below) is how it lays the ground for the

In fact strife is fundamental to the myth-world of archaic Greek hexameter epic more generally. In his second-century CE summary of the Epic Cycle (*Chrestomathia*), Proclus traces the ultimate cause of the Trojan War all the way back to Eris:

παραγενομένη δὲ Ἔρις εὐωχουμένων τῶν θεῶν ἐν τοῖς Πηλέως γάμοις νεῖκος περὶ κάλλους ἀνίστησιν Ἀθηνᾷ, Ἥρᾳ καὶ Ἀφροδίτῃ αἳ πρὸς Ἀλέξανδρον ἐν Ἴδῃ κατὰ Διὸς προσταγὴν ὑφ' Ἑρμοῦ πρὸς τὴν κρίσιν ἄγονται· καὶ προκρίνει τὴν Ἀφροδίτην ἐπαρθεὶς τοῖς Ἑλένης γάμοις Ἀλέξανδρος.

Strife appears while the gods were feasting at the marriage of Peleus and sets in motion a *conflict* over beauty between Athena, Hera, and Aphrodite, who, at the command of Zeus, are led by Hermes to Alexandros on Ida for *judgment*. Alexandros decides in favor of Aphrodite, excited over a marriage with Helen.

Proclus' identification of the cause of the Trojan War represents the transposition of strife among the gods (Eris, herself a goddess, personifies the effects to which she gives rise) to the human realm. The language that Proclus uses and the pattern that he establishes for this transposition are telling. Conflict (*neikos*), the physical manifestation of strife (*eris*), is envisaged as deriving from rival divine claims to receiving honor in a social setting (a wedding); this is, in turn, resolved by a judgment (*krisis*) that has the effect of disrupting human codes of honor through another marriage (of sorts). These underlined words—*eris*, *neikos*, and *krisis*—are metonyms for other story patterns. Using them we can isolate interformulaic and intertraditional resonances that are critical in the formation of the epics we have from Homer and Hesiod, and, as we will see, also important for what we know of the lost Theban epics. That is to say, they encapsulate patterns significant to understanding not only the poems we have but also the competitive environment that shaped both them and, relatedly, the poems that *we no longer have*.[6]

The question of strife's role in Greek epic is even more pointed if we plot it within the logic of Hesiod's sense of cosmic history. In his *Works and Days*, Hesiod's insertion of the race of heroes into the myth of ages disrupts the clear serial decline (based on a ranking of metals from gold through silver and bronze to iron), in which each successive age of humankind recedes ever further away

---

institutions that follow in the wake of the death of heroes and man's new covenant with the gods, as represented by, and enacted in, Homer's epics and hymns: see Chapter 5, below.

[6] For an exploration of these themes as compositional features of early Greek poetry: Christensen 2018a. Sections of this chapter and the following one are based in part on this analysis.

from a golden age of ease and moral probity to resemble ever more closely the world of the audience. The end point, the thesis of this poem, is the (iron) age of austerity, in which the common people must toil even to eke out a living, and whose morally bankrupt leaders Hesiod rails at. As well as subverting the pattern by being "better and more just" (δικαιότερον καὶ ἄρειον, 158) than the previous generation of bronze, Hesiod's race of heroes fulfills a clear teleological function within this explanatory framework. On the one hand, heroes must disappear because the audiences of Homer and Hesiod only know them through their cult rites and tales—and, of course, by definition the heroes are unlike us in terms of their status as "demigods" or their physical strength.[7] On the other, precisely by being larger than life, heroes have the potential to be not only a benefit to society but also a danger, or at the very least a problem in it.[8] Implicit here is a cosmic history that both explains the necessity of limiting the powers of heroes and sets out where we, Hesiod's audience, come from.[9] This includes, we suggest, a critical reframing of conflict. For it is the appearance of strife and its connection to our two famous locations—Troy and Thebes—that specifically separates *this* generation of heroes from others. And it is strife and its themes, we suggest, that help to make these stories particularly *epic*.[10]

In the rest of this chapter we explore in more detail Hesiod's representation of strife, mapping out a framework in which we can read early Greek hexameter poetry as a whole and trace its shifting manifestations. We suggest that the movement through epic history from the *Theogony*, via the Homeric poems, to the *Works and Days* offers a dramatic treatment of the matrix of themes that Proclus identifies as seminal for understanding the cause of the Trojan War. Each step in the narrative sequence, we argue, inquires into the origins of strife, examines attempts to mediate conflict through the distributions of rights and honors, and explores the exigencies of incomplete or problematic resolutions. Relatedly, we identify themes of strife (*eris* and *neikos*), distribution (*dasmos*),

---

[7] On Hesiod's description of the heroes as "demigods": Nagy 1990:36–82. This seems to be a generic description of the age of heroes, since not all heroes are divine born. One who is not, Hektor, is nevertheless able to pick up a rock that it would take "two men nowadays" to lift (*Iliad* 12.447–449).

[8] For heroes as those who both suffer and cause suffering, see above on Herakles (Chapter 2, "The Epic Herakles") and Oedipus/Odysseus (Chapter 3, "Oedipus of Many Pains"). Note that the tension is encapsulated in epic phraseology: "the leader destroys his people" (e.g. ἐπεὶ πολὺν ὤλεσα λαόν, *Iliad* 2.115). See further Haubold 2000:20 and *passim*.

[9] Cosmic history: see the Introduction, "Why Thebes?" In the process of myth, the Iliadic crisis of these values stands as a midpoint between the *Theogony* and the *Works and Days*. Cf. Mondi 1980 for an extended discussion of the *Theogony* as a cosmological text.

[10] In the Near Eastern tradition, mass destruction of mankind most often takes the form of natural disasters, such as lightning or floods. The Greek epic tradition is unusual by putting the emphasis on humans' involvement in their own destruction: See Barker 2008; cf. Haubold 2002.

and judgment (*krisis*) as central compositional features of the Greek epic tradition, as represented by both Hesiodic and Homeric poetry, and—as we shall see in the following chapter—in extant fragments of the Theban tradition and its surviving testimonia.[11] One manifestation will be of particular significance for our study of Homer's Thebes: the process by which the strife that appears destructive and cosmically threatening in the *Theogony* is transformed into a striving that is both formative for, and espoused by, the other epics—the two Homeric poems and the *Works and Days*—that deal with mankind's place in the cosmos. For the divine realm, these related motifs allow audiences to gain an insight into how the Olympians achieved their strong and stable government; for humankind, the questions remain unresolved, the solutions only partial or temporary. Revolving around the struggle in words—or in other words *politics*—these issues reflect, interrogate, and help structure the experiences and concerns of audiences throughout the early Greek world.

The Eris Revolution

Being in wonder at also this the Greeks praised Homer, because his epic poetry was beyond what could be naturally expected, and they were clamoring to give him victory. But the king crowned Hesiod, saying that it was just for the one who was issuing an invitation to farming and peace to have the victory, not the one who was describing wars and slaughter. They report that Hesiod happened on victory this way and add that, once he took the bronze tripod and inscribed it, he dedicated it to the Muses.

The Contest of Homer and Hesiod, 204–212[12]

Among the many elements of the cosmos that Hesiod's *Theogony* establishes and catalogues is the origin of strife (223–232):

τίκτε δὲ καὶ Νέμεσιν, πῆμα θνητοῖσι βροτοῖσι,
Νὺξ ὀλοή· μετὰ τὴν δ' Ἀπάτην τέκε καὶ Φιλότητα
Γῆράς τ' οὐλόμενον, καὶ Ἔριν τέκε καρτερόθυμον.

---

[11] On the compositional nature of theme from the perspective of oral-poetry, see the Introduction and Christensen 2018a.

[12] θαυμάσαντες δὲ καὶ ἐν τούτῳ τὸν Ὅμηρον οἱ Ἕλληνες ἐπήνουν, ὡς παρὰ τὸ προσῆκον γεγονότων τῶν ἐπῶν, καὶ ἐκέλευον διδόναι τὴν νίκην. ὁ δὲ βασιλεὺς τὸν Ἡσίοδον ἐστεφάνωσεν εἰπὼν δίκαιον εἶναι τὸν ἐπὶ γεωργίαν καὶ εἰρήνην προκαλούμενον νικᾶν, οὐ τὸν πολέμους καὶ σφαγὰς διεξιόντα. τῆς μὲν οὖν νίκης οὕτω φασὶ τυχεῖν τὸν Ἡσίοδον καὶ λαβόντα τρίποδα χαλκοῦν ἀναθεῖναι ταῖς Μούσαις ἐπιγράψαντα. See Graziosi 2002:168–180; Barker and Christensen 2013:195–196.

αὐτὰρ Ἔρις στυγερὴ τέκε μὲν Πόνον ἀλγινόεντα
Λήθην τε Λιμόν τε καὶ Ἄλγεα δακρυόεντα
Ὑσμίνας τε Μάχας τε Φόνους τ᾿ Ἀνδροκτασίας τε
Νείκεά τε ψευδέας τε Λόγους Ἀμφιλλογίας τε
Δυσνομίην τ᾿ Ἄτην τε, συνήθεας ἀλλήλῃσιν,
Ὅρκον θ᾿, ὃς δὴ πλεῖστον ἐπιχθονίους ἀνθρώπους
πημαίνει, ὅτε κέν τις ἑκὼν ἐπίορκον ὀμόσσῃ.

After she bore Nemesis too, a pain for mortal men,
Ruinous Night then gave birth to Deception and Sex
And destructive Old Age, and also strong-hearted Strife.
Then hateful Strife gave birth to grief-causing Toil,
And Forgetfulness, and Hunger, and tearful Pains,
Battles, Wars, Murders, and Man-killings,
Conflicts, Lies, Arguments, Doubletalk,
Bad-government, Blindness, each other's bosom companions,
And Oath, who pains mortal men the most of all
Whenever someone willingly swears falsely.

In this rogue's gallery, Strife, "strongwilled" (καρτερόθυμον) and "hateful" (στυγερή), is identified as the daughter of "destructive Night," along with her ugly sisters Deception, Sex, and destructive Old Age. Far more fecund than her mother, she gives birth to Toil, Forgetfulness, Hunger, and Pains, as well as "Battles and Wars and Murders, and Man-killings, / Conflicts and Lies and Arguments and Doubletalk, / Bad-government and Deception," and finally Oath. While the sources of strife are thus general ills that afflict humans (dishonesty, desire, and mortality), its results manifest themselves in both individual and *societal* struggle, including both physical and verbal violence. While the rest of the poem addresses the remaining problem of Strife among the gods (as befits its theogonic perspective), this passage on her birth and affiliations demonstrates forcefully the extent to which Strife is thematically linked to conflict, specifcally the total wars of the age of heroes.

Hesiod provides further background to Strife in *Works and Days*, where a rather different picture of this productive goddess emerges. Most conspicuous is the new information that "there was not just one birth of Strifes after all, but upon the earth there are two" (οὐκ ἄρα μοῦνον ἔην Ἐρίδων γένος, ἀλλ᾿ ἐπὶ γαῖαν / εἰσὶ δύω, 11–12). The one, Hesiod explains, "a man would praise once he got to know it, while the other is blameworthy, and they have a spirit split in two" (τὴν μέν κεν ἐπαινέσσειε νοήσας, / ἣ δ᾿ ἐπιμωμητή: διὰ δ᾿ ἄνδιχα θυμὸν ἔχουσιν, 12–13). The latter Strife, the type which incurs blame, recalls her

Theogonic genealogy: fostering "evil war and conflict" (ἣ μὲν γὰρ πόλεμόν τε κακὸν καὶ δῆριν ὀφέλλει, 14), she receives honor from mortals "out of compulsion" (ὑπ' ἀνάγκης, 15) and "by the plans of the immortals" (ἀθανάτων βουλῆσιν, 16). This latter phrase may bring to mind the *dios boulê* and the association of Zeus' plotting with the strife-ful narratives of the *Iliad* and also, by what we can tell from its proem, the *Cypria*, and specifically Zeus' role in destroying the race of heroes.[13]

Evidently we should already be familiar with this "burdensome" Strife, for Hesiod provides a genealogy for only the second kind of Strife, the one that would be praised, were we to get to know it.[14] Hesiod sets about putting us in the know. She too is born of Night (though this time Night is more ambiguously "dark" not "destructive"); but Zeus is said to have "set her in the roots of the earth" where she turns out to be "much better for men" (γαίης ἐν ῥίζῃσι, καὶ ἀνδράσι πολλὸν ἀμείνω, 19). Exactly how Strife could be a good thing is the idea to which Hesiod next turns his attention (20–26):

> ἥ τε καὶ ἀπάλαμόν περ ὁμῶς ἐπὶ ἔργον ἐγείρει·
> εἰς ἕτερον γάρ τίς τε ἴδεν ἔργοιο χατίζων
> πλούσιον, ὃς σπεύδει μὲν ἀρόμεναι ἠδὲ φυτεύειν
> οἶκόν τ' εὖ θέσθαι· ζηλοῖ δέ τε γείτονα γείτων
> εἰς ἄφενος σπεύδοντ'· ἀγαθὴ δ' Ἔρις ἥδε βροτοῖσιν.
> καὶ κεραμεὺς κεραμεῖ κοτέει καὶ τέκτονι τέκτων,
> καὶ πτωχὸς πτωχῷ φθονέει καὶ ἀοιδὸς ἀοιδῷ.

> She awakens even those who are lazy to do work:
> For a man who shirks work sees another
> Who is wealthy, who hastens to plow and plant
> And order his house well. Neighbor envies his neighbor,
> The two of them hastening to wealth. This is the good Strife for men.
> And potter begrudges potter, and carpenter carpenter—
> And beggar envies beggar, and singer singer.

In its very insistence on disambiguation, Hesiod re-creates a figure of some ambiguity, a Strife whose role doubles up in the world of men both as the destructive propagator of arguments and war and, it seems, as a stimulus to

---

[13] See the discussion in the previous chapter, "Strife and the Age of Heroes."

[14] For the disambiguation of the two *Erides* as programmatic for the poem, see Hamilton 1989:64; cf. Nagler 1992:79. On Hesiod "correcting" his view in the *Theogony*, see Most 1993: 76–80; against this view, see Thalmann 2004; cf. Nagler 1992:87. For the doubling of Eris as an innovation: West 1978:142; Gagarin 1990:173; Zarecki 2007:10; cf. Thalmann 2004:364 for earlier bibliography.

compete in more constructive ways.[15] The reason for this doubling is complex and uncertain, though it must have something to do with Hesiod's supplementary biography for the goddess. By explicitly locating this second Eris on earth, Hesiod emphasizes her connection to mankind, and perhaps even more directly to his *Works and Days*, which addresses the epic endeavor facing the everyday man working the land.[16]

Strife's connection to human beings is rooted in cosmic history and the growing distinction between the mortal and immortal realms. In the story that unfolds in the *Theogony*, the gods who always are attain honors that never cease. Their world (from this point on, because of the narrative told in the poem) remains unchanging; the distribution of their (rightful) honors remains forever the same.[17] Among men, who live briefly and die, the story is quite different. To get on in life, no matter what it is they do, humans must continually *strive*. At one level, this distinction is about the daily grind of human subsistence in contrast to the gods' carefree existence, which may again recall the myth of the ages, specifically the contrast between a golden age of ease and bliss and the present iron age of toil and misery. At another, it contributes to an important debate on the dynamics of competition.[18] The Theogonic destructive Eris signifies a "zero-sum game" wherein one party can gain only if another loses. In contrast, the earth-bound Eris represents a type of struggle whose outcome, rather than being zero-sum, increases the material and social position of its participants—in similar game-theory terminology, one might call this a "positive-sum game." This *supplementary* aesthetic, a binary opposition in contrast to the polar opposition intrinsic to the zero-sum game, is both competitive *and also* cooperative.[19]

---

[15] Nagler 1992:88–89 argues that the distinction is between "what is simplex and complex" and notes that Hesiod never calls one good and bad, but rather says that one should be praised and the other blamed. "The problem is that the Erides, or rather the two outcomes of acting under the eristic impulse, are often distinguishable only in their effects."

[16] For the roots of the earth as having to do with agriculture: West 1978:144; cf. Zarecki 2007:9–10; and Thalmann 2004:364, who notes that the roots of the earth (*Theogony* 728) are also where Night resides.

[17] Thalmann 2004:376: "Hesiod's description of the two *Erides* thus makes explicit the multiple potentialities in competition, conflict, and violence that are implicit elsewhere in hexameter poetry and in the narrative and formulaic traditions that underlie it, and that are obscured by the tradition (if such it was) reflected in the *Theogony*."

[18] For connections between Hesiod's good strife and Greek agonistic culture: Hogan 1981:35, 57–58; cf. Thalmann 2004:367. For strife's social functions in heroic poetry, see Nagy 1999 [1979]:213–242, 309–312.

[19] We approach a similar phenomenon from a different perspective in our analysis of fight-or-flight debates common to the Homeric epics and the new Archilochus fragment: Barker and Christensen 2006. In that work we also emphasize the importance of rivalry and play to the development of poetic motifs and the emergence of separate poetic perspectives.

Significantly, Hesiod's double take on strife performs this very notion of the supplement. The *Works and Days* revision is both a *competitive* take on the (conceptually) earlier *Theogony* by virtue of correcting, even *countermanding*, its definition and, at the very same time, a *cooperative* move in the sense that it represents *an extension* of the original idea. The passages on strife taken together (assuming that they can be regarded as having coexisted in a common performance tradition) represent macro-level extensions of what Fenik has called "the anticipatory doublet," where an idea is expressed and then repeated in an expanded or altered form.[20] Such a pairing can both implicitly signal the greater importance of the second element (akin to Kakridis's "ascending scale of affection") and facilitate the advancement of themes from one example to another.[21] With regard to the two *Erides*, the *second* strife builds on the first, encompasses or retains all of its prior characteristics, but has something extra added or supplemented to it. The additional material in this case is that, while strife (in its original form) is wholly to be blamed (and shunned), it is also (in its second form) praiseworthy (and to be practiced) insofar as it can be useful. In essence strife as *competition* encompasses both the good and bad strife, but here Hesiod uses a tool of early Greek poetic thought—the anticipatory doublet—to disambiguate the single concept into two in order to home in on its positive aspects.

The complexity and profundity of these poetic moves in all likelihood has to do with the nature of oral poetry—in this case, the function of poetic *themes*. Eris in its single and double forms functions as a metonym that both evokes and invokes story patterns. A basic revelation from oral-formulaic studies, articulated first by Albert Lord, is that oral poetry of the kind represented by the early Greek hexameter epic tradition exhibits the phenomenon of *composition by theme*.[22] Conventional formulae are often intricately—and sometimes exclusively—connected to given themes, so much so that the themes' meanings may be felt even in their absence.[23] Themes are said to be compositional in that they carry within them patterns that can be expanded or compressed, re-ordered and re-arranged, with elements either obscured or magnified; outcomes can differ according to the execution.[24] A process like this in the context of multiple song traditions, such as we find in early Greek poetry more broadly, lends itself

[20]   See Fenik 1974:142–207; Scodel 1984:55–58; Kelly 2007; Sammons 2014:302. For a fuller bibliography, see Tsagalis 2014:357.

[21]   See Kakridis 1949:43–49. For the doublet's cooperative nature, see Sammons 2014:310: "Besides their anticipatory function, such doublet pairs can be used for the progressive development of themes."

[22]   See Lord 1960:68–98; cf. Muellner 1996:15; Ebbott 2014:320.

[23]   See Lord 1960:94–97; cf. Ebbott 2014.

[24]   See Lord 1960:81–82; cf. Ebbott 2014:322.

to a competitive imperative, wherein the song being sung is heard in tension with the expectations established by those that have come before.[25] In addition, just as individual utterances accrue meaning through their history of potential uses, so too do thematic motifs derive their most affective force from both their diachronic and synchronic axes—the process that we've been calling (following Bakker) *intertraditionality*. From the perspective of enjoying or analyzing an oral poem, compositional themes and their intrinsic intertraditionality allow us to understand that narrative patterns are metonymic retellings, or recombinations of similar conventional story "genes," for specific contexts and new creations.

For Eris, this means that its meaning and power derives in part from a repertoire of traditional meanings deployed in other performances. The performance context and the function of theme, then, are inherently both cooperative (individual meanings depend upon prior iterations) and competitive (each new invocation potentially redefines and replaces what came before). In this way, both the nature of Eris as defined by Hesiod in *Works and Days* and the way it functions in that particular instance directly engage with the act of poetic composition and performance. That is to say, in his redefinition of Eris, Hesiod gestures toward what he is doing as a poet. By drawing on the description of the nature of Strife, he recalls a theme from a putatively earlier performance (of the *Theogony*). At the same time, even as he integrates this theme into the current performance (of the *Works and Days*) he contests its relevance to his poem by adding to it, thereby changing not only its form, but also meaning and significance. In the act of performance the contested topos is made subordinate to, but remains underneath and underpinning, the new one. Hesiod's redefinition is thus both cooperative in the sense that the two definitions are mutually dependent, but also competitive insofar as the second seeks to contain and thereby supplant the "original." This is, in short, a model for poetic rivalry. Among different traditions and iterations of these themes, we see a dynamic rivalry that motivates each new instantiation to integrate and add to what came before, facilitating the development of new perspectives in traditional forms and contexts.

Above we noted the titular aspect of Eris in epic poetry as defined by Proclus, who (re)defines the Trojan War as Eris writ large, setting in motion a conflict (*neikos*) over beauty.[26] Though a late witness to the resonance of epic, Proclus uses vocabulary that is highly resonant within an epic cosmos, such as that found in another fragment from the Hesiodic tradition (Hesiod fr. 43.36-39):

αἶ]ψα [δ' ἄ]ρ' ἀ[λλ]ήλοισ[ι]ν ἔρις καὶ ν[εῖκος] ἐτ[ύχθη
Σισύφωι ἠδ' Αἴθωνι τανισφύρο[υ εἵ]νεκα [κούρης,

---

25 See Lord 1960:75–80; cf. Ebbott 2014:334–335.
26 For a similar tour through instances of *eris* with a different emphasis: Thalmann 2004:360–374.

ο]ὐδ' ἄρα τις δικάσαι [δύ]νατο βροτός…

And soon *strife and conflict* arose for them both,
Sisyphus and Aithon, over the fair-ankled girl.
No mortal was able to make a judgment for them.

Preserving a glimpse into another story of conflict that centers, this time, on an unnamed girl, the fragment again presents the formulaically matched pair *eris* and *neikos* (ἔρις καὶ ν[εῖκος]). Furthermore, the conflict worsens in the absence of someone who can resolve it through judgment (ο]ὐδ' ἄρα τις δικάσαι [δύ]νατο βροτός). In this case, however, the warring parties agree to entrust the conflict to Athena, who settles the case by pronouncing proverbial wisdom on the importance of honoring agreements and not taking back what had been given.[27] That combination of the use of proverbial wisdom to resolve conflict also fits a pattern of Hesiodic poetry more generally, whereby destructive conflict tends to be avoided or negotiated, or sublimated in the poetic representation of a law court case.

If this fragment pointedly represents what we might consider a Hesiodic avoidance, deferral, or sublimation of conflict, Homeric poetry directly engages with conflict, though always staying alert to its destructiveness. Several lines after headlining *mênis* as its theme, the *Iliad* begins its narrative from "that time when those two men were *striving*" (ἐξ οὗ δὴ τὰ πρῶτα διαστήτην ἐρίσαντε, 6), and immediately asks: "which god caused those two to fall into *strife*?" (Τίς τάρ σφωε θεῶν ἔριδι ξυνέηκε μάχεσθαι, 8). Both Homeric epics also refer to further conflicts in other story traditions using the language of *neikos* or *eris*.[28] Nestor, the hero with one foot in the epic past, calls a conflict from his youth a *neikos* ("as when a conflict arose among between us and the Eleans," ὡς ὁπότ' Ἠλείοισι καὶ ἡμῖν νεῖκος ἐτύχθη, 11.671; cf. 11.721, 737), while in the *Odyssey* he recalls how Athena created *strife* between the sons of Atreus ("she who set strife on both the sons of Atreus." ἥ τ' ἔριν Ἀτρεΐδῃσι μετ' ἀμφοτέροισιν ἔθηκε, 3.136). *Eris* and *neikos* are also used interchangeably to describe the Trojan War in the *Iliad*. Paris is said to be the cause of the conflict (*neikos*) ("Paris, on whose account this strife arose," Ἀλεξάνδροιο, τοῦ εἵνεκα νεῖκος ὅρωρεν, 3.87; cf. 7.374, 388), which shortly afterwards Menelaos redefines as *eris* ("on account of my strife and Alexandros' beginning," εἵνεκ' ἐμῆς ἔριδος καὶ Ἀλεξάνδρου ἔνεκ' ἀρχῆς, 3.100). Achilles describes his quarrel with Agamemnon in similar terms: "I think that the Achaeans will remember our *strife* for a long time" (…αὐτὰρ Ἀχαιοὺς / δηρὸν ἐμῆς καὶ σῆς ἔριδος μνήσεσθαι ὀίω, 19.64–65). Given that Achilles is here

27 This text uses the readings and emendations provided by Most 2007.
28 For *neikos* as a synonym of *eris* to indicate verbal conflict: Hogan 1981 *passim*.

looking back at and reflecting on his actions in the course of *this* poem, *eris* may be taken as a thematic judgment on the *Iliad*'s narrative.[29] In a similar metapoetic moment in the *Odyssey*, when the narrator mentions the conflict between Achilles and Odysseus, he uses *neikos* to describe it as a "tale of men, whose fame has reached wide heaven" ("the song, whose fame has reached the wide sky, the conflict of Odysseus and Peleus' son." οἴμης, τῆς τότ᾽ ἄρα κλέος οὐρανὸν εὐρὺν ἵκανε, / νεῖκος Ὀδυσσῆος καὶ Πηλεΐδεω Ἀχιλῆος, *Odyssey* 8.74–75).

Evidence in other early Greek poetry further points to the metapoetic valorization of strife as a metonym for Homer's kind of epic. Anacreon (fr. 2) expresses his disdain for anyone who, while drinking, sings of "*conflicts* and tearful war" (<u>νείκεα</u> καὶ πόλεμον δακρυόεντα λέγει, 2). Theognis similarly advises his audience that those "who tell stories well around the mixing bowl / keeping away *strife* with one another for a long time" (ὑμεῖς δ᾽ εὖ μυθεῖσθε παρὰ κρητῆρι μένοντες, / ἀλλήλων <u>ἔριδος</u> δὴν ἀπερυκόμενοι, 493–494). The kind of song that constitutes heroic epic—with its emphasis on strife, conflict and suffering—is not appropriate to the sympotic context of men drinking together. As the narrator of one of the fragmentary Anacreontea makes clear, using the very pairing that we have been exploring together, Troy and Thebes won't conquer him ("you speak the tales of Thebes, but he sings of the Phrygians' battle-shouts, and I sing of my conquests," Σὺ μὲν λέγεις τὰ Θήβης, / ὁ δ᾽ αὖ Φρυγῶν αὐτάς, / ἐγὼ δ᾽ ἐμὰς ἁλώσεις, fr. 26). Instead, for the symposiasts, love conquers all. In heroic epic, strife is not only the tagline and thematic marker; it belongs to a matrix of associations based on interformular and intertraditional meanings that position the poems in and against the backdrop of an evolving cosmos.

The status of *eris* as a compositional theme with cycles of distribution and judgment, resulting at times in resolution and at others in further strife,[30] improves our understanding of the methods by which such metapoetic debates operated in early Greek poetry and influenced the shape of various poetic traditions, particularly the difference between Hesiodic and Homeric epic. Thus an audience familiar with the theme of *rage* (*mênis*) might expect a certain type of story-pattern from the first line of the *Iliad*—one, say, involving divine anger, cosmic conflict, and mortal suffering; in this way, *mênis* represents both a headline and a poetic frame.[31] Alternatively, when Hesiod redefines Eris in the *Works and Days*, he is both drawing on familiar narrative patterns and realigning their cosmic traditions, meaning that the new genealogy of Eris assumes a latent,

---

[29] See Chapter 5. Hogan 1981:21 relates Achilles' words at *Iliad* 18.107-108 to the *eris* of the proem (1.6, 8) and that of Athena's request (1.210).

[30] Hogan 1981:36: "A salient feature of an *eris* is that it is self-perpetuating."

[31] For the importance of the *mênis* theme in Homer, Hesiod and early Greek myth: Muellner 1996.

even if imperfect, understanding of its "other" status. Hesiod does not so much erase the memory of the first Eris as add to its semantic range. It is supplementary to the other version rather than its replacement.[32]

The reason for dwelling on Hesiod's ambiguous description of strife is its relevance for rethinking notions of epic rivalry. Famously, Hesiod ends his rumination on strife with the detail of singer rivaling singer, pointing to a performance aesthetic that is individually competitive and yet culturally cooperative. The Hesiodic revision and re-versioning of strife as somehow constructive—what we might call a *domestication of Eris*—is taken up and dramatized in the Homeric epics,[33] though the extent to which it ever manages to escape its more destructive twin is open to constant examination and question. Even here in the *Works and Days*, where Hesiod establishes competition as a cornerstone of human existence, it should be noted that the broader context is a rivalry *that has gone awry*: the poet's brother and addressee has cheated him of his inheritance; the kings who should be judges have swallowed bribes. How the essential ambiguity of strife is managed in Hesiod's epic cosmos more broadly is the subject of the next section.

Managing Strife in Hesiod's Cosmos

I think that Homer and Hesiod lived four hundred years before my time and not more. These are the poets who created a theogony for the Greeks and who gave to the gods their names, while also dividing up their honors and skills and telling their forms. Poets who are said to have come earlier than these men, it seems obvious to me, came later.

Herodotus II 53[34]

---

[32] Cf. Derrida 1997:144. Culler 1982:103 explains the "supplement" as "an inessential extra, added to something complete in itself, but the supplement is added in order to complete, to compensate for a lack in what was supposed to be complete in itself." In these terms, what is complete in itself cannot be added to: a supplement can occur only where there is an originary lack. In any binary set of terms, the second can be argued to exist in order to fill in an originary lack in the first.

[33] For other analyses of the shared characteristics of Homeric and Hesiodic *eris*, see: Munding 1955 who suggests that the Homeric epics influenced Hesiod's representation of Eris; and Havelock 1966:66–69, who argues that the roots of the Eris passage in the *Works and Days* lie in the *Iliad*; cf. Thalmann 2004:364–367; See Hogan 1981:57 for the implicit relationship (although he maintains *passim* that the Homeric *eris* must be analyzed on its own).

[34] Ἡσίοδον γὰρ καὶ Ὅμηρον ἡλικίην τετρακοσίοισι ἔτεσι δοκέω μέο πρεσβυτέρους γενέσθαι καὶ οὐ πλέοσι· οὗτοι δέ εἰσι οἱ ποιήσαντες θεογονίην Ἕλλησι καὶ τοῖσι θεοῖσι τὰς ἐπωνυμίας δόντες καὶ τιμάς τε καὶ τέχνας διελόντες καὶ εἴδεα αὐτῶν σημήναντες· οἱ δὲ πρότερον ποιηταὶ λεγόμενοι τούτων τῶν ἀνδρῶν γενέσθαι ὕστερον, ἔμοιγε δοκέειν, ἐγένοντο. For an outline of how central the Hesiodic *Theogony* is even to the few examples of other theogonic tales extant: Fowler 2013:35.

Though we have just said that Hesiod tends to defer strife, we are really only talking about its manifestation on earth in the form of total war among men. Some of the essential features of the *Iliad*'s treatment of conflict—the language of strife (*neikos*, *eris*); the thematic conflict over prizes and honors (*gera*, *timai*); the structural distribution of social position (*dasmos*)—are explored first (conceptually) on Olympos in the *Theogony*. In many ways this poem, which projects its priority in the early Greek hexameter corpus by narrating the origins of the cosmos, helps to establish a poetic baseline for the deployment of the *eris* story pattern in the rival Theban and Trojan traditions. Although the basic plot of the *Theogony* narrates the genealogical succession from Ouranos and Gaia to Zeus, large-scale conflicts largely associated with Zeus, once he's already assumed power, punctuate and give structure to narrative. Significantly these conflicts largely manifest themselves as political issues, giving rise to questions about leadership, social organization and in particular the proper distribution of honor.[35]

The story that the Hesiodic narrator requests from the Muses concerns "how the gods *divided* the wealth and how they distributed their *honors*" (ὥς τ᾿ ἄφενος δάσσαντο καὶ ὡς τιμὰς διέλοντο, *Theogony* 112).[36] After being flagged at the beginning of the poem, this point is not reached until well after the birth of Eris discussed above, the overthrow of Kronos by Zeus, and the Titanomachy. At this juncture, in the brief respite before Zeus takes a series of women for the purpose of populating the world with heroes (and ordering human society), the narrator describes Zeus' (re)ordering of the world of gods (881–885):

αὐτὰρ ἐπεί ῥα πόνον μάκαρες θεοὶ ἐξετέλεσσαν,
Τιτήνεσσι δὲ τιμάων κρίναντο βίηφι,
δή ῥα τότ᾿ ὤτρυνον βασιλευέμεν ἠδὲ ἀνάσσειν
Γαίης φραδμοσύνῃσιν Ὀλύμπιον εὐρύοπα Ζῆν
ἀθανάτων· ὁ δὲ τοῖσιν ἐὺ διεδάσσατο τιμάς.

Then, when the blessed gods accomplished their toil
and achieved a *judgment of honors* with the Titans by means of
strength,
They went and urged the Olympian, wide-seeing Zeus, to be king
And to rule the immortals at the advice of Gaia.
Then he *divided the honors* among them well.

---

[35] On the politics of Hesiod's succession myth: Holway 1989. On the poetics of the succession myth as connected to the *Iliad*'s *mênis* theme: Muellner 1996. Cf. Clay 2003.

[36] In their analysis of the prolonged proem, Harden and Kelly 2014:9 show that part of the topic of the poem is "the division of *timai*."

Although the lexical items *eris* and *neikos* are absent, perhaps reflecting Zeus' uncontested primacy at this point in the narrative, cognate terms such as toil (πόνον) and strength (βίηφι) provide an echo of former troubles. Toil is harshly juxtaposed midline with the gods' epithet "blessed" (μάκαρες), while it is through a trial of strength (βίηφι) that the gods receive judgment (κρίναντο). After their battle with the Titans, the gods look to a new world order, namely the (now legitimized) kingship of Zeus.[37] Connecting these two moments is honor, over which the gods received judgment (in their conflict with the Titans), and for which they now turn to Zeus.

Zeus' first act is to distribute "portions of honor" (διεδάσσατο τιμάς). The poem has already shown that Zeus has form in this regard. When Hesiod first mentions the *honor* that the Olympians newly receive (ὅσσοι γὰρ Γαίης τε καὶ Οὐρανοῦ ἐξεγένοντο / καὶ <u>τιμὴν ἔλαχον</u>, 421–422), he is at pains to point out that Hekate retains her portion "of all of these things" (τούτων ἔχει αἶσαν ἁπάντων, 422), because of Zeus (423–425):

> οὐδέ τί μιν Κρονίδης ἐβιήσατο οὐδέ τ' ἀπηύρα,
> ὅσσ' ἔλαχεν Τιτῆσι μέτα προτέροισι θεοῖσιν,
> ἀλλ' ἔχει, ὡς τὸ πρῶτον ἀπ' ἀρχῆς ἔπλετο <u>δασμός</u>.

> Neither did Kronos' son do violence to her nor deprive her of the
>   rights,
> All those which she was allotted among the Titans who were the
>   gods from before,
> But she possesses what she did from the beginning at the first
>   division.

Latent in the possibility that Zeus might deprive Hekate of her *timê* is a threat of *eris*—a threat that is hinted at by the description of Zeus *not doing violence* to Hekate. Equally, Zeus is careful not to disturb a prior distribution (*dasmos*). In the *Theogony* Hesiod attributes the success of Zeus' rule, particularly its persistence, to his ability to negotiate the nexus of associations between strife, judgment, and division. He uses his powers of judgment to secure the latter and avoid the former.

A more complex instance of distribution and conflict negotiation is dramatized in Zeus' dealings with the Titan Prometheus. Not coincidentally, this example is bound up with the world of mortals: indeed, it is the distribution where humans and gods are separated definitively. Introducing the episode

---

[37] For a darker reading, see Thalmann 2004:386: "Zeus establishes his rule by might and intelligence and is then in a position...to head off further strife by inflicting it on mortals."

through Herakles' rescue of Prometheus, Hesiod describes how Zeus, "though especially angry desisted from his anger, which he held before on account of the fact that [Prometheus] used to *strive* [with him] in counsel" (καί περ χωόμενος παύθη χόλου, ὃν πρὶν ἔχεσκεν, / οὕνεκ' <u>ἐρίζετο</u> βουλὰς ὑπερμενέι Κρονίωνι, 533-534). The reference to βουλάς hints again at the idea of plotting, as if Prometheus were a potential rival author to Zeus, whose epic song would take a very different path from this theogony. Hesiod provides a glimpse of what that might look like by tracing Zeus' power back to when "gods and mortal men were *separated for judgment* at Mêkônê" (ὅτ' <u>ἐκρίνοντο</u> θεοὶ θνητοί τ' ἄνθρωποι / Μηκώνῃ, 535-536). At this critical juncture of cosmic history, when there appears to be a universal settlement of some kind, Prometheus apportions the sacrifice in such a way as to deceive the mind of Zeus ("after making a division he set it out, hoping to deceive the mind of Zeus," <u>δασσάμενος</u> προύθηκε, Διὸς νόον ἐξαπαφίσκων, 537): he offers only the bones (wrapped in fat) for the gods, while making sure that mortals would receive the best cut of meat. This deception does not escape the mind of Zeus, however, who calls him out for having "so unfairly *divided up* the portions" (ὡς ἐτεροζήλως <u>διεδάσσαο</u> μοίρας, 543-544). The language and context should be by now familiar: one figure strives with another in the context of a distribution and scene of judgment, and uses deception—one essential cause of strife, we earlier learned—to try to get his way. Yet in spite of all this, and in spite of Zeus' anger, open conflict does not materialize. Instead, Zeus remains in control of the situation/narrative and trumps Prometheus' trickery with his own, by fashioning all-giving woman (Pandora) to be a bane to men forevermore and after. Hesiod's structuring of the episode underlines Zeus' authority by introducing us to Prometheus in the act of being freed by Zeus. Though he may get angry, Zeus can control that anger because *he no longer strives*. Later we learn that Zeus has even laid down the means to forestall the cunning wiles of any future Prometheus. "Whenever *conflict and strife* arise among the gods" (ὁππότ' <u>ἔρις καὶ νεῖκος</u> ἐν ἀθανάτοισιν ὄρηται, 782), they are obliged to take a mighty oath on the river Styx. Here Zeus establishes the oath as an institutional means of managing conflict for the gods and, moreover, installs himself as its guarantor and executor. By these means Zeus removes himself from the fray and stands *outside* any (and all) future quarrels.[38]

---

[38] The phrase recalls the *Iliad*'s description of Thoas, whom few could surpass in the assembly "whenever the young men were striving in debate (ὁππότε κοῦροι ἐρίσσειαν περὶ μύθων, *Iliad* 15.284): according to Barker 2009:65-66, the use of "whenever" (ὁππότε) demonstrates the institutionalization of dissent in the institution of the *agora*. At any rate, the indefinite temporal clause definitely gives it a feeling of custom if not of law. On the *Iliad*'s Zeus as somehow "outside" strife: Barker 2009:75-78.

The fair allotment of honors to individual Olympian gods is largely told else-where, in the corpus of epic poetry known as the *Homeric Hymns*, which collectively explore much of the same thematic matrix as Hesiod's *Theogony*.[39] In the *Hymn to Demeter*, for example, Helios tries to curb Demeter's anger (χόλος, 83) at Hades' abduction of her daughter by arguing that Hades enjoys honor (τιμή, 85) from the original distribution of rights (ἔλλαχεν ὡς τὰ πρῶτα διάτριχα δασμὸς ἐτύχθη, 86).[40] Like Achilles' anger in the *Iliad*, Demeter's anger has the potential to be socially destabilizing. In her case she withdraws her powers of fertility, which leads to the death and dearth of crops and animals, and which in turn threatens the sacrifices that are a part of each god's *timê*.[41] The *Hymn to Hermes* expressly addresses the lack of honor felt by this latest son of Zeus (166–172). His potential strife, however, is sublimated by a (playful) quarrel with Apollo (μή τις τοῦτο πύθοιτο πόθεν τόδε <u>νεῖκος</u> ἐτύχθη, 269), and judgment is made by Zeus (322–396) at his own request ("give me justice and take me to Zeus, Kronos' son," δὸς δὲ <u>δίκην</u> καὶ δέξο παρὰ Ζηνὶ Κρονίωνι, 312). In the *Hymn to Aphrodite*, Zeus pre-emptively moves against the goddess to ensnare her in her own power precisely because of the threat that it carries. For she can potentially lead even him, the greatest god with "the greatest share of honor" (μεγίστης τ᾽ ἔμμορε τιμῆς, 37) astray, by the power of love to reignite strife on Olympus.[42] Taken together as a collection, the *Hymns* along with the *Theogony* map out a cosmos in which each god has found or been allotted their own portion of honor and Zeus has secured his almighty power, forever and ever.[43]

Amen to that: for, by the end of the *Theogony*, the Eris that has been generated as part of the necessary cosmogonic imperative towards Zeus' hegemony has been terrifyingly manifest in the violent successions of and titanomachic struggles among the gods. Significantly, however, it has also been mediated through Zeus' (re)distribution (*dasmos*) of honors and rights (*timai* and *gera*) and managed via institutional mechanisms of judgment (*krisis*) and the oath. This concern to carefully frame the parameters of strife and redirect it towards more socially cohesive results is evident right from the beginning of the poem. In a passage noteworthy for its rumination on poetry and politics Hesiod articulates

[39] On Zeus' division of *timai* in the *Homeric Hymns*: Clay 1989. On the Hesiodic cosmos: Clay 2003.

[40] Walsh 2005:147 argues that *kholos* is the type of anger that leads to *neikos*. On the meaning of *kholos* in general see Walsh 2005:109–231 and Muellner 1996:9, 83–4, and 111 (for its thematic importance in the *Theogony* and the *Iliad*).

[41] *Hymn to Demeter* 311–312. Zeus resolves this danger by compensating Demeter for her lost position, by increasing both her and Persephone's *timai*.

[42] Consider similarly how Nestor's (unsuccessful) attempt at mediation includes the warning to Achilles "not to strive" with the king, "since it is no like honor that is the portion of a sceptered king" ("ἐπεὶ οὔ ποθ᾽ ὁμοίης ἔμμορε τιμῆς / σκηπτοῦχος βασιλεύς," *Iliad* 1.278–279).

[43] Cf. Clay 1989; 2003.

the triangular relationship between Zeus, the Muses, and the god-raised kings (79–93):

Καλλιόπη θ'· ἣ δὲ προφερεστάτη ἐστὶν ἁπασέων.
ἣ γὰρ καὶ βασιλεῦσιν ἅμ' αἰδοίοισιν ὀπηδεῖ.
ὅν τινα τιμήσωσι Διὸς κοῦραι μεγάλοιο
γεινόμενόν τε ἴδωσι διοτρεφέων βασιλήων,
τῷ μὲν ἐπὶ γλώσσῃ γλυκερὴν χείουσιν ἐέρσην,
τοῦ δ' ἔπε' ἐκ στόματος ῥεῖ μείλιχα· οἱ δέ τε λαοὶ
πάντες ἐς αὐτὸν ὁρῶσι διακρίνοντα θέμιστας
ἰθείῃσι δίκῃσιν· ὃ δ' ἀσφαλέως ἀγορεύων
αἶψά κε καὶ μέγα νεῖκος ἐπισταμένως κατέπαυσεν·
τοὔνεκα γὰρ βασιλῆες ἐχέφρονες, οὕνεκα λαοῖς
βλαπτομένοις ἀγορῆφι μετάτροπα ἔργα τελεῦσι
ῥηιδίως, μαλακοῖσι παραιφάμενοι ἐπέεσσιν.
ἐρχόμενον δ' ἀν' ἀγῶνα θεὸν ὣς ἱλάσκονται
αἰδοῖ μειλιχίῃ, μετὰ δὲ πρέπει ἀγρομένοισιν·
τοίη Μουσάων ἱερὴ δόσις ἀνθρώποισιν.

Kalliope is the Muse who attends kings worthy of reverence.
Whomsoever of the god-raised Kings the daughters of great Zeus
Honor and look upon when he is born,
On his tongue they pour sweet dew
And gentle words flow out of his mouth. Then the people
All look upon him as he separates out the laws
With straight judgements. He speaks securely
And swiftly halts even a great conflict with skill.
For this reason kings are sensible, so that whenever the people
Are harmed they may accomplish retributive actions in the assembly
Easily, persuading everyone with gentle words.
When he walks into the contest ground people propitiate him
Like a god with gentle reverence, and he stands out among the
      assembled.
Such is the sacred gift of the Muses for men.
(trans. after Evelyn-White)

In this passage we find a fully expressed articulation of the interrelationship between conflict (*eris, neikos*), judgment (*krisis, dikê*), and distribution (*dasmos*). Central to this account of what it is to be the good king (the one who is *honored* by the Muses and Zeus) is an anatomization of how to control strife. Managing strife depends on both the king's innate persuasive abilities ("On his tongue they pour sweet dew / And gentle words [ἔπεα μείλιχα] flow out of his mouth") and his performance within a rudimentary institutional framework.[44] The latter involves the king not only judging laws (διακρίνοντα θέμιστας) but also interceding in the *agora* to exact punishments that reflect the crimes (μετάτροπα ἔργα) and being honored in his community's contest space (ἀγῶνα). Thus, even should a great conflict (μέγα νεῖκος) arise and cause harm for the people (*laos*), the king's performance of remunerative—or, perhaps better, *redistributive*—acts would forestall the emergence of the kind of destructive Eris that will be documented exhaustively in the cosmogonic narrative of the *Theogony*. Honored by the Muses and Zeus, the king acts as a kind of surrogate for Zeus on earth.

In his *Works and Days*, Hesiod explores the alternative scenario—when the king is not being a good representative of Zeus. There he bluntly criticizes the kings who take bribes and fail to make fair judgments. In the *Theogony*, too, even as Hesiod uses an idealized representation of Zeus as king as a paradigm for mortal rulers, poetry and poetically marked speech emerges as a tool for managing Strife. Sweet dew is poured on the tongue of Hesiod's model ruler and gentle words (ἔπεα μείλιχα) flow from his mouth. In making conflict management contingent on the effective use of words, Hesiod makes *how you speak* matter.[45] Poetry and politics are configured as two sides of the same coin.[46] Indeed, Hesiod's description may be particularly charged. The type of words, *epea* (ἔπε᾽), that flow from the king's mouth are those that give the description to this kind of verse: *epic* poetry. It is as if Hesiod is offering (his) epic as a way of negotiating conflict. While this description establishes the framework through which to read the *Theogony*'s cosmogony and has obvious relevance for Zeus, as *the* king who must use words to negotiate strife (to achieve and then secure his reign), it resonates equally powerfully for the poetic voice that appears in the

[44] West 1966:44 concludes that the difference in the treatment of kings between Hesiod's *Theogony* and his *Works and Days* is the result of different target audiences—the former was composed for a performance before kings and the latter for a performance before "the people." For us, the theogonic work praises kings while contemplating the evolution of a divine political order; the *Works and Days* excoriates kings for failing to fulfill the *promise* of this order and to carry out the duties *imposed* on them in the *Theogony*'s proem.

[45] On the importance of understanding the correlation between the poet's ability in speech and the king's: Gargarin 1991:65–66. He argues that the king's judgment is linked to the skill he uses to communicate it, and that the justice of the decision is based in part on its acceptability to the complainants who are persuaded by the king; cf Christensen 2018a.

[46] The traditionality of this passage is buttressed in part by very similar lines in Homer's *Odyssey* where Odysseus describes the advantages that accrue to a man blessed by the gods with power of speech (8.165–177). For discussions about the relationship between the Hesiodic and Homeric passages: Solmsen 1954; West 1966:183; Edwards 1971:166–189; Janko 1982; Martin 1984. See especially Rosen 1997 for a bibliography and summary of prior arguments.

Works and Days. There, Hesiod the poet laborer is embroiled in a conflict over a corrupt judgment on inheritance, which he (re)enacts through the very performance of this poem. Read in this way, it would be as if the *Works and Days* were a trial and Hesiod its plaintiff.[47]

We will return to this image in due course. For the present it is enough to note that if this passage is proleptic for the type of ruler Zeus could, and *should*, be by the end of the *Theogony*, then it also prepares the ground for the failures of kings elsewhere in the epic cosmos. The tradition outside Hesiodic epic obsessively interrogates the idealization of kingship anatomized here. The unexpressed possibility that not all men will judge with skill or that the judgment will not be expressed with gentle words is, for example, explored most rigorously in the Homeric poems, whether we think of the disastrous strife that explodes in the Achaean community at the beginning of the *Iliad*, as both Agamemnon and Achilles fail in their protective duties to the people,[48] or the equally socially destructive strife that infects the Ithacan community in the prolonged absence of its leader.[49] How this thematization of strife might have been articulated and explored in the Theban tradition is the subject of our final section in this chapter.

Honor, Division, and Strife: A Theban Tale

> The epic called *Thebais* was composed about this war. Kallinos, when he comes to mention this epic, says that Homer composed it. Many authors of considerable repute have believed the same thing. In my opinion too I praise this poem especially, after the *Iliad* and *Odyssey* at least.
>
> Pausanias IX 9.5[50]

From our survey of Hesiod's cosmos, it has become apparent that the thematization of Eris, along with its attendant associations of division (*dasmos*), honors (*timai, gera*) and judgment (*krisis*), is fundamental at a compositional level in

---

47 Walker 1996:250-251. For *epos* as a title for poetic discourse: Nagy 1999 [1979]:265-275.

48 Particularly striking in this context is Agamemnon's later failure to win Achilles around. In preparing the ground, Nestor had counseled Agamemnon to be persuasive with "both glorious gifts *and gentle words*" (δώροισίν τ' ἀγανοῖσιν ἔπεσσί τε μειλιχίοισι, 9.113); commenting on Agamemnon's subsequent offer, Nestor mentions only the gifts (164). Judged only on the terms of the *Theogony*'s proem, Agamemnon makes a very poor leader. For the *Iliad*'s narrative, this is the reason why some other political settlement than a single king pronouncing on all has to be pursued: see Chapter 5 below.

49 For comparisons between this passage and Nestor's introduction into the *Iliad*: Havelock 1966:71-73; Gagarin 1992:64; Walker 1996:246-248. Cf. Martin 1984:43; Nagy 1999 [1979]:311-312.

50 As cited above (epigraph to Chapter 1, "The Battle for Thebes").

early Greek hexameter poetry. Viewed in the context of cosmic construction, the Theogonic treatment of strife "sets the table" for poetic feasting. The allotment of proper honors for the gods, no less, is explored and reified at the foundational scene of sacrifice described in the *Theogony*, suggesting an indelible thematic connection between the sacrificial feast (δαίς) and the proper apportionment of "cuts" (δάσσαντο is the iterative form of the verb δαίομαι).[51] Transgressions arising from unjust divisions result in strife and war; as we saw from Proclus, Eris attends banquets and portions out conflict.

The table motif will play a critical role as we pick over the scraps left of the Theban tradition. We have already seen that Hesiod groups Thebes and Troy together etiologically. As early as Herodotus, poems whose titles evoke a Theban tradition to rival that of Troy—the *Thebais* and the *Epigonoi*—were attributed to Homer, presumably on the basis of a similarity in thematic content and poetic style to the two Homeric poems that have come down to us.[52] Whatever precise form these poems took—and it is by no means clear that their narratives were ever as fixed or quite as large and *epic* as those of the *Iliad* and *Odyssey*—the two traditions share various points of contact, not least of all in their cast list. We have already seen (in Chapter 1) that the *Iliad* represents the sons of the Seven against Thebes fighting at Troy; other accounts record that a bastard brother of Atreus and Thyestes, by the name of Chrysippus, was raped by Laios, the king of Thebes. It was for this insult that Hera cursed him to be killed at the hands of his own son and replaced by him as king.[53]

Saying anything certain about the contents and especially the plot of any notional Theban epic is fraught with hazard, given the paucity of non-Homeric evidence, which is one reason why we have focused in this book almost entirely on what Homer does with Thebes. Anything that can be said derives from the few surviving hexameter fragments, later testimonia (including Proclus' much later summary), reworkings (especially tragic), and, in our opinion most fraught of all, Theban material in the surviving epic corpus, primarily the *Iliad* and *Odyssey*. In each case, critics face the problem of interpreting Thebes through the distorting lens of other perspectives—interpretations that, to a certain extent, are conditioned by our understanding of these other sources.[54] Still, some broad and informative outlines seem tantalizingly in reach, especially with regard to the pervasively tragic treatment of Thebes' sack. If this suggests

---

[51] Nagy 1999 [1979]:127–139. Cf. Muellner 1996:33–34.

[52] See Davies 2014:133–143; Bernabé 1996:20, 28.

[53] See our discussion in Chapter 3, "Oedipus in Epic Fragments." This story itself is contested, since some story traditions record that Chrysippus was rather murdered by Atreus and Thyestes: Gantz 1993:489, 548–552.

[54] See our discussion of Thebes the Introduction, along with the bibliography cited there.

the gravitational pull of a strong, possibly unitary composition (like an epic poem),[55] then we also have to consider the possibility that a tradition of Theban poems also existed. Perhaps these were not as extensive as the collection that appears to have been a Trojan Cycle, but nevertheless we can postulate a range of poems or versions of particular stories based at or around Thebes: ancient evidence would seem to attest to nearly a half-dozen different named Theban epics. Again the anomaly is the survival of the *Iliad* and *Odyssey* as complete texts of heroic epic.

A way forward may be to identify and reflect on the type of dynamic engagement that we have been exploring in the Homeric poems. First, however, we must deal with the sparse nature of our evidence, taking the fabula related to Oedipus as an example. In Chapter 3 we discussed the *Odyssey*'s engagement with the idea of Oedipus as a hero to rank alongside Odysseus: our focus here lies rather on how Oedipus' story may have been told in his own epic, the *Oedipodea*.[56] A chief obstacle of doing any full comparative analysis of the Oedipus story in Homer and in a Theban epic is that all our evidence of the latter has been furnished explicitly for comparison to or explication of the former. Homer's extant epics have provided the frame by which the lost epic is judged and the lens through which its contents are judged as strange or memorable.

The difficulty of retrieving any Theban archetype is demonstrated by the fact that only two ancient witnesses mention the epic, and both are late. The one, Pausanias, explicitly uses Homer (the *Odyssey*) to judge that Oedipus' sons were born of Euryganeia not Iokasta (IX 5.10).[57] The other, a scholion to Euripides' *Phoenican Women*, preserves only the tale of Laios' sexual transgression against Chrysippus that we have just noted, along with the single quotation that survives: "the most beautiful and desire-inducing of all men / the dear child of blameless Creon, shining Haimon."[58] The context that the scholion provides relates to the Sphinx, sent by Hera as punishment for Laios' transgression, which implies that Haimon is its victim.

---

[55] See Davies 2014:70–71.

[56] The title is attested on the *Tabula Borgia* (IG XIV 1292) and the scholia to Euripides' *Phoenican Women*. See Bernabé 1996:17; Davies 2014:1.

[57] See Bernabé 1996:20; Davies 2014:132. Recent authors, e.g. Fowler 2013:404–405, follow Deubner 1942:16–17 and argue that the epic did not present the incest or children as an issue—the tragedians likely magnified these horrors. Davies is more sceptical: "it is hard to see how an epic whose very title implies a detailed account of the career and suffering of the hero could ever have similarly avoided these basic issues" (17). Modern scholars have also used the *Odyssey* to reconstruct the plot of the *Oedipodea*. See Davies 2014:13–17 for a discussion of the various scenarios.

[58] ἀλλ᾽ ἔτι κάλλιστόν τε καὶ ἱμεροέστατον ἄλλων / παῖδα φίλον Κρείοντος ἀμύμονος, Αἵμονα δῖον, Scholion to Euripides *Phoenican Women* 1760.

Admittedly all this, such as it is, is not much to go on.[59] However, if we use our earlier chapters' ideas of interformularity and intertraditionality, rather than basing any reconstruction on a unidirectional notion of, say, Homeric precedence, then some interesting points of contact emerge. On the one hand, the death of a younger hero clearly reflects a common trope in heroic epic (such as Patroklos in the *Iliad*, or Antilochus in the so-called *Aithiopis*). On the other, the story arc, at least as represented by the scholion, befits an epic cosmos: in the first movement ("book") of the *Iliad*, for example, a (sexual) transgression by a king leads to a god sending a plague against the people; we might further note that the leader, having sought a prophetic interpretation of the events, finds that he is the cause of the plague. While these elements also evoke the plot of Sophocles' *Oedipus Tyrannos*, the *differences* from the play provide circumstantial evidence that an *Oedipodea* may have taken a form along the lines suggested by viewing the fragment's potential intertraditionality. Indeed, if we take the *dynamism* of this approach seriously, we might even speculate that motifs and thematic patterns from an *Oedipodea* may well have been appropriated by the *Iliad*, on the basis that the plot relating to Agamemnon's transgression lies outside the core Trojan War material.[60] Or, to put that another way, the idea of a leader finding himself implicated in a prophetic judgment on the basis of his sexual transgression *sounds* Oedipal.

Of all the lost Theban epics, the *Thebais*, which was most often attributed to Homer, provides our largest sample of fragments.[61] The fragment that is purportedly its opening line preserves the epic invocation of the Muse:[62] Ἄργος ἄειδε, θεά, πολυδίψιον, ἔνθεν ἄνακτες.... "Sing, goddess, about very thirsty Argos, from where the lords..." (fr. 1). The headline subject—to sing about *Argos*—comes as somewhat of a surprise given the fact that this opens a tale about *Thebes*. Indeed, such a striking beginning may have had something to do with its memorialization (in the *Contest of Homer and Hesiod*).[63] The capacity to

---

59 Many scholars accept Peisander's summary of the tale in the scholia as accurate: Bernrbé 1996:17–19; Davies 2014:7–8 with bibliography.

60 Discussions of the lost epics can be determined by a circularity based both on the fact that their remains were largely preserved with reference to the Homeric poems and on the desire of interpreters to create objects worthy of study: see Davies 2018. This reason—among others—is why we have primarily been concerned with the use of Theban material by Homer.

61 On the testimonia: Bernabé 1996:20–22; cf. Davies 2014:135–136.

62 Cf. the apparent opening line of the *Epigonoi*: "Now, Muses, let us sing in turn of the younger men" (Νῦν αὖθ' ὁπλοτέρων ἀνδρῶν ἀρχώμεθα, Μοῦσαι, fr. 1): Davies 2014:107–108. For an outline of the typical events and sources: Gantz 1993:522–528.

63 For the surprise of a poem about the sack of Thebes starting with an invocation of Argos: Davies 1989:23.

surprise or to misdirect, even in the presentation of a tale that can be recognized as being traditional, is a feature that characterizes both Homeric epics.[64]

It is the second fragment of the *Thebais*, the longest that we have, that is particularly notable in the light of our discussion on epic strife in Hesiod (fr. 2 B/D):[65]

αὐτὰρ ὁ διογενὴς ἥρως ξανθὸς Πολυνείκης
πρῶτα μὲν Οἰδιπόδηι καλὴν παρέθηκε τράπεζαν
ἀργυρέην Κάδμοιο θεόφρονος· αὐτὰρ ἔπειτα
χρύσεον ἔμπλησεν καλὸν δέπας ἡδέος οἴνου.
αὐτὰρ ὅ γ' ὡς φράσθη παρακείμενα πατρὸς ἑοῖο
τιμήεντα γέρα, μέγα οἱ κακὸν ἔμπεσε θυμῶι,
αἶψα δὲ παισὶν ἑοῖσιν ἐπ' ἀμφοτέροισιν ἐπαρὰς
ἀργαλέας ἠρᾶτο· θοὴν δ' οὐ λάνθαν' Ἐρινύν·
ὡς οὔ οἱ πατρώϊ' ἐνηέι <ἐν> φιλότητι
δάσσαιντ', ἀμφοτέροισι δ' ἀεὶ πόλεμοί τε μάχαι τε.

Then the divine-born hero, blond Polyneikes
First placed before Oedipus a fine silver platter,
A thing of god-minded Cadmus. And then
He filled a fine golden cup with sweet wine.
But, when he discerned that lying before him were the
Honorable gifts of his own father, a great evil fell upon his spirit.
Swiftly he uttered grievous curses against both
Of his own sons—and he did not escape the divine Erinys' notice—
That they would not divide their inheritance in kind friendship
But that they would both always have wars and battles.

The language of this fragment reveals motifs and structuring familiar from other extant epics.[66] The term hero (ἥρως) immediately locates these events in a heroic story world, just as in the proem to the *Iliad* or in Hesiod's age of heroes. It is fitting too that the emphasis is on conflict,[67] here manifest in the form of a curse that "that they would not *divide* their patrimony in friendship,

---

[64] On misdirection in Homer: Morrison 1992. On the importance of composing a tale in oral performance that sounds traditional: Scodel 2002.

[65] The fragment is preserved in Athenaeus' *Deipnosophists* XIV 465b. The context is discussing *eris* as a thematic marker, the stories of Thebes being reduced to a "thumbnail" for the participants of the *Iliad*.

[66] The lines throughout the fragment have parallels in extant epic: Davies 2014:49–51.

[67] Thalmann 2004:385: The *Iliad* remembers a sack of Thebes and its quarrel, "an extremely pointed example of the destructive power of *eris*."

but *always wars and battles* would be *between* them" (ὡς οὔ οἱ πατρῷαν εἴη φιλότητι / <u>δάσσοντ᾽, ἀμφοτέροισι δ᾽ ἀεὶ πόλεμοί τε μάχαι τε</u>). Division and strife are again coupled together, as they had been in Hesiod. A divided patrimony is a latent threat in Homer's epics too, both with the characterization of the troubled half-brothers, Ajax and Teucer (a story more fully told in Sophocles' *Ajax*) and in the very insistence on the uniqueness of the line of descent from Laertes through Odysseus to Telemachus—single sons all.[68] Nor is fraternal strife far away: in the *Odyssey*, Nestor recounts how Athena sets strife on *both* sons of Atreus (ἥ τ᾽ ἔριν Ἀτρεΐδῃσι μετ᾽ <u>ἀμφοτέροισιν</u> ἔθηκε, 3.136), the results of which cause the catastrophic division in the Achaean army that fatally compromises the safe returns of the many. It is easy to imagine such a tale of conflict between the Atreidae that, like our *Iliad*, starts with a problematic assembly (as too in Nestor's account) and leads to a prolonged exploration of their troubled home-comings.[69] The conflictual nature of Oedipus' patrimony, however, seems to be of a different order: just as both Achilles and Odysseus contain the seeds of their stories within their names, so too does Oedipus' son, Poly-neikes, "much strife."[70] The strife between brothers is essential to conflict in the *Thebais*.

Perhaps less obviously epic is the catalyst for conflict. There seems to be little in the way of conflict in the opening lines, where Polyneikes serves his father food and wine. On the contrary, the accumulation of positive epithets—divine-born, blond, fine silver, god-minded, fine golden, sweet wine—serves to create a mood of fine dining. It is all the more shocking—that element of surprise again—when a great evil fell upon Oedipus' spirit. The reason appears all too elusive (and allusive?): "his father's honored gifts had been set before him" (παρακείμενα πατρὸς ἑοῖο / τιμήεντα γέρα). With this line, the scene of conviviality is shattered, and Oedipus "swiftly" (αἶψα) curses his sons and divides their patrimony in strife.

A third fragment from the Thebais (3.1) lingers on the moment, even if the details remain frustratingly *elliptical*:

ἰσχίον ὡς ἐνόησε, χαμαὶ βάλεν εἶπέ τε μῦθον·
"ὤ μοι ἐγώ, παῖδες μέγ᾽ ὀνειδείοντες ἔπεμψαν..."
εὖκτο Διὶ βασιλῆϊ καὶ ἄλλοις ἀθανάτοισι
χερσὶν ὑπ᾽ ἀλλήλων καταβήμεναι Ἄϊδος εἴσω.

---

[68] See Chapter 3; cf. Goldhill 2010.

[69] West 2013:244–250 imagines that the "Return of the Atreidai" mentioned by Athenaeus is actually the same as a single Cyclic poem called the *Nostoi*. Davies 2014:61 places this fraternal struggle in the larger context of Mediterranean fratricide myths.

[70] On the speaking names of Achilles and Odysseus: Higbie 1995; Kanavou 2015: 29–35 and 91–100; and Chapter 3, n35.

> When he noticed the cut of meat, he hurled it to the ground and
> > spoke a word:
> "Alas, my children have sent this as a reproach to me..."
> He prayed to King Zeus and the other gods
> That they would go to Hades' home at each other's hands.

Given the overlap in content, it is quite possible that this fragment comes from a different source and provides an alternative account of Oedipus' cursing of his sons;[71] on the other hand, it is equally plausible that what it does is complementary to the previous fragment, in effect doubling the sons' offense and giving voice to the curse. In either case what exactly provokes Oedipus' furious response remains unclear, and we should perhaps not discount a sense of the uncanny or inexplicable.[72] What is apparent from both fragments, however, is the epic theme of strife and, more particularly, its network of associations that we have previously identified in Hesiod—specifically the division or distribution (*dasmos*) of honors (*timai, gera*) at a *feast*.

We observed above that the strife between Zeus and Prometheus in *Hesiod* also occurs at a feast: indeed, as the original "settlement" between the gods and humans, the feast in the *Theogony* represents and replays a foundational moment, when mortal and immortal are definitively separated. The idea of the feast as a source of conflict occurs too in the *Odyssey*. In Book 8, Demodokos' song places the "strife of Odysseus and Achilles" at a feast. For three whole books Odysseus then sings about his strife (as he strives to return) in the banqueting halls of the Phaiakians. Within that frame, feasting plays a curiously prominent role in the death of his companions. They perish when they feast on the beach after sacking the city of the Kikonians; when they help themselves to Polyphemus' provisions, only to be feasted on themselves; and when they slaughter the cattle of the Sun—their fatal demise which the narrator headlined as early as the proem.[73] Finally, back on Ithaca, with the return of the king, the suitors are slaughtered in Odysseus' banqueting hall, as they feast.[74] While scenes of conflict at feasts are (arguably unsurprisingly) absent from the *Iliad*'s war narrative, another Trojan War epic, the *Aithiopis*, apparently included a

---

[71] For a discussion of the relationship of the two fragments: Davies 2014:54–62. Fowler 2013:408–409 suggests that it is easier to view them as fragments of different poems.

[72] Oedipus' rage derives from his sons' disobedience and being reminded of his murder of Laios: Davies 2014:138; cf. 45–48. Taking the evidence more literally, a scholion to *Oedipus at Colonus* 1375 explains that Oedipus curses his sons after being denied a customary portion of sacrificial meat. See Davies 2014:138–139; Bernabé 1996:23–24.

[73] See Barker and Christensen 2006 for a discussion of how generic rivalry with sympotic poetry might be at play. We might note too that Odysseus' men are turned into pigs when they accept food from Circe.

[74] See Pucci 1987:128–138; Barker 2009:123–126; cf. Rutherford 1991:44.

scene of feasting where Achilles kills Thersites for mocking him over his desire for the Amazon queen Penthesileia.[75] The *Iliad* perhaps preserves a memory of such a conflict in its introduction of Thersites as "always abusing Achilles and Odysseus especially" (2.220). What is important in the *Iliad*, however, is the institutionalization, or *domestication*, of strife in scenes of meetings between the Achaean leaders, which are all framed by the formulaic line: "when they had put aside their desire for food" (e.g. 9.92: αὐτὰρ ἐπεὶ πόσιος καὶ ἐδητύος ἐξ ἔρον ἕντο).[76] The intimate connection between meal taking and political deliberation, suggested by that formula, can be read as an extension of the Hesiodic contemplation on distributing honors at the sacrifice—as if providing different points of view in a safe environment were a distribution of honors of sorts.[77] In this way the *Iliad* recoups feasting as a socially unifying moment. Conflict at the feast becomes sublimated in the institutional, and formulaically framed, scene of council.

We will discuss some of the implications of viewing strife as a common theme for reading Homer in more detail in the next chapter; here we might note how the language and ideas of these two Theban fragments also resonate with the opening movement of the *Iliad*, and not only because of the honor (*geras*) of which Achilles is deprived.[78] In his quarrel (*neikos*) with Achilles, Agamemnon savages him for "always being in love with strife and *wars and battles*" (αἰεὶ γάρ τοι ἔρις τε φίλη πόλεμοί τε μάχαι τε, 1.177), a line that Zeus repeats in his criticism of Ares (5.891) and that recalls Oedipus' curse against his sons. What happens to the brothers in the Theban poems when their father promises them continual war and battles (ἀεὶ πόλεμοί τε μάχαι τε) we don't know: what we do know is that in the *Iliad* Agamemnon deploys the formula in a context of *verbal* battle, a conceptual extension of the motif of physical strife. Indeed, when Agamemnon reworks this line, he does to emphasize the *social threat* posed by Achilles, as Zeus too does later in relation to the god of war.[79] The interesting twist on Agamemnon's perception of Achilles as a danger to all is that it is Achilles who, at least initially, stands up for a proper and *communal* distribution of goods (before *his* prize specifically is threatened).[80] We have no way of telling

---

[75] See Rosen 2002.

[76] See Barker 2009:63 with n85.

[77] Cf. the famous scene between Glaukos and Sarpedon (*Iliad* 12.310–328), in which the pair articulate the necessity to fight in the front line since they get the choicest cuts of meat. On this scene: Adkins 1970:34–35 and Pucci 1998:49–68.

[78] Cingano 2004:278 places Oedipus and Achilles alongside each other as heroes who are deprived of a previously sanctioned γέρας and who experience wrath as a result.

[79] On the comparison between Achilles and Ares: Nagy 1999 [1979]:131 and Christensen 2012:236. On the latent cosmic threat presented by Ares: Muellner 1996:5–13.

[80] See our discussion of Achilles and the Achaean assembly in the next chapter.

how the theme of strife played out in the *Thebais*, though it is true to say that the emphasis in the fragment is on *familial* conflict. In the *Iliad*, as we shall see, the manifestation of *eris* is complex, fluid, and socially oriented, an ambiguous figure that owes something to its double genealogy in Hesiod.

The fragments of the remaining Theban epics—that is to say, those not held to be thoroughly "Homeric"—do not appear to exhibit the kind of interformular thematics of strife that we have been discussing, so far as any conclusion can be drawn from a fragmentary corpus. Even then, however, there are interesting intertraditional echoes in the corpus. The longest fragment of the *Alcmeonis*, for example, starts with the brothers Peleus and Telamon, fathers of the Homeric Achilles and Ajax, murdering their half-brother Phokos (fr. 1):[81]

ἔνθα μιν ἀντίθεος Τελαμὼν τροχοειδέι δίσκωι
πλῆξε κάρη, Πηλεὺς δὲ θοῶς ἐνὶ χειρὶ τινάξας
ἀξίνην εὔχαλκον ἐπεπλήγει μέσα νῶτα.

There, godlike Telamon struck him in the head
With a rounded discus and Peleus raised in his hands
Swiftly a bronze ax to strike him down through the middle of the
    back.

On the face of it, murdering one's half-brother hardly seems to rank in the same heroic category as the actions of their sons, the *Iliad*'s most famous warriors.[82] But not only is it rather befitting of the savagery attributed to the fighters around Thebes where Tydeus famously eats brains;[83] it resonates strongly with the theme of fraternal strife and violence that is central to the *Thebais*. Elsewhere in the corpus of early Greek poetry more generally the idea of Thebes as a locus for strife is also prominent. A very good reason why Thebes proved such rich pickings for the Athenian tragedians relates to its tradition of thematizing internal strife, a particularly charged and fertile idea when explored through an individual (ruling) family.

The Lille Stesichorus provides further evidence for understanding these lexical markers and their attendant themes as an integral part of the story

---

[81] For the content and scholarly history: Davies 2014:116–117.
[82] Davies 1989:25–26 suggests that the fragments indicate that, unlike Homer's *Iliad* where both sides are presented with sympathy, the attackers in the *Thebais* were "portrayed...as semi-monsters."
[83] For Tydeus' brain eating, see fr. 5; Davies 1989:26.

tradition around Thebes.[84] In addition to the poem's clear Homeric diction,[85] *neikos* features prominently, appearing on no fewer than three occasions (μ]έγα νεῖκος, 188; νεῖκος ἔμπεδον, 206; νείκεος ἐμ μεγάροις, 233), which serves to structure the narrative around an Eris theme. The second of those instances is put in the mouth of a female speaker,[86] who complains that "the immortal gods have established constant strife throughout sacred land for mortals" (θεοὶ θέ σαν ἀθάνατοι κατ' αἶαν ἱρὰν / νεῖκος ἔμπεδον βροτοῖσιν, 205–206). The phrase κατ' αἶαν ἱράν, "through the sacred land," echoes and, at the same time, reworks the epithet and noun combination "sacred Thebes" in hexameter epic, as if conflict were no longer contained in the city alone but has spread throughout the land.[87] The fragment continues with a proposal to end the conflict through a proper division of the spoils: one son should keep the household, while the other takes the goods (220–221).[88]

As well as directly addressing the issue of fair distribution preserved in the *Thebais* fragments that come down to us, this scene of arbitration engages with the Hesiodic nexus of themes relating to *eris, krisis,* and *dasmos* that we identified and discussed above. Using the kind of "gentle words" (μύθοις ἀγ[α]νοῖς ἐνέποίσα, 232) attributed by Hesiod to his adjudicating king, or requested by Nestor for his,[89] Iocasta's (or is it Epikastê's or Euryganeia's?) act of arbitration attempts to redistribute inheritance in much the same way as we might imagine the absent kings doing in the beginning of Hesiod's *Works and Days,* even if

---

[84] For the text: Parsons 1977; Bremer 1987; Finglass 2014. The papyrus is dated by Finglass 2014:369 to the mid-third century BCE. According to Russo 1997 it may be a mistake to think of Stesichorus as operating outside the epic tradition. He addresses problems in our understanding of the poet's genre and argues that Stesichorus occupies a space between epic and lyric that pre-dates the regular hexameter and (re)performances of Hesiod and Homer. In addition, he proposes that the performances of Demodokos in the *Odyssey,* which mix subjects later generations might see as deriving from these different genres, point to the Homeric depiction of this sort of figure.

[85] See Parsons 1977:7 and 12.

[86] Parsons 1977 identifies her as Epikastê. Finglass 2014:364–366, following Bremer 1987:139, believes it to be Euryganeia, on the basis that evidence for Oedipus' mother living on after the shocking revelation is lacking until Euripides, and that in the tradition it was Oedipus' second wife who gave birth to his children.

[87] See the Introduction, "Why Thebes?" Bremer 1987:139, observing that the adjective "sacred" is attached to a city everywhere else in archaic poetry but here modifies generic "land," finds the usage "curious."

[88] The division is repeated and expanded upon at 235–246: Finglass 2014:377.

[89] See Bremer 1987:162 for Homeric parallels to "gentle speech." Oedipus appears absent from the poem: Finglass 2014:366–367 suggests that he is dead already; Burnett 1988:115 argues that the poem has made "the queen the head of the house." Bremer 1987:167 relates Iocasta's adjudication of the conflict to the situation between Hesiod and Perses in the *Works and Days.* He also points to a historical example of fraternal distribution by lot: in the seventh century BCE, Cyrene sent out colonists by having families with more than one male heir draw lots to stay or go.

here the rightful distribution will ultimately be decided by lot ("whoever drew first with the willingness of the Fates," πρᾶτος λάχηι ἔκατι Μοιρᾶν, 324).[90] In both cases—in Hesiod and in this reworking of the Theban story—an outbreak of conflict (*eris*) has been addressed through a judgment (*krisis*) that attempts resolution through some kind of a distribution (*dasmos*). The problem in both situations is that (at least) one of the brothers cannot or will not adhere to the results of the *krisis* and attempts to take more than what has been apportioned. The result of this initial failure of distribution will be the renewal of conflict. While for Hesiod the *eris* is reworked and sublimated into his poem, for the story of Oedipus this is the *eris* that will forever go on destroying the city of Thebes.

Conclusion

In this chapter we have discussed the importance of the bifurcation of *eris* and its connection to both the form and the content of epic poetry. By unpacking its constituent parts we have identified and explored a series of thematic moves that appear to be shared and shaped by both Trojan and Theban epics. On this basis we believe that investigating the *content* of the thematics of *eris* has been a useful and hermeneutically productive exercise for thinking about the agonistics of these rival traditions. However, we also want to emphasize the fundamental impact of the thematics of *eris* on the *form* of epic as well. In rivalry with and in response to other traditions, each epic poem builds on and develops motifs and themes in a process that is both competitive and cooperative. In our last example we have observed some of the ways in which both the Theban tradition of the Oedipus tale and the poetic conceit of the conflict between Perses and Hesiod depend upon and draw on the same themes, motifs and, in some cases, even the same language. Yet their deployment of these elements differs radically. Where Hesiod integrates *eris* to make his epic words a type of settlement, inviting his audience to a *krisis* within the regulatory framework offered by his poem, the Stesichorus fragment anticipates further conflict and destruction.

In a storyworld where we imagine the sacks of Thebes and Troy as coexisting, the intertraditionality that leads both narrative traditions to integrate similar themes into their representative poems results in mirrored explorations of the primeval force of strife. An integral part of the dynamic rivalry between these traditions was the inversion of theme and the juxtaposition of context and content. Where the nominal Theban epic, the *Thebais*, turns an internecine

---

[90] The rest of the poem first narrates the drawing of the lots and then prepares the ground for the renewed outbreak of strife as the sons protest and Teiresias prophesies their future doom. On the former: see Parsons 1977:27; Finglass 2014:385; on the latter: Parsons 1977:24 and 26. Finglass 2014:367 suggests that Teiresias' prophecies replace the curses of Oedipus.

struggle into an international war of sorts, Homer's response, as we shall see in the next chapter, is to integrate extraneous Trojan War motifs like civil strife into what initially appears to be a tale of a foreign expedition and the return home. Thus, the *Iliad* turns an international war into an internecine struggle of sorts, redirecting the focus of conflict from scenes of battle with enemy combatants to a war of words between the best of the Achaeans, with important political, foundational consequences for the people of Achaean society. In turn the *Odyssey* even more rigorously interrogates the social institutions that are supposed to protect society from destructive disintegration, all the time reflecting metapoetically on the role of song in the management and negotiation of strife, particularly civil war.

5

Theban Palimpsests[1]

Strife that gives birth to strife *prosmnatai* ('wins over') reason.
Ἔρις ἔριν τίκτουσα προσμνᾶται λόγον.

Suda s.v. Eris; *Mantissa Proverbiorum* 1.60

T HIS PROVERB ON STRIFE, preserved in both the *Suda* and the *Mantissa Proverbiorum*, is unusually cryptic for a maxim. The verb προσμνᾶται is not attested anywhere else but clearly relies on a metaphor of wooing;[2] *logos* can be translated in any number of ways, but here probably means something along the lines of "reason";[3] both texts gloss the proverb as applying "to those who chatter on because of friendship" (ἐπὶ τῶν ἐκ φιλίας ἀδολεσχούντων). The language, if we understand it correctly, is deeply ambiguous, implying, it seems, that strife pursues or tries to win over reason, like a persistent suitor. The difficult point may just be that conflict in multiple forms is always in the process of inviting or courting argumentation and reason to challenge or support it, or otherwise reflect upon it in some way.

Indeed, we find in this proverb a useful reflection on the story of strife that we set out in the last chapter. First, the opening three words ("strife that gives birth to strife," Ἔρις ἔριν τίκτουσα) represents, in a pithy axiomatic form, the interpoetic resonance of *eris* that we discussed above, where one type or manifestation of conflict has the thematic tendency to lead to or be sublimated in

---

[1] The title of this chapter acknowledges the debt to Christos Tsagalis's 2008 *The Oral Palimpsest*. Explaining the oxymoron (using a term from the manuscript tradition to describe oral poetics), he writes (xi): "During a long process of shaping, the Homeric tradition has absorbed, altered, disguised, and reappropriated mythical, dictional, and thematic material of various sorts and from different sources. In that sense it is like an oral palimpsest, 'to be erased' and re-'written' in accordance with traditional structure and within the limits of the multiform idiom."

[2] It is glossed in the *Mantissa Proverbiorum* as προξενεῖ καὶ προμηθεύεται ("manages and takes care over").

[3] The paroemiographer Arsenius adds: "this is applied to those striving over philosophy" (ἤτοι ἐπὶ φιλοσοφίᾳ ἐριζόντων, *Apophthegmata* 7.94a).

another. Second, there is a progressive development in the valence of *eris* over the course of the proverb itself. Where the first three elements appear to denote an escalation of conflict and recalls Hesiod's negative representation of strife as destructive, the verb and its object offer a somewhat a different moral. No matter what προσμνᾶται means precisely or how *logos* is to be translated—to disambiguate and render it in English as, say, either "reason" or "conversation" detracts (and distracts) from the overlapping meanings available in the Greek— the violence anticipated fails to materialize and we are left with something more productive. In this subtle transformation, we come closer to Hesiod's second, more positive kind of strife. Significantly, further comment provided by both encyclopedia entries performs this verbal domestication of strife. The gloss interposes friendship (*philia*) as an essential state or motivation to generate and direct the productive kind of *eris*—an attempt to explain (and control) strife that recalls the desired actions of Hesiod's king.

The previous chapter laid out the fragmentary remains of the Theban tradition and the thematic framework of Eris. While it is clear that we have no way of knowing how the epics about Thebes told their story, there is enough evidence from the extant fragments and later summaries to suggest that their main focus was on internecine and interfamilial strife over rule and honor. In particular we have identified a nexus of associations with the idea of strife—distribution, judgment, more conflict—whose thematic resonances are broadly shared with Hesiod's representations both of strife and of the settlement between gods and mortals more specifically.

In this chapter, we pick up the story of Homer's engagement with these same themes, motifs, and larger story-patterns. Our aim is not to argue that our Theban epic fragments or cognate poems necessarily influenced the plot and shape of our Homeric epics, as a neoanalytical approach might. Rather, we believe that the resonances of the *eris* theme in the *Iliad* and the *Odyssey*, and in particular its "secondariness," supports the claim that these epics are responding in part to the *kind* of thematics implied by the fragments of the Theban epics. That response, as we have already anticipated, is a political one.[4]

---

[4] This is not to argue that the Theban epics did not deploy political themes: if the Athenian tragedies are anything to go by, stories about Thebes were intensely interested in questions of power, social relations, etc. But, if there is a difference between these stories and those relating to Troy, it seems to be that the interest of the Theban stories appears to lie in exploring issues of distribution and judgment through a framework not so much of *coalition* as of the *family*. Other mythical stories whose details are now lost to us, such as the Calydonian boar hunt or the voyage of the Argo, equally provide ample opportunity for considering how heroes band together. Our evidence, meager though it is, implies that a *Seven Against Thebes* tradition and the *Epigonoi* did not develop this element in depth, though that again may be largely due to the warping effect of the Homeric poems.

As we observed at the end of the last chapter, the *Iliad* starts with a plague caused when Agamemnon refuses a ransom. This plot-device is integral to the Theban story, where personal transgressions on the part of the king (Laios or Oedipus) lead to a plague being cast on the city. In this chapter we explore how the *Iliad* doubles down on the thematic trope by transforming a communal conflict (the war) motivated by personal enmity (the abduction of Helen) into a personal conflict (the quarrel) over public concerns (common distribution of spoils). As such, we will see that the *Iliad* engages and competes with and *through* what we might call "Theban themes." Where the *Iliad* marks a distinct, and in its terms superior, contribution is through its representation of the political consequences of strife—namely, the series of institutional forms that emerge in direct response to the cosmic problem of strife and man's attempt to manage it: the institutions of the assembly, law court, oath, and burial.

In pursuing the theme of Eris in the homecoming narrative of the *Odyssey*, we draw upon our conclusions in Chapter 3, which suggested the importance of Oedipus as a countermodel to Odysseus, acting in much the same way as the more commonly observed (faulty) paradigm of the triad Agamemnon-Clytemnestra-Orestes in relation to Odysseus-Penelope-Telemachus: the *Odyssey* is at pains to avoid the tangled familial history of the Thebes of Oedipus, another returning hero of sorts. Arguably the *Odyssey* is even more insistent on the need to regulate strife, by largely sidelining it from its narrative and relegating it to a heroic past, in the epic-like stories that are sung. The reason is in part the *Odyssey*'s post-*Iliad*, post-war position in cosmic history: its rivalry is with both Thebes *and* Troy, and as much with the *Iliad* as a foundational narrative as with the thematic fragments belonging to the nebulous Theban poems. Nevertheless, the extent of its obsession with the failure of institutions like the assembly to manage strife adequately may also be due to the specter of Thebes haunting the narrative. We explore the *Odyssey*'s thematic resonances with Thebes in its many scenes of feasting, the poem's notoriously difficult final lurch towards a Theban-style civil strife, and the prophecy from a figure of Theban myth who heralds no end to the theme of Odysseus' wanderings. With the sudden outbreak of potentially catastrophic strife averted, just as suddenly, through direct divine intervention, the *Odyssey* leaves its audiences to ponder questions relating to the extent to which, and how, strife has been (or can be) mediated by and transformed into some kind of good for the community.

All of these thematic strands interweave within the conceptual history that we have discussed several times in this book. Within this framework, the strife of both the Theban and Trojan wars is part of a broader cosmic plan—the plan of Zeus—to rid the world of heroes and bring the age of heroes to an end. Picking up on this end point, we conclude the chapter by returning to Hesiod's *Works and Days* and his conflict with Perses, which marks—and to a certain extent ushers into existence—a putative end to that cosmic history. Even though both Homeric epics look forward to institutions and futures outside the race of heroes, in Hesiod's post-heroic poem these institutions emerge as a disappointment, ultimately frustrating attempts to resolve human conflict to the satisfaction of all those involved in it, poet included. Strife, though somewhat transformed and domesticated, persists nevertheless and continues to demand a whole range of differing responses.

Enabling Strife, Founding Politics

The elements marshaled together at the beginning of the *Iliad* contribute to what we imagine to be a thoroughly conventional epic framework for the latest telling of the war at Troy (*Iliad* 1.1–8):

> μῆνιν ἄειδε θεὰ Πηληϊάδεω Ἀχιλῆος
> οὐλομένην, ἣ μυρί᾽ Ἀχαιοῖς ἄλγε᾽ ἔθηκε,
> πολλὰς δ᾽ ἰφθίμους ψυχὰς Ἄϊδι προΐαψεν
> ἡρώων, αὐτοὺς δὲ ἑλώρια τεῦχε κύνεσσιν
> οἰωνοῖσί τε πᾶσι, Διὸς δ᾽ ἐτελείετο βουλή,
> ἐξ οὗ δὴ τὰ πρῶτα διαστήτην <u>ἐρίσαντε</u>
> Ἀτρεΐδης τε ἄναξ ἀνδρῶν καὶ δῖος Ἀχιλλεύς.
> τίς τ᾽ ἄρ σφωε θεῶν <u>ἔριδι</u> ξυνέηκε μάχεσθαι;

> Goddess, sing the rage of Peleus' son Achilles,
> The ruinous rage which made endless griefs for the Achaeans
> And sent many stout souls of heroes to Hades
> As it made their bodies into food for the dogs
> And all the birds. And Zeus' plan was being accomplished.
> Start from when those two men first stood apart in *strife*
> Atreus' son, lord of men, and shining Achilles.
> Which god sent them together to fight in *strife*?

The notes of this proem chime with themes that we have heard in Hesiod and were likely activated by poems of the Theban tradition. The reference to heroes immediately locates the *Iliad* in a heroic epic cosmos, tasked with addressing (at its core) the death of the race of the demi-gods; the formulaic half-hexameter line, "and the will of Zeus was being accomplished," provides an assurance that the plot will unfold according to the plan of Zeus which, along with the invocation to the Muse, gives an authoritative backing to this version of events.[5] Within this frame, the narrator traces a direct line from the first word "wrath" to the headline of strife at the proem's end, from which point the tale will begin ("from when those two men first stood apart *in strife*," ἐξ οὗ δὴ τὰ πρῶτα διαστήτην <u>ἐρίσαντε</u>, 6) and the question of divine agency which marks the beginning of the narrative proper (τίς τάρ σφωε θεῶν <u>ἔριδι</u> ξυνέηκε μάχεσθαι, 8). It is in the unveiling of what this strife entails that the *Iliad* immediately issues a challenge to its own tradition: Achilles' wrath sends the spirits of *his own people* to Hades; it is his strife with Agamemnon, "lord of men," that is under scrutiny, not (so much) the conflict with the Trojans. This provocative turn inwards, a Theban kind of strife, questions and threatens the very constitution of Achaean epic society.

The short first episode establishes the terms and wide-ranging scope of this focus. A Trojan priest by the name of Chryses arrives in camp and appeals to the Achaeans and the twin sons of Atreus for his daughter, in return for whom he offers a boundless ransom.[6] His offer is hailed by the Achaeans en masse only to be immediately, and forcefully, countered by Agamemnon, who sends the priest away "with a mighty word" (κρατερὸς μῦθος, 1.25). Not only does the king's rejection of consensus bode ill for his relations with his people; as David Elmer points out, the very expression of communal judgment is problematic. The verb used to denote the Achaeans' reaction, ἐπευφήμησαν (*Iliad* 1.22), which apparently means "they expressed approval," is, in Elmer's words, "ungrammatical" (Elmer 2013:74). It only occurs once more, when Achilles narrates this episode to his mother (*Iliad* 1.376), and *jars*, even if its sense can be deduced. The combination of the group's singular reaction and the king's willful assertion of his own desire critically divides the judgment and violates the most fundamental principle of the poem's grammar of reception—the principle that "collective will should be decisive in scenes of collective decision making" (Elmer 2013:66).[7] The fallout from this "state of exception" (Elmer 2013:68–69) anticipates in form and content the ensuing quarrel between Agamemnon and Achilles, as strife begets more strife. This next episode, out of which the rest of the poem is moulded, reveals two important indicators of the *Iliad*'s own striving within its tradition: the (foundational) idea of assembly and the (communal) issue of distribution.

---

[5] On the generic force of the term "heroes": Haubold 2000:3–11. On the *Dios boulê* in the wider epic tradition, see Chapter 3, n39, above.

[6] On the meaning and stakes of this boundless ransom: Wilson 2002a:40–53.

[7] "But it wasn't pleasing to Atreus' son, Agamemnon in his spirit" (ἀλλ' οὐκ Ἀτρεΐδῃ Ἀγαμέμνονι ἥνδανε θυμῷ, *Iliad* 1.24).

If the first scene of judgment seems to take place within an institutional vacuum (Chryses simply arrives in the Achaean camp and makes his appeal), the next scene is more conspicuously introduced (*Iliad* 1.53–58):

ἐννῆμαρ μὲν ἀνὰ στρατὸν ᾤχετο κῆλα θεοῖο
τῇ δεκάτῃ δ᾽ ἀγορὴν δὲ καλέσσατο λαὸν Ἀχιλλεύς.
τῷ γὰρ ἐπὶ φρεσὶ θῆκε θεὰ λευκώλενος Ἥρη.
κήδετο γὰρ Δαναῶν, ὅτι ῥα θνήσκοντας ὁρᾶτο.
οἳ δ᾽ ἐπεὶ οὖν ἤγερθεν ὁμηγερέες τε γένοντο,
τοῖσι δ᾽ ἀνιστάμενος μετέφη πόδας ὠκὺς Ἀχιλλεύς.

For nine days the deadly barbs of the god rained down on the army,
And on the tenth Achilles called the people to assembly.
For the white-armed goddess Hera put it into his mind:
Her heart went out to the Danaans, as she saw them dying.
When they had gathered and were all gathered together,
Then swift-footed Achilles stood up and spoke to them.

In our Introduction we analyzed the resonance of the phrase "swift-footed Achilles" and argued that this first example sets the tone for the rest of the epic in that the *Iliad* depicts an Achilles who, for the most part, is paradoxically motionless (literally) and immovable (figuratively). Here, the "misuse" of the epithet, applied to his act of having risen to his feet to speak, places emphasis on the precise nature of his immobility: that is to say, his gathering of the people to assembly. As Johannes Haubold (2000:33) has argued, "One of the basic facts of social life in early Greek hexameter poetry is that the people [*laoi*] need to be 'gathered'. They do not assemble regularly or of their own accord." This event is further emphasized by the doublet ἤγερθεν ὁμηγερέες τε γένοντο. (To bring out the redundancy we ungracefully translate this as "they had gathered and were all gathered together.")

We see a far more elaborate description of the people gathering in the next book, when "Agamemnon ordered the clear-voiced heralds / to gather the long-haired Achaeans to assembly. / They gave the order, the people gathered quickly."[8] The formularity of these lines (repeated almost verbatim at *Odyssey* 2.6–8) implies that the idea of the assembly as a gathering of the people for debate—that is to say, as a socio-political institution—was well known in early Greek hexameter epic; the idea is embedded in the language itself. In addition, these lines delineate the agents and their roles: the instituting figure

---

[8] αὐτὰρ ὁ κηρύκεσσι λιγυφθόγγοισι κέλευσε / κηρύσσειν ἀγορήνδε κάρη κομόωντας Ἀχαιούς / οἳ μὲν ἐκήρυσσον, τοὶ δ᾽ ἠγείροντο μάλ᾽ ὦκα, *Iliad* 2.50–52.

(the shepherd), the heralds who deliver the instructions, and the group who are (to be) gathered, "the long-haired Achaeans"—itself a resonant phrase representing the epic group of Greeks who fought at Troy. Indeed, the event of assembly seems to be so familiar that it can be exploited for effect. In this later episode, Agamemnon interrupts the process of gathering by first calling a council meeting (βουλὴν δὲ πρῶτον, *Iliad* 2.53). The effects of this intervention not only disrupt the institutional formation but are felt on the language itself, as the formulaic expression of civic coordination under the authority of the king unravels to present *laoi* now "hurrying on by their own accord," urged on by the new instituting agent, Rumor; as "the kings' heralds try to wrest back control," the "*agora* was in turmoil." Haubold regards this episode as "a beginning of communal action", a "[replay of] the 'original' assembly at the beginning of the Trojan War."[9] Yet it seems more likely that Agamemnon has (again) willfully trumped the expression of communal will (here, the apparatus of assembly) in pursuit of his own ends, as he will do (again) in his subsequent speech.[10]

In fact, the change "from unstructured to structured social life" (Haubold 2000:55), we argue, comes before, in the assembly that "swift-footed Achilles" calls.[11] We have just seen that the very presence of a formula for assembling shows that there is prior knowledge of the institution of the agora in early Greek hexameter poetry. However, through its careful framing of this first assembly in the poem, the *Iliad* creates the fiction of its foundation, that this *is* the first moment of assembly among the Achaeans. This framing has several components. First, Achilles is the instituting figure, not Agamemnon, the "shepherd of the people" and "lord of men." This makes the event not only unusual but potentially untraditional, in the sense that such an act of social formation isn't what "swift-footed Achilles" is famous for—and the use of that epithet to introduce the hero's speech in this assembly underlines the disjunction. At the same time, convoking the assembly seems to be beyond the scope of the king whose very status is defined by his relationship to the people (as their shepherd or lord); instead, it requires the hero with a special connection to the gods ("godlike Achilles," δῖος Ἀχιλλεύς 1.7) to make the decisive intervention in the crisis. This brings us to our second observation: the *gods* are involved in the establishment of this assembly. Hera puts the idea into Achilles' mind, as if calling an assembly to resolve a community's crisis is not (yet) the course of action that would occur

---

[9] Haubold 2000: 54, 55.

[10] As Haubold (2000:56) goes on to argue: "In what follows, Agamemnon turns a structured world of groups and leaders, in which all the responsibility for success or defeat rests on him, the 'shepherd of the people', into a homogeneous social world of equally interested single agents... qua 'heroes'."

[11] This argument was first proposed in Barker 2004 (cf. 2009); the focus here is rather different.

"naturally" to the hero. Hera's mediation marks the moment as significant, extraordinary in some way.

Lastly, Homer uses the resonant term *laos* as the group whom Achilles calls to assemble.[12] This is the only instance of *laos* being used in the convocation of the assembly, though it is again they who are assembled when Achilles later establishes the agon; "long-haired Achaeans" is more usual in the context of debate. The *laoi*, Haubold argues, are the people of epic, importantly—when thinking about moments that establish a precedent—a group undifferentiated by social distinction. They are the group before institutions, reliant solely on an individual for protection and salvation. Yet here they are being gathered into an institution. The unique, founding moment is set off by a further manipulation of traditional meter, as Achilles steps "into the protected metrical space of 'the people of the Achaeans' (λαὸν Ἀχιλλεύς)" at the end of the line.[13]

After gathering the people together (in response, lest it be forgotten, to a crisis that is putting their very existence at risk), Achilles not only speaks on their behalf but creates the conditions for speech on the public good to take place. He first invites whoever knows what crisis is inflicting the people to speak;[14] then, when the response comes back from Calchas that he fears to reveal his knowledge, Achilles steps in to guarantee his safety and valorize his speech. In essence he establishes the parameters for debate to take place in the assembly by enabling dissent from (the king's) authority to happen.[15] Therefore, while Haubold is right to say that "none of the major figures in the *Iliad*—Agamemnon and Achilles among them—can in fact provide the institutional continuity that would rescue the people permanently," Achilles *does* establish the parameters and sets the precedent in which the people can gain salvation themselves. His primeval gathering of the people makes possible the moment of institutional transformation and establishes the assembly as an institution that will offer the people protection once the race of heroes is dead and gone.[16]

---

[12] We thank Mary Yossi for this observation.

[13] Haubold 2000:79. As Haubold notes, the only other character to do so is Athena, who, in Nestor's story, is said to have "turned the host back again" (ὅθεν αὖτις ἀπέτραπε λαὸν Ἀθήνη, 11.758).

[14] Initially addressing Agamemnon (59), Achilles immediately refers to the welfare of the Achaeans as a whole (61), and proceeds to use the first person plural subjunctive ("let us ask," 62) to invite "whoever" (64) to speak up—as heralds will later formally do in convoking the Athenian assembly: see Sommerstein 1980:160 on Aristophanes *Acharnians* 45.

[15] See Barker 2009:40–52. Scenes of the Trojan assembly lack any kind of foundational moment like this, with the result of the crippling, and catastrophic, consensus that greets Hektor's final speech in the assembly, when he commits them to staying outside the walls. The narrator feels compelled at this point to step in and say "fools" (νήπιοι, 8.311): Barker 2009:67–74.

[16] Haubold (2000:75). For him, "the *laoi* leave behind their suffering to become what we might call the 'founding people' of successful institutional structures" only outside Homer (144). The later

In addition to the assembly that he establishes, Achilles—initially at least—pointedly frames his strife as socially constructed in a way that recalls Hesiod's other strife and the Theban concern with proper division which we saw in the previous chapter. Even if it is his godlike status that gives him the license to strive (with words) with the lord of men,[17] he emphasizes that the community as a whole have been involved in the *division* of booty. "All the things we sacked from the cities, *all that has been distributed*" (ἀλλὰ τὰ μὲν πολίων ἐξεπράθομεν, τὰ δέδασται, 1.124), he asserts; "it is not proper that *the people* gather these things together again" (λαοὺς δ' οὐκ ἐπέοικε παλίλλογα ταῦτ' ἐπαγείρειν, 1.125). This is not the language one might have expected from an exceptional hero, nor the manner in which we might have imagined the subject of distribution would be central to an epic about the attempt to reclaim Helen.[18] This political refocusing on events at Troy is enabled through the repurposing of the nexus of themes around *eris*—primarily *dasmos* and *krisis*, as well as the good kind of strife—that we have seen operate in the Hesiodic and Theban traditions.

How to *read* the strife between the two Achaean heroes is particularly at issue. By the end of the assembly, Achilles has hurled to the ground the scepter—the symbol of the right to speak before the community on behalf of the community[19]—and sworn an oath that would see his people destroyed. The oath institution, established by the Theogonic Zeus to contain strife, here becomes the means of expressing it and devastatingly extending its destructive potential, as the plague sent by Apollo gives way to huge (Achilles-less) Achaean losses in the war as promised by Zeus. Significantly, immediately after Achilles swears this oath, Homer introduces Nestor, the voice of the tradition, in terms that strikingly recall Hesiod's description of the Zeus-blessed king. Where Hesiod's ideal king has honey poured on his tongue by the Muses so that from his mouth gentle words flow (τῷ μὲν ἐπὶ γλώσσῃ γλυκερὴν χείουσιν ἐέρσην, / τοῦ δ' ἔπε' ἐκ στόματος ῥεῖ μείλιχα, *Theogony* 83–84), Nestor is the "sweet-spoken, clear-voiced orator whose words flow more sweetly than honey from his tongue" (ἡδυεπὴς ἀνόρουσε λιγὺς Πυλίων ἀγορητής / τοῦ καὶ ἀπὸ γλώσσης μέλιτος γλυκίων ῥέεν

---

[17] emphasis of Graziosi and Haubold 2005 on the Homeric epics as foundational narratives accords better with our emphasis on the foundational character of Achilles' act of gathering the people. Hera puts it into his mind to call an assembly (*Iliad* 1.55); Athena prevents him from striking down the king, and redirects his violence into words (*Iliad* 1.207–214); it is Zeus to whom Achilles turns (through his mother) to make sure that his honor will be recognized (*Iliad* 1.352–356, 393–412).

[18] Achilles asserts his individual effort and poor return: though he does the lion's share of the work, "whenever the *distribution* happens, for you [meaning Agamemnon] the prize is by far greater, and I have little but dear" (ἀτὰρ ἤν ποτε δασμὸς ἵκηται / σοὶ τὸ γέρας πολὺ μεῖζον, ἐγὼ δ' ὀλίγον τε φίλον τε, 1.166–167). In response to Agamemnon's willful assertion of authority, this complaint does not detract from the political implications of his argument.

[19] On the significance of the scepter for assembly speech, see Detienne 1996:95. Cf. Easterling 1989.

αὐδή, *Iliad* 1.248–249).[20] Nestor *sounds like* the ideal king, intervening in strife to resolve the crisis with his judgment. Yet the situation differs markedly, as does the outcome. His is just another (albeit a particularly authorized) voice attempting to resolve the striving of other kings, equal or superior to him; and he fails. Nestor cannot restrain Agamemnon from continuing his affronted criticism of Achilles' insubordination; because of this, we never learn whether Nestor's words had achieved their desired effect on Achilles, but, given the furiousness of his own parting shot, we may doubt it. In this interformular *and* intertraditional moment, the *Iliad resonates* dissonantly, marking the Theogonic presentation of a sweet-talking all-powerful (and ideal) king as insufficient for dealing with strife in this new political world, where there is not one single authoritative figure but many, each with competing claims.[21]

And it does so with a further redeployment of a Theban theme. For Agamemnon, Achilles' dissent equates to the antisocial kind of strife seen before in Hesiod's genealogy of strife, the kind that promises "Battles, Wars, Murders, and Man-killings" (Ὑσμίνας τε Μάχας τε Φόνους τ' Ἀνδροκτασίας τε, *Theogony* 228). According to Agamemnon, "strife, war, and battle are always dear [to Achilles]" (αἰεὶ γάρ τοι ἔρις τε φίλη πόλεμοί τε μάχαι τε, 1.177). This phrase and the sentiment expressed by it resonate strongly with a fragment of the so-called *Thebais*, which we discussed in the last chapter. Oedipus, feeling cheated of his prize (*geras*, 6), utters a curse that his children "would not divide their inheritance in kind friendship / but both always have wars and battles" (ὡς οὔ οἱ πατρώϊ' ἐνηέι <ἐν> φιλότητι / δάσσαιντ', ἀμφοτέροισι δ' ἀεὶ πόλεμοί τε μάχαι τε, fr. 2 B/D, 9–10).[22] In the *Iliad*, Achilles similarly swears an oath, but its scope encompasses the entire community, not just one family. Even if at various points the *Iliad* invites us to see Agamemnon and Achilles as a warring father and son, clearly their striving raises broader, political issues.[23]

Indeed, the *Iliad*'s interest in the broader political settlement align it more with the concerns of distribution that we saw operating in Hesiod's *Theogony*, but inflected to address the world of men and the founding of communal institutions. Achilles' oath not only condemns his people to further (and greater) suffering, but critically also leaves unresolved what to make of his intervention. On the one hand, Achilles is both responsible for calling the assembly in the

---

[20] On the Hesiodic Nestor, see Martin 1989:81; Dickson 1995; Mackie 1996:132.

[21] See Taplin 1992:6–7; cf. Hammer 1997; Wilson 2002a; Roisman 2005; Barker 2009; Christensen 2009; Elmer 2013.

[22] Chapter 4, "Honor, Division, and Strife." Whether this fragment derives from the *Thebais* or whether the *Iliad* was aware of this passage, the importance of the oath to the Theban tradition is well testified: Oedipus swears an oath that curses his sons and leads to strife between them.

[23] In the catalogue of gifts that he promises Achilles, Agamemnon expressly says that he takes him as a son and honors him like Orestes: *Iliad* 9.142.

first place, and subsequently establishing it as an institution that can and must accommodate dissent—essentially striving with the king—for the well-being of the community, as if dissent here is equated with Hesiod's second kind of strife.[24] On the other hand, his own striving with the king in the end merely replaces one crisis (the plague) with another (war without him). Far from being safely domesticated, this strife—Hesiod's primary destructive kind—transforms assembly debate into a raging war of words.[25]

This critical open-endedness in judging strife is the fundamental means by which the *Iliad* not only represents Hesiod's positive strife, but reproduces it, engaging the audience in realizing its narrative of institutional foundation. When at the beginning of Book 9 a tearful Agamemnon announces to the assembled people that he intends to give up on Troy, it is the Theban hero Diomedes who this time contests his authority. Significantly, he frames his rejoinder with the words (9.32–33):

"Ἀτρεΐδη σοὶ πρῶτα μαχήσομαι ἀφραδέοντι,
ἣ θέμις ἐστὶν ἄναξ ἀγορῇ· σὺ δὲ μή τι χολωθῇς."

"Son of Atreus, with you I'll fight first in your foolishness:
It's the custom, lord, in the assembly. And you, don't get angry."

Applying the phrase "it is the custom" prescriptively to authorize his capacity to speak in opposition to Agamemnon, Diomedes institutionalizes the assembly as a place where disagreement is allowed.[26] Furthermore, by making the conflict with words in the assembly critical for its own narrative fulfillment, in the assembly of Book 9, the *Iliad* puts a *political* stamp on the epic theme of strife. Like the Theban epics discussed above, the action of the *Iliad* is motivated in part by a disagreement over distribution of common goods. Where the Theban epics turn a domestic (intrafamilial) conflict into an international one, the *Iliad* reversions the Trojan tale and reverses this movement, by transforming it from an international conflict into a domestic one that focuses on internal conflict,

---

[24] On the argument here and below, see Barker 2009:61–66; Christensen 2009. Cf. Barker and Christensen 2011:61–88.

[25] The narrator caps the assembly with the description, "so the two of them, having fought with violent words, stood up" (ὣς τώ γ᾽ ἀντιβίοισι μαχεσσαμένω ἐπέεσσιν / ἀνστήτην, 1.304–305). See Barker 2009:49–51.

[26] On the phrase "it is the custom," see Kirk 1985:122–123; Griffin 1986:38. When the narrator next mentions strife in the assembly, it is in the context of introducing a skilled young speaker, Thoas, whom "few of the Achaeans could vanquish in the assembly, whenever the young men strived with words" (ἀγορῇ δέ ἑ παῦροι Ἀχαιῶν / νίκων, ὁππότε κοῦροι ἐρίσσειαν περὶ μύθων, 15.283–284)—the "whenever" marking "striving with words" a normal event in the maturation of a young man. See Barker 2009:65–66; Christensen 2018b.

and promotes its own value as a foundational narrative for political institutions and action.

By *Iliad* 9, given Achilles' absence from battle, the Achaeans have been in such dire straits that they have taken defensive measures and—at the behest of Nestor, the *Iliad*'s link to the heroic past and other traditions—have built a (Theban) wall around their ships. The besiegers have become the besieged, the Trojan War Achaeans Achaeans of Thebes.[27] Following another convention also reflected in Theban tradition, which we discussed in Chapter 1, the Achaeans now send to Achilles an embassy.[28] The change in setting (from the public assembly to a private audience in Achilles' camp) has a similarly transformative effect on the theme of strife. Taking his cue from Odysseus' appeal to him as the Achaeans' foremost warrior, as if he were a hero from a bygone age, Achilles now describes the division of spoils rather differently than before. He attributes the act of the *dasmos* to Agamemnon alone, who "gives out a little but holds on to the most" (διὰ παῦρα δασάσκετο, πολλὰ δ' ἔχεσκεν, 9.333); when other Achaeans are mentioned, it is as the beneficiaries of Agamemnon's largesse ("he was giving the other gifts to the best men and the kings," ἄλλα δ' ἀριστήεσσι δίδου γέρα καὶ βασιλεῦσι, 9.334). Achilles even goes on to reframe the Trojan War as a conflict carried out for the benefit only of the sons of Atreus (9.337–341), casting into doubt the very value of this epic poem.[29]

Achilles' rejection of Agamemnon's catalogue of gifts (renumerated by Odysseus) is so shocking that it has been regarded as kind of a conceptual break in the valorization of heroic action itself.[30] However, thinking of this scene in terms of interformularity and intertraditionality can shed further light on the *Iliad*'s poetic agonistics. Achilles begins his rejection of Agamemnon's offer—an offer that bypasses the communal distribution of goods and that would, if accepted, establish a personal contract with and dependency on the king[31]—by musing that the man who works hard and the one who does not both die alike (κάτθαν' ὁμῶς ὅ τ' ἀεργὸς ἀνὴρ ὅ τε πολλὰ ἐοργώς, 9.320). For Hilary Mackie, the odd-sounding emphasis on manual labor in a martial epic, as if Achilles

---

[27] See Singor 1992; Tsagalis 2008:25; cf. Pache 2014; Barker and Christensen 2014:270–273. On the destruction of the Achaean Wall: Scodel 1982.

[28] But not the two emissaries that one would expect according to traditional referentiality (cf. Ebbott 2014: see Chapter 1, "On Not Being Alone"). In fact, the *Iliad*'s use of duals in this episode seems deliberately to play on and confront such audience expectations. On the aspect of the troubling duals, see e.g. Griffin 1995:51–53.

[29] Perhaps heralded by what Achilles is doing when the embassy arrives: he's singing about the κλέα ἀνδρῶν (9.189)—the glories of (other) men.

[30] Expressed most forcefully by Parry 1973. Cf. Friedrich and Redfield 1978; Scully 1984; and Martin 1989.

[31] Wilson 2002: 71–108.

were some laborer on the land, resonates with a Hesiodic tradition of hard agrarian work. She suggests that by adopting this "Hesiodic stance, and the language associated with it," Achilles is criticizing "the system of distribution (*dasmos*) that is practiced among the Achaeans"—or, we would say, criticizes Agamemnon's flouting of that distributive system.[32] In the manner of a Hesiod, Achilles anatomizes strife and locates its destructive origins in the unjust distribution of goods (*gera*)[33] by a bribe-swallowing king.[34] When he announces that he will go home where he will not lack for anything, it is no coincidence that he brings to mind the world of the *Works and Days*, of rightful patrimony, and of peace (9.401–403). In fact, to cap it all, the hero of war puts at stake his future fame by singing about his valorization of the good (long) life of honest toil and labor (410–416).[35] Perhaps it should come as no surprise that the existential threat to Achilles' fame (and to this poem) finds articulation in the Hesiodic poem of peace, one of the many traditions in and against which this version of the Troy story is being composed.[36]

It takes Ajax to keep Achilles at Troy, and the death of his best friend, Patroklos, to finally stir him to action again.[37] Achilles' (re)entry into battle is not only much anticipated (for having been much delayed); the intervention is marked as decisive for cosmic history. Because of the events that the *Iliad* has represented (namely, Achilles' withdrawal from battle), Hektor believes that he

---

[32] Mackie 1996:143. This includes casting "Agamemnon in the role of a hybristic king of the type Hesiod's audience is warned against" (144) and assuming the role himself of an "'exterior insider,' a *metanastês*" (145), with reference to how Agamemnon has treated Achilles as "an alien without honor" (ἀτίμητον μετανάστην, 9.648; cf. 16.58–59). Kelly 2008:193, 197–198 discusses the relationship between Odysseus' self-presentation as a metanast (in his Cretan tales) and Hesiod, whose father was a metanast (*Works and Days* 633–640). Cf. Martin 1992.

[33] Mackie 1996:142–143. On Agamemnon's flouting of the system: Wilson 2002a: 54–55.

[34] Achilles calls Agamemnon "a *people-eating* king who rules over nobodies" (δημοβόρος βασιλεὺς ἐπεὶ οὐτιδανοῖσιν ἀνάσσεις, *Iliad* 1.231). Cf. Hesiod *Works and Days* 221 and 264 for "bribe-eating kings" (δωροφάγοι). See also Scholia bT to *Iliad* 1.231 *ex.* for the explanation that, "This disturbs the masses. For the most serious accusation is making the common goods your own" (δημοβόρος: κινητικὰ ταῦτα τοῦ πλήθους· μεγίστη γὰρ κατηγορία τὸ σφετερίζεσθαι τὰ κοινά).

[35] If anything, the dead Achilles is even more dismissive of (Iliadic) glory and even more desperate to have lived a Hesiodic life, even as a slave to another (*Odyssey* 11.488–503). But, then, this is the *Odyssey*. See Edwards 1985.

[36] Another candidate is the *nostos* tradition best represented (for us) by the *Odyssey*. In Achilles' first words in the *Iliad*, he suggests that the Achaeans will be leaving for home (if a solution to the plague is not quickly found); it is his threat to go home that provokes Agamemnon's dismissive threat to take his prize. Achilles returns to the idea of leaving here, in response to Odysseus' delivery of Agamemnon's offer of recompense. It is also noteworthy that Odysseus takes a leading role in the epic in the direct fallout from each of Achilles' decisions to withdraw from battle: See Haft 1990; cf. Barker 2009:55–61.

[37] Patroklos is persuaded to fight in his friend's place by Nestor, reworking a story from his epic past that featured Herakles: see Chapter 2, "Out of Time."

fights with Zeus' favor and refuses to retreat to Troy (*Iliad* 18.285–309). Thus he condemns his men—apparently for the first time in the war—to face Achilles head-on. The resulting carnage, particularly the bloodbath in Scamander's choked waters, marks a critical stage in the instantiation of Zeus' plan to destroy the age of heroes, which will leave Troy's champion dead and Achilles doomed.

Before we witness this pivotal moment, Homer provides a reflection on strife in one of the scenes depicted on the shield that Hephaestus makes for Achilles (*Iliad* 18.497–508):

λαοὶ δ' εἰν <u>ἀγορῇ</u> ἔσαν ἀθρόοι· ἔνθα δὲ <u>νεῖκος</u>
ὠρώρει, δύο δ' ἄνδρες <u>ἐνείκεον</u> εἵνεκα ποινῆς
ἀνδρὸς ἀποφθιμένου· ὃ μὲν εὔχετο πάντ' ἀποδοῦναι
<u>δήμῳ</u> πιφαύσκων, ὃ δ' ἀναίνετο μηδὲν ἑλέσθαι·
ἄμφω δ' ἱέσθην ἐπὶ <u>ἴστορι</u> πεῖραρ ἑλέσθαι.
<u>λαοὶ</u> δ' ἀμφοτέροισιν ἐπήπυον ἀμφὶς ἀρωγοί·
<u>κήρυκες</u> δ' ἄρα <u>λαὸν</u> ἐρήτυον· οἳ δὲ <u>γέροντες</u>
εἵατ' ἐπὶ ξεστοῖσι λίθοις ἱερῷ ἐνὶ κύκλῳ,
σκῆπτρα δὲ κηρύκων ἐν χέρσ' ἔχον ἠεροφώνων·
τοῖσιν ἔπειτ' ἤϊσσον, ἀμοιβηδὶς δὲ δίκαζον.
κεῖτο δ' ἄρ' <u>ἐν μέσσοισι</u> δύω χρυσοῖο τάλαντα,
τῷ δόμεν ὃς μετὰ τοῖσι <u>δίκην ἰθύντατα</u> εἴποι.

> The people were gathered in a crowd in the assembly, where a *conflict*
> had arisen: two men were in conflict over the penalty for
> a man who had been killed; the first one was promising to repay
>   everything
> as he was testifying to the people; but the other was refusing to take
>   anything;
> and both men longed for a judge to make a decision.
> The people, partisans on either side, applauded.
> Then the heralds held the people in check; the elders
> sat on smooth stones in a sacred circle
> as they held in their hands the scepters of clear-voiced heralds;
> each one was leaping to his feet, and they pronounced judgments in
>   turn.
> In the middle there were two talents of gold to give
> to whoever among them uttered the straightest judgment.

Not only is strife headlined: a conflict *had already arisen* (νεῖκος / ὠρώρει) and *was still* unresolved (ἐνείκεον); the scene of two antagonists fighting with words in an assembly clearly recalls the opening *neikos* of the *Iliad*. Equally clearly, however, the scene on the shield depicts an institutional framework far more developed than anything represented in the story-world of the *Iliad*.[38] Two plaintiffs testify to the people (*demos*) in the assembly (*agora*); the people (*laos*) support either side; an arbitrator (*histor*) adjudicates; elders pass judgment; prizes are "in the middle,"[39] ready to be given to the elder who passes the "straightest judgment." Given this picture of a community working together to resolve strife without a role for named individuals (far less for heroes), this seems to be a far cry from Homer's world of warring heroes. In fact, the emphasis on communal performance, to the erasure of individual identities, amounts to something of an anti-heroic-epic aesthetic.

If this scene on the shield seems to depict a world beyond Homeric epic, it resonates strongly with Hesiod's cosmos. In the *Theogony*, as we have seen, Hesiod articulates a similar interest in "straight judgments" being made, but from the perspective of the "divine born kings" who resolve disputes in the assembly and prevent their people from coming to harm (89–90). The *Iliad* scene is closer to the *Works and Days*, in which Hesiod documents and laments the extent to which this potential has not been fulfilled: the "divine-born kings" take bribes, issue crooked judgments, and generally fail to live up to Zeus'—and the poet's—expectations (248–273). The whole poem is both an argument for institutionalizing justice in society and, to a certain extent, the very demonstration of that act (Hesiod addresses his poem to an addressee, his brother Perses, as if presenting a case: see the final section in this chapter). The shield scene is thus further evidence of the *Iliad* positioning itself in the cosmic evolution mapped out between Hesiod's *Theogony*, in which the only humans to play a role in the world of gods are divine-born kings and heroes, and the *Works and Days*, in which only the gods that feature are Zeus and the abstract goddess "Justice." Achilles' shield offers a brief glimpse of a world in-between, a time beyond the age of heroes, where people rely instead on institutions for conflict resolution.[40] In its continued engagement with the Hesiodic tradition, the *Iliad*, we might

---

[38] For extensive discussion (and further bibliography) on Achilles' shield: see Edwards 1991:200–204; Becker 1995:5; Hammer 2002:107–109. For the juridical scene in particular, see Westbrook 1992. Cf. Muellner 1976:105–106 and Nagy 2003:72–87.

[39] Detienne 1996:91–102. Cf. Barker 2009:17–18, 86–87.

[40] For these comparisons, see Christensen 2018a. There are historical parallels for emphasizing the performance of the judges, just as Hesiod's *Works and Days* provides a poetic outcome for when their judgments are wrong. A fifth-century BCE inscription from West Lokris (IG IX, 1² 3:718.41-45 = Nomima 1, 43 = Koerner, *Inschriftliche Gesetzestexte*, no. 49) preserves a law to disenfranchise an archon who did not pursue a case; an earlier inscription from Chios (Meiggs and Lewis, no. 8 = Nomima 1, 62 = Koerner, *Inschriftliche Gesetzestexte*, no. 61) sets fines for the poor execution of judicial duties. See Papakonstantinou 2004:14.

suppose, is showing that such scenes owe a debt to Achilles (whose shield this is), for setting in motion the move towards a participatory form of politics, when he stood up to Agamemnon.

As Achilles re-enters the fray, plunging this peaceful scene of a community forever frozen in the process of coming to judgment back into the ferocity of war,[41] he carries on his shoulders a world known better to the audience than to himself, a world worth fighting for, a world which the *Iliad* can claim as its legacy.[42] It is, though, a precarious future. Balanced with this city at peace is a city at war, where strife is neither contained nor mediated, but violently escalating, a Thebes in bronze.[43] If the *Iliad* presents some way of managing strife within a community, extension of such institutions beyond the community remains an unattainable fantasy. For, when Achilles re-enters battle, he encapsulates the savagery of a man free of all institutions, a man whose *distribution* is that of human bodies to birds and dogs (ἀλλὰ κύνες τε καὶ οἰωνοὶ κατὰ πάντα <u>δάσονται</u>, 22.354), a disturbing realization of the proem's promise that "the bodies of heroes [will be] food for dogs and birds" (αὐτοὺς δὲ ἑλώρια τεῦχε κύνεσσιν / οἰωνοῖσί τε πᾶσι, 1.4–5), and a man whose meat-sacrifice is Hektor's body ("and after dragging Hektor here, I will give him to the dogs to split up raw," Ἕκτορα δεῦρ᾽ ἐρύσας δώσειν κυσὶν ὠμὰ <u>δάσασθαι</u>, 23.21). Yet, by putting the emphasis on judgment, the carefully framed scene on the shield prepares the audience for the poem's final movement towards achieving some kind of strife-resolution, to balance its opening focus on who *started* the conflict. This scene not only challenges the contents of the epic itself, but it also productively contests the theme of *eris* as it has been pursued within the tradition as a whole. By placing a potential resolution outside the heroic world's actions, Homer also contests the notion that epic poetry can be a sufficient vessel for disarming strife's violence. Such a move builds upon the destruction of both Thebes and Troy.

When these mythical cities have been destroyed, and the heroes associated with them are dead and buried, what should be built in their place? The *Iliad* has already offered its audience the assembly as a venue for *dasmos*, to which we may now add the related juridical scene on the shield as a model for *krisis*. As the *Iliad* draws to a close, Achilles offers a reflection on the poem's exploration of *eris* within two kinds of institutional frame.

---

[41] Lynn-George 1988:197.

[42] In his reworking of the shield scene, Virgil makes explicit his hero's legacy by representing the future historical battle for Rome, Actium (*Aeneid* VIII 617–731). When Aeneas re-enters the fray, he carries on his back Augustus' new world order.

[43] Pache 2014:288: "The city at war depicted on the shield of Achilles is in many ways generic, and as such could stand in for various cities, but the epithet ἐπήρατος is unusual and echoes the Odyssean passage about πολυήρατος Thebes." See Chapter 3, n109.

The first occurs at the beginning of Book 19, when Achilles, resolved now to re-enter the fray after the death of his best friend, again calls an assembly. The narrator marks the convocation of this assembly in the most elaborate terms yet. First, it conspicuously involves everyone, even those who before used to wait behind "in the contest (*agon*) of the ships"—a curious phrase which occurs only for the duration of Achilles' absence from battle and seems to be used metaphorically to indicate the battle over or contest for the Achaean ships (νεῶν ἐν ἀγῶνι, 19.42).[44] Homer also creates the fiction that Achilles has been absent for a long time:[45] though in reality it has only been a mere three days, for an audience, now possibly into its third day of performance, it has been a test of almost epic endurance.[46] Moreover, the group Achilles gathers is neither the long-haired Achaeans, nor even the people (*laoi*), but the "Achaean heroes" (ἥρωας Ἀχαιούς, 19.41)—a kind of generic marker, we noted above, of epic poetry. The combined effect is to frame this assembly as having something to say about the *Iliad*'s performance within the epic world. Befitting such a broadly self-reflexive framework, Achilles' opening assembly speech addresses the key theme of the poem and introduces his initial contemplation of it. The theme that Achilles identifies is his striving with Agamemnon. The Achaeans, Achilles ponders, will remember the strife between them for a *long time* (αὐτὰρ Ἀχαιοὺς / δηρὸν ἐμῆς καὶ σῆς ἔριδος μνήσεσθαι ὀΐω, 19.64–65). Here Achilles, the cause of that strife, acknowledges both his role in its generation and its destructive outcome: but, more importantly, he makes the claim that it will be this theme which will live on in the memory.

Achilles may be the one hero to reflect directly on the thematization of strife in the *Iliad*, but he is not alone in pondering its importance and finding ways to respond to it. This process began in the quarrel scene itself, as represented by the diverging interventions of Athena and Nestor; besides Diomedes' studious repurposing and formalization of Achilles' striving with the king to legitimize his own dissent, which we analyzed above, one might also consider Thersites' less successful aping of Achilles' complaints, which prompts his brutal suppression. It is in the games that Achilles puts on in honor of his fallen comrade, Patroklos, however, that the poem's contemplation on strife comes to the fore.[47]

---

[44] See Ellsworth 1974; Barker 2009:78–81.

[45] "Even they at that time came to the agora, since Achilles had appeared, / and for a long time he had ceased from grievous battle" (καὶ μὴν οἳ τότε γ᾽ εἰς ἀγορὴν ἴσαν, οὕνεκ᾽ Ἀχιλλεὺς / ἐξεφάνη, δηρὸν δὲ μάχης ἐπέπαυτ᾽ ἀλεγεινῆς, 19.45–46).

[46] On the most convincing argument for an *Iliad* in three divisions, see Heiden 2008.

[47] On *eris* in the games, see Hogan 1981:42–43 For a comparison between Achilles' management of this strife and Hesiod's "good" Eris, see Gagarin 1991:66–69; Thalmann 2004:372; and Christensen 2018a.

Achilles formally convokes the games in language that recalls his establishment of the assembly. Achilles held back the *laos* and sat them down in a wide contest space or *agon* (εὐρὺν ἀγῶνα, 23.258). We again see an instituting figure acting on the *laos* to bring them into an institutional process.[48] In addition, Achilles converts the *agon*—which before had been used as a metaphor for the existential threat to the Achaean people in the "contest" for their ships, into a safe space where individuals can show off their physical prowess and win honor without fear of death. More than ever the emphasis lies on group activity. It is a curious detail that, while the language of contest (*agon*) marks out the events in the games,[49] it is not restricted to denoting those contests. For the first and lengthiest contest, the chariot race, competition spills over the boundaries of the delineated contest space and breaks out among the spectators (448, 451, 495). Markedly, the contest among the spectators recalls the opening quarrel between Achilles and Agamemnon.[50] "Then there would have been further conflict between them" (καί νύ κε δὴ προτέρω ἔτ᾽ ἔρις γένετ᾽ ἀμφοτέροισιν, *Iliad* 23.490), Homer narrates, had not Achilles intervened. Significantly, he draws on the experience of his own strife with Agamemnon to recommend that they should defer judgment until one of them knows for sure what is happening among the charioteers. It is also significant for the *Iliad*'s metapoetic reflection that the conflict which Achilles successfully defers relates to who is best at reading the signs.[51]

Further strife threatens to break out when the prizes are awarded. It is Achilles who initially subverts his own newly minted meritocracy, when he judges that Eumelos, who comes last after suffering a crash while leading,

---

[48] As before, once the agon is dissolved, the various groups go their separate ways: the people go back to their ships to eat, Achilles goes back to abusing Hektor's body (24.1–2).

[49] For the first event (the chariot race), he puts forth prizes into the contest-space (τάδ᾽ ἄεθλα δεδεγμένα κεῖτ᾽ ἐν ἀγῶνι, 273) to be competed over; it is into "the middle of the contest-space" (μέσῳ ἐν ἀγῶνι, 23.507) that Diomedes enters to claim his first prize. For the second event (boxing), he "sets forth prizes... into the contest-space" (θῆκεν ἄεθλα...ἐν ἀγῶνι, 23.653–654), and so on: at 685 competitors step forward to fight; at 696 the defeated man is led out; at 710, two more competitors step forward; at 799 Achilles sets up the next prize; at 847 a discus is thrown out of the agon; at 886 Achilles sets up the next prize. On the language of the *agon*, see Barker 2009:86–87; cf. Detienne 1996:95. On the agon as marking the "contest" for the Achaean ships: Ellsworth 1974.

[50] Idomeneus challenges the rest of the Achaeans to disagree with who he thinks is leading; dismissing his claim the lesser Ajax, Agamemnon-like, criticizes his big mouth (23.474–479; cf. 1.291); in turn, like Achilles, Idomeneus "gets angry" (23.482; cf. 1.244) and lays down a wager using Achilles' phrase "so that you may know" (23.487; cf. 1.299). The echoes between Book 1 and Book 23 were sensed in antiquity: Richardson 1993:228–299.

[51] On the *agon*'s emphasis here on the problems of conduct for contestants *and* spectators alike: Scott 1997:221. Hammer 1997 argues that Achilles resolves the crisis by getting the two parties to imagine themselves as onlookers to a quarrel (cf. 23.494). Farenga 2006:150 talks of the "intersubjective perspective" that Achilles introduces to this scene of judgment.

should be awarded second because he was "the best man" (536). This judgment provokes the second-place Antilochus to angrily proclaim that he will be deprived of what is rightfully his. While his objection echoes Achilles' very words to Agamemnon,[52] he is also careful both to frame his dissent[53] and to offer an alternative judgment: Achilles should reward Eumelos from his *own* store of booty, not from the common pool.[54] Achilles, as if hearing a younger version of himself, smiles and accepts the compromise.[55]

This is not quite the end of the matter either. (As tends to happen in conflict resolution, one issue gets resolved only for another to spring up.) Menelaos, so long the injured party in the *Iliad*, berates Antilochus for almost running into him and forcing him off the racing line. His concern that he is being cheated out of a prize recalls again the strife of Book 1 and in particular Agamemnon's angry response to Achilles' challenge;[56] again, however, his register strikes a radically different note. After voicing his anger with Antilochus, Menelaos turns to the assembled Achaeans and appeals to *them* for judgment "in the middle" (ἀλλ᾽ ἄγετ᾽ Ἀργείων ἡγήτορες ἠδὲ μέδοντες / ἐς μέσον ἀμφοτέροισι δικάσσατε, 23.573–574). In addition, keen to avoid the accusation of seeking to gain through deceit (576), Menelaos calls upon Antilochus to swear an oath that he used no guile. Important here is his gloss, "as is the custom" (ἢ θέμις ἐστί, 581)—like Diomedes, when making dissent institutional in the assembly, Menelaos lays down the principle of swearing an oath before the community to resolve conflict. This is a far cry from the oath that Achilles swore condemning his group to suffering; rather it is the thematic equivalent of Zeus' establishment of the river Styx as

---

[52] Just as Achilles threatens to fight any man who would take from him anything more than Briseis, so Antilochus threatens the same, only he won't even give her (the feminine pronoun this time signifying a horse) up (23.553; cf. 1.161).

[53] He warns Achilles that he may get angry should his complaint not be heard: cf. Diomedes' careful framing of his contest of words with Agamemnon that we explored above.

[54] Of course, such a proposal reflects a kind of political fantasy. The strife between Achilles and Agamemnon occurs because all of the prizes have already been distributed—how one manages scarce resources is a fundamental fixture of political debate. Here Achilles is able to sidestep the problem by introducing new resources to address the scarcity. Even so, Antilochus is able to make this proposal in this way precisely because the situation among the Achaeans has changed. As a direct consequence of Achilles' challenge to the king in Book 1, it is now possible to dissent from the figure in power. (Agamemnon could have given up part of his booty, as Achilles does here, to maintain the public good—but he doesn't.)

[55] For Achilles recognizing his own words in Antilochus', see Martin 1989:188–189. It is also noteworthy that the Trojan War tradition depicts Antilochus and Achilles as great friends. In the *Aithiopis* it is apparently the death of Antilochus at the hands of Memnon that drives Achilles into a(nother) destructive rage.

[56] Agamemnon believes Achilles is trying to trick him out of a prize (1.131–132). The potential for this scene to re-examine the conflict between Agamemnon and Achilles was not lost on ancient commentators: see Richardson 1993:230. Finley 1954:80–81 believes that the dispute between Antilochus and Menelaos is merely a private issue. Cf. Hammer 1997:19.

the guarantee of divine oath in Hesiod's *Theogony*.[57] Where the gods have some supernatural institution to enforce the faith of their pledge, men require a community and the institutional memory of the assembly. The communally witnessed oath thus emerges as a tool in the resolution of strife, to contrast pointedly with the oath used in Book 1 to divide and destroy the community.

Whereas the quarrel of the assembly in Book 1 escalates to a point at which the two greatest Achaeans take up polarized positions to the detriment of the community, in Book 23 conflict is re-imagined as a typical case of claim and counter-claim. The prevailing spirit is of mediation and negotiation rather than one of status-posturing and dominance,[58] a kind of political environment[59] born of and immersed in competing interests, none of which are easily resolvable, and in which the judge's judgment also comes under constant consideration and scrutiny. Moreover, this new political settlement directly resonates with, and derives from, the strife of Book 1, which the characters seem to draw upon as a paradigm and invite the audience to do the same. Similar themes and issues are replayed, and words repeated, even as other elements show up the difference between the two situations. The characters—and the audience with them—engage in a process of recouping strife over the course of the narrative. Menelaos' speech is the clearest example of the continuing progress that the *Iliad* makes towards the world of today. He addresses the man he has charged, appeals to the jury, and then recommends a formal solution, the oath. Not only does this again show how integral the Achaeans-at-large are to the assigning of prizes and rights; it is also proto-forensic in its anticipation of a legal settlement, such as we saw on Achilles' shield.[60]

Arguably, it is not only important that this new kind of politics is realized under the jurisdiction of Achilles, the *Iliad*'s protagonist. Where it happens is also noteworthy: the games. We have already identified the extent to which Achilles formally establishes the games as an institutional form of contest (*agon*). It should also be observed that the foundation of the games in early Greek society is usually assigned to *Herakles*. That figure is conspicuous by his absence

---

[57] See Chapter 4, "Managing Strife in Hesiod's Cosmos."

[58] Antilochus' reaction reflects this difference. He chooses to diffuse the situation by addressing Menelaos with due respect and admitting to his own inexperience. Indeed, by this strategy, Antilochus actually succeeds in retaining his prize, while also allowing Menelaos to keep his honor. That is to say, both Antilochus and Menelaos, like Achilles, seem to have learned from the earlier events of the epic.

[59] Hammer 1997, 2002:140; cf. Barker 2009:86–88; Elmer 2013:187–197.

[60] Farenga 2006:145 connects the two scenes for their ideal solutions to intractable conflicts, though his emphasis lies on how they "dramatize ways a *basileus* may perform a *dikê* consistent with *themis*." This fits his overall focus on individuals who perform "scripts" (8) of justice on the way to establishing of an idea of citizenship: he does not regard the institutions that Achilles sets up as the place where the people may find security.

from this section of the poem; interestingly, however, the one figure whose funeral games *are* mentioned as a precedent is another Theban hero, Oedipus. In his only reference in the *Iliad* (23.679), it is the burial of Oedipus in Thebes at which a certain Mekisteos excelled, and "there defeated all the sons of Cadmus" (ἔνθα δὲ πάντας ἐνίκα Καδμείωνας, 23.680). Where the *Iliad* does not make the claim that it invents the games, in its formalization of the games as an *agon* and through its representations of adjudication and disagreement, it transforms this particular type of domesticated strife into something much more valuable—a political moment of debate, reflection, and negotiation. As for the hero whose father had defeated all comers at Thebes (like Tydeus)—Euryalos is knocked out cold by the boxer Epeios who receives no externally relevant genealogy. So much for the relevance of Thebes and the men of Tydeus' ilk.

The final book of the *Iliad* further hints at the poem's role in the epic cosmos and, in particular, at the shadow of Thebes that lies not far beneath the surface. It does so through the theme that later characterizes Theban myth: (the denial of) burial. As has been well documented, Book 24 begins in ways that strongly recall the opening of the epic.[61] Where the poem's catalyst for strife was Apollo's anger at Agamemnon for disrespecting his priest, Apollo intervenes again now, but this time neither directly nor unilaterally. Instead, reflecting the *Iliad*'s movement towards a new political settlement, he calls the gods to an assembly and puts his case to them (24.33–54). Equally significantly, he intervenes here *not* because of a personal tie (the insult suffered by *his* priest) but in defense of a *general* principle—the right to burial.[62]

In the *Cypria*, Zeus (apparently) "took pity on Earth" (Ζεὺς δὲ ἰδὼν ἐλέησε, *Cypria* fr. 1.4) and planned to relieve her burden by destroying the race of heroes; now, according to Apollo, "because Achilles has destroyed pity" (ὡς Ἀχιλεὺς ἔλεον μὲν ἀπώλεσεν, *Iliad* 24.44) by not allowing Hektor's burial, "Achilles shames the dumb earth in his wrath" (κωφὴν γὰρ δὴ γαῖαν ἀεικίζει μενεαίνων, 24.54).[63] The implication that Achilles' wrath, the catalyst of the poem, knows no bounds hints at the poem's own borders and poses the question how this story of strife will, or can be, brought to a close. In opposing the motion Hera tries to maintain a critical distinction between the mortal Hektor and godlike Achilles,

---

[61] See Macleod 1982 for an in-depth discussion of this ring composition.

[62] Significantly the *Iliad* uses the language of the prize, *geras*, to describe burial *rites*. The first occasion is when Hera resists Zeus' attempt to save his son, Sarpedon, from his fated death: she insists instead on rescuing his body so that his family and kinsmen can bury him, "for this is the *right* of those who have died" (τὸ γὰρ γέρας ἐστὶ θανόντων, 16.457). The paradoxical idea of "saving" a body for burial is most explicitly articulated by Apollo here, when he calls upon the other gods to "save him [Hektor], though a corpse" (24.35). Zeus supports this claim, precisely because Hektor had made due sacrifice, "for that we gods have received as our right" (24.70).

[63] On the *Cypria*, see above and Chapter 4, "Strife and the Age of Heroes."

by invoking the pre-Iliadic marriage of Peleus and Thetis, at which Apollo too feasted as he held his lyre (24.62–63). Zeus' arbitration confirms that the *Iliad* has moved on from this bygone era of gods and heroes: while Achilles will always be more honored, Hektor is "dearest" of all, because of the sacrifices he made—or, as Zeus puts it, his altar "was never lacking an equal cut" (οὐ γάρ μοί ποτε βωμὸς ἐδεύετο δαιτὸς ἐΐσης, 24.69). At the end of *Iliad* 1, strife on Olympos fails to break out because Zeus has already assigned each god his or her due: "they feasted and their spirits were not lacking an equal cut" (δαίνυντ', οὐδέ τι θυμὸς ἐδεύετο δαιτὸς ἐΐσης, 1.602), nor indeed were they lacking the lyre that Apollo held (1.603). This portioning out of honor for the gods takes place in the *Theogony* and *Homeric Hymns*. Here, in *Iliad* 24, we receive an important gloss on that equal share. While the gods no longer dine at our table, we may gain their favor by making due sacrifice. With this intervention, the *Iliad*'s gods make it clear that the corpse, even that of an enemy, deserves to be buried: or, to put it in the language of epic, a proper burial is the "allotment" or "portion" due the dead. The refusal to grant burial results in an ongoing *eris* between mortals and threatens to escalate the strife to the world of the immortals. The theme of an unburied body as the locus for potentially yet more conflict recalls most famously the stories associated with Thebes and the (non-)burial of the seven.

It is with such a potential Theban story as both the backdrop to and threatening model for the *Iliad*'s last movement that we now come to the scene between Achilles and Priam, when Homer's hero finally relinquishes his anger and returns Hektor's body. His last act of redistribution is to share with Priam all the things that are his due ("I will [give him back] to you and in turn offer as much of these things as is proper," σοὶ δ' αὖ ἐγὼ καὶ τῶνδ' ἀποδάσσομαι ὅσσ' ἐπέοικεν, 24.595). This moment not only represents the resolution of the theme of ransom that was again a catalyst for strife at the poem's beginning; it also operates within a storyworld of strife between fathers and sons, shared with some of our Theban tales. Throughout the *Iliad*, various characters have sought to influence Achilles either by assuming the mantle of his father, Peleus, or else by ventriloquizing his words.[64] Priam's direct appeal to "remember your father" (μνῆσαι πατρὸς σοῖο, *Iliad* 24.486) resonates with those earlier, failed attempts. But, given the circumstances, where Achilles will offer Priam what he is due—his son's body, goods, a *meal*—it also potentially resonates with and corrects the episode in the *Thebais* (as represented by the fragments discussed

---

[64] Odysseus reminds Achilles of his father's (pre-war) advice: 9.252–259; Phoenix's autobiography subtly corrects this (mistaken) move in a way that establishes him as the true surrogate father: 9.434–447, 485–495. See Wilson 2002a:97–98. Throughout the argument of her book, Wilson perceptively demonstrates how Agamemnon consistently tries to subordinate Achilles through relations of dominance that a father would enjoy over a son.

in the previous chapter) where a meal between a father and his sons leads to conflict and a curse. We say correct, because the scene between Achilles and Priam not only brings strife to an end (formally, if not substantively) in the *Iliad*; it also emphasizes appropriate distribution within the context of the feast—a significant and fraught moment in early Greek hexameter epic as we have seen, including for our Theban sources.

The *Iliad* ends in the burial of Hektor. Given heroic epic's focus on the death of the race of heroes, it is no surprise that burial should play such a key role in the *Iliad*. Yet, its thematization may also be highly charged in the context of a Theban tradition.[65] Evidence from Athenian tragedy about Theban plots suggests a particular emphasis on burial, whether it is the denial of burial (Sophocles' *Antigone*) or its acceptance (Sophocles' *Oedipus at Colonus*). In fact there is a tradition that Herakles was the first to give back a body under truce (Plutarch *Life of Theseus* 29.4–5), in and against which Athenian tragedians may have been working when representing Theseus preserving the rites of the dead.[66] The *Iliad* reverses the association of burial with strife by not only ending its anatomization of the latter with the former, but pointedly also by disavowing strife through having Achilles promise Priam a truce for the days of the burial (*Iliad* 24.656–670; 779–781). And yet, even as the *Iliad* closes with the peaceful, if somber, image of burial, strong hints of the strife remain, as the Trojans post guards just in case the Achaeans attack (*Iliad* 24.798–801).[67]

The *Iliad* starts out as a tale of Eris set in a larger tradition about a particular famous strife: the conflict between Menelaos and Paris for Helen. This personal vendetta sets multiple communities into turmoil, results in a massive redistribution of humanity and wealth, and brings to an end the race of heroes. In all likelihood, the versions of poems about Thebes used the Eris theme to illustrate similar conflations of private conflicts and public costs—indeed, this is a clear dynamic that emerges from tragic versions of Oedipus' family story. But the *Iliad* appropriates and deploys these themes in a monumental fashion, exploring multiple angles on the costs of *eris*, incomplete or problematic *dasmos*, and failed judgment over the course of its unfolding, only to anticipate and control its own reception at the end. Moreover, it resonates with Hesiod's *Theogony* in its depiction of the assembly as an imperfect ground for resolution, anticipates the *Works and Days* with its objections over the use of public means for private ends during the embassy to Achilles, and produces variations on intra-familial

---

[65] For the burial of the Seven, see the Conclusion.

[66] Steinbock 2013:172 notes that Theseus' help to the fallen Argives may have been an answer to the tradition.

[67] "In spite of the assurance there is a sense of apprehension, insecurity and urgency on the borders of the text": Lynn-George 1987:254.

wrongs and sinful banquets familiar to Theban tales throughout the poem. In its closing focus on the oath, the importance of burial, and the need for a leader like Achilles putting public good before his private interest, the *Iliad* appears to end the story of strife. How could a city like Thebes produce anything to compete with this?

Just as the *Iliad* complicates and tries to control its own reception, so too does the Homeric tradition contest its own resolutions. Not only are the ideals explored in the *Iliad* put firmly to the test in the *Odyssey*; the very construction of a narrative about managing strife is made the subject of the tale.

Enduring Strife, Surviving Epic

Given that the *Iliad* reworks the Eris theme as the basis of a foundational narrative that dramatizes the establishment of institutions for managing conflict once heroes are no more, we may have expected to see a similar emphasis on political strife in the homecoming narrative. Far from it. Not only is the *Odyssey* relatively uninterested in institutions, it seems to show little interest in strife per se. In part its reticence is due to a far more complicated political picture, where it is not altogether clear that strife can be the relatively constructive force that the *Iliad* had seemed to suggest.[68] In part, too, it is because the potential for intrafamilial rivalry is so strongly denied, in the epic's assertion that Laertes, Odysseus, and Telemachus are single sons (16.117–120), an unrivalled genealogy in Greek myth.[69] In that very insistence, however, one can detect a particular element of the *Odyssey*'s striving—a striving in *poetic form* (as we saw in Chapter 3). This is manifest in the poem's representation of institutional strife as a binary opposition, between those fighting for Odysseus and his family, and those against.[70] Furthermore, where strife tends to be absent, the motif of distribution (as part of the thematic nexus around strife) is present as an urgent idea in both Odysseus' speeches and Telemachus' inquiries, both of which take place during scenes of feasting. These resonant strains, which lurk just beneath

---

[68] For overviews of political ideology in the *Odyssey*, see Rose 1975, 2012; Thalmann 1998; cf. Barker 2009:85–93 for the movement from the *Iliad* through the *Odyssey*. Halverson 1986 and Silvermintz 2004 discuss issues of succession in the monarchy, while Chaston 2002 examines different models of authority within the poem. See also Whitman 1958:308 for Ithaca as being in a permanent state of flux; and generally Finley 1954 on the difficulty of talking about politics in the *Odyssey*.

[69] For the comparatively limited importance of the *laos* in the *Odyssey*, see Haubold 2000:101–103. For this passage as encapsulating the "functions of patronymics and genealogies in Homer," see Higbie 1995:147; cf. 176 for the epic's end with the three standing together to fight as a fulfillment of the three-generational image.

[70] For the *oikos* dominating the idea of the *polis* in the *Odyssey*, see Scully 1990:87 and Haubold 2000:102–103. For civil strife as emerging from the transgressions of the boundaries between the *oikos* and the *polis*, see Agamben 2015:10–16.

the surface of those episodes, explode on the scene at the end of the *Odyssey* in the form of civil conflict over the denial of burial and Odysseus' leadership. If this sounds Theban, then it is all the more noteworthy that it is a Theban hero whose strange prophecy anticipates the problematic closure of the poem by prophesying still more wandering for Odysseus.

As the epic of homecoming, the *Odyssey* explores a post-*Iliad*, post-war world in which the difficult returns of the Trojan War heroes come into focus—the trauma faced by war veterans, the loss (imagined or real) of their loved ones waiting at home, the disruption to ordinary life experienced by their communities, the stories that they tell to make sense of their involvement of conflict.[71] Conflict itself, particularly as manifested by the Trojan War, is deceptively consigned to the world before. Demodokos sings of the "conflict of Achilles and Odysseus" (νεῖκος 'Οδυσσῆος καὶ Πηλεΐδεω Ἀχιλῆος, 8.75); Odysseus himself describes the Trojan War to Penelope as a "great conflict" (ἔκριναν μέγα νεῖκος ὁμοιΐου πτολέμοιο, 18.264). From the perspective of the *Odyssey* the Trojan War is as much in the past as the conflict between men and Centaurs (ἐξ οὗ Κενταύροισι καὶ ἀνδράσι νεῖκος ἐτύχθη, 21.303) from the poem's ideological perspective. In place of armed conflict, strife is transformed into an attempt to win a woman in marriage ("they wanted to woo a good wife and the daughter of a rich man and were striving with one another," οἵ τ' ἀγαθήν τε γυναῖκα καὶ ἀφνειοῖο θύγατρα / μνηστεύειν ἐθέλωσι καὶ ἀλλήλοισ' ἐρίσωσιν, 18.276-277).[72]

Yet destructive strife is never that far away, especially when the woman in question is already married; as the Trojan War has shown, the wrong kind of wooing can lead to a destructive conflict, fit for epic song.[73] Thus the *Odyssey*'s thematization of strife investigates what happens when the very fabric of society—institutions both social (hospitality, the household) and political (the assembly)—is torn asunder by men (or monsters). In many ways this poem's contemplation of strife is even more radical than the *Iliad*'s, juxtaposing its own fantastic reimaginings of social order with the situation on the ground, so to speak. It both represents an unraveling of Achilles' redistributive fantasy and re-evaluates from the ground up the causes and consequences of human striving.[74]

---

[71] On combat trauma in Homer and the use of stories to make sense of pain: see Shay 2003; Race 2014. Cf. Christensen 2018c.

[72] See the description by the suitors of their wooing in 2.85-128.

[73] See our discussions of the Hesiodic *Catalogue of Women* in Chapter 6 below. Cf. Haubold 2000:140–141.

[74] Hogan 1981:45: "The concept of eris in the *Odyssey* does not differ from that in the *Iliad*. What is changed is neither the passions nor attitudes accompanying it, but the kinds of context in which it appears."

The idea of conflict in the assembly is explored in the scenes back on Ithaca, though not quite in the way that the *Iliad* had depicted. On the advice of a loyal retainer, Mentes (Athena in disguise), Telemachus calls an assembly of the Ithacans, in which he lays out to the people his case for the impropriety of the suitors' behavior (2.40–79).[75] If in the *Iliad* we see the gradual institutionalization of the assembly (and the management of physical conflict in the form of debate), the *Odyssey* takes this as its premise: the gods Zeus and Themis—Law/Custom—"dissolve and establish the assemblies of men" (ἥ τ' ἀνδρῶν ἀγορὰς ἠμὲν λύει ἠδὲ καθίζει, 2.69), as if now assemblies are fully institutionalized and overseen by the divine powers who ensure the proper workings of a society's customs.[76]

Only here on Ithaca, such institutions have fallen into disuse. An assembly has not been called since Odysseus left for Troy (2.26–27). In spite of Telemachus' appeal to the Ithacans, they remain silent, leaving the assembly to be hijacked by the suitors, who care only about forcing Penelope's hand and nothing about the state of Ithaca. Two other speakers do speak up for Telemachus to the public, but their appeals and threats have little effect on the assembled group. What should be the occasion for an open exchange of views in the public management of strife becomes a demonstration of the futility of debate, as the suitors show no interest in constructive discussion (nor indeed any unity among themselves).[77] Arguably this assembly is not only a condemnation of Ithacan social practice; at times the assembly resembles, and sometimes sounds like, the opening assembly of the *Iliad*.[78] The institutional framework promised by the *Iliad* as a way of negotiating disputes is exposed as badly lacking, particularly when no figure emerges who is not already implicated in the struggle to make a fair judgment. The *Odyssey*'s prolonged rumination on the conditions necessary to obtain fair

---

[75] Importantly he speaks over the heads of the suitors directly to the people: "you too must feel indignation yourselves and shame before others" (νεμεσσήθητε καὶ αὐτοί, / ἄλλους τ' αἰδέσθητε, 2.64–65); and they should fear the wrath of the gods (θεῶν δ' ὑποδείσατε μῆνιν, 2.66). Here, Telemachus speaks to an audience—a group to whom the Iliadic heroes pay lip-service but never directly address—and seeks to use the weapons of public cohesion—shame and fear of the anger of the gods—to bring about a change for the better in society, in the proper arena for effecting such change, the public assembly. On the Ithacan assembly, see Barker 2009:92–119. Cf. Haubold 2000:110–115.

[76] See too Homer's fully formulaic description of the setting up of the assembly (2.6–14).

[77] "The suitors' repeated rejections of Telemachus' attempts at mediation serve to underline their obdurate self-regard. In marked contrast to the cohesive support for Odysseus, they consistently represent themselves as individuals contesting for the right to marry Penelope: a different suitor speaks each time; individually they try only to silence the previous speaker, and fail to appeal to the people" (Barker 2009:105). In the words of Haubold 2000:111, "the suitors resist social formation."

[78] Telemachus throws the scepter down in an Achillean show of temper (2.80–81; cf. *Iliad* 1.245–246): Barker 2009:101–102.

judgment insistently probes the limits of the positive Eris developed in the *Iliad* and interrogated in Hesiod's *Works and Days*. Telemachus declares that he will pursue justice by other means—outside the assembly.[79]

Instead, the *Odyssey* approaches the theme of strife indirectly, through moments of distribution. Telemachus' search for a solution to the crisis on Ithaca takes him on an Odyssean voyage to two of the Trojan War veterans who have survived and made it back home. When Telemachus first meets Nestor, he is in the process of *dividing out* the correct portions for an orderly feast in Pylos ("After they divided the portions, they dined on a luxurious feast," μοίρας δασσάμενοι δαίνυντ' ἐρικυδέα δαῖτα, 3.66). Similarly, when Odysseus arrives washed up on the shore of Skheria, the narrator informs us that King Nausithoos had equitably *distributed* its lands among men and gods ("he built the temples of the gods and distributed the farmlands," καὶ νηοὺς ποίησε θεῶν καὶ ἐδάσσατ' ἀρούρας, 6.10), the result of which seems to guarantee the Phaiakians a Hesiodic golden-age life of ease and plenty.[80] Seemingly conscious of the problem of distribution suffered by the Achaeans in the *Iliad*, Odysseus himself emphasizes that he and his men *divided things up* correctly after sacking the city of the Kikonians, "so that none in my power might be robbed of his fair share" (ἐκ πόλιος δ' ἀλόχους καὶ κτήματα πολλὰ λαβόντες / δασσάμεθ', ὡς μή τίς μοι ἀτεμβόμενος κίοι ἴσης, 9.41–42). Even after barely extricating his companions from the clutches of Polyphemos, Odysseus' thoughts immediately turn again to the proper distribution of goods ("once we took the flocks from the Cyclops' deep cave, we divided them up so that no one left without a share," μῆλα δὲ Κύκλωπος γλαφυρῆς ἐκ νηὸς ἑλόντες / δασσάμεθ', ὡς μή τίς μοι ἀτεμβόμενος κίοι ἴσης, 9.548–549). Similarly, too, in the troubled scenes of feasting on Ithaca, there remains the concern to distribute the portions all round ("they cooked the portions skillfully and divided them up," ὤπτησάν τε περιφραδέως δάσσαντό τε μοίρας, 19.423).

This obsession with due allotment not only recalls the badly managed division of spoils that proved the catalyst for the *Iliad*—at which Odysseus' distribution of spoils after sacking the city of the Kikonians seems pointedly aimed—but resonates also with Hesiodic and especially Theban anxieties about proper division. Beneath these expressions of ideals the situation turns out to be far more complex and troubling, and owes much to the kind of issues that we saw being explored in our remaining Theban fragments. Odysseus' equitable

---

[79] In fact Telemachus doesn't just seek a fair distribution but vengeance or payback (*tisis*, 2.76)—a watchword of the *Odyssey* that brings to mind that older, more destructive, zero-sum strife. Telemachus will achieve this by becoming more like his father—going on his own odyssey (cf. 2.209–213) and learning to use deception.

[80] Cf. Austin 1975:153–162.

sharing-out of goods after sacking the Kikonian city ironically leads to ruin, since his companions (against his advice) insist on enjoying their newly-won spoils there and then rather than fleeing—and soon find themselves embroiled in a second, even more destructive, battle.

It is Odysseus especially who articulates problems with epic *dasmos*. When he first interviews Eumaios, he laments (in his Cretan persona) that he loved raiding so much that he neglected the affairs of his home (13.222–223).[81] When embellishing his tale shortly afterwards, he identifies how his men "yield to hubris and are overcome by their strength" (οἱ δ᾽ ὕβρει εἴξαντες, ἐπισπόμενοι μένεϊ σφῷ, 14.262).[82] The language of excess is also projected onto the suitors whose transgressive behavior is thematized as a type of raiding.[83] Beyond the *Odyssey*'s flagrant fantastical presentation of idealized golden-age society, on the one hand, and its world of supernatural beings on the other, we find the emergent reality of life outside of war—or, more to the point, a step further on from the heroic age of the war at Troy. In *Iliad* 9, while Achilles pays lip-service to the Hesiodic ideal of hard work, the picture that he presents of his home, Phthia, is of a world of plenty. Moreover, though deprived of his home and unable to enjoy that patrimony, by virtue of his hard work in the field of battle at Troy he has gained many other possessions (even if Agamemnon failed to distribute that booty equitably). Thus, Achilles' solution to *eris* in *Iliad* 23, in which he offers prizes in compensation for heroic effort, enables him to construct a political fantasy of equitable redistribution based on merit. In the *Odyssey*, however, Ithaca is not a land of endless resources. This is not only a post-conflict world, but also a post-heroic one. One problem with the endless feasting enjoyed by the suitors is the fact that it threatens to eat Telemachus out of house and home. There is a critical limit on what can be distributed. On meeting Nestor, Telemachus contrasts the scene of proper distribution by which he is greeted with the scene back on Ithaca, warning Nestor not ever to leave home "lest arrogant men eat up all your household / and *divide* all your possessions" (οὕτω ὑπερφιάλους, μή τοι κατὰ πάντα φάγωσι / κτήματα <u>δασσάμενοι</u>, 3.316–317; cf.

---

[81]   For King 1999:81–83 the Cretan figure is an evocation of "the greatest of the Greek heroes" but also a caricature. For similarities between the Cretan persona and Odysseus, see Walcot 1977:14. For Newton 2015:270 "the beggar confirms for Eumaios that marauders who succumb to excess do indeed bring on their own ruin."

[82]   For an overview of Odysseus' Cretan "lies" see Haft 1984; Emlyn-Jones 1986. For their common elements and connection to the epic's themes, see Reece 1994; cf. Walcot 1977:9–12; Higbie 1995:170–171; King 1999; and Newton 2015.

[83]   For Newton 2015:271 Odysseus' narrative resolves the "adversarial relationship between raiding and hospitality" by focusing on the excess of the men. King 1999:80 argues that "Odysseus' tale invents and vividly depicts a hero who aspires to the ideal of the other great Homeric epic (or epic tradition) and therefore serves as a countertype to the hero of the *Odyssey*."

15.12–13 and 20.215–216). Far from enjoying an epic world of plenty, the characters are acutely aware of a Hesiodic precarity to their existence.

Such concerns are never far from Odysseus' mind. On gaining access to
the royal couple ruling Skheria, Odysseus prays that Arete's guests may always
keep their "possessions in their homes and the prize (*geras*) which the *demos*
grants them" (κτήματ' ἐνὶ μεγάροισι <u>γέρας</u> θ', ὅ τι δῆμος ἔδωκεν, 7.150)—a
rather curious aside that betrays an anxiety about the precarity of his own
position. Later he asks his mother's shade whether his father or son or some
other person has his *geras* already ("does my *geras* still reside among them /
or does some other man already have it while they claim I will not come home?"
ἦ ἔτι πὰρ κείνοισιν <u>ἐμὸν γέρας</u>, ἦέ τις ἤδη / ἀνδρῶν ἄλλος ἔχει, ἐμὲ δ' οὐκέτι
φασὶ νέεσθαι, 11.175–176). Ever his father's son, Telemachus reveals the same
concern, worrying whether it will be Eurymachus who "marries [his] mother
and receives the *geras* of Odysseus" (μητέρ' ἐμὴν γαμέειν καὶ <u>Ὀδυσσῆος γέρας</u>
ἕξειν, 15.522). In this tale of a world in flux, caught between the Iliadic Trojan
conflict and an everyday Hesiodic existence, the characters are keenly aware
that the objects of *dasmos*—goods, and social position—are not fixed in perpe-
tuity. Strife remains latent in anxiety and speculation throughout the poem.
Arguably the most striking, and certainly the most jarring, example occurs when
Odysseus describes the moment he meets Charybdis for a second time as "late,
when a man rises from the assembly to go to dinner, one who has been *judging
many conflicts* while men were *seeking judgments*" (ὄψ'· ἦμος δ' ἐπὶ δόρπον ἀνὴρ
ἀγορῆθεν ἀνέστη / <u>κρίνων νείκεα πολλὰ δικαζομένων</u> αἰζηῶν, 12.439–440). The
harsh juxtaposition between an incomprehensibly horrific encounter with an
otherwordly monster and the drudgery of routine life does not merely suggest
that Odysseus' mind is returning to the everyday world back at home, as the
fantastical part of his journey is about to end; the simile acts as a bridge between
the two worlds, as if the ordinary life that Odysseus yearns for both depends
on his action here and informs it. Judging conflict *is like* surviving a horrific
monster. Survival in the *Odyssey* here strongly recalls the picture of everyday
hard labor in *Works and Days* coupled with the Theogonic emphasis on the king
who bestows judgment, but inflected: the emphasis lies on every man making
judgments for himself, since judgment is too important to be left to some ideal
king (when they're usually not). Through such resonances Odysseus, the now
lone survivor still making it back from the Trojan War, is represented as making
the (necessary) transition from Achaean hero to everyman figure, a quintessential "middle" *man*.[84]

---

[84] On *andra*—the first word of the poem—see Goldhill 1991:1–5; cf. Slatkin 1986:262–263. On
Odysseus the "middle" man: Peradotto 1990.

The absence of a political means of settlement for Telemachus is addressed directly when Nestor welcomes him in Pylos, and will be later repeated by Odysseus when he first meets his son back on Ithaca: could it be that he is so easily subdued, or that the people hate him, because of some divine word? [85] In a follow-up question to that later scene, Odysseus coyly asks whether the blame lies with Telemachus' relatives, "in whom a man / can trust, when there are struggles and a *great conflict* arises?" (οἷσί περ ἀνὴρ / μαρναμένοισι πέποιθε, καὶ εἰ <u>μέγα νεῖκος</u> ὄρηται;, 16.97–98). [86] Placing the emphasis on *family* in nego-tiating strife, the disguised Odysseus marks his means of gaining redress to the unlawful redistribution that has occurred in his absence. [87] Initially conflict is direct; first when Iros threatens to fight Odysseus for the position of palace beggar (ἀλλ' ἄνα, μὴ τάχα νῶϊν <u>ἔρις</u> καὶ χερσὶ γένηται, 18.10), and then when Odysseus declares that given the opportunity he would best the suitors in a competition of work ("If there could be a work-contest between us...,"εἰ γὰρ νῶϊν <u>ἔρις</u> ἔργοιο γένοιτο, 18.366). If the first example represents an instantia-tion of Achilles' complaint about the treatment he has received at the hands of Agamemnon, the image of a farming competition strongly reverberates with echoes of Hesiod's *Works and Days*. Both instances represent strife sublimated, through either a sporting or an agricultural contest, but the threat of real strife hangs over the suitors should they fail to restrain their physical or verbal abuse ("so that no conflict and strife might arise..." ἵνα μή τις <u>ἔρις καὶ νεῖκος</u> ὄρηται, 20.267). The warning is not heeded, and Odysseus' halls soon echo instead to the sound of martial contest, in the form of an Iliadic battle where the flower of Ithaca is put to the bow and sword. [88] When an assembly is called in the wake of the slaughter, again the community ruptures on partisan lines (24.412–466), again any middle ground is erased. (You are either for us or against us.) Far from resolving the crisis, Odysseus' actions threaten to unleash civil war on Ithaca. With kinsmen facing kinsmen, and the bodies of fallen Achaeans lying unburied, the shadow of Thebes looms ever larger.

It is worth reiterating that the conflict is represented by and perpetuated through feasting within a single household. When Odysseus comes in disguise to test the suitors, he dons another persona and declares: "I once lived in a house among men, a blessed man in a wealthy house, and I used to give much

---

[85] *Odyssey* 3.214–215; 16.95–96.

[86] When Nestor asks Telemachus about the political situation at home, he follows up the same question asked by Odysseus in Book 16 with an express hope that Odysseus may someday return (3.216–217).

[87] Pucci 1987:128–38. Rutherford 1993:44 describes *Odyssey* 22 as "'Iliadic' warfare transferred to the domestic setting." On the importance of Odysseus suffering insult at home, see Emlyn-Jones 1984:6–7.

[88] Chapter 3, "A Great Deed."

to a beggar" (καὶ γὰρ ἐγώ ποτε οἶκον ἐν ἀνθρώποισιν ἔναιον ὄλβιος ἀφνειὸν καὶ πολλάκι δόσκον ἀλήτῃ, 17.419–420). He promises that upon receiving similar care he will make Antinoos famous (418). The suitors, in a gesture perhaps echoing Oedipus' recalcitrant sons, refuse to give the king-in-disguise a portion at their (his) feast. This is transgressive hospitality at its worst. But Odysseus' veiled threat communicates that another type of distribution is in play and anticipates the epic's final movement. When declaring that he could make "Antinoos" famous, Odysseus uses the verbalized form of *kleos*, κλείω. The Ithacan youth have found themselves barred from heroic life by circumstance. Too young to go to (the Trojan) war, they have turned back to a pre-(Trojan) war scenario of wooing a woman. But the war hero has returned: even as he declares that he has control over fame, so, by virtue of his return, his epic asserts its fame over other potential stories. In its engagement in strife with the epic tradition the *Odyssey* implies that the product of epic songs, *kleos* itself, is a limited resource over which it has control.

This is, in fact, part of the challenge offered by the false resolution of strife in *Odyssey* 24. For a brief moment, we find the story suspended as the families of the suitors bury their dead and gather in the assembly to contemplate their options. One of the suitors' fathers, Eupeithes, openly condemns Odysseus' failure as an epic leader of people, deploying epic poetry's own care for the people against him: Odysseus lost all the people whom he had led to Troy; on his return he has killed the people at home. Eupeithes presents a calculus of Strife that reflects both on the zero-sum game and on epic poetics. First, he encapsulates the epic theme of revenge, which can only function by taking satisfaction or payment for another. This ethos countermands Ajax's assertion from *Iliad* 9 (632–638) that men can live together after a murder once restitution has been made. The problem at the end of the *Odyssey* is eerily similar to that at the beginning of the *Iliad*: who is going to judge this *eris* and effect a new *dasmos* when the conflict is between the king and his people? Second, Eupeithes' behavior is driven in part by shame, in part by a fear of infamy. His positive fame can emerge only from ending Odysseus' story. The *Odyssey* here reflects the very issue of epic rivalry itself—to replace or contest another entity's fame is in part to erase it.

Such competitive erasure is part of the experiment of the epic's end. Eupeithes' speech proves radically divisive: half of them go home, half gather to attack Odysseus' supporters. When they are routed and Odysseus rampages after them in an Achillean (Heraklean) killing spree, Athena is forced to intervene directly and bring the poem to a shuddering halt (*Odyssey* 24.543–545):

"διογενὲς Λαερτιάδη, πολυμήχαν' Ὀδυσσεῦ,
ἴσχεο, παῦε δὲ <u>νεῖκος ὁμοιΐου πτολέμοιο</u>,
μή πώς τοι Κρονίδης κεχολώσεται εὐρύοπα Ζεύς."

"Divine-born son of Laertes, many-wiles Odysseus,
Hold back, stop the *conflict of a like war*,
Lest Zeus, the wide-browed son of Kronos, get angry in some way."

Little more than 60 lines before, Zeus ordained such an ending (24.482–486):

ἐπεὶ δὴ μνηστῆρας ἐτείσατο δῖος Ὀδυσσεύς,
ὅρκια πιστὰ ταμόντες ὁ μὲν βασιλευέτω αἰεί,
ἡμεῖς δ' αὖ παίδων τε κασιγνήτων τε φόνοιο
ἔκλησιν θέωμεν· τοὶ δ' ἀλλήλους φιλεόντων
ὡς τὸ πάρος, πλοῦτος δὲ καὶ εἰρήνη ἅλις ἔστω."

"Since Odysseus has paid back the suitors,
let him be king again for good after they all take faithful oaths.
Let us force a forgetting of that slaughter of children and relatives.
Let all the people be friendly towards each other as they were.
Let wealth and peace be abundant."

In the very formalization of its closure,[89] the *Odyssey* suggests there is never any simple, easy or even final resolution to strife; any judgment to resolve strife inevitably implicates the act of the judgment. At one level this final word on strife (or, more particularly, on the "strife of a like war") signifies the threat of a conflict that respects no distinctions, a war with one's own kind, a *civil war*. It is as if the poem were threatening to take something like a Theban turn, where the very likeness of its combatants—brothers who are sons—is the catalyst for strife.[90] At this metapoetic level, it also directly recalls Odysseus' description of the war between the Trojans and Achaeans, which he designates as a "great conflict of a like war" (18.264)—a war that by respecting no age or status distinctions has effectively killed off the race of heroes. Through such an abrupt and explicitly marked endgame, the *Odyssey* implies that no other Troy story like it should be told, lest, we should not forget, the gods disapprove. By ending strife

---

[89] The end of the *Odyssey* has been viewed as notoriously problematic: see Moulton 1974: 154–157; Wender 1978; Marks 2008, Chapter 3; Kelly 2007: 382–387. For arguments strongly in favor of Book 24's authenticity, see Lord 1960: 177–185; Kullman 1992: 291–304; Henderson 1997.

[90] See Odysseus' description of the conflict between the Trojans and Achaeans at 18.264: ἔκριναν μέγα νεῖκος ὁμοιΐου πτολέμοιο. Cf. *Lexikon des frühgriechischen Epos* s.v. ὁμοίιος for the meaning "gemeinschaftlich"—the formula seems to imply necessarily a difficulty of judgment.

with a divinely imposed *krisis* amid the chaos of transgressed institutions, the *Odyssey* uses the divine judgment as a kind of placeholder for the *krisis* to come as audiences absorb and respond to the epics' attempted domestication of *eris*.

At the same time, the artificiality of the ending demands reflection not only because of its form but also its content. In Zeus' final declaration, the promise of peace and wealth is possible only by forgetting—or, rather, through "forcing a forgetting" (ἔκλησιν θέωμεν). This conceit is the very opposite of the promise of fame which epic poetry usually holds out. And, although this noun comes from *lanthanô*, the same root as the river of forgetfulness *Lêthê*, the sound *e-klê-sis* might make audiences think of that which is being generated by this loss: *kleos*.

The end of the *Odyssey*'s political narrative thus brings an abrupt, and not altogether satisfactory, resolution to issues of the distribution of life, public and private goods, and fame. The final *dasmos* to forestall future *eris* limits the political power of the people in exchange for the promise of mutual benefit: it is a solution which encourages audiences to value stability and common prosperity over and against all else. Or, to put that in the terms of Hesiod's *Works and Days*, hard work and just behavior.

This is not, however, the end of Odysseus' odyssey (even if it is the end of ours). During his underworld adventure, Odysseus receives a prophecy about his return. In fact, it was for this reason that he undertook this labor in the first place. And yet the prophecy that he receives reveals very little about *how* he will return home and *what* he needs to do, even if that had been the aim.[91] Instead, in addition to learning that his *nostos* will not be complete when he sets foot back on his island, Odysseus also discovers that his journeying will not be at an end even then (11.119–137).[92] Once home, he must depart again for a final odyssey, carrying with him an oar, until he comes upon a people who know nothing about the sea or ships: there, when a passing wayfarer confuses his oar for a winnowing fan, he is to plant the oar in the ground and sacrifice to Poseidon, before (finally) returning home.

A number of features framing this strange prophecy make it suggestive for our argument. The figure of the seer has some pedigree in heroic epic as well as in later tragedy. Early in the *Iliad*, Homer introduces the key testimony of the Achaian seer Calchas, with the momentous line: "who knew the things that already are, and that will be, and that had been before" (ὃς ἤδη τά τ' ἐόντα

---

[91] Torres 2014:343: "It is striking that Teiresias does not actually explain to Odysseus what Circe had promised (see, 'your journey, and the distances to be covered, and the return'), and that it is Circe herself who will later (*Odyssey* 12.37–141) outline the particularities of the return voyage. Circe had made clear that Odysseus needed to consult Teiresias, but the question is: why necessarily Teiresias?"

[92] Odysseus later retells the prophecy to Penelope back on Ithaca (23.267–277).

τά τ' ἐσσόμενα πρό τ' ἐόντα, *Iliad* 1.70). Shortly afterwards, Odysseus appeals to Calchas' prophecy that Priam's city would fall only in the tenth year, in order to keep the host at Troy (*Iliad* 2.301-335). A seer's words, however challenging for a king or difficult to interpret, are the very definition of efficacious: they are always borne out. In this case, the seer Teiresias looms large in the testimonia and later tragedies associated with Thebes and its ruling family. It seems significant, then, that "Odysseus" is careful to denote Teiresias as "the Theban,"[93] exclusively associating him with the city, Thebes, not with its ruling house.[94] The identification of Teiresias as the Theban seems designed to bring to mind the rival tradition at more or less the center point of Odysseus' tale (and the poem itself). If this is suggestive of interpoetic rivalry, the fact that Teiresias delivers his prophecy standing on the "borders" (11.13) of the world next to the great sea "Oceanus" makes it appear as though we are on the edge of epic poetry itself.[95]

Within this metapoetic framework, Teiresias' prophecy is particularly striking. As Alex Purves has argued, the prophecy does not merely map out Odysseus' continued journeying beyond the limits of this poem; "to travel inland in such a way is to travel 'off the map' of archaic poetics" and "toward a new literary landscape."[96] When Odysseus later recounts this prophecy to his wife, he describes his continued toil as "unmeasured" (ἀμέτρητος, *Odyssey* 23.249). In *Works and Days*, Hesiod announces that he will show the measure (*metra*) of the resounding sea, although he is not skilled in sailing and ships (648-649), in what recent critics have taken to be a metapoetic distancing of his kind of epic from Homer's.[97] "Unmeasured" or, better, "unmetrical," then, suggests a kind of poetry without meter (or at least not the steady beats of hexameter of epic). Moreover, when Teiresias glosses a key signifier in the prophecy, "the well-fitted oar" (121, 129), as the "wings of a ship" (οὐδ' εὐήρε' ἐρετμά, τά τε πτερὰ

---

[93] Teiresias the Theban: *Odyssey* 10.492, 565; 11.90, 165; 12.267; 23.323.

[94] Torres 2014:355: "It should be noted that, when Teiresias appears in the *Odyssey*, the role he may have played as the counselor to Laius or his son is irrelevant. In the Homeric poem, he is characterized as the 'Theban' Teiresias, which connects him to the city, not with the Labdacids; he is even 'lord Teiresias' (Τειρεσίαο ἄνακτος)."

[95] According to Purves 2010:79, "to speak of the domain (or *metra*) of Homeric poetics is also, in the same breath, to talk of the *metra* of the sea."

[96] Purves 2010:71.

[97] For the connection between the *Odyssey* (23.249: *ametrêtos ponos*) and *Works and Days* (648-649, *metra* 'measures' of the sea): Purves 2010:76. On Hesiod: Nagy 1982:62-65 for the Hesiodic association and rejection of sailing wisdom and Homeric poetics; Rosen 1990 for Aulis as suggesting a connection between sailing and song-making; Dougherty 2001:13, 21-25 for the similarities between shipbuilding and poetic composition. As Barbara Graziosi 2002:169 has shown, this summary of the *Iliad* is rather pointed: "unlike Hesiod, the Achaeans did not know when the right time for sailing was."

νηυσὶ πέλονται, 11.125; cf. 23.272)—using a typical poetic figure from Homeric epic—the passing wayfarer gets the wrong end of the stick. This wanderer in a world far from the sea—far from Homeric epic, that is—mistakes the oar as a land-based tool for agriculture, mistranslating the poetic figure ("the wings of a ship") as a prosaic object ("a winnowing fan").[98] Taken together, Teiresias' prophecy and Odysseus' translation of it point to a storied terrain far removed from the *Odyssey*, far even from the kind of heroic epic that Homer's poem represents.

The prophecy concerning the oar "meditates on the idea of the end of epic." At first glance we might think that Teiresias, as the representative of the Theban tradition, is critically limiting the *Odyssey*, by suggesting that Odysseus' *nostos* is not yet over; that is, that this poem fails even to tell that story right. Or that, in the words of Purves: "The logical consequence of Tiresias' prophecy is that there exists somewhere upon the earth a group of people who, although they are human and 'eaters of bread,' have never heard of the Trojan War or a hero who fought in it called Odysseus."[99] That may be true, but the Cyclops had not heard of Agamemnon and the Achaean sackers of Troy either, and he soon came to learn the *mêtis* of Odysseus. Here we should remember that Teiresias is not speaking in his own voice: his prophecy is being relayed, and translated later, by Odysseus himself. Another way of reading this prophecy, then, is (ironically) straight—as a prophecy that Odysseus will survive beyond epic. Through appropriating the Theban seer of legend, Homer/Odysseus stakes out—literally in the form of the oar—the ground for Homer's hero's transition from epic to prose. And, if the never-ending story of Odysseus' wandering is a journey into other literary forms, epic as a genre will not survive beyond the (abrupt) end of our *Odyssey*.

Odysseus' death, it is foretold, will come "gently from the sea" (ἐξ ἁλὸς / ἀβληχρὸς), and the people round about will be happy or "blessed" (ἀμφὶ δὲ λαοὶ / ὄλβιοι ἔσσονται). In epic, the people (*laos*) are always under threat of being killed or not being protected by their leaders and shepherds. The fact that Odysseus' people are now blessed suggests that they live in a time beyond epic, when they no longer need to rely on the blessed heroes for security. It looks forward to an age of men that follows hard on the race of heroes, a world in and of our time, Hesiod's *Works and Days*.

---

[98] Purves 2010:80.
[99] Purves 2010:85.

Hesiod's Domestic Striving

After articulating the potential of the beneficial Strife to balance its evil twin, Hesiod turns to his brother Perses and laments their own conflict (*Works and Days* 27–41):

Ὦ Πέρση, σὺ δὲ ταῦτα τεῷ ἐνικάτθεο θυμῷ,
μηδέ σ᾽ Ἔρις κακόχαρτος ἀπ᾽ ἔργου θυμὸν ἐρύκοι
νείκε᾽ ὀπιπεύοντ᾽ ἀγορῆς ἐπακουὸν ἐόντα.
ὤρη γάρ τ᾽ ὀλίγη πέλεται νεικέων τ᾽ ἀγορέων τε
ᾧτινι μὴ βίος ἔνδον ἐπηετανὸς κατάκειται
ὡραῖος, τὸν γαῖα φέρει, Δημήτερος ἀκτήν.
τοῦ κε κορεσσάμενος νείκεα καὶ δῆριν ὀφέλλοις
κτήμασ᾽ ἐπ᾽ ἀλλοτρίοις. σοὶ δ᾽ οὐκέτι δεύτερον ἔσται
ὧδ᾽ ἔρδειν· ἀλλ᾽ αὖθι διακρινώμεθα νεῖκος
ἰθείῃσι δίκῃς, αἵ τ᾽ ἐκ Διός εἰσιν ἄρισται.
ἤδη μὲν γὰρ κλῆρον ἐδασσάμεθ᾽, ἄλλα τε πολλὰ
ἁρπάζων ἐφόρεις μέγα κυδαίνων βασιλῆας
δωροφάγους, οἳ τήνδε δίκην ἐθέλουσι δικάσσαι.
νήπιοι, οὐδὲ ἴσασιν ὅσῳ πλέον ἥμισυ παντὸς
οὐδ᾽ ὅσον ἐν μαλάχῃ τε καὶ ἀσφοδέλῳ μέγ᾽ ὄνειαρ.

O Perses, keep these things in your mind
and don't let the evil-hearted strife keep your heart from work
while you lurk about observing conflict in the assembly.
For the season of conflicts and assemblies is a short one
for any man whose means of living is not abundantly stocked at
      home
in time, which the earth produces, Demeter's grain.
After you have made your fill of that, you can add to the store of
      conflicts and strife
over another's possessions. But it will not be possible for you a
      second time
to act like this. No, let us bring our conflict to a resolution
with straight judgments, which are best from Zeus.
For we have already divided up our inheritance, and you
made off with much besides, glorifying the bribe-swallowing
kings, the men who long have judged this kind of case.
The fools, they do not know how much more half is than everything
Nor how much wealth is in mallow and asphodel.

Many of the critical themes that we have been discussing in this chapter appear in this passage: the problem of evil-hearted strife (κακόχαρτος) and quarrels in the assembly (νείκε'… ἀγορῆς; νεικέων τ' ἀγορέων τε); the desirability of separating out strife with straight judgements (διακρινώμεθα νεῖκος / ἰθείῃσι δίκῃς); the distribution of allotments (κλῆρον ἐδασσάμεθ'); and the corrupting influence of bribe-swallowing kings (βασιλῆας / δωροφάγους).

However, on this occasion, the narrator is speaking as someone who has suffered from strife and is (still) negotiating its destructive nature.. According to Hesiod, he has been deprived of his rightful share of what has already been distributed (ἤδη μὲν γὰρ κλῆρον ἐδασσάμεθ'), because his brother has skewed the settlement by "bigging up" (μέγα κυδαίνων) those who are supposed to oversee the distribution with straight judgments. These bribe-swallowing kings apparently now intend to issue a new judgment (οἳ τήνδε δίκην ἐθέλουσι δικάσσαι) that will unjustly favor his brother. Frustrated by the institutional corruption, Hesiod is left to wield poetic tropes to express his dismay—paradox ("they don't know how much more half is more than everything") and figure ("nor how much wealth is in mallow and asphodel").

Hesiod's anatomization of strife and criticism of society's efforts to manage it is an important corrective not only to the impression that might have been given in the *Theogony* that strife was *only* bad and that kings deliver *only* good judgments, but also to the *Iliad*'s domestication of strife. The particular comment that Perses should avoid "looking out for conflict in the assembly" (νείκε' ὀπιπεύοντ' ἀγορῆς ἐπακουὸν ἐόντα) seems pointedly aimed at an Iliadic take on strife, which is—as we have seen—so characterized by striving in debate. Moreover, where in the *Iliad* the prizes are stored up for the man who makes the best judgment, Hesiod makes the point that there is no store of prizes for the combatants, and the judges are corrupted by gifts. The political imaginary at the end of the *Iliad* made possible by the separation from the zero-sum game unravels when faced with the material reality of Hesiod's Ascra or, as we have seen, of Odysseus' Ithaca.

At one level this is about promoting farming and peace over wars and battles, the *Works and Days* over the war at Troy (or the *Iliad*).[100] But Hesiod goes further. He makes Iliadic striving *dependent on* the aesthetic of self-reflection and hard work that he is promoting. The time (or, better, "season," for that captures the thematics of this poem) for quarrels in the assembly is short (ὥρη γάρ τ' ὀλίγη πέλεται νεικέων τ' ἀγορέων τε); only once one has a year's grain of supply in hand (again the language of farming) can one raise disputes and conflict

---

[100] As the narrator of the *Contest of Homer and Hesiod*, cited above, puts it at any rate. For Hesiodic rivalry with Homer, and in particular the significance of the narrator's hostility to sailing and criticism of Aulis, see Graziosi 2002:169–171.

over another's possessions (τοῦ κε κορεσσάμενος νείκεα καὶ δῆριν ὀφέλλοις / κτήμασ' ἐπ' ἀλλοτρίοις). According to Hesiod, it is the evil, non-productive Eris that compels men away from work and reduces them to audience members to someone else's striving instead of their own. It is as if Hesiod is accusing Perses of being distracted by Homeric epic from doing the work that is inspired by the better Eris. What Perses really needs to do is to attend to his own affairs and pay more attention to his brother by hearkening to *this* poem.

We should further note that Hesiod gives advice to his brother in the context of a *fraternal dispute*. After establishing the principles of the good strife, Hesiod turns back to his personal conflict: though they have already divided their inheritance, his brother has engaged bribe-taking officials to make a judgment against him. As we explored above, fraternal disputes over an inheritance are a feature of the fragments of the Theban tradition that have come down to us. In fact, judgment of distribution is arguably even more of an issue in the Theban storyworld than it is at Troy, since in Thebes the king casting judgment is both father and brother, both victim of a familial curse and agent of one.[101] In the *Works and Days* it is as if Eteocles had taken up farming and sought to deprive his brother of his fair share of their father's inheritance by going back on the deal—and finds himself challenged by a Hesiod of "many conflicts" (Polyneikes). When Hesiod later aligns both traditions, he defines the Trojan War as striving over Helen, and the Theban conflict as a war over the "flocks of Oedipus." These phrases not only summarily domesticate the rival epic traditions; they even suggest a Hesiodic *Works and Days* appropriation.[102] In the Hesiodic cosmos, the conflicts of the age of heroes relate to the concerns of the everyday man, the theft of valuable property—a woman on the one hand, sheep on the other. By offering his reader guidance on observing the basic rules of living a just life, the *Works and Days* offers a rumination on epic conflict that has resonance for the men of now, engaged in inheritance disputes, getting a wife, or skirmishing or with neighboring groups.

The *Odyssey* shares many of these concerns with Hesiod's *Works and Days*. Though a returning hero from the Trojan War, Odysseus is presented—and presents himself—as a beggar in rags, mixing in the company of the people who work the land. When he is faced by the violent arrogance of the suitors, he challenges them to a farming contest. Where Hesiod longs to separate out conflict with straight justice (ἀλλ' αὖθι διακρινώμεθα νεῖκος / ἰθείῃσι δίκῃς) and cannot because of the corrupt kings, so Odysseus cannot simply return to a world where

---

[101] Notice how much of Sophocles' reworking of the Theban field highlights the king's *judgment*—whether that king is Oedipus or Kreon—as the issue at stake.

[102] Such strategies of conflict domestication occur throughout the *Iliad*, especially in the speeches of heroes. See Christensen 2009 and 2018b.

he can just work harder (in spite of the fantasy of his metaphorical challenge to the suitors); he must violently regain what is his. Here we might think that this is where the comparison ends, as Odysseus' removal of his beggar's disguise ushers in an Iliadic scene of frenzied slaughter. Yet Odysseus' assumption of a heroic mantle represents a last raging against the dying light of the heroic age. From now on, as Zeus and Athena make clear, conflicts cannot be resolved in such individualistic shows of strength; some kind of community judgment, as shown on Achilles' shield, and as promoted here by Hesiod, is needed.

This starts with the audience themselves. Strife is left to be adjudicated— and to be contested over and over again—by the audiences who receive it and by the next singers who will add to these tales. Homer's audience departs mulling over the end of the *Odyssey* and weighing the guilt assigned to each party; Hesiod's audience is presented with the case of the striving brothers followed by traditional advice on good living, and, most importantly the story of the end of the race of heroes. Their task is to figure out how to achieve a better life, the good life, in their worlds.

Conclusion

> Polyidos marries Eurydameia the daughter of Phyleus, the son of Augeas. His sons were Eukhênôr and Kleitos who sacked Thebes with the Epigonoi. Then they went to Troy with Agamemnon where Eukhênôr died at Alexander's hand.
>
> Pherecydes, fr. 115[103]

The T Scholia credit to Pherecydes the mythographer a genealogy that combines Thebes and Troy. Two otherwise unknown brothers, Eukhênôr and Kleitos, sack Thebes with the Epigonoi and then go on to fight at Troy. There, the "Boasting-Man" (Εὐχήνωρ) is killed by Paris, but his brother, "Mr. Famous" (Κλεῖτος), survives. The pairing and the generational overlay helps to explain why even an early mythographer like Pherecydes found the intersection of the two traditions useful and insightful. The destruction at Thebes was not enough; *more* perishing was necessary to erase the race of heroes. Troy is not offered to replace Thebes but rather as a supplement to finish the work that was begun.

In this chapter we have explored critical Homeric and Hesiodic themes that are securely identified within the corpus of extant Theban fragments. A key

---

[103] Πολύιδος...γαμεῖ Εὐρυδάμειαν τὴν Φυλέως τοῦ Αὐγέα· τῷ δὲ γίνονται Εὐχήνωρ καὶ Κλεῖτος, οἳ Θήβας εἷλον σὺν τοῖς ἐπιγόνοις ἔπειτα εἰς Τροίαν ἔρχονται σὺν Ἀγαμέμνονι, καὶ θνήσκει Εὐχήνωρ ὑπ' Ἀλεξάνδρου. See Fowler 2000:337 for this fragment and its attestations; for the scholion, Erbse 3.526.28; Schol. T *Iliad* 13.663.

feature of this thematic overlap is poetic rivalry as the poems draw on ideas and issues from their common traditions and from each other to deploy and explore in their own ways. Just as Hesiod's good strife (cf. Chapter 4) enables neighbors to compete with each other and create greater wealth than they might have in isolation, the competitive aesthetic of Greek poetry facilitated repeated and repeatedly more complex explorations of similar themes in contexts and inter-relations where the performance of a new version was at least partly deriva-tive from, and built on, prior and competing visions. Such results, we suggest, are characteristic of an artistic marketplace where poet strives against poet, working to maintain audience interest as they sing "the latest song." Yet, among competing visions there resides too a certain cooperative outcome. By drawing on and reworking similar themes and characters in reaction to audience interest, political contexts, and social trends, they help develop a cultural gestalt.[104]

Throughout this chapter we have been exploring the heroic epic deploy-ment of the theme of *eris* and its attendant features of division (*dasmos*) and judgment (*krisis*). These aspects rely on the intrinsic interformularity and inter-traditionality of Greek epic and they are present through Homer, Hesiod, and the fragments of the Theban tradition. The contrasting presentations of Strife in *Theogony* and *Works and Days* offer different ways of thinking about rivalry not only in the Hesiodic but also Homeric tradition. In addition to the zero-sum game that exists in both, there is another supplementary competitive spirit that can be useful for communities, a domesticated Eris disambiguated from violence and destruction. Though we have lost the Theban epics, their frag-ments and parallels in poems on similar subjects imply that they too were part of this process. Speculation about how and why they were eventually fall out of the epic tradition handed down to us is the subject of our last chapter.

---

[104] Consider the character of the criminal anti-hero on American television from the past 20 years, through which, from Tony Soprano to Walter White, competing networks and writers have explored similar themes for similar audiences. The success of these characters and their stories in appealing to modern audiences is dependent not just on the nature of post-industrial capi-talism, Western-style democracy, and eroding religious faith, combined with ultimately impo-tent frustration at the pace and state of the world; they are also interdependent: one counter-cultural narrative depends upon the inroads made by others.

6

Beyond Thebes

"And what about you, Nikêratos—what kind of knowledge do you take pride in?" And he said: "My father, because he wished for me to be a good man, compelled me to memorize all of Homer. And now I can recite the whole *Iliad* and *Odyssey*."

Xenophon *Symposium* III 5[1]

LYKOURGOS, A GREEK from the Peloponnese, is famous for having traveled to Crete to return with the institutions that would be critical for establishing Sparta's new constitution. This, however, was not the only journey that Lykourgos took, nor the only benefit he brought back for his people. In a story related by Plutarch, Lykourgos is said to have discovered the Homeric poems during his travels among the Ionians and, after writing them down, to have brought them home to the Spartans for their "educational and political value" (τὸ πολιτικὸν καὶ παιδευτικὸν). "At the time," Plutarch writes, "the epics had a slight reputation among the Greeks: a few possessed certain portions of the poems which had been circulated randomly. But Lykourgos was the first to make the poetry especially well-known."[2] Solon, who was comparably regarded as the founder of the Athenian constitution, is reputed to have traveled abroad in a similar fashion, while it was his kin, the Peisistratids, who famously established the performance of Homeric epic in Athens.[3] Homer was even said to have wandered from city to city performing his tales in rivalry with other poets, which, while doubtful as an accurate biography (by modern standards), stands as evidence for the universal reception of his poetry in diverse and scattered communities throughout the Greek-speaking world.[4]

---

[1] ἀλλὰ σὺ αὖ, ἔφη, λέγε, ὦ Νικήρατε, ἐπὶ ποίᾳ ἐπιστήμῃ μέγα φρονεῖς. καὶ ὃς εἶπεν· Ὁ πατὴρ ὁ ἐπιμελούμενος ὅπως ἀνὴρ ἀγαθὸς γενοίμην ἠνάγκασέ με πάντα τὰ Ὁμήρου ἔπη μαθεῖν· καὶ νῦν δυναίμην ἂν Ἰλιάδα ὅλην καὶ Ὀδύσσειαν ἀπὸ στόματος εἰπεῖν.

[2] Plutarch *Life of Lykourgos* 4.4.

[3] On overlap in accomplishments attributed to Peisistratus and Solon, see Higbie 1997:282.

[4] See Graziosi 2002.

This process of developing shared myths, cult cites, and festivals among various dialectical groups, as well as very different political, economic, and social communities, has been identified as a feature of Panhellenism.[5] The idea of Panhellenism has helped scholars to think about how the Homeric and Hesiodic poems were shaped by and shaped in turn Greek culture over a long period of engagement with local traditions,[6] and has contributed to the discussion over the eventual textualization and survival of these poems.[7] For the reasons outlined in the introduction, primarily regarding the paucity of evidence, using Panhellenism to explain why the Theban epics failed to gain a comparable currency is fraught with difficulties.[8] Nevertheless, even if its explanatory power is open to doubt, it remains a useful framework to explore the process through which mythical tales were transformed from local and particular traditions into the authorities that would one day be prized by Greeks like Herodotus or Plutarch. While a scenario that lays emphasis on gradual text formation of the Homeric poems (rather than, say, their recording by a one-time act of transcription) supports Gregory Nagy's evolutionary model, we remain in the dark about the precise process by which the Homeric poems were formed.[9] In the end they are texts that need to be analyzed, even if—as we have argued throughout—that analysis is best achieved through an oral framework of traditional referentiality.

[5] For Panhellenism, see our discussion in the Introduction, "Rivalry and Panhellenism." For a classic statement of Greekness, see Herodotus VIII 144.2, where the Athenians point to the common blood, language, gods, and customs of the Greek world. The rhetorical nature of this speech should not, however, be overlooked: Barker 2009:196–198.

[6] "It has become an established tenet of Homeric criticism that the *Iliad* and the *Odyssey* are to be understood as Panhellenic in scope," Elmer 2013:205. On the relationship between Homer and Panhellenism, see Nagy 1990:52–81, and for the exploration of the Panhellenizing tendencies of Homeric epic and the local orientation of hero cult Nagy 1999 [1979]; cf. Scodel 2002:45–46.

[7] On the basis of the Homeric epics' notional Panhellenism, Nagy 2004 offers a model whereby our *Iliad* evolves in form over time until finally being fixed by the editorial practices of the Hellenistic age; cf. Nagy 1996a:62–112. Contrast West 2001:3–4, who places the textualization of the *Iliad* in the Troad as far back as the eighth century BCE. Gentili 1988:4–19 opts for a much later date (fifth century BCE) on the basis of classical *topoi* regarding the Homeric epics (such as the Peisistratid recension and the fluidity of the texts in the Alexandrian era). For the dictation of the poems under the Peisistratids in 522 BCE, see Jensen 2011 *passim*. Cf. Reece 2005, whose overview of the debate regarding textualization (39–53) is the basis for an argument in favor of the dictation model (54–88).

[8] As is, for example, using aesthetic considerations based largely on judging the quality of fragments: Griffin 1977. Similarly Nagy 2015:63 argues that Homer is Panionic and proto-Panhellenic, as opposed to the Cyclic poems which are more localized.

[9] Primarily this is because we want to avoid the impression that the Homeric poems cannot (or should not) be studied as coherent and organic wholes. Therefore, we draw a distinction between a long tradition of, say, Iliadic tales (songs about Troy and even Achilles) that developed over time and *our Iliad* (this particular song about Achilles that we have) that was created out of it.

In the first three chapters of this book we have argued that, by looking at the Homeric poems' use of Theban mythic material, we can better appreciate the poetic strategies through which they consistently appropriate, manipulate, and implicitly suppress rival poetic traditions.[10] In our last two chapters we further suggested that, through a cultural agonistics of succession and replacement, our extant examples of epic poetry communicate and interrogate the nature and importance of *eris*, acknowledging its devastating potential even while trying to domesticate it for mankind in some way.

The foundational text for anatomizing strife is the *Works and Days*, which, as we have seen, establishes the origins of a second kind of cooperative strife, even as it represents—and reproduces in its very form—the destructive strife of a divided patrimony. In the light of our discussion of the Eris theme, let us return to the passage in which Hesiod describes the "race of heroes" (ἀνδρῶν ἡρώων θεῖον γένος) that we first considered in our Introduction (161–172):

καὶ τοὺς μὲν πόλεμός τε κακὸς καὶ φύλοπις αἰνὴ
τοὺς μὲν ὑφ᾽ ἑπταπύλῳ Θήβῃ, Καδμηίδι γαίῃ,
ὤλεσε μαρναμένους μήλων ἕνεκ᾽ Οἰδιπόδαο,
τοὺς δὲ καὶ ἐν νήεσσιν ὑπὲρ μέγα λαῖτμα θαλάσσης
ἐς Τροίην ἀγαγὼν Ἑλένης ἕνεκ᾽ ἠυκόμοιο.

Evil war and dread battle destroyed them,
some at seven-gated Thebes in the land of Cadmus,
when they fought for the flocks of Oedipus,
and others when it had led them in their ships over the great deep
      sea
to Troy for lovely-haired Helen.

In addition to the pairing of Troy and Thebes together (τοὺς μέν and τοὺς δέ), the repetition of the *casus belli* in the genitive (μήλων ἕνεκ᾽ Οἰδιπόδαο; Ἑλένης ἕνεκ᾽ ἠυκόμοιο) and the chiastic order (Thebes - men who died there - others - Troy) suggest a careful structuring of the material that repays closer attention. It may be argued that the ordering of Thebes first, then Troy, points to the prioritization of the former tradition, a result, perhaps, of the Boiotian perspective afforded by Hesiod's poem.[11] Alternatively, the pairing could be a

---

[10] See, for example, Larson 2007; Barker and Christensen 2008; Ebbott 2010; the essays collected in Tsagalis ed. 2014; and Berman 2015.

[11] "This is a non-Homeric, non-Troy-centric perspective that shows the primacy of Thebes as a legendary city under siege, previous to Troy," Berman 2015:30–31. Earlier, he asserts, "In the Hesiodic poems, Thebes has a presence equal to, or perhaps more prominent than, that of Troy" (29).

manifestation of what we observed in Chapter 4: that is, Fenik's "anticipatory doublet," where a pattern is introduced and then repeated in expanded form to signal the greater importance of the second element.[12] In this interpretation Troy is offered as the same *kind* of event as Thebes, but arguably greater in magnitude, requiring ships and a journey overseas. Or to put that differently, Thebes is not (epic) enough to wipe out the race of heroes; the conflagration at Troy is needed to finish the job.[13] Similarly, while the mention of "the flocks of Oedipus" might be suggestive of sub-heroic conflicts of the kind Nestor recalls in Homer, the reference to Helen—daughter of Zeus, the most beautiful woman in the world—opens up any number of grand cosmic narratives, including the Hesiodic *Catalogue of Women*.[14] The pull of Troy, even here, seems greater.

In this final chapter we reflect on the cultural rivalries that may have helped to shape and valorize the Homeric treatment of Thebes. To do this we use a series of case studies to help us think about the multilayered and multi-directional ideological aspects that constituted the process of Panhellenic culture-making. We first consider local epichoric traditions—specifically Boiotian—in order to think about how the practice of contesting Thebes may have been a part of Greek culture before the epics reached their final form. Then, drawing on this image of Hesiod as the "Boiotian poet" par excellence, we use resonant elements of the two other ("heroic") poems attributed to him, the *Shield* and the *Ehoiai*, to provide a framework for reconsidering the relationship between Boiotian traditions, Panhellenic authority, and the presence of Thebes. In short, we explore how Homeric opposition to *and* partnership with Hesiodic traditions helped these epics absorb and instrumentalize a Boiotian perspective.[15] Next, we turn to a brief examination of Erginos of Orkhomenos and specifically the ways in which his story is integrated into extant Pan-Boiotian and Panhellenic narratives respectively. Not only do we suggest that his mythical career provides some insight into the complex rivalries and negotiations that must have taken place between epichoric Theban material and Panhellenic representations, we also show how many of their latent properties were primed to respond to

---

[12] See Chapter 4 above, "The Eris Revolution." In addition to Fenik 1974:142–207 and Kakridis 1949:43–49, see e.g. Scodel 1984:55–58; Kelly 2007; Sammons 2014:302, 310; and Tsagalis 2014:357 for a fuller bibliography.

[13] In fact not the entire race of heroes is wiped out at Thebes and Troy: "dread war" destroys only "some of them" (τοὺς μέν); Zeus has settled "the others" in the blessed isles (τοῖς δέ, 167).

[14] The balance is disrupted by a contrast between the clear identification of Helen as the cause of the Trojan War and the rather oblique phrase "around the flocks of Oedipus" with which the war at Thebes is described: which war around Thebes sent the heroes to their doom? On this lack of clarity and earlier interpretations, see Cingano 1992, who concludes nevertheless that these lines refer to the later, more monumental battles.

[15] Cf. Finkelberg 2012:142: the Homeric epics were "intended to supersede the other traditional epics from the very beginning."

historical events in the late sixth and early fifth centuries BCE. Finally, we turn back to Homer to reflect on the ways in which the *Iliad*'s catalogue of ships presents its Boiotian contingents. Using the processes that emerge from our analysis of the Boiotian Hesiod and a layered Erginos, we provide a further glimpse into how the *Iliad* selectively presents and suppresses material to tone down or even mute entirely traditions about Thebes.

The Boiotian Hesiod

For truth's sake it is right to praise
Only after pushing envy away with both hands
if some mortal man fares well.
The Boiotian man says these things,
Hesiod, servant of the sweet Muses:
Whichever man the gods honor,
Mortal fame will follow.

Bacchylides 5.187–194[16]

While the Homeric poetry of the Trojan War narrative is often suggested to have its epichoric[17] origins in Ionian Asia Minor,[18] Hesiod's poetry is in part both linguistically and self-consciously Boiotian in character. He is, as Bacchylides names him, the "Boiotian Man."[19] His poetry seems to valorize local traditions and assert Boiotian identity.[20] In spite of the anonymizing character and effect

---

[16] [χρὴ] δ' ἀληθείας χάριν
αἰνεῖν, φθόνον ἀμφ[οτέραι-]
[σιν] χερσὶν ἀπωσάμενον,
εἴ τις εὖ πράσσοι βροτῶ[ν.]
Βοιωτὸς ἀνὴρ τάδε φών[ησεν, γλυκειᾶν]
Ἡσίοδος πρόπολος
Μουσᾶν, ὃν <ἂν> ἀθάνατοι τι[μῶσι, τούτῳ]
καὶ βροτῶν φήμαν ἔπ[εσθαι.]
[17] According to Nagy 1990:66, "myths that are epichoric...are still bound to the rituals of their native locales, whereas the myths of Panhellenic discourse, in the process of excluding local variations, can become divorced from ritual."
[18] For the Ionian character of Homer, see Frame 2009; West 2001:6–7; Nagy 2004. For the "obviously Ionic character" of its dialect, see Horrocks 1997:194.
[19] Berman 2015:32. On the Boiotian perspective of the *Theogony* and *Works and Days*, see West 1966; Larson 2007:50-52. On the Panhellenic character of the Hesiodic *Ehoiai*, in contrast to a local poem like the *Naupactica,* see Lulli 2014:85-86.
[20] See Larson 2007; Larson 2014; Berman 2013; and Berman 2015. Larson 2007:195–196 proposes that hexameter poetry is a vehicle for exploring real-world rivalries as demonstrated in Boeotia.

of Panhellenism, "Hesiod" retains something of a local, Boiotian character in contrast to the Ionian and more broadly international "Homer."[21]

Yet, at the same time, as we have consistently assumed in this book, Hesiod's poems share a Panhellenic outlook with Homer and are perhaps, therefore, best thought of not so much in competition with the Homeric poems as complementary to them and in competition instead with other Boiotian traditions such as the Herakles cycle or the tradition of the offspring of Minyas from Orkhomenos.[22] As several scholars have suggested, the process of Panhellenism was not an absolute, consistent phenomenon. Rather, it operated in part as a type of cultural discourse, a pressure to conform and fit in that motivated stories and storytelling traditions to coalesce more or less into similar forms communicating widely applicable and broadly interlocking content. In this regard, Panhellenism was, until the end of the Classical period at least, an ideology in motion, a complex and ever shifting negotiation of different interests and needs.[23] According to Jose González (2015:257–258), when Hesiod reveals that the Muses "know how to tell many lies similar to the truth / but also know how to utter true things when [they] want to" (ἴδμεν ψεύδεα πολλὰ λέγειν ἐτύμοισιν ὁμοῖα, / ἴδμεν δ' εὖτ' ἐθέλωμεν ἀληθέα γηρύσασθαι, *Theogony* 27–28), he is marking himself out as a truth-teller of epic (Panhellenic) universals in contrast to local (epichoric) traditions. In setting out this striking poetic conundrum within the opening frame of a poem that narrates the very origins of the (epic) cosmos, Hesiod makes the claim that this performance is seeking to create a common poetic inheritance, which may well (and arguably must) transgress or countermand stories that have come before.

The process of Panhellenization was not a simple one; there were likely many turns and (mis)steps in the reception, appropriation, and deployment of (universalizing) themes, ideas, and stories that are now lost to us. In the next two sections we offer a range of examples to think through some of the ways in which local traditions may have linked to regional communal tales before being incorporated within (or subsumed by) larger panhellenic narratives. The

---

[21] Nagy 1990:79: "the Panhellenic tradition of oral poetry appropriates the poet, potentially transforming even historical figures into generic ones who represent the traditional functions of their poetry. The wider the variation and the longer the chain of recomposition, the more remote the identity of the composer becomes. Extreme cases are Homer and Hesiod."

[22] For our evidence of lost epic traditions centering on the city of Thebes, see our discussions in the Introduction, at the beginning of Chapters 1–3, and in the final section of Chapter 4. On these "submerged" traditions, see especially Lulli 2014:77–90, who suggests that the fragments of the other epics betray a local focus, such as Peisander's *Herakles,* which being recognizably more Doric implies a local performance context at a disadvantage with Homer, or the *Capture of Oechalia* by Creophylus of Samos.

[23] See Elmer 2013:202–205; Cf. Nagy 1999 [1979]:7. Cf. Scodel 2002:45–46.

process that we sketch out, however, is not a blandly hierarchical one: we envision moves in multiple directions as Boiotian tales jockey for position in their regional narratives only to have the putative winner of these struggles downgraded in Homeric narrative. This is, ultimately, another way of looking at the rivalry between Troy and Thebes, as a lens through which to view how its many manifestations capitalized upon *already existing* competitive dynamics.

Hesiod is a good starting point for this investigation, precisely because, as recent scholarship has suggested, the poetic material assigned to Hesiod at times appears to consist of individual entries in the competition over local identities. Here, in particular, we are thinking of the *Shield (Aspis)* and the *Catalogue of Women (Ehoiai)*, two fragmentary poems which, while radically different in theme, both belong to a Hesiodic tradition but lack the authority ascribed to the *Works and Days* and *Theogony*. Essentially what they lack is, precisely, a foundational, Panhellenic outlook. The differences that they display from each other may, nevertheless, be best explained by their prolonged and dynamic engagement among local traditions *and* with more Panhellenic versions. While Thebans may be Boiotian, all Boiotians are *not* Theban.[24] Moreover, although these poems *could* be said to be working in concert by giving both broad and specific views of Boiotian myths, they also have different relationships to Panhellenic myth that illustrate a degree of the complex interplay that poetic and epichoric identities enjoyed in the pre-classical period.

We discussed the *Ehoiai* earlier in the context of thinking about its position as somewhere between the Homeric heroic tradition of the Trojan War and the genealogical narratives associated with Hesiod's cosmos construction, where the catalogue of suitors for Helen provides a genealogy of heroes of those who fought at Troy.[25] The important point to make is that the *Ehoiai* establishes a genealogy connecting the Boiotians with the heroic past, as represented by Homeric epic and the larger Panhellenic mythical storyworld relating to the Trojan War and the Achaean coalition.[26] A prominent aspect of this process is the development of an expansive genealogy for the daughters of Asopos, which relates the Boiotians to Aiakos and the genealogy of the eponymous Boiotos,

---

[24] For the genealogy of Boiotos in Hesiod and its importance to Boiotian collective identity, see Larson 2007, Chapter 1.

[25] Chapter 3, "A Theban Catalogue of Women."

[26] Larson 2007:9: "The Boiotian *ethnos* claimed its identity through genealogy, traditions of territory and epic, shared dialectical features, ties to panhellenic epic tradition, shared symbolism, a common name, and common cult." Larson (*passim*) shows how these narratives make sense of a legendary migration to Boiotia while also exploring ties with and claims to parts of Thessaly. For a similar process in quasi-Greek areas like Epirus where *nostos*-narratives are used to connect royal families to Panhellenic pedigrees, see Malkin 1998:140–145. For the *Catalogue*'s possible origin in northern-central Greece, see Rutherford 2005:114.

a son of Hellen, who establishes kinship between the Boiotians and the rest of Greece.[27] In turn, in Chapter 2, we discussed the *Shield* in the context of its establishing of Herakles as a Homeric-sounding, but very Theban-looking, hero to rank alongside those who fought at Troy. The *Shield*'s presentation of an ultra-Theban Herakles may well be a response to the First Sacred War, one which positions Thebes as a protector of Delphi against external brigands, and the Theban hero as fighting the "first war to end war."[28]

Crucially, the two fragmentary poems share a considerable number of lines with each other: the opening of the *Shield* (1–56) also appears in the *Ehoiai* (fr. 195.8–63), the section of the catalogue focusing on the biography of Alkmênê. "Most critics," Richard Martin (2005:173) observes, "have automatically assumed that the *Shield* was composed by some poetaster, who copied or borrowed the Alkmênê biography in the *Catalogue* and clumsily pegged onto this the story of Herakles' fight against Cyncus."[29] Put in less pejorative terms, one could regard the *Shield*—the poem centered on Thebes and its hero, Herakles—as writing itself into a Pan-Boiotian tradition.[30] Martin himself provocatively suggests that the opposite was true: using an analogy with the shield *ekphrasis* in Homer, he argues that "the *Aspis* [*Shield*] was a part of the *Catalogue* just as much (and as separably) as Achilles' shield was within the *Iliad*."[31] For us the point is rather that the "clumsily" rendered appropriation—no matter which way one perceives it as taking place—leaves starkly exposed the kind of interformular and intertraditional interplay that tends to remain hidden or erased from view elsewhere. What is unusual in this case is that both appropriating texts, though fragmentary, remain paradoxically intact, enabling us to see this process in action and their working out, so to speak, of their rivalry.

The repeated verses tell the basic story of Zeus' deception of Alkmênê. Before sleeping with his new bride, Amphitryon must depart in order to avenge the murder of Elektryon; while he's away, Zeus comes to inform her of the tale of vengeance meted out, and sleeps with her himself (the details are humorously reworked in Plautus' *Amphitryo*). The shared fragment terminates with the

---

[27] Larson 2007:81–84: The Hesiodic catalogue relates Aigina to many cities in Boiotia; "Through Asopos, then, the Aiakid genealogy is relevant both to Aigina and also to Thebes and wider Boiotia, especially the southeast, one of the most important areas of activity in the Late Archaic and early classical periods" (84).

[28] Janko 1986:46. See Janko 1986:43–48 for a summary of the pro-Theban character of the poem. Cf. Stamatopoulou 2017:14–16 for the *Shield* as "consciously post-Homeric" (14).

[29] Cf. Janko 1986:39.

[30] Larson 2007:50–51 and 114. The poem is generally dated c. 570–520 BCE: West 1985:136; Janko 1986:38–39. Martin 2005:172–175 makes *Ehoiai* and *Shield* Hesiod's; Janko 1986:47–48 proposes that *Shield* is Theban. For a recent discussion of the poem focusing on the modeling of Herakles as a *theomachos* after Homer's Diomedes, see Stamatopoulou 2017:11–16.

[31] Martin 2005:173.

double-conception of Iphikles and Herakles. From there, the *Ehoiai* continues with its catalogue, while the *Shield* takes up the story of one of Herakles' exploits, the killing of Kyknos, a son of Ares.

In (re)using the same verses as part of either a genealogical catalogue or the story of a heroic action, the *Ehoiai* and *Shield* also disclose a common strategy for engaging with what we know as the dominant epic tradition. In both, Alkmênê is marked out for her beauty: "she surpassed the race of womanly women in form and stature" (ἥ ῥα γυναικῶν φῦλον ἐκαίνυτο θηλυτεράων / εἴδεΐ τε μεγέθει τε, 3–4). If this description might suggest that other famous beauty of myth, Helen—particularly through the use of the generic description "race of women" (γυναικῶν φῦλον) and the doubling up of her (desirable) womanliness—then the rest of the line, which adds that "none could strive with her in intelligence" (νόον γε μὲν οὔ τις ἔριζε, 4), brings to mind Penelope. If so, *eris* (again) would be an indication of intertraditional rivalry and οὔ τις ("no one") perhaps even a distant echo of Odysseus' famous trick in Cyclops' cave. In these terms, Alkmênê is immediately framed as a potential rival to, arguably, the two women most representative of the Trojan War sack and return. Moreover, she is clearly positioned as the Theban response to this other tradition. Her husband, Amphitryon, travels to Thebes as a suppliant (13), from which he leads a grand(ish) coalition of Boiotians, Lokrians, and Phocians against the Taphians and Telebaoians (24–26). Thus, while both the *Shield* and the fragment use the story of Zeus' rape of Alkmênê to provide a genealogy for Herakles, the narratives also show an intense interest in Thebes and in establishing it as a principal location for heroic action. Thebes is not only the city at which a coalition of Boiotians and their allies gathers, but it also acts as a safe haven to which people come as suppliants—an arresting inversion of its status in Athenian tragedy where bad stuff happens, and where Athens supplants it as the suppliant city and home for alliances. In this way both narratives function as foundational texts for establishing the local importance of Thebes in the cultural imagination of the central Greek mainland.

At the same time, the two texts depart significantly from each other in their rivalry with Homer. Though the *Ehoiai* is clearly positioned as a bridge to the world of heroic epic (represented by the *Iliad*), in that it sets up the story and introduces the Achaean heroes of the Trojan War, in its catalogue form and genealogical interest it also owes much to the Theogonic ordering of the cosmos. And, where the *Ehoiai* provides a catalogue of genealogies structured around women, the *Shield* tells the stories of famous heroes—tribes who war against Herakles (161–167), the battle of the Lapiths and Centaurs (with Theseus at the center), the adventures of Perseus (216–234)—in a dramatic, mimetic form, like Homer. More particularly, it features Athena helping a son of Zeus against an opponent, two heroes flyting, Athena conspiring against Ares (as in *Iliad* 5), and, in its longest, climactic segment (148–319), which provides the name of the poem, the *ekphrasis* of the shield. The *ekphrasis*, moreover, implies a clear inter-traditional relationship with the shield of Achilles, not only in presenting a city at war and at peace, as in the *Iliad*, but also in the details of festivities (272–285), agricultural activities (286–300), and athletic contests (301–314).

A final difference is worth considering in more detail. We have already mentioned that, where the *Catalogue* is interested in establishing genealogical relationships, the *Shield* dramatizes a series of (heroic-style) martial conflicts. Significantly, these depictions can be understood as reflecting geographical realities of armed conflict as refracted through the conflict between Kyknos and Herakles. Twice in the poem, the narrator pans out to place the conflict between Herakles and Kyknos in the context of the wider region. The cities listed on the first occasion are telling (379–383):

πᾶσα δὲ Μυρμιδόνων τε πόλις κλειτή τ' Ἰαωλκὸς
Ἄρνη τ' ἠδ' Ἑλίκη Ἄνθειά τε ποιήεσσα
φωνῇ ὑπ' ἀμφοτέρων μεγάλ' ἴαχον· οἳ δ' ἀλαλητῷ
θεσπεσίῳ σύνισαν· μέγα δ' ἔκτυπε μητίετα Ζεύς,

The entire city of the Myrmidons and famous Iaôlkos,
Arnê, and Helikê, and grassy Antheia,
Rang with both of their voices. Then they rushed ahead
With divine roaring. And Zeus, the counselor, thundered greatly.

These cities each tell different stories about the relationship between the tale of the *Shield* and the cultural position of Thebes. Arnê, Helikê, and Antheia are Boiotian cities, the first of which is listed in the *Iliad*'s catalogue of ships; Iaôlkos and Phthia (the "entire city of the Myrmidons") are cities in southern Thessaly. The connection of these cities with Thebes might seem fleeting, but it is likely evidence of a Panboiotian version of Panhellenism. Phthia was, of course, famous as the home of Achilles—the home that he imagines going back to in *Iliad* 9 and where he reflects that his father will live out his dying days alone (now that his son is condemned to die at Troy), surrounded by enemies, in *Iliad* 24. Two other fragments of the *Ehoiai*, however, provide more details about Phthia and specifically the reason behind its pairing here with Iaôlkos. These fragments (211 and 212b) depict Peleus coming to Phthia for his marriage to Thetis, "bringing many possessions from wide-wayed Iaôlkos" (πολλὰ] κτήματ' ἄγων ἐξ εὐρυχόρου Ἰαωλκοῦ, fr. 211.1; cf. fr. 212.9), whose city he has just sacked. Indeed, the "accomplishment of his charming marriage" is paired with his sack of Iaôlkos' "well-founded city" (ὥς τε πό]λιν [ἀ]λάπαξεν ἐύκτιτον, ὥς τ' ἐτέλεσσεν / ἱμερόεν]τα γ[ά]μον, fr. 211.4-5; cf. fr. 212.7). Both epithets recall Troy.[32] Moreover, if this association of marriage with the sack of a city encourages us to think of his (arguably more) famous city-sacking son, fragment 212 tantalizingly mentions the Skaian gates (again of Troy?) and something (the subject is unfortunately lost) "for men in the future to learn" ([ ]ε..θεν ι.[....].. Σκαιῆισι πύληισι [/ [ ]..ρω[.....κα]ὶ ἐσσομένοισι πυθέσθαι· [, fr. 212.5-6). And, if we are thinking of Iaôlkos as some kind of substitute for Troy, it is all the more significant that the *Shield* pairs it with a Phthia that is conspicuously *unnamed*, but instead described periphrastically as the "entire city of the Myrmidons." The poem's hedging around Phthia's name while recounting by name the other city of southern Thessaly reduces Achilles' home city to a silent (or *silenced*) witness of Herakles' actions, at the service of a Boiotian story.

The same cities reappear at the conclusion of the *Shield* (in a disputed fragment), which narrates the burial of the defeated Kyknos (472–476):

> Κύκνον δ' αὖ Κήυξ θάπτεν καὶ λαὸς ἀπείρων,
> οἵ ῥ' ἐγγὺς ναῖον πόλιος κλειτοῦ βασιλῆος,
> [Ἄνθην Μυρμιδόνων τε πόλιν κλειτήν τ' Ἰαωλκὸν
> Ἄρνην τ' ἠδ' Ἑλίκην· πολλὸς δ' ἠγείρετο λαός,]
> τιμῶντες Κήυκα, φίλον μακάρεσσι θεοῖσιν.

> Kyknos, Kêyx and his boundless host buried,
> They who live near the city of the famous king,
> [In Anthê and the city of the Myrmidons, and famous Iaôlkos
> And Arnê and Helikê. A great host gathered,]
> Honoring Kêyx, dear to the blessed gods.

As is clear from the detailed story in Ovid (*Metamorphoses* 11.410–749), the ancient testimonia attributing a *Wedding of Kêyx* to Hesiod (see Most 2007:278–283), and several other fragments from the *Ehoiai*, Kêyx, the son of the Dawnstar, was an important figure in southern Thessalian myth, who was integrated into the stories of Boiotia in part through his guest-friendship with Herakles.[33] His traditional geographical association with Trachis further cements a connection between Boiotia and Thessaly. His position in the poem as one who accepts

---

[32] Troy, along with other cities, is often described as "well-built" in Homer (e.g. Ἰλίου ἐξαλαπάξαι ἐϋκτίμενον πτολίεθρον; *Iliad* 4.33). Troy is also "wide-wayed," but with the epithet εὐρυάγυια in the *Iliad* at 2.12, 29, 66, 141, 329; 9.28; 14.88; *Odyssey* 4.246 and 22.320. Mycenae is wide-wayed at *Iliad* 4.53.

[33] Hesiod fr. 10d; see also fr. 10a 89–98; and fr. 71a. For fuller versions of the story, see Apollodorus I 52; scholion to Aristophanes *Birds* 250; Eustathius *Commentary on Homer's Iliad* II 2.8.

suppliants is crucial to the Theban narrative as well: Trachis is where either Herakles or his children go for shelter after he must leave Thebes.[34] In making this story of Kêyx about his wealth and magnanimity (and not his arrogance or tragic marriage, as the Hesiodic fragments do), the *Shield* departs again from the tone and focus of the catalogue tradition.

In this section we have seen how taking two of the marginal narratives ascribed to Hesiod together, the *Shield* and the *Ehoiai*, and comparing their varied engagements with both epichoric and Panhellenic traditions, can be useful for thinking about the dynamic relationship between and symbiotic development of story traditions relating to Thebes and Troy. On the one hand, the local (Pan-Boiotian) and the communal (Panhellenic) elements are *partners* in the creation of a shared, corporate identity. On the other, as a secondary part of this process, local narratives continue to serve the needs and interests of their local audiences. They adapt communal narratives to epichoric contexts and weave their own traditions into the evolving Pan-traditions. It is not only impossible to resolve the question whether the first lines of the *Shield* were borrowed from the *Ehoiai*, or vice versa; posing such a question misses the point that the lines and the cultural frames, which gave each poem purchase, developed in concert and were then re-adapted to different needs. This illustrates well the type of eristic self-styling that we imagine characteristic of interactions between local and larger traditions in the archaic age.[35]

Though a culturally authoritative narrative form, early Greek hexameter epic was born out of a series of oppositions based on geographical (local vs. Panhellenic), temporal (past vs. present) and ethnic (e.g. Ionians vs. Dorians; "Greek" vs. non-Greek) considerations. Our contention is that the development of what in retrospect we regard as a Panhellenic standard was not a vertical, top-down or bottom-up, process, but an oblique and chaotic negotiation of cultural narratives working in multiple directions. Thebes, for example, was not the only city to try to wrest "Hesiod" from a larger Boiotian claim: Orkhomenos had its own hero, through whom we can see the integration of a localized Boiotian event within the larger cultural frame of Panhellenism.

---

[34] See Bacchylides fr. 33b; cf. scholion to Sophocles *Trachinian Women* 40: "[Trachis] is a Thessalian city in which Herakles settled according to the law after the murder of Iphitos. He stayed there with his guest-friend Kêyx who was the child of the brother of Amhpitryon." Cf. Diodorus Siculus IV 57.2: "After the apotheosis of Herakles, his children settled in Trachis with Kêyx, the king," μετὰ τὴν Ἡρακλέους τοίνυν ἀποθέωσιν οἱ παῖδες αὐτοῦ κατῴκουν ἐν Τραχῖνι παρὰ Κήυκι τῷ βασιλεῖ.

[35] Although Janko sees the poet of the *Shield* as imitating Homer and Hesiod—rather than participating in a cultural debate and appropriation—his emphasis on the shield's "false archaisms" and stylistic imitation presents useful evidence for the poetic dynamics of the age. See Janko 1986:42–43.

Local Hero

So far in this chapter we have discussed different narrative strategies of poems attributed to Hesiod as they participate in the creation of larger affinitive identities. This process has been useful because it affords us the opportunity to consider how our sources can be used to shed light on the complex ways in which ancient poetic traditions responded to one another in both theme *and* form (building on our analysis in Chapter 3). The details of such a process serve to support our claim that the creation of Panhellenic narratives was neither simple nor monodirectional. Instead, it involved the negotiation of different geographic, genealogical, and ideological identities.

Understanding how this process works with our Theban heroes can give us some indication of how Panhellenic narratives used and reused Theban material. As we suggested in the previous section, the Herakles narrative moved away from genealogical catalogue, downplayed the importance of female characters (and characteristics), and used poetic strategies and devices familiar to us from the Homeric poems. Until now, however, we have largely ignored local, intra-Boiotian competition and the ways in which Panhellenic narratives (here, Homer) may have manipulated rival strains within local narratives in the forging of their own identity. In this section we return to the figure of Oedipus to find his family narrative further contested and complicated by the introduction of a third party, the hero Erginos.

Evocative of this intra-Boiotian rivalry and its potential impact on the process of Panhellenization is a fragment of Pherecydes:

> Pherecydes says these things about the children of Oedipus and the women who married him: "Kreon," he says, "gave the kingdom and Laios' wife, his own mother Iokasta, to Oedipus, and from her were born *Phrastôr and Laonytos, who died thanks to the Minyans and Erginos.* Then a year had passed, Oedipus married Euryganeia, the daughter of Periphas, and from her were born Antigone and Ismene, the girl Tydeus took at the stream and the stream is called Ismene after her. The sons Eteokles and Polyneikos were also born to Oedipus from her. When Euryganeia died, Oedipus married Astymedousa, the daughter of Sthenelos." And some people add that Euryganeia was the sister of Oedipus' mother Iokasta. [36]

---

[36] γαμεῖ δὲ τὴν τεκοῦσαν: Φερεκύδης τὰ κατὰ τοὺς Οἰδίποδος παῖδας καὶ τὰς γημαμένας οὕτως ἱστορεῖ· "Οἰδίποδι," φησὶ, "Κρέων δίδωσι τὴν βασιλείαν καὶ τὴν γυναῖκα Λαΐου, μητέρα δ' αὐτοῦ Ἰοκάστην, ἐξ ἧς γίνονται αὐτῷ <u>Φράστωρ καὶ Λαόνυτος, οἳ θνήσκουσιν ὑπὸ Μινυῶν καὶ Ἐργίνου.</u> ἐπεὶ δὲ ἐνιαυτὸς παρῆλθε, γαμεῖ ὁ Οἰδίπους Εὐρυγάνειαν τὴν Περίφαντος, ἐξ ἧς γίνονται αὐτῷ

This fragment is revealing of differences among ancient traditions concerning what might be considered two of the key elements of the myth of Oedipus—his family and his death.[37] In a twist on the marriage theme, Oedipus enjoys no fewer than three wives. His third wife, "some people add," turns out to be the sister of Oedipus' mother (and therefore his aunt); he is a hero who seems peculiarly defined by his conjugal relations, especially *incestuous* relationships. It is the deaths of the first set of sons, however, that catch the eye. There is no mention here of the infamous pairing of Polyneikes and Eteocles; instead, Phrastôr and Laonytos are the doomed pair. Moreover, while their demise is appropriate for the theme of internecine strife that we have seen dominate Thebes, their deaths are ascribed to two new figures in the tradition, the Minyans and the hero Erginos.

Further details of these figures are provided by later mythographers like Apollodorus (II 68–71) and Pausanias (IX 37). According to these accounts, Minyas was a legendary founder of Orkhomenos, which was an important city in the early Greek world, and where he may have enjoyed his own local epic tradition.[38] As for Erginos: another local hero, he attacks Thebes after his father Klymenos is killed there while celebrating a festival to Poseidon; after sacking the city, he imposes a yearly indemnity of one hundred oxen.[39] On the basis of this evidence, the story related in Pherecydes would seem to suggest an inter-city, intra-Boiotian rivalry—a local, Orkhomenos-centered, narrative applying motifs, familiar from other cities' myths, to assert its preeminence over its rival Thebes.[40] Such a tale may indeed reflect a cultural memory of a period when

---

Ἀντιγόνη καὶ Ἰσμήνη, ἣν ἀναιρεῖ Τυδεὺς ἐπὶ κρήνης καὶ ἀπ' αὐτῆς ἡ κρήνη Ἰσμήνη καλεῖται. υἱοὶ δὲ αὐτῷ ἐξ αὐτῆς Ἐτεοκλῆς καὶ Πολυνείκης. ἐπεὶ δὲ Εὐρυγάνεια ἐτελεύτησε, γαμεῖ ὁ Οἰδίπους Ἀστυμέδουσαν τὴν Σθενέλου." τινὲς δὲ Εὐρυγάνειαν ἀδελφὴν λέγουσιν εἶναι Ἰοκάστης τῆς μητρὸς Οἰδίποδος. This passage (Pherecydes fr. 95) comes from a scholion to Euripides' *Phoenician Women* 53; see Fowler 2000. On the passage and its agreement with other early sources, see Cingano 1992:9–10.

37 Cingano 1992:2: "The death of Oedipus is alluded to in a passage in the Iliad (23.677 ff.)... Clearly, the *Iliad* version is in direct contrast to the version immortalized by Sophocles in the *Oedipus Coloneus*, in which the wretched Oedipus died in exile in Athens; according to epic tradition as reported in Homer and Hesiod (fr. 192 M.-W.), Oedipus, still king (*Odyssey* 11.271 ff.), died at Thebes and was commemorated by funeral games, a traditional honour accorded to epic heroes."

38 For Pherecydes' passage as reflecting an Orkhomenian tradition colored against Thebes, see Cingano 1992:10; cf. Buck 1979:59–60. On this war as the subject of the local epic the *Minyas*, see Severyns 1928:183.

39 This narrative is similar to the tale of Minos' indemnity on Athens for the death of his son. See Pausanias IX 37; Diodorus Siculus IV 10.2-6; and Apollodorus II 67. Cf. Berman 2013; Fowler 2013:386–387.

40 Berman 2013:52: "It is again a type of genealogical negotiation with implications for regional identity, perhaps in this case in the context of the longstanding rivalry between Thebes and Orkhomenos." For the political use of these myths, see Bearzot 2011, who sees the narrative

Orkhomenos was a pre-eminent city, while also engaging with the mythical tradition of Theban hubris.[41] The archaeological record shows that during the Mycenaean period, Boiotia was dominated by Orkhomenos in the north and Thebes in the south. Orkhomenos' economic power is clear from the massive engineering works that went into draining Lake Kopais. In post-Mycenaean myth Theban myth, the breaking of these works—and thus the breaking of Orkhomenian power—is credited to Herakles, who went to avenge the city of his birth against the Minyans.[42]

In the regional engagement between Thebes and Orkhomenos, then, we can identify generational layers of myths reflecting possible historical memories. In response to the disastrous events at the funeral games and the indemnity imposed on Thebes by Orkhomenos, mythical events speak to local, Boiotian, *and* Panhellenic layers of the story's reception. In many accounts, after the indemnity is imposed, the Panhellenic hero par excellence steps in. When Herakles discovers that Thebes has been sacked by its neighbors, he attacks Orkhomenos. At this point, Pausanias (IX 37) has Erginos make peace with Herakles; other authors, however, take a different line. Eustathius (*Commentary on Homer's Iliad* II 417) records that Herakles kills Erginos. Apollodorus (II 67) agrees, but not before he has Herakles cut off the ears and noses of the heralds of Orkhomenos when they come to collect the tribute. Diodorus Siculus adds the detail that Creon awards his daughter Megara to Herakles in gratitude for his service to the city (IV 40). It is only after the death of this wife that Herakles' labors truly begin.

Although many of these sources derive from later authors and summaries, they reveal an array of different responses to an early local tale—the dominance of Orkhomenos over Thebes—and various attempts to link that local narrative into a more inter-regional story. The tale at home in Orkhomenos, which depicts the Minyans as holding sway in Thebes through the defeat of Oedipus by Erginos, enters into a Pan-Boiotian dialogue about the eminence of the region's chief cities. The return of the Panhellenic Herakles redresses the balance to reflect both historical and mythical realities from a larger Hellenic perspective: Thebes *was* more important than Orkhomenos in the Archaic and Classical periods and its prominence in later myth reflects this. Thus, we get a sense of how mythical

---

as attesting to shifting powers in Boeotia (277–278) and an early anti-Theban character corresponding with the expansion of Orkhomenos in 700 BCE (273–274).

[41] There is evidence of historical conflict between Orkhomenos and Thebes: see Buck 1979:38–49. Cf. Cingano 1992:3.

[42] See Kountouri et al. 2012 for a description of the earthen works under excavation at Orkhomenos and their reflection in Herakles myths. Cf. Apollodorus II 4.11 and Diodorus Siculus IV 18.12 for Herakles' expedition against Orkhomenos. We are grateful to Aleydis Van de Moortel for bringing this excavation to our attention.

rivalry might have played out: one local tradition projects its superiority over another through a narrative of its hero (here, Orkhomenos' Erginos over the Theban Oedipus), before this relationship in turn is re-contested through the introduction of a Theban Herakles, which re-connects the heroic action to a Panhellenic storyworld.

This brief discussion shows the importance of recognizing that the interpenetration of local and communal myths happened over time and in multiple directions. When one story tradition was integrated into another, its salient features were not entirely lost. Indeed, one element that facilitates the process of Panhellenization is the fact that the local narratives are in part retained by the whole.

The description we have offered so far, even if it can appear somewhat bewildering, still oversimplifies the process. Homer's Trojan narrative was not the only Panhellenic narrative machine in archaic Greece. The deeds of Erginos were not only integrated into Herakles narratives, but they also form part of Argonautic myth. Erginos remains well enough known in the fifth century for Pindar to refer to him allusively as "child of Klymenos" (Κλυμένοιο παῖδα, *Olympian* 4.19) in a *paradeigma* in which the hero's (Achillean?) speed of foot rescues him "from the dishonor [ἐξ ἀτιμίας] of the Lemnian women" (20). Even as he hints at Erginos' epic career (and in particular his association with the Argonautic myth),[43] Pindar casts doubt on, if not the veracity then the persuasiveness of, his account by insisting that he "will not lie" (οὐ ψεύδεϊ τέγξω / λόγον). Throughout the extant accounts, Erginos is integrated into a wider Panhellenic tradition through genealogy,[44] which—in the same way as "collective memories of historical events"—were vital to the continued maintenance and continual (re)negotiation of social status, kinship relations, and the collective identity of local communities.[45]

---

[43] Erginos is cited among the Argonauts by Apollonius of Rhodes (cf. the scholion on *Argonautica* II 196, p. 193 Wendel: Erginos was the helmsman of the *Argo* after Tiphys' death, according to Herodoros). Erginos and the Minyans also appear in Pindar. Two scholia to Pindar *Olympian* 4 (29d6 and 31c7) provide a suitably epic coda to his tale: when Erginos was an old man, he went to compete in the funeral games for Thoas. Laughed at by the crowd because of his age, Erginos, out-odysseusing the Odysseus of the games in honor of Patroklos (where he wins the footrace), as well as those in Phaiakia (where he wins the discus after an ageist insult), won the race in *full armor*.

[44] Many scholars have articulated the critical importance of genealogy during the archaic and classical ages: see Larson 2007:17 and Hall 1997:41; cf. Thomas 1989 and Higbie 1997.

[45] Steinbock 2013:27: "Aristocratic families increased their social status and prestige by claiming descent from famous Homeric heroes. Local heroes functioned as eponyms for fictive kinship groups or local communities... All these heroes had mythical stories attached to them that provided the members of the group with a shared image of their past and fostered group identity. The social memory of these mythical heroes was manifested and transmitted by, among

These intertwined Panhellenic narratives, drawing on traditions like those of the Hesiodic *Ehoiai* or the Argonaut myth, integrate and subsume the Minyans by having the daughters of Minyas marry descendents of Aiolos. Their ethnonym is associated with the Argonauts through settlement in Iolcus,[46] genealogical association with Athamas (a founder, according to Pausanias IX 34.7) and Aiolos, and shared geographical association with Thessaly and Thrace (the scholia on *Olympian* 14.5a3 and *Pythian* 4.122). In addition, they also reveal relationships with Ionian city-states, in all likelihood influenced by colonization during the early archaic period. Although he writes that the Minyans settled in Teôs (a city between Miletus to the south and Phokaia to the north), Pausanias adds that they joined the Athenian expedition against Persia because they were related to Codrus; in turn, Codrus' son Neileus took his contingent to Miletus.[47]

The continued importance of Erginos in the Panhellenic tradition is expressed through genealogy. His children Agamêdês and Trophonios appear in the Homeric *Hymn to Apollo* to lay the first stone for his temple (296–297).[48] What is particularly striking is the fact that of all the heroic families, these sons of Erginos are the only mortals mentioned on Apollo's tour of Boeotia. Fragment 70 (18–40) of the *Ehoiai* similarly presents a genealogical tour through Boiotian geography, where Orkhomenos appears to occupy a special place, although the fragmentary nature of this testimony makes it difficult to assert anything with confidence.

This last passage brings us back to Hesiod, the *Ehoiai,* and the dynamic relationship among local and communalizing traditions. As we discussed in the previous section, it seems clear that the remains of poems attributed to Hesiod attest to competition and cooperation in the formation of poetic and mythical identities within Boeotia. The story of Orkhomenos and Thebes has illustrated some of the ways in which such narrative traditions might clash and then

---

other things, religious cults and festivals, which deserve special attention when dealing with the orators' allusions to the mythical past."

[46] Fowler 2013:191 calls the Minyans the *"magni nominis umbra* of Greek Myth...[who] left enough traces to suggest that they were at one time a major presence both in mythology and history."

[47] So, as far as we can see, the likely reason that there are traditions for a Milesian and a Orkhomenian Erginos, both of whom could fairly be called Minyan, is that local narratives were carried by Minyans in their settlements to Ionia and connected as part of several layers of collective, Panhellenizing narratives to larger Greek traditions including the Argonauts, the Herakles cycle, and the Trojan War narratives. As the Minyans were subsumed into other regions and the importance of Orkhomenos declined, their heroic narratives were similarly subsumed and fragmented. One version of Erginos became associated with the Argonaut myth as part of a conceptual Minyan Diaspora; similarly, he became dissociated from the Boiotian Erginos as the Theban-centered Herakles tales rose into prominence.

[48] According to "Plato" *Axiochus* 367c, the two were rewarded for their service to the god by a quick death in their sleep.

reconcile. The Homeric *Hymn* and the Hesiodic fragment, however, reveal that this was not a clean and simple process: despite losing to Thebes and Herakles in the Panhellenic traditions, through his local traditions Erginos lives on long enough to be integrated into other genealogical and ritual traditions.

Both this process and its players—here the family of Erginos and his city—have implications for the relationship between Troy and Thebes as well. The Homeric epics enter into this Boiotian fray and offer yet another viewpoint on the local traditions. As many critics have remarked, the Boiotian contingents in the Catalogue of Ships (2.494–516) are noteworthy for their position at the head of the catalogue, the number of named locations, and the wealth and power indicated by the size of their armies. Less frequently discussed is Homer's description of the leaders of the contingent from Orkhomenos, which identifies the pair Askalaphos and Ialmenos as Erginos' descendents (*Iliad* 2.511–512). It is this passage to which we turn now.

Homer's Boiotian Catalogue

Who doesn't know the well-built city
Of dark-haired Thebe?

Bacchylides 9.53–54[49]

Local rivalries between a larger Boiotian identity and the city of Thebes, such as we have just seen played out both in Hesiod and in the mythical tradition of Erginos the hero of Orkhomenos, were likely constantly at play in the development of Panhellenic culture.[50] When it comes to understanding the development of the *Iliad* and the *Odyssey*, we can safely assume that part of the process of achieving their Panhellenic imprimatur depended upon their ability to respond to local traditions and integrate them into a cohesive whole that retained its appeal across diverse audiences. Engagement with—and often resistance to—Panhellenic narratives, which were sensed to eclipse or undermine local traditions, was an essential part of poetic rivalries in the late archaic age, especially in generic struggles between lyric and epic.[51] While we have received only the products of these competitions, and few examples at that, we can nevertheless

---

[49] τίς γὰρ οὐκ οἶδεν κυανοπλοκάμου Θή- / βας ἐΰδμα[τον πόλι]ν;

[50] The Hesiodic tale of the daughters of Asopos, as Stephanie Larson (2007) argues, demonstrates how local genealogies were integrated into non-local traditions as individual Greek cities began to conceive of a larger Greekness and to compete with their neighbors in appropriating this identity.

[51] See Collins 2006:31.

observe some of the processes at work in the ways in which Boiotian elements are embedded within Homer.

One place where the presence of Boeotia is keenly felt is in the *Iliad*'s Catalogue of Ships, where its contingent is the first mentioned. It is commonly pointed out that the priority, size, and wealth of the Boiotian contingents in the Catalogue seem out of place with the actual contributions of their members in the epic itself.[52] One reason that might be offered to explain the apparent anomaly relates to our theme in Chapter 3—the formal association of Boiotia with catalogue poetry through the epics of Hesiod. Homer's Boiotian catalogue, however, repays closer attention, since its use of genealogy and toponyms reveals a metapoetic awareness of rival traditions.

Homer's account of the Boiotian contingent runs to some 17 lines (2.494–510):

Βοιωτῶν μὲν Πηνέλεως καὶ Λήϊτος ἦρχον
Ἀρκεσίλαός τε Προθοήνωρ τε Κλονίος τε,
οἵ θ' Ὑρίην ἐνέμοντο καὶ Αὐλίδα πετρήεσσαν
Σχοῖνόν τε Σκῶλόν τε πολύκνημόν τ' Ἐτεωνόν,
Θέσπειαν Γραῖάν τε καὶ εὐρύχορον Μυκαλησσόν,
οἵ τ' ἀμφ' Ἅρμ' ἐνέμοντο καὶ Εἰλέσιον καὶ Ἐρυθράς,
οἵ τ' Ἐλεῶν' εἶχον ἠδ' Ὕλην καὶ Πετεῶνα,
Ὠκαλέην Μεδεῶνά τ' ἐϋκτίμενον πτολίεθρον,
Κώπας Εὔτρησίν τε πολυτρήρωνά τε Θίσβην,
οἵ τε Κορώνειαν καὶ ποιήενθ' Ἁλίαρτον,
οἵ τε Πλάταιαν ἔχον ἠδ' οἳ Γλισᾶντ' ἐνέμοντο,
οἵ θ' Ὑποθήβας εἶχον ἐϋκτίμενον πτολίεθρον,
Ὀγχηστόν θ' ἱερὸν Ποσιδήϊον ἀγλαὸν ἄλσος,
οἵ τε πολυστάφυλον Ἄρνην ἔχον, οἵ τε Μίδειαν
Νῖσάν τε ζαθέην Ἀνθηδόνα τ' ἐσχατόωσαν·
τῶν μὲν πεντήκοντα νέες κίον, ἐν δὲ ἑκάστῃ
κοῦροι Βοιωτῶν ἑκατὸν καὶ εἴκοσι βαῖνον.

Pêneleôs and Lêitos were leaders of the Boiotians
As well as Arkesilaos, Prothoênôr, and Klonios
And those who inhabit Hyriê and rocky Aulis,

---

[52] See S. Larson 2007:31–41 for her full characterization of the catalogue of ships. The Boiotian contingents are second numerically only to Agamemnon's forces. For the epic's depiction of the Boiotians as a wealthy and large cooperative community, see Larson 2007:32–33. For the Boiotian "coloring": Kirk 1985:178. For the Catalogue as having an earlier Boiotian origin, see Willcock 1978.

Skoinos, Skôlos, and many-ridged Eteônos,
Thespeia, Greia, and wide-wayed Mykalêssos,
And those who dwell around Harma and Eilesion and Erythrai,
And those who hold Eleôn, Hylê, and Peteôn,
Ôkale, Medeôn, the well-built city,
Kôpai, Eutrêsis, and Thisbê with its many pigeons,
The people who live in Korôneia, and grassy Haliartos,
Along with those who holdlove Plataia, and inhabit Glisas,
And the people who keep Hypothebai, the well-built city
And holy Onkhêstos, the sacred grove of Poseidon,
And those who keep Arnê of many-grapes, and Mideia,
Holy Nisa, and Anthêdon, which is way out there.
Of these fifty ships came and in each came
One hundred and twenty Boiotian youths.

There are two striking absences in this catalogue, and they give further weight to the argument of this book. The first is notably Thebes itself. The absence of the city from the Boiotian catalogue is conspicuous, and not only because it is so pointedly hinted at in the toponym *Hypothebai* ("lower" Thebes). If plotted on a map, the places mentioned here form a circle emanating from a single, missing, focal point—Thebes.[53] It is as if the *Iliad* cannot bring itself to mention the other city, which for the purposes of this epic has been replaced by the Thebes on the Troad. Indeed, from the perspective of the *Iliad*, Thebes does not exist because it has *already* been sacked—destroyed, moreover, by members of this very expedition. In this way the Homeric Catalogue of ships, when it omits a Theban contingent, communicates a broader Panhellenic perspective by establishing a continuity with Hesiod's sequential pairing of the destruction of Thebes and Troy.

Equally conspicuous by its absence is the most famous river in Boiotia, the Asopos.[54] This in spite of the fact that the *Iliad* shows some knowledge of the association between the river Asopos and the city Thebes, mentioning it twice in relating the tale of Tydeus' exploits.[55] The *Odyssey* confirms a Homeric grasp of the genealogy by making Antiope, the mother of Amphion and Zethus, the

---

[53] In a thought-provoking use of digital technology, Jenny Strauss Clay has shown how Homer's spatial description of the Boiotian contingent contrasts with the other contingents in the catalogue by being visualized as if on spokes coming out of an absent central point (as opposed to a more hodological route). That absent center turns out to be Thebes, erased from the geography of the catalogue and from the memory of epic. See http://ships.lib.virginia.edu/neatline/show/the-boiotian-plain.

[54] Diodorus Siculus (IV 77) lists twelve daughters for the Boiotian river Asopos.

[55] See *Iliad* 4.386; 10.288.

daughter of Asopos.[56] Furthermore, the other daughters of Asopos appear as the toponyms of Aigina (2.562) Salamis (2.557) and Kleone and Orneia (2.570–571), all listed as part of Agamemnon's contingent. Also missing is the eponymous hero Boiotos.[57] While occupying first place in the catalogue *seems* impressive, then, the narrative is critically disconnected from certain key features of Boiotian tradition. Boeotia's major city, river, and hero are all missing, suggesting that its local traditions have been first *de*-constructed before being (re)incorporated into the master narrative.

In this context it is worth pondering the contingent who follow directly after the Boiotian catalogue (2.511–515):

Οἳ δ' Ἀσπληδόνα ναῖον ἰδ' Ὀρχομενὸν Μινύειον,
τῶν ἦρχ' Ἀσκάλαφος καὶ Ἰάλμενος υἷες Ἄρηος
οὓς τέκεν Ἀστυόχη δόμῳ Ἄκτορος Ἀζεΐδαο,
παρθένος αἰδοίη ὑπερώϊον εἰσαναβᾶσα
Ἄρηϊ κρατερῷ· ὃ δέ οἱ παρελέξατο λάθρη.

The men who inhabited Asplêdon and Minyan Orkhomenos
Askalaphos and Ialmenos the sons of Ares led.
Their mother, the reverent maiden Astyokhê, bore them in the
home
Of Aktôr the son of Azeus, after ascending to the bed chamber
With powerful Ares—but he laid next to her in secret.

Rather than leaving Boeotia unrepresented, the Catalogue draws on extant local traditions by giving Orkhomenos prominence, singling it out from the other Boiotian communities, with no mention of the overlapping tales of conquest fought between Thebes and Orkhomenos. Moreover, her leaders are given a divine parentage with their own miniature heroic narrative. Missing, however, is the figure of Erginos, who appears to have been written out of the picture: in his place are the twin sons of Ares, Askalaphos and Ialmenos. In turn, their double parentage recalls the tradition of Herakles, though, in this case, not one but two sons are produced when a god lies in secret with a reverent maiden. Yet in the *Iliad* Ares is hardly the ideal father to have. And the deeds of these sons of Ares—just like those all of the other Theban captains—do not add up to much

---

[56] τὴν δὲ μέτ' Ἀντιόπην ἴδον, Ἀσωποῖο θύγατρα, *Odyssey* 11.261.
[57] S. Larson 2007:45 suggests that "it is possible in the mid-sixth century environment in which the epic reached its transcript form of fixity, the figure Boiotos, the eponymous hero of one of Athens' main sixth-century rivals, was purposefully omitted from the poem in a spirit of hostile competition and as a subtle slight against the collective which bore his name."

in the epic that follows.[58] The entire heroic tradition of Minyas is reduced to a simple epithet: Μινύειον. We are left with a dissonance between the emphasis placed on the numbers and genealogy of the Boiotians in the Catalogue and their actual presence in and impact on the rest of the poem.

In selecting from available narrative traditions in the effort to create a different type of non-local identity, Homer engages with local traditions in Boeotia and integrates their genealogies and heroic narratives into his tale. In part, this strategy may suggest the importance of collective identity over and against the exceptionality of their leaders.[59] It may also be true that Homer's Catalogue presents a realistic world with plausible reasons for *not* featuring a strong Theban contingent. Whatever the case, the *Iliad* acknowledges the impressive power of Boeotia only to minimize it by staying relatively mute on its heroic pasts or achievements in the narrative, while simultaneously redeploying it to overshadow Thebes.[60] In offering the Trojan War as the end of the race of heroes, the Homeric epics work in concert with Hesiodic traditions to subsume and consume local Boiotian narratives in order to make them serve the poem-in-performance, the story of Troy.

Burying the Seven and Heroic Remains

And they add that [Ariadne] was left by Theseus because he loved another. "A terrible love for Aiglê, the daughter of Panopeus, plagued him" (fr. 105). For Hereas the Megarian says that Peisistratus deleted this line from Hesiod just as he inserted the following into Homer's *Nekyia*: "Theseus and Peirithoos, the outstanding children of the gods."

Plutarch *Life of Theseus* 20[61]

Appropriating the Panhellenic traditions, which both Homeric and Hesiodic epic represented, by connecting them to local genealogies or attempting to rival their accounts, was a signal way for emerging *poleis* to establish their

---

[58] On the weakness of the Boiotian heroes, see S. Larson 2007:34–35.
[59] S. Larson 2007:32-39. Cf. Heiden 2008b.
[60] The emphasis may be different in the *Odyssey*. Larson 2014:419: "In light of these Boiotian connections to Thessaly and the Aeolids through traditions of migration, collective cult, and the genealogy of Boeotus, the *Odyssey*'s emphasis on Thessalian tradition takes on new meaning and can be read as a reflection of sixth-century Boiotian concerns." Nevertheless, as we discuss in Chapter 3 above, this representation of Boiotian women need not be read so positively.
[61] ἀπολειφθῆναι δὲ τοῦ Θησέως ἐρῶντος ἑτέρας: "Δεινὸς γάρ μιν ἔτειρεν ἔρως Πανοπηίδος Αἴγλης." τοῦτο γὰρ τὸ ἔπος ἐκ τῶν Ἡσιόδου (fr. 105 Rz.) Πεισίστρατον ἐξελεῖν φησιν Ἡρέας ὁ Μεγαρεύς ὥσπερ αὖ πάλιν ἐμβαλεῖν εἰς τὴν Ὁμήρου νέκυιαν "τὸ Θησέα Πειρίθοόν τε θεῶν ἀριδείκετα τέκνα" χαριζόμενον Ἀθηναίοις.

own prestige.[62] In his *Life of Solon*, for example, Plutarch famously provides an account of a debate over the use of Homer in a contemporary political dispute (10.2–3).[63] The verses in question relate to the presence of Ajax in the Catalogue of Ships, with the accusation being that Solon interpolated the line, "He brought and stationed his ships where the Athenians' battle-lines were" (στῆσε δ᾽ ἄγων ἵν᾽ Ἀθηναίων ἵσταντο φάλαγγες, *Iliad* 2.558), following the mention of Ajax's Salaminian contingent. By making this alleged interpolation, Solon was thought to be strengthening the Athenian claim to the island of Salamis, an action that Plutarch describes as "contesting the reputation of Homer" (συναγωνίσασθαι λέγουσι τὴν Ὁμήρου δόξαν). According to Strabo, the Megarians responded with their own lines from the catalogue, reflecting a tradition in which Ajax led an array of Megarian toponyms.[64] It is this type of competitive engagement that features in the passage cited above from Plutarch's *Theseus* where Peisistratus is accused by Megarian historians of altering the texts of both Hesiod and Homer to control the perception of the local hero Theseus.[65] The Panhellenic authority of Homer and Hesiod did not stop such wrangling over the past; rather, they were a continual stimulus to local traditions to adopt and adapt the cultural *koine*.[66]

One attractive explanation for the popularity of the Homeric poems, and in particular the acceleration and reification of their Panhellenic identity, is their larger, more synoptic perspective on a world that was much more than simply Boiotian or Athenian, or indeed merely Greek. Again, without anything but the fragmentary remains of a Theban tradition, we cannot tell for certain how its epics represented the siege of the city; there does seem to have been an attempt to portray coalitions of heroes and cities that might well have appealed

---

[62] Nagy 1990:67: "As an institution, the polis mediates between the epichoric and the Panhellenic: although it *contains* what is epichoric, it also *promotes* what is Panhellenic...The polis can best promote its prestige by promoting its own traditions in poetry and song on a Panhellenic scale." Finkelberg 2012:146 argues that "the codification of the *Iliad* and the *Odyssey* in Athens of the sixth century BCE granted the Athenian state a monopoly over the standard text of Homer."

[63] For other versions of this "trial," see Aristotle *Rhetoric* 1335b26-30; Strabo IX 1.9-10; and Diogenes Laertius I 48. See Higbie 1997 for how this episode illustrates Greek use of the past.

[64] Strabo IX 1.10. On this exchange, see Higbie 1997:283-286 and especially 285 for the suspicion that the Athenians also altered 2.553-555 in the Catalogue.

[65] Other fragments show historians from Megara disputing Athenian accounts of the deeds of Theseus, specifically the hero or brigand Skeiros: see Higbie 1997:281. Based on the absence of Theseus in iconography before the mid-sixth century BCE, Steinbock argues that Theseus was a rather minor local hero whose narratives were intentionally adapted under the Peisistratids to rival the Theban Herakles. Theseus is not on Attic pottery until 570 BCE. From 550–510 things change; his new exploits were modeled on Herakles. See Steinbock 2013:169-174.

[66] Lulli 2014:82: the attributions of various poems to Homer shows that "Homer's name must have stood with the public as a guarantee of the standards of a narrative."

to audiences on the ground.[67] Nor perhaps was there anything so new about the global world in which the emerging Greek *poleis* found themselves at the end of the archaic age, other than in its representation.[68] Nevertheless, evidence from the Homeric poems does reveal how well equipped they were to (continue to) speak to as broad an audience as possible.

Most notable is the *Iliad*'s depiction of the Achaeans' political situation, which appears to have no historical precedent.[69] Agamemnon is in charge overall, as the brother of the injured party, Menelaos; but he does not (and cannot, it seems) enjoy unquestioned authority over his peers, notably Achilles. Instead, Achaean society appears to operate on a "first among equals" principle, whereby the leaders of the many contingents of the coalition vie for honor and glory from their peers. From the beginning of the epic to the point when Achilles finally enters the fray, the public assembly has been the venue for the strife. It is not only that Homer depicts elite heroes (Achilles and Agamemnon) at odds with each other; he also shows an intense interest in the situation of the people who depend on their leaders for salvation (as epic narrative puts it). Accordingly, the quarrel plot, which extends through and motivates much of the *Iliad*'s action, provides a frame for considering questions of a political nature (who should be prominent, when, where, how, and why), the consequences of failing to resolve internal conflicts, and the strengths and weaknesses of man-made solutions, such as ad hoc compromises or even institutional innovation. Its characters are not uncivilized heroes who do what they want, who go on quests, and who reap the benefit of their individual labors. Instead, we find men who can only profit by working together in coalitions and who suffer more if they cannot organize their co-operation effectively. In part, the epic provides what we might consider an explanatory myth for the origin of human political conventions within a dramatization of why they are so crucially needed. In the wake of the death of the race of heroes, the *Iliad* traces out the need for and development of institutions.

From this perspective, Achilles' act of establishing an assembly in the first episode of the epic poses general questions important for any community. The drama of the *Iliad* resides not so much in an aristocratic argument over relative honor as in its fallout, in the continuing negotiations and renegotiations as men try to resolve and/or manage the consequences of conflict. It is in the aftermath

---

[67] See Ebbott 2014 for a discussion of the gathering of a coalition in terms of traditional referentiality.

[68] For the Mediterranean-wide extent of the early Greek world, see Malkin 2011.

[69] See Konstan 2001; cf. Finley 1954. For Osborne 1996:33, the *Iliad*'s heroic world of the past is useful "for the way in which it can, as a purely fictional world also can, cast light upon the structures of the present world." For the discussion here, see Barker and Christensen 2013:29–31.

of the strife introduced in its opening movement that the poem unfolds the business of governing.[70] By posing serious challenges to the rule of one man, exposing flaws in the intense rivalry between competing heroes, and showing the predicament of the group at large, the *Iliad* responds to, engages in, and may even have helped shape contemporary political concerns. In fact, it is precisely by projecting these concerns onto a previous age that Homer encourages his audience(s) to explore and make sense of their own experiences of strife through the conflicts of prior mythical figures. Most importantly, by posing difficult questions and providing no easy answers, the *Iliad* fosters political conversation, facilitating as many responses as there were different cities in the Greek world. Rather than attempting to portray the realistic workings of an assembly or, more generally, the real-life political situation in the Greek world of the time, the *Iliad* provides audiences with a past that they can recognize as transitional to their present, whether conservative oligarchs or radical democrats.

This same engagement with, and departure from, the real-world experiences of the audience can be seen in the *Odyssey*'s adventurous geographical scope. By having Odysseus chart out the known places of the real world, as the hero returns home to Ithaca from Troy, gathering stories from places like Crete, Egypt, and Sidon, the *Odyssey* belongs to a series of stories (including the labors of Herakles and the voyage of Jason and the Argonauts) that reflect an expanding Greek awareness from the eighth century BCE onwards of geography, place, and civilization. For this was an age of discovery, as Greeks took to the sea to settle in far-off places or to trade wares much as Odysseus trades stories, rendering the Mediterranean Sea the ancient equivalent of the world wide web. And, in his own account of his adventures, we can see Odysseus giving voice to these pioneering concerns, when he reflects upon the favorable harbor and uncultivated land of the Cyclopes' island (*Odyssey* 9.132–139). Here Odysseus comes across as possessing the same kind of inquisitive spirit that propelled Greeks on through the Mediterranean and beyond, with an eye always on the possibilities of settlement, cultivation, and profit. Paradoxically, however, Odysseus' description acts as a prelude to a series of adventures (in *Odyssey* 9–12) that become ever more fantastical (starring one-eyed monsters, a witch who turns men into pigs, ghosts of heroes past, etc.). The *Odyssey* hardly aims at a realistic depiction

---

[70] Indeed, ingeniously Homer's epics imitate the evolutionary nature of political institutions. Rarely are whole-scale political settlements created at a single stroke, as in the framing of the US Constitution. The United Kingdom, for example, lacks a written constitution. There is the Magna Carta, but how this thirteenth-century text relates to current Parliamentary democracy, let alone the notion of the United Kingdom itself, is a moot point. Rather, political institutions tend to develop over time in reaction to cultural demands from the bottom up; they are not imposed top-down. The *Iliad*, we suggest, invites its audience to think about this process and get involved in making sense of its song of strife.

of voyaging. But, by portraying a world beyond what was known and recognizable, Odysseus can act as a model for all adventurers. Even as the map of the Greek world gets ever larger and ever more detailed, the ambiguous locations of Odysseus' wanderings allow them to continue to speak to those charting new ground or waters.

Homer's epics transform tales about a war and a return into *foundational* narratives that can speak to the concerns of all Greek communities regardless of their specific political constitutions and allegiances, and regardless of where they were to be found in the Greek-speaking world. They are of course helped by the subject matter of a great international war. But the precise details—the *Iliad*'s focus on strife within political institutions, the *Odyssey*'s intense interest in correct behavior in civil society—enable these *Trojan War* narratives to remain contemporary in what might otherwise seem to be the rapidly changing historical conditions of the sixth through fourth centuries BCE.[71] In the context of the rise of Greek-bloc coalitions—Athenian hegemony with claims to and relations with entities among the Aegean islands, in Thessaly, Chalcidice and the Ionian states; Spartan hegemony in the Peloponnese and close connections to Sicily— we can imagine that the allure of this shared past was stronger than similar but localized coalition narratives like the tale of raiding in Jason and the Argonauts, the adventure of the Calydonian Boar Hunt, or the Boiotian traditions of the *Seven Against Thebes* and the *Epigonoi*.[72]

Against the conservative idea of epic as being traditional, *foundational*, there is a strong refrain praising the song that remains current. Telemachus announces that the most recent song is always on men's lips in the *Odyssey*, while in the *Iliad* Sthenelos brazenly suggests that they are better than their fathers. Even as they use a rhetoric of traditionality,[73] both Homeric poems address a fast-changing contemporary world, where their audiences were engaged in the same process of adding to and improving on what came before.[74] No matter how Panhellenism is to be conceived—as emerging from the construction of the barbarian in the period of the Persian Wars,[75] or in the long interplay of local communities in

---

[71] We are not here making an argument about the composition of the *Iliad* and the *Odyssey* during the fifth century but instead about the *selection* of these epics under the conditions of the fifth century to render them Herodotus' cultural authorities.

[72] For the textualization of the *Odyssey* under the Peisistratids, see Larson 2014:426; cf. Jensen 2011; West 1989:36–38. West 2014:43 places the composition of the *Odyssey* at the end of the seventh century BCE (though still near Attica in Euboea, see 90–91).

[73] Scodel 2002.

[74] Berman 2013:50. Herodotus famously compares his Persian Wars to Homer's Troy, with the more recent wars gaining by magnitude and reliability. Thucydides makes the Peloponnesian War the "latest and the greatest."

[75] For this see E. Hall 1989 *passim*; Cartledge 1995:75–82; for the "aggregate" character of Panhellenism prior to the Persian War, see J. Hall 1997; cf. Malkin 1998:18, 60–61.

unified and unifying expressions of shared identity in religious contexts such as games and oracular consultations[76]—the two Homeric poems communicate a process of moving among local and shared identities, of a multiplicity within a shifting unity.[77] The *Iliad* dramatizes the struggle of integrating the one into the many; the *Odyssey* of the many returning home to become "local" again. What we think likely is that epic poetry—along with certain cult sites and beliefs—possessed a certain level of prestige in the early archaic age that had the effect of creating a sort of aspirational ground of contest. In this process, local narratives joined local dialects in a de-centered community that, through their interaction, not only represented but played an active role in realizing a pluralistic commonwealth whose shared characteristics over time became more familiar and more fixed. This more amorphous, competitive Panhellenism then rigidified under the influence of world events beginning with the struggles between the Ionian Greek city states and Persia and metastasizing during and after the Persian invasions.[78] The internationalization of Homer's epics didn't stop with their institutionalization in Athens or their textualization in Alexandria. If anything, once written down they were able to perform even better as international foundational texts, where the "plan of Zeus" could be more directly linked to other disaster narratives more familiar from Near Eastern and Biblical traditions.[79]

How Theban epics continued to engage with contemporary events or presented themselves as foundational is something that we cannot know. But we can see how any attempt to appeal to an audience beyond Thebes must have been severely curtailed by two factors. First, the Persian Wars had the effect of leaving Thebes outside the coalition of Greek states. Arguably this may not have been decisive—Macedon was able to reinvent itself as a supporter of Hellenic ideals, and Thucydides presents the Thebans as blaming their medization on

---

[76] For Panhellenism as beginning in the eighth century with the founding of the Olympic Games, see Snodgrass 1971:55–57; Nagy 1990:52–53. For this as "Proto-Panhellenism" reflected in the *Iliad*, see Ross 2005:301–307. For a later date, but still prior to the Persian Wars, see Hall 1997.

[77] For a "non-oppositional but shared Greek identity" indicated by linguistic distinctions among the Homeric characters and reflecting the beliefs of the late eighth century BCE, see Ross 2005:299–300. For the absence of a sense of Panhellenism in the Homeric epics see Cartledge 1993 and 1995:77–78; Konstan 2001:31–32. In the heterogeneity within unity of the Greeks at Troy, others have seen reflections of Panhellenic notions: see Finley 1954:18; Haubold 2000:43–45. In narratives of *nostoi* circulating during the ninth and eighth centuries BCE, Malkin 1998:53–54 sees a type of "proto-Pan-Hellenic focus"; cf. 117–118.

[78] For the sixth century BCE as an important period in the gradual development of Panhellenic identity, see Hall 1997:47–51; cf. Kurke 1992 for the importance of sixth-century values among the elite.

[79] See Barker 2008 on the D scholia's connection between the *Iliad*'s plan of Zeus, the *Cypria*, and other Near Eastern epics.

their previous form of government—had it not been for the growing power of Athens, a city which had been fighting with Thebes (in ideological rivalry as much as in war) for a generation before the invasion.[80] Following the Theban capitulation to Persia, not only did the Athenians continually depict the Thebans as medizers who betrayed the Greeks, *and who betrayed Panhellenic identity*, right up to the destruction of the city by Alexander in 335 BCE;[81] Athenian rhetoric and official commemoration seems to have elided the victory over Persia with a victory over Thebes.[82]

Second, and relatedly, the period of the Persian Wars also witnessed the development and flourishing of a new, post-epic genre: tragedy. Athenian soft power has arguably proven more influential than her fifth-century military might. Thebes in tragedy is not only represented as the city always being besieged (in contrast to Troy as the city always in the process of being sacked); it is critically an *anti*-Athens. This tragic reinvention, and distortion, of Thebes in the popular imagination seems to have occurred early in this genre's emergence (perhaps in generic contest with Pindar). For example, prior to the performance of Aeschylus' now lost *Eleusinians* there is no literary or even cult record of Athenian involvement in the expedition against Thebes or for the burial of the dead.[83] The burial monuments that existed near Eleusis were likely re-purposed as the graves of the Seven around the end of the sixth century BCE.[84] Nor was this process localized at Eleusis: the Attic border-town of Eleutherai similarly displayed tombs in the fifth century that were dedicated to the common soldiers of the Seven. Critical to this mythologizing was the material assistance the Athenians gave to the Plataeans, which played an important role in shaping their self-image of protecting "the rights of suppliants" against hubristic Greek powers like Thebes (Steinbock 2013: 54).[85] In this way, the narrative that Oedipus and his sons symbolized everything that was wrong with Thebes took center

---

[80] Steinbock 2013:105: by the end of the sixth century Thebes was the leading power in Boeotia. Plataea didn't want to join the Boiotian league. Athens made an alliance with Plataea in 519 BCE.

[81] See Steinbock 2013 *passim* for an analysis of the importance of this negative depiction of Thebes in Athenian collective memory.

[82] Steinbock 2013:110–111: the shrine built from the spoils (Plutarch *Life of Aristides* 20.3) showed the victory of Odysseus over the suitors by Polygnotus with another painting by Onasias showing the expedition of Adrastus and Argives against Thebes (Pausanias IX 4.1–2).

[83] See Steinbock 2013:159–160.

[84] Finglass 2014:358 calls these tombs the earliest evidence of the myth about the Seven, whereas Steinbock 2013:160 argues that many tombs during this period had their identifications altered to cohere with local narratives. As Finglass notes, Argos also added a tomb for the Seven during the sixth century. For Pindar's seven pyres and records of monuments to the Seven in Thebes, see Berman 2015:61–65; cf. Steinbock 2013:165.

[85] For a full treatment of this theme, see Steinbock 2013:174–189. Steinbock adds later that this antipathy may have been increased by the fact that the Athenians directly faced the Thebans at the battle of Plataea in 479 (106–107).

stage in Athenian drama,[86] and continues even (or especially) as the Athenians make Oedipus *theirs* by cleansing him at Colonus.[87]

As a thought experiment within this framework, consider the relationship between the cities of Thebes and Troy through the lens of epic intertraditionality and interformularity. There is, apart from the genealogies and chronologies imposed later, no *prima facie* reason for Thebes to be destroyed before Troy. Indeed, it could be argued that Herakles' destruction of Troy was an attempt to subordinate the Ionian tradition to the local Theban one, as if making Troy, the first city to be sacked, to play second fiddle to the later—and thus more important—sack of Thebes. If we then imagine Theban and Trojan narratives on roughly equal footing in the early archaic period, what emerges is a pattern of cultural and political forces that gradually combine to attenuate the popularity of one while strengthening the other. For Theban epic, competition with Orkhomenos, coupled with notions of Pan-Boiotian identity, created rivalries *within* its narratives across Boiotia and central Greece. (And, though we have less evidence, Achaean, Argive, and Laconian traditions must have faced similar challenges.) For Trojan epic, as interest in the wider world continued to grow in the light of trade and conflict, rivalries were created *outside* its narratives. Since local traditions were not controlled by central authorities, there was nothing stopping pluralistic responses to new narratives with larger perspectives: Greek communities all throughout the Mediterranean were "writing" themselves and their traditions into the Trojan War, just as they were also engaging with broader narratives about Herakles, the Argonauts, and the multiple wars around Thebes.[88] The growing contact with and influence of Persia, coupled by the outbreak of hostilities with this overseas power, only served to increase the prestige and gravity of the Trojan War tradition and—along with the economic and political power concentrated in cities opposed to Thebes (e.g. Athens)—helped to valorize and centralize these epics as opposed to those associated with Thebes. The *Iliad* and *Odyssey* emerged as "better to think with," just at the time when a new technology (writing) was being adopted, which would be able to preserve oral performance for posterity.

The city of Thebes and its story-traditions suffered for multiple reasons. One is that it was already subject to rivalry within its own region. Another is that the scope of its narrative as a coalition tale and as a vehicle for the concerns of a broader Greek world was limited by its geography. The tale of Troy, by virtue

---

[86] For Thebes as the "anti-Athens" on stage, see Zeitlin 1986. Cf. Steinbock 2013:61

[87] Berman 2013:50. In a similar way the Athenians make Orestes, the Argive hero, theirs, in his legal cleansing at the court of the Areopagus in Aeschylus' *Eumenides*, on which see Sommerstein 1989:3–6.

[88] Malkin 1998.

of its geographical range, was simply more responsive to a broader vision of the world that included non-Greeks and distant lands while also allowing more flexibility in adding communities from around the Greek world and in altering the importance of different regions (e.g. Achaea) over time. In the light of historical developments and traumatic events, not only did other cities rise to political and economic power and incorporate themselves into Panhellenic traditions; there was also an incentive for other Greeks to downplay the prominence of Thebes.[89]

Homer does not become exclusively a Trojan War poet until the fourth century BCE. Indeed, an author as late as Pausanias still believed him to be the poet of the *Thebais*. The treatment of Theban myth is thus partly about origins, if we accept the Ionian character of the *Iliad* and the *Odyssey*. Yet it is also about the aesthetics of Homeric poetry, the chance opportunities of narrative rivalry operating on different levels of locality, and the influence of selection and preference exercised by historical events and successive constructions of self-identity throughout the Greek-speaking world.

---

[89] The gradual development of Panhellenism described above also echoes the evolutionary movement of the Homeric tradition towards fixity proposed by Gregory Nagy. See Nagy 2004:27–28 for the simplest presentation. His "evolutionary model" posits a formative "Panhellenic" stage from the eighth through sixth centuries BCE followed by a "definitive period centralized in Athens"; we are imagining an analogous set of stages for Panhellenism roughly coterminous with these middle steps. Nagy 1990:53 similarly notes that "the hermeneutic model of Panhellenism must be viewed as an evolutionary trend extending into the Classical period, not some fait accompli that can be accounted for solely in the terms of, say, the eighth century," and later that "Panhellenic poetry would have been the product of an evolutionary synthesis of traditions" (54).

Conclusion: Endgame

"Simonides said that Hesiod is a gardener while Homer is a garland-weaver—the first planted the legends of the heroes and gods and then the second braided them together in the garland of the *Iliad* and the *Odyssey*."

Simonides[1]

One of the issues shadowing this book throughout—and one with which we have sparred constantly—is the *how*; that is, how the complex associations between poems of different traditions (and within the same tradition) originated; how the *Iliad* and *Odyssey* came to be the only heroic epic poems left standing; and how, in turn, the Theban epics were lost to time. This question is all the more pressing, when so many resonant cases of engagement may be identified between the poems that we have—the *Iliad* and the *Odyssey*—and the stories, motifs, and structures we believe were in those that we have lost.

In the last chapter we suggested that Homer's use of Thebes and, ultimately, the city's suppression, were in all likelihood connected to the Panhellenic horizons of the Homeric poems, oriented towards an ever-expanding world of external struggles and adventures, where the communities on the margins of the Greek world held all the faster to those foundational narratives that most efficiently (or authoritatively, or provocatively, or...) told of heroes fighting in war or struggling to return home.[2] To highlight the efficacy of this storytelling is also to acknowledge that the narrative dynamics of the Homeric poems actively repurpose and reshape other traditions' story patterns, themes, and elements. Seen in this light, a Theban focus on internal strife in a story like the *Seven Against Thebes* comes across as somehow less able to respond or speak to a

---

[1] Σιμωνίδης τὸν Ἡσίοδον κηπουρὸν ἔλεγε, τὸν δὲ Ὅμηρον στεφανηπλόκον, τὸν μὲν ὡς φυτεύσαντα τὰς περὶ θεῶν καὶ ἡρώων μυθολογίας, τὸν δὲ ὡς ἐξ αὐτῶν συμπλέξαντα τὸν Ἰλιάδος καὶ Ὀδυσσείας στέφανον (T91b Poltera [*Vatican Appendix*, p. 217 Sternbach]).

[2] On this dynamic, see Malkin 2011: a central concern of his book is to explain (through network theory) the observation that "the more the Greeks dispersed, somehow the more 'Greek' they became" (5). In Malkin 1998 he devotes much of his network analysis to tracing the ways in which Odysseus is reinvented as a hero for communities across the Mediterranean, and not only Greek ones.

world of expanding horizons; at the same time such a story is already covered by the *Iliad*'s treatment of strife between of Achilles and Agamemnon.

We close by offering a viewpoint through an alternative Theban lens, which we believe best helps us to rethink the continually renewed "afterlives" of the *Iliad* and *Odyssey* and their epic rivals. Our interest lies not so much in the intrinsic value of this alternative account as in how it potentially sheds light on the processes of change undergone and endured by Homer's poems.

The Orchard

In the Introduction we used the image of the rhizome, popularized by Deleuze and Guattari, to think about the process behind the emergence of the Greek epic oral tradition. In *A Thousand Plateaus*, they reject the familiar idea of the knowledge tree, in which origins may be traced back to a single point and influence is conceived of as hierarchical and uni-directional, in favour or the rhizome—an understanding of cultural objects as multiple, heterogeneous and diffuse. For us, this image best captures the oral tradition, whose beginnings are not singular or discrete, and whose individual components (poems) are a product of endless struggles over and links between shared storyworlds, narrative patterns, themes and language. We believe that this metaphor has been helpful for better understanding the process of cultural and poetic development that helped to produce our epics, and then for using that understanding to provide a reading of those epics. But this metaphor does not adequately account for why (or how) the Homeric epics outgrew their rivals to choke out all other life.[3]

To address this specific question, the metaphor of the tree may still hold a value for thinking about Homer's poems.[4] In the *Iliad*, trees are often used in a metaphorical sense by the poet to denote the death of a warrior, an association underlined by Glaukos, who uses the image of trees shedding their leaves to describe the passage and passing of generations of man.[5] The emphasis in the *Odyssey* lies, in contrast, on trees that are still standing and their use as material for human goods of survival and identity. Trees indicate Odysseus' location and represent his progress towards home, describing in turn the topography of Kalypso's island (1.51), where he is to be found languishing at the beginning of the epic, and the view he spies when finally landing back on Ithaca, whose trees

---

[3]   Seen from the perspective of Homeric reception, the metaphor of the tree remains useful for suggesting how the trunk of the poems' knowledge sprouted innumerable branches of cultural flowering.

[4]   Purves 2010: 225–226; cf. Pucci 1996: 5–24.

[5]   *Iliad* 11.155–159; 13.178–181, 389–393; 14.414–415; 16.482–486; 17.53–60. On Glaukos: 6.146–149.

he initially fails to recognize (13.196).[6] When Odysseus first makes the steps necessary to embark upon his *nostos*—understood as both the passage home and the narrative told about it[7]—he must cut down the trees on Ogygia and carve out his own vessel (5.228–262). His skill in fashioning his means of return from wood is also highlighted in the gloom of Cyclops' cave, where he makes the stake from an olive tree with which he and his men will blind the monster and enable their great escape (9.375–388). In Book 23, the bed that *was* a tree is both a token of Odysseus' skill—he crafted his marriage bed from an olive tree— and a symbol (σῆμα, 23.202) of the rootedness of his relationship with his wife; indeed, Penelope's trick to reveal her husband's identity is the claim to have moved their bed, which in fact has remained throughout everything "in place" (or "in the ground": ἔμπεδον, 23.203).[8] The pattern culminates in the reunion of father and son in their walk through their family's orchard, where Laertes "reads the *sure-grounded symbols* Odysseus had pointed out " (σήματ᾽ ἀναγνόντος τά οἱ ἔμπεδα πέφραδ᾽, 24.346) to prove who he is.[9]

How to read these sure signs shared between father and son is a challenge of semantics and semiotics. To gain his father's recogition, Odysseus immediately shows his scar. We have already witnessed the sigificance of this sign for indicating Odysseus' heroic credentials, when. accidentally exposed by his nurse, it threatens to expose the beggar as the returning hero. What worked before (inadvertently) seems insufficient now, as Odysseus quickly changes tack and instead provides details of the trees in the orchard that his father has been tending (ἕκαστα…ἕκαστα… ἕκαστος, 24.337, 339, 343). In the cataloguing of each species, it is difficult to see the wood for the trees. What is clear is that this secondary supplementary sign plots out Laertes' inheritance for his son.[10] John Henderson draws attention to the specialized vocabulary of διατρύγιος ('bearing grapes in succession' 24.342), a hapax which appears to signify "expertise in tending the vintage through to its ultimate garnering" (1997: 105); and to the game of number crunching the orchard; and indeed to the act of naming (ὠνόμασας…ὀνόμηνας, 339, 341) the trees, which in itself needs to be glossed (as in to "*name* the species": 1997:108n78). Alex Purves (2010:228) retraces these

[6] "Trees have been playing their part all along in constructing the *Odyssey*'s many-layered ledger of human identity," Henderson 1997:98.
[7] On this double meaning of *nostos*, see Barker and Christensen 2016.
[8] On the paradox of the trickster's identity being revealed by a trick: Goldhill 1991:18.
[9] On the economic energizing of the "faded etymological image" of ἔμπεδα to mean "in the ground," see Henderson 1997:89, with n9 on ἔμπεδον as indicating the rootedness of the marriage bed.
[10] Goldhill 1991:19. Henderson 1997, also noting (95) the significant change in signs (from scar to orchard), writes about challenge of reading this additional proof: "the meaning is not in the sign, but in the 'bodily practices' that bring the sign's signification to fruition" (107).

steps as Odysseus "taking an imaginary walk through the orchard in his mind just as [Elizabeth] Minchin has suggested that Homer takes a cognitive walk through the Peloponnese in order to recount the Catalogue of Ships (2001: 84–7)." In this recounting of the catalogue, the trees were "'planted' in Odysseus' mind when he was just a boy before the frame of the *Iliad* had begun," which in turn suggests that the *Odyssey*'s catalogue of trees is somehow some kind of response to the *Iliad*'s great Catalogue of Ships, by which means Homeric epic encapsulates the launch of the Achaean expedition against Troy. Trees are also present in (and responsible for) that launch, in the form of the ships—trees that have been felled—that carry the soon-to-be-felled Achaean heroes to Troy.[11]

Whether or not Laertes' list of trees bookends the world of Homeric epic by bringing to mind the *Iliad*'s Catalogue of Ships, the orchard evocatively resounds within an epic cosmos, where trees are suggestive of the stories that are or could be told.[12] In announcing his intention to test his father, Odysseus hands over his "warlike arms" (ἀρήϊα τεύχε', 24.219) to his slaves, as if Laertes' farmstead represented a "temporary retreat and seclusion from epic struggle" (Henderson 1997:99). The toil showcased here is Laertes' (epic) work on the land (ἐπεὶ μάλα πόλλ' ἐμόγησεν,[13] 24.207)—Odysseus finds his father "digging about a plant" (λιστρεύοντα[14] φυτόν, 24.227)—and the care (κομιδή,[15] 24.245) he has shown his orchard. Not only does this picture suggest an adjournment to the "anti-heroic margins" (Henderson 1997:112) of the poem; it resonates with the everyday humdrum world of Hesiod's *Works and Days*, towards which the narrative arc of the *Odyssey* has been building. The vines "named-and-promised by Laertes are dwelt on...in *lyrical* rapture on the promise of a seasonal abundance" (Henderson 1997:104, our italics), with "the *seasons* [ὧραι] of Zeus' sky weighing them down to the ground from on high" (24.344, our italics), as if the hard labor countenanced in Hesiod's *Works and Days* finds its instantiation and ultimate reward in the

---

[11] Purves 2010: 225–226.

[12] Cf. Henderson 1997:87 for the trees as "epic wood."

[13] πόλλ' ἐμόγησεν is used in the *Iliad* to denote the labors of Achilles in war (*Iliad* 1.162; 2.690; 9.492), an echo of which is found in Menelaos' praise of Antilochus (23.607). In the *Odyssey* all instances relate to Odysseus' long time suffering in trying to make it home (*Odyssey* 2.343; 4.170; 5.223, 449; 6.175; 7.147; 8.155; 15.489; 19.483; 21.207; 23.101, 169, 338), along with two other examples that resonate with this theme (3.232, where the disguised Athena advises Telemachus that it's better to suffer hardships than to return home quickly and be killed, like Agamemnon; and 16.19, where a simile relates Eumaios' fatherly welcome of Telemachus with a barely disguised nod towards Odysseus). The only exception is here, in the description of Laertes' (heroic) agricultural work. The one other example in archaic Greek hexameter epic, in Hesiod's *Theogony*, describes Jason's long toil in capturing Medea.

[14] Like διατρύγιος a hapax, as if revealing the strain of incorporating non-martial scenes of everyday life into heroic epic.

[15] Cf. Henderson 1997:97 with n40.

gods' favor here in Laertes' "Works and Seasons." When, therefore, hostilities are renewed (which only ever remains an indefinitely deferred promise at the end of the *Iliad*[16]), the scene is all the more shocking after this walk through the orchard, as if Hesiod's discontentment with his brother had transmogrified into full-blown civil strife, or additionally the ever-present threat of a Theban tale interrupts the bucolic setting. No wonder it takes renewed plotting by Zeus and Athena to (literally) put an end to the conflict and bring this poem to a shuddering halt.

These closing metapoetic ruminations are rooted in the poem's beginning, where Odysseus fashions a sailing craft to (re)start his journey home (*nostos*) and, thus, begin (again) his narrative (*nostos*). In the previous chapter we explored the metapoetic associations in Teiresias' prophecy, where, following Alex Purves, we suggested that the prophetic announcement of (yet) more wanderings for Odysseus (until his oar is confused with a farming tool), points to a world beyond heroic epic, to the agricultural poetics of Hesiod's *Works and Days*.[17] Here, as the *Odyssey* itself runs to a close, the oar is returned to the soil in the form of the trees of Laertes' orchard.[18] Laertes himself is silent on his careful tending. Instead, it is what these trees mean to the on-looking Odysseus that is articulated.

In this way, the trees may stand metonymically for epic poems, but not in the way that the arboreal metaphor is usually imagined. Instead, these trees/poems represent the combined product of nature and nurture which have been shaped by the judgment (aesthetic and political) of countless constant gardeners. To point to one instance in this process and claim any one to be the most formative for the creation of these specific trees is to underplay the contribution of others and to overlook and appeal to and significance for generations of people who experience them right now, each time.

The challenge of the way we invite people to think about Homer is part of the point. As readers and thinkers we are attracted to and distracted by the object we can see so powerfully that it is hard for us to think about what *had* to be before what is there developed. In this way, the *Iliad* and the *Odyssey* are but two outcroppings—or trees—tended and grown in an unknown number of wild groves and family orchards. The work we have done in this book, we believe,

---

[16] *Iliad* 24.799–800; cf. Lynn-George 1988:230–276.

[17] Purves 2010 suggests that the *Odyssey*'s expansion into a world beyond its border charts a path "from heroic to agricultural poetics" (88), and represents a meditation "upon the *idea* of the end of epic" (89), if not its actual end. For the ambiguity of this sign of the oar and the prophecy, see Peradotto 1990:75–77. For the oar as a symbol of Odysseus' passage from the world of the living to the world of the dead, see Segal 1994:44.

[18] Henderson 1997:89 sees a connection between the soil that gives rise to the trees and that into which the oar will be planted.

functions in part both to trace the impression of what might have been on the poems we have and to help us think and talk about them better. It seems only fitting, therefore, that before we close this book, to speculate on what might have happened following the epics' textualization.

A Theban Revenge?

One suggestion that we pursued throughout this book and that was explored most fully in our last chapter is that individual manipulations of mythical traditions preserved in historical records are likely to have played a role in the privileging of one tradition over another. As such, the process of (pan)Hellenization—to be conceived not as a direct and teleological flow but rather as a chaotic series of negotiations in multiple directions—clearly exercised an influence on the formation of the epics that we now possess and on the traditions which we believe they appropriated.[19]

During the period of the development and institutionalization of epic poetry, different cities laid competing claims to the burial sites of heroes, including those of Theban myth. One material consequence of this inter-civic rivalry was the urgent pursuit to acquire the remains of heroes, which in turn became increasingly important for helping to establish or promote a city's political identity. In a similar way to the role that holy relics played in the formation and consolidation of the Catholic faith in communities throughout medieval Christendom, bones represented tangible connections with the larger-than-life figures from the age of heroes. At the same time, the cults that grew up around these remains provide further evidence of the use of genealogies to define and redefine identities in relation to one another.[20]

Within such a context of a maturing institutional framework and claims on dominion, Herodotus provides an account of Spartan hegemony in the Peloponnese. Critical to this tale of growing Spartan power is a venture to find and bring back the bones of Orestes[21]—an importance signaled by consultation of the Delphic oracle, a special-forces mission, and careful decoding of the oracular

---

[19] For a recent discussion of the political use of relics, see Salapata 2014:23–27. She draws attention especially to evidence in Pausanias of communities doing battle over claims to host the same hero cults. See Pausanias I 22.1 (Athens and Troizen over Hippolytos' tomb); Pausanias III 12.7 (grave of Talthybios in Sparta and Aigion); cf. Plutarch *On the Sign of Socrates* 5 and Pausanias I 41.1, 9.2.1 (Alkmênê at Haliartos, Athens, and Megara). On the multilocality of heroes and hero cults, see Hall 1999:52, who notes that "the Seven had nonexclusive cult worship at both Argos and Athens."

[20] See Salapata 2014:96–100 for an overview of the thirteen historical and fictional examples of bone transfer in the ancient Greek world.

[21] Cf. Herodotus I 67–68; Pausanias III 3.6. For the political implications of the manipulation of the bones of Orestes, see Phillips 2003. For an overview of the transfer of bones from Tegea to Sparta

text (Herodotus I 67–68).[22] Orestes was important, in the words of Gina Salapata, because he "was a favorite hero of all Peloponnesians and had achieved what Sparta aspired to: the hegemony of the whole Peloponnese under legitimate claim" (2014:37). For Salapata, the Spartans embraced both Dorian and Achaean origins to affiliate with both Homeric and Heraclid identities (2014:35; cf. Herodotus V 72).

Evidence from other sources reveals a similar tale of body snatching elsewhere across the Greek world, in order to justify territorial claims and/or hegemony over other groups. Not surprisingly, the Spartans' most serious rivals during this period of consolidation and retrenchment, the Athenians, seem to have been most active in this regard—a point that befits both their acquisitive character (as commented on by Thucydides) and their appropriation of the Homeric poems within the institution of the Great Panatheneia. According to Pausanias, the Athenians claimed the tombs of several heroes and may have made unsuccessful attempts to acquire the bones of Aiakos. More certain are the records of the Athenians "recovering" the bones of Theseus from Skyros in the fifth century BCE, immediately after the Persian invasion.[23] Thus, just as recovering the bones of Orestes allowed the Spartans to appeal to a more indigenous royalty as they asserted themselves throughout the Peloponnese, so the Athenians used the bones of Theseus to justify their emerging hegemonic position at the head a renewed Ionian naval alliance with the islands of the Aegean . Equally, such claims could play a role in internal politics: for Cimon, recovering the bones of Theseus was a political coup for the family of Miltiades and helped bolster the standing of their faction in the city.[24]

Among these many tales of claim and counterclaim on the body of heroes, there is one that directly informs and impinges on our investigation into the ongoing struggle between Troy and Thebes. This is the strange tale recorded in the scholia to Lykophron which implies that competition between Troy and Thebes may have persisted outside the Homeric poems for some time:

> They say that when there was a famine in Greece Apollo decreed that they should transfer the bones of Hektor, which were at a place in the Troad called Ophrynos to some city in Greece which had not taken part in the expedition against Troy. When the Greeks realized that Thebes in

---

(Orestes) and from Skyros to Athens (Theseus) as well as eleven other recorded instances and their political ramifications, see McCauley 1999.

[22] On heroic bones as a motif in the Greek use of the past, see Higbie 1997:299–302.

[23] Plutarch *Life of Cimon* 8.57; *Life of Theseus* 36.1–4; Pausanias I 17.6, III 3.7. See Pausanias II 29.6–8; Higbie 1997:296; Kearns 1989:47.

[24] See Salapata 2014:88–91.

Boiotia had not fought against Troy, they retrieved the remains of the hero and installed them there.[25]

Isaac and John Tzetzes on Lykophron *Alexandra* 1194

This evidence is interesting, for it not only represents a literal Theban appropriation of a Homeric hero, as the bones of Hektor are dug up and reburied in Thebes; it also relies on a detailed understanding of the *Iliad* in which Boiotian Thebes is conspicuous by its absence—and all the more so when, as we saw in the previous chapter, the Catalogue of Ships circles around Thebes but studiously avoids naming the city. The familiar trope of an oracular proclamation as a response to some crisis also invites the reader to ponder the cause and effect: here, the implication seems to be that the Greeks are suffering from famine because of their assault on Troy, as if it hadn't enjoyed the full support of the gods after all. Again such an explanation both corrects the *Iliad* (where Zeus oversees the fall of Troy) *and* draws on it for its legitimacy (where Apollo, indeed, favors the Trojans and is represented largely acting against the Achaeans). Using the *Iliad* against itself, then, this account finds in favor of Thebes, the one (mainland) Greek city not to have joined in the (now) discredited expedition against Troy.

The tradition of the transfer of Hektor's bones reappears in other sources. The historian Aristodemos of Thebes, whose work only survives in fragments, is recorded in a scholion to the *Iliad* providing an account largely similar to the one just cited. On this occasion, however, the (unspecified) crisis is restricted to the Thebans alone, whose oracular injunction to move the bones to "a place in their land" suggests an (overdue) anxiety to be involved in the Trojan War.[26] Pausanias too identifies a grave of Hektor near Thebes, along with the oracle

---

[25] φασὶν ὅτι λοιμοῦ κατασχόντος τὴν Ἑλλάδα ἔχρησεν ὁ Ἀπόλλων τὰ τοῦ Ἕκτορος ὀστᾶ κείμενα ἐν Ὀφρυνῷ τόπῳ Τροίας μετενεγκεῖν ἐπί τινα πόλιν Ἑλληνίδα ἐν τιμῇ <οὖσαν> μὴ μετασχοῦσαν τῆς ἐπὶ Ἴλιον στρατείας. οἱ δὲ Ἕλληνες εὑρόντες τὰς ἐν Βοιωτίᾳ Θήβας μὴ στρατευσαμένας ἐπὶ Ἴλιον ἐνεγκόντες τὰ τοῦ ἥρωος λείψανα ἔθηκαν αὐτὰ ἐκεῖσε.

[26] FGrHist 383 F 7 [=Schol. AB to *Iliad* 13.1]: "'the Trojans and Hektor': He has separated Hektor especially from the rest of the Trojans. After the sack of Troy, Hektor the son of Priam obtained honor from the gods even after death. For the Thebans in Boiotia were beset by evils and solicited a prophecy about their deliverance. The oracle told them that they would stop their troubles if they would transfer the bones of Hektor from Ophrynion in the Troad to a place in their land called the 'birthplace of Zeus.' They, once they did this and were freed from the evils, maintained the honors for Hektor and during hard times they used to call for his manifestation. This is the account in Aristodemos." Τρῶάς τε καὶ Ἕκτορα] κεχώρικε τῶν λοιπῶν Τρώων τὸν Ἕκτορα κατ' ἐξοχήν. μετὰ δὲ τὴν Ἰλίου πόρθησιν Ἕκτωρ ὁ Πριάμου καὶ μετὰ τὸν θάνατον τὴν ἀπὸ θεῶν εὐτύχησε τιμήν· οἱ γὰρ ἐν Βοιωτίαι Θηβαῖοι πιεζόμενοι κακοῖς ἐμαντεύοντο περὶ ἀπαλλαγῆς· χρησμὸς δὲ αὐτοῖς ἐδόθη παύσεσθαι τὰ δεινά, ἐὰν ἐξ Ὀφρυνίου τῆς Τρωάδος τὰ Ἕκτορος ὀστᾶ διακομισθῶσιν εἰς τὸν παρ' αὐτοῖς καλούμενον τόπον Διὸς γονάς. οἱ δὲ τοῦτο ποιήσαντες καὶ τῶν κακῶν ἀπαλλαγέντες διὰ τιμῆς ἔσχον Ἕκτορα, κατά τε τοὺς ἐπείγοντας καιροὺς ἐπικαλοῦνται

that had supported it. Significantly, he combines the tale of Hektor's bones with the tale of Oedipus (IX 18.5):

Ἔστι δὲ καὶ Ἕκτορος Θηβαίοις τάφος τοῦ Πριάμου πρὸς Οἰδιποδίᾳ καλουμένῃ κρήνῃ, κομίσαι δὲ αὐτοῦ τὰ ὀστᾶ ἐξ Ἰλίου φασὶν ἐπὶ τοιῷδε μαντεύματι·

Θηβαῖοι Κάδμοιο πόλιν καταναιετάοντες,
αἴ κ' ἐθέλητε πάτραν οἰκεῖν σὺν ἀμύμονι πλούτῳ,
Ἕκτορος ὀστέα Πριαμίδου κομίσαντες ἐς οἴκους
ἐξ Ἀσίης Διὸς ἐννεσίῃσ' ἥρωα σέβεσθαι.

τῇ δὲ Οἰδιποδίᾳ κρήνῃ τὸ ὄνομα ἐγένετο ὅτι ἐς αὐτὴν τὸ αἷμα ἐνίψατο Οἰδίπους τοῦ πατρῴου φόνου.

At Thebes there is also the grave of Hektor, Priam's son. It is next to a spring called the Oedipus Spring. The Thebans say that they brought the bones from Troy to this place because of the following oracle:

Thebans living in the in the city of Cadmus,
If you want to live in a country with blameless wealth
Bring the bones of Hektor, Priam's son, home
From Asia to be honored as a hero at Zeus' urging.

The spring was named after Oedipus because Oedipus washed off the blood from his father's murder into it.

There is some debate about whether or not there was an actual cult practice centered around Hektor's bones in Thebes and, if there was, when it actually began.[27] For our purposes what it represents is a continuation of some of the same real-world struggles and tensions that helped to shape the Homeric poems. However secure (or not) these texts are as witnesses to an ancient

---

τὴν ἐπιφάνειαν αὐτοῦ. ἡ ἱστορία παρὰ Ἀριστοδήμωι. Other sources include Strabo XIII 1.29; Aristotle fr. 640 R³.

[27] Hornblower agrees with Jacoby (*FGrHist* 383 F 7 *Kommentar*, 177–8) that the story of the transfer of Hektor's bones to Thebes circulated from the fourth century BCE onwards and accepts that the cult was historical (2013:422–424). Hornblower (427) also posits the tale as an instance of rivalry between Thebes and Athens as part of Thebes establishing a connection in the Hellespont to challenge Athenian commercial interests in the region. The first suggestion places the bone transfer tale after 316 BCE; the second dates it back to 365. Hornblower suggests that there were two stages: an oracle c. 465 BCE (428) followed by the retrieval of the bones near the end of the century. Cf. Schachter 1981; Ziehen 1934.

tradition, they reflects an ongoing understanding of the absence of Thebes in the Trojan War narrative, a reflection of the importance of Thebes right up to and beyond the composition and institutionalization of the Homeric poems, and, despite the city's absence in the extant heroic epic corpus, an indelible connection between the two chief cities of ancient Greek myth.

In Homeric epic, the destruction of Troy is built upon the destruction of Thebes, both by coming after it and by subordinating the role of that other city in its own narrative. In these later accounts of Hektor's bones, we see the future of the Greek world being determined by the continued rivalry between the two cities, based now on the possession of the material remains of the past. In this putative victory of the "real-world" Thebes over the imagined Troy, we find a metaphor for our relationship with the past and a demonstration of the results of Homer's competitive practice. The *Iliad* may end with the interment of Hektor, but later traditions would not let these bones lie in peace. In Aristodemos' fragment, the Trojan War narrative is reified as a material object that can relieve the suffering of the physical inheritors of the world of Thebes. While this could be viewed as a victory of the power of the story of Troy over the Theban tale (since the former functions as a magic talisman in the very homeland of the latter), Pausanias offers a somewhat different take. Here, the tales of Hektor and Oedipus are materialized and collocated together, two sets of relics of a past with various shades of relevance. The relics are metonyms for their narrative traditions, nestled together in a way similar to the collocation of Thebes and Troy in Hesiod's myth of the ages in the *Works and Days*. From our distant perspective, the continued cultural relevance of Theban myth seems less powerful, thanks largely to the long history of the reception of Homer's poems.

Even in the way we read these objects and their relationships to the narratives that might have been, we too are engaging in a weighing of their meaning that has no universal measure. They shift depending upon our knowledge of the traditions for which they are metonyms and, by being placed alongside each other in our vision of Homer's Thebes, create other levels of meaning anew. This dynamic process wherein meaning shifts from viewer to viewer recalls the emphasis that we have previously placed on traditional referentiality as an interpretive approach that facilitates multiple axes of time, authority, and audience engagement. While this book has certainly been *about* the use of Theban myths in the Homeric epics, its subtext—how to "read" Homer and situate that meaning in larger hermeneutic traditions—has been our endgame all along.

To address such a weighty task has meant approaching the topic obliquely rather than head on, precisely because of the absence of evidence and the gravity exerted on the missing bodies of Theban myth by the overwhelming presence of Homer's two poems, at once both so paradigmatic of the genre of heroic epic and so exceptional within it. In this sideways wander through Homeric epic, we have moved back and forth through different themes to force ourselves to think in terms of the subjects presented by the poems as both content and form.

The first chapter considered the question of how Homer's epics orient themselves toward the past, specifically in the creation of a *Theban* past that (re)defined that city's epic scope and relevance. This chapter's emphasis on the *Iliad*'s creation of a Thebes it needs for its own themes fluidly transitions to questions of what different heroic traditions mean and how their identities, affinities, and affiliations are negotiated, not with reference to another city or place, but almost exclusively with reference to the story being told. In these terms, the *Iliad*'s Herakles is recognizably Theban primarily to deny him a Panhellenic currency that the *Iliad* claims for itself (Chapter 2). Such a process of selection and suppression is evident too from Odysseus' mercurial use of other narrative traditions in his epic, as he bends and remakes them for his own ends (Chapter 3).

If these first three chapters focused on Theban heroes and the themes of politics, time, and form, one critical element of epic poetry more generally—strife—has helped us think about Homeric composition and structure on a bigger canvas. Chapters 4 and 5 explored how the emergence and containment of strife is a signal topic of Greek epic poetry; in our final chapter, we observed its importance in the very process of Panhellenization and the formation of cultural continuities. This contemplation of strife has suggested that such continuities almost always must contain within themselves discontinuities and elisions that make their existence possible. The story of how the *Iliad* and *Odyssey* came to be will also always be a type of cenotaph, a eulogy or a lament for the stories that came to be, those that were lost, and for all the stories that never were fully realized.

In our reading of the epics and our attempt to approach the problematic hermeneutics of Homer askance, we have been engaging in a different type of domesticated strife, of the kind that Timon the Philiasian calls "The paper-pushers behind their palisade waging endless contest / in the bird-cage of the Muses" (βιβλιακοὶ χαρακῖται ἀπείριτα δηριόωντες Μουσέων ἐν ταλάρῳ, fr. 60W = Athenaeus *Deipnosophistae* I 22). As collaborators, we have constantly challenged each other to consider new angles and to force ourselves to consider and reconsider what kind of stories Homer's epic presents. Just as Odysseus tries to articulate what he had learned from his father in their walk through the orchards, so we too retrace the steps of our predecessors, recounting how these powerful poems, whose fruits we continually enjoy, have been lovingly tended and passed down to us. And, every so often, a trace of some other presence in the shadows or soil detains us.

Works Cited

Adkins, A. W. H. 1970. *Merit and Responsibility: A Study in Greek Values.* Oxford.

Agamben, G. 2015. *Stasis: Civil War as a Political Paradigm.* Stanford.

Alden, M. 2000. *Homer Beside Himself: Para-narratives in the* Iliad. Oxford.

Allan, W. 2006. "Divine Justice and Cosmic Order in Early Greek Epic." *The Journal of Hellenic Studies* 126:1–35.

Andersen, Ø. 1978. *Die Diomedesgestalt in der Ilias.* Oslo.

———. 1987. "Myth Paradigm and Spatial Form in the *Iliad*." In *Homer Beyond Oral Poetry: Recent Trends in Homeric Interpretation*, ed. J. Bremer and I. J. F. De Jong, 1–13. Amsterdam.

———. 2012. "Older Heroes and Earlier Poems: The Case of Herakles in the *Odyssey*." In Andersen and Haug 2012: 138–151.

Andersen, Ø., and D. T. T. Haug, eds. 2012. *Relative Chronology in Early Greek Epic Poetry.* Cambridge.

Antovic, M., and C. P. Cánovas. 2016. *Oral Poetics and Cognitive Science.* Freiburg

Apthorp, M. J. 2000. *The Manuscript Evidence for Interpolation in Homer.* Heidelberg.

Arend, W. 1975. *Die typischen Scenen bei Homer.* Berlin.

Arft, J. 2014. "Immanent Thebes: Traditional Resonance and Narrative Trajectory in the *Odyssey*." *Trends in Classics* 6:399–411.

Arft, J., and J. M. Foley. 2015. "The Epic Cycle and Oral Tradition." In Fantuzzi and Tsagalis, 78–95.

Austin, N. 1975. *Archery at the Dark of the Moon: Poetic Problems in Homer's* Odyssey. Berkeley.

Bakker, E. J. 1997. *Poetry in Speech: Orality and Homeric Discourse.* Ithaca.

———. 2005. *Pointing at the Past: From Formula to Performance in Homeric Poetics.* Hellenic Studies 12. Washington, DC.

———. 2013. *The Meaning of Meat and the Structure of the Odyssey.* Cambridge.

Barker E. T. E. 2004. "Achilles' Last Stand: Institutionalising Dissent in Homer's *Iliad*." *Proceedings of the Cambridge Philological Society*: 92–120.

———. 2008. " 'Momos Advises Zeus': The Changing Representations of *Cypria* Fragment One." In *Greece, Rome and the Near East*, ed. E. Cingano and L. Milano, 33–73. Padova.

—————. 2009. *Entering the Agon: Dissent and Authority in Homer, Historiography and Tragedy*. Oxford.

—————. 2011. "The *Iliad*'s Big Swoon: A Case of Innovation within the Epic Tradition." *Trends in Classics*, ed. F. Montanari and A. Rengakos, 1–17.

Barker, E. T. E., and J. P. Christensen. 2006. "Flight Club: The New Archilochus Fragment and its Resonance with Homeric Epic." *Materiali e Discussioni per l'Analisi dei Testi Classici* 57:19–43.

—————. 2008. "Oedipus of Many Pains: Strategies of Contest in Homeric Poetry." *Leeds International Classical Studies* 7.2. (http://www.leeds.ac.uk/classiscs/lics/)

—————. 2011. "On Not Remembering Tydeus: Diomedes and the Contest for Thebes." *Materiali e discussioni per l'analisi dei testi classici* 66:9–44.

—————. 2014. "Even Herakles Had to Die: Epic Rivalry and the Poetics of the Past in Homer's *Iliad*." *Trends in Classics: Homer and the Theban Tradition*, ed. Christos Tsagalis, 249–277.

—————. 2015. "Odysseus' *Nostos* and the *Odyssey*'s *Nostoi*." G. *Philologia Antiqua* 87–112.

Bearzot, C. 2011. "L'Antica egemonia di Orcomeno in Beozia: fortuna di un tema propagandistico." In L. Breglia, A. Moleti, and M. L. Napolitano, 171–189. Pisa.

Beck, D. 2005. *Homeric Conversation*. Hellenic Studies 14. Washington, DC.

Becker, A. S. 1995. *The Shield of Achilles and the Poetics of Ekphrasis*. Lanham.

Beekes, R. 2010. *Etymological Dictionary of Greek*. Leiden.

Bergren, A. 1981. "Helen's 'Good Drug', *Odyssey* iv. 1–3–5." In *Contemporary Literary Hermeneutics and Interpretation of Classical Texts*, ed. S. Kresic, 201–214. Ottowa.

—————. 1983. "Language and the Female in Early Greek Thought." *Arethusa* 16:69–95.

Berman, D. W. 2013. "Greek Thebes in the Early Mythographic Tradition." In *Writing Myth: Mythography in the Ancient World*, ed. S. M. Trzaskoma and R. S. Smith, 37–54. Leuven.

—————. 2015. *Myth, Literature, and the Creation of the Topography of Thebes*. Cambridge.

Bernabé, A. 1996. *Poetorum Epicorum Graecorum*. Leipzig.

Boardman, J. 1975. "Herakles, Peisistratos, and Eleusis." *The Journal of Hellenic Studies* 95:1–12.

Bolmarcich, S. 2001. "*Homophrosune* in the *Odyssey*." *Classical Philology* 96:205–13.

Braswell, B. K. 1971. "Mythological Innovation in the *Iliad*." *The Classical Quarterly* 21:16–26.

Breglia, L., A. Moleti, and M. L. Napolitano, eds. 2011. *Ethne, identità e tradizioni: La "terza" Grecia e l'Occidente.* Pisa.

Bremer, J. N. 1987. "Stesichorus, the Lille Papyrus." In *Some Recently Found Greek Poems,* ed. Bremer and van Taalman, 128–172. Leiden.

Buck, R. 1979. *A History of Boeotia.* Edmonton.

Burgess J. S. 2001. *The Tradition of the Trojan War in Homer and the Epic Cycle.* Baltimore.

———. 2006. "Neoanalysis, Orality, and Intertextuality: An Examination of Homeric motif Transference." *Oral Tradition* 21:148–189.

———. 2009. *The Death and Afterlife of Achilles.* Baltimore.

———. 2012. "Belatedness in the Travels of Odysseus. " In Montanari, Rengakos, and Tsagalis, 269–290.

Burkert, W. 1985. *Greek Religion.* Cambridge.

Burnett, A. P. 1988. "Iokasta in the West: The Lille Stesichorus." *Classical Antiquity* 7:107–154.

Carlier, P. 1996. "Les Basileis homériques sont-ils des rois?" *Ktèma* 21:5–22.

Cartledge, P. 1993. *The Greeks: A Portrait of Self and Others.* Oxford.

———. 1995. "'We Are All Greeks'? Ancient (Especially Herodotean) and Modern Contestations of Hellenism." *Bulletin of the Institute of Classical Studies* 40:75–82.

Chaston, C. 2002. "Three Models of Authority in the *Odyssey.*" *The Classical World* 96: 3–19.

Christensen, J. P. 2009. "The End of Speeches and a Speech's End: Nestor, Diomedes, and the *Telos Muthôn.*" In *Reading Homer: Film and Text,* ed. K. Myrsiades, 136–162. Madison.

———. 2010. "First-Person Futures in Homer." *The American Journal of Philology* 131:543–571.

———. 2012. "Ares: ἄϊδηλος; On the Text of *Iliad* 5.757 and 5.872." *Classical Philology* 107:230–238.

———. 2013. "Innovation and Tradition Revisited: The Near-synonymy of Homeric ΑΜΥΝΩ and ΑΛΕΞΩ as a Case Study in Homeric Composition." *The Classical Journal* 108:257–296.

———. 2015. "Diomedes' Foot-wound and the Homeric Reception of Myth." In *Diachrony,* ed. Jose Gonzalez, 17–41. Berlin.

———. 2018a. "Eris and Epos: Composition, Competition and the 'Domestication' of Strife." *YAGE.*

———. 2018b. "Speech Training and the Mastery of Context: Thoas the Aitolian and the Practice of Múthoi." In *Homer in Performance: Rhapsodes, Narrators and Characters,* ed. C. Tsagalis and J. Ready. Austin.

————. 2018c. "Learned Helplessness, the Structure of the Telemachy and Odysseus' Return." In *Psychology and the Classics*, ed. J. Lauwers, J. Opsomer, and H. Schwall. Leuven.

————. 2018d. "Human Cognition and Narrative Closure: The *Odyssey*'s Open-End." In *The Routledge Handbook of Classics and Cognitive Theory*, ed. Peter Meineck, 139-155. New York.

Cingano, E. 1992. "The Death of Oedipus in the Epic Tradition." *Phoenix* 46:1–11.

————. 2000. "Tradizioni su Tebe nell'epica e nella lirica greca arcaica." In *La città di Argo: Mito, storia, tradizioni poetiche*, ed. P. A. Bernardini, 59–68. Rome.

————. 2004. "The Sacrificial Cut and the Sense of Honour Wronged in Greek Epic Poetry: Thebais frgs. 2-3D." In *Food and Identity in the Ancient World*, ed. C. Grotanelli and L. Milano, 269–279. Padova.

————. 2005. "A Catalogue within a Catalogue: Helen's Suitors in the Hesiodic Catalogue of Women." In *The Hesiodic Catalogue of Women: Constructions and Reconstructions*, ed. R. L. Hunter, 118–152. Cambridge.

————. 2014. "Oidipodea." In Fantuzzi and Tsagalis 2014:213–225.

Clarke, M. I., B. G. F. Currie, and R. O. A. M. Lyne, eds. 2006. *Epic Interactions: Perspectives on Homer, Virgil and the Epic Tradition*. Oxford.

Clay, J. S. 1983. *The Wrath of Athena: Gods and Men in the* Odyssey. Princeton.

————. 1989. *The Politics of Olympus: Form and Meaning in the Major Homeric Hymns*. Princeton.

————. 1999. "The Whip and the Will of Zeus." In *Literary Imagination*, 1.1:40–60.

————. 2003. *Hesiod's Cosmos*. Cambridge.

————. 2011. *Homer's Trojan Theater*. Cambridge.

Clayton, B. 2004. *A Penelopean Poetics: Reweaving the Feminine in Homer's* Odyssey. Lanham.

Collins, D. 1998. *Immortal Armor: The Concept of* Alkê *in Archaic Greek Poetry*. Lanham.

————. 2004. *Master of the Game: Competition and Performance in Greek Poetry*. Hellenic Studies 7. Washington DC.

————. 2006. "Corinna and Mythological Innovation." *The Classical Quarterly* 56:19–32.

Combellack, F. M. 1976. "Homer the Innovator." *Classical Philology* 71:44–55.

Cook, E. F. 1994. *The* Odyssey *in Athens: Myths of Cultural Origins*. Ithaca.

————. 1999. "Active and Passive Heroics in the *Odyssey*." *The Classical World* 93:149–167.

Culler, J. 1982. *On Deconstruction: Theory and Criticism after Structuralism*. New York.

Currie, B. 2016. *Homer's Allusive Art*. Oxford.

Currie, B. G. F. 2006. "Homer and the Early Epic Tradition." In *Epic Interactions: Perspectives on Homer, Virgil and the Epic Tradition*, ed. M. Clarke, B. Currie, and R. Lyne. Oxford: 1–45.

D'Alessio, G. B. 2005. "Ordered from the Catalogue: Pindar, Bacchylides, and the Hesiodic Genealogical Poetry." In R. L. Hunter, 217–238. Cambridge.

Danek, G. 1998. *Epos und Zitat: Studien zur Quellen der Odyssee*. Vienna.

———. 2002. "Traditional Referentiality and Homeric Intertextuality." In *Omero tremila anni dopo*, ed. F. Montanari and P. Ascheri, 3–19. Rome.

Davidson, O. M. 1980. "Indo-European Dimensions of Herakles in *Iliad* 19.95–133." *Arethusa* 12:197–202.

Davies, M. 1988. *Epicorum Graecorum Fragmenta*. Göttingen.

———. 1989. *The Greek Epic Cycle*. London.

———. 2014. *The Theban Epics*. Hellenic Studies 69. Washington, DC.

———. 2016. *The Aithiopis: Neo-Analysis Reanalyzed*. Hellenic Studies 71. Washington, DC.

———. 2018. Review of *Device and Composition in the Greek Epic Cycle*, by B. Sammons.

de Jong, I. J. F. 2001. *A Narratological Commentary on the* Odyssey. Cambridge.

Deleuze, G. and F. Guattari. 1987. *A Thousand Plateaus: Capitalism and Schizophrenia*. Minneapolis.

Derrida, J. 1997. *Of Grammatology*. Trans. G. C. Spivak. Baltimore.

Detienne, M. 1996. *The Masters of Truth in Archaic Greece*. New York.

Deubner, L. 1942. "Oedipusprobleme." *Abhandlungen der Preussischen Akademie der Wissenschaften* 4:1–43.

Dickson, K. 1995. *Nestor: Poetic Memory in Greek Epic*. New York.

Dodds, E. R. 1957. *The Greeks and the Irrational*. Boston.

Doherty, L. 1991. "The Internal and Implied Audiences of *Odyssey* 11." *Arethusa* 24:145–176.

———. 1992. "Gender and Internal Audiences in the *Odyssey*." *The American Journal of Philology* 113:161–177.

———. 1995. *Siren Songs: Gender, Audiences, and Narrators in the* Odyssey. Ann Arbor.

Donlan, W. 1979. "The Structure of Authority in the *Iliad*." *Arethusa* 12:51–70.

———. 2002. "Achilles the Ally." *Arethusa* 35:155–172.

Dougherty, C. 2001. *The Raft of Odysseus: The Ethnographic Imagination of Homer's* Odyssey. Oxford.

Downing, E. 1990. "*Apatê, Agôn*, and Literary Self-Reflexivity in Euripides' *Helen*." In M. Griffith and D. J. Mastronarde, 1–16.

Doyle, A. 2010. "'Unhappily Ever After?' The Problem of Helen in *Odyssey* 4." *Akroterion* 55:1–18.

Drout, M. D. C. 2011. "Variation Within Limits: An Evolutionary Approach to the Structure and Dynamics of the Multiform." *Oral Tradition* 26.2: 447–474.

Dué, C. 2002. "Achilles' Golden Amphora in Aeschines' *Against Timarchus* and the Afterlife of Oral Tradition." *Classical Philology* 96:33–47.

———. 2011. "Maneuvers in the Dark of Night: *Iliad* 10 in the Twenty-First Century." In F. Montanari, A. Rengakos, and C. Tsagalis, 165–173.

Dué, C., and M. Ebbott. 2009. *Iliad 10 and the Poetics of Ambush*. Hellenic Studies 39. Washington, DC.

Dunkle, R. 1997. "Swift-Footed Achilles." *The Classical World* 90: 227–234.

Easterling, P. E. 1989. "Agamemnon's *Skêptron* in the *Iliad*." In *Images of Authority: Papers Presented to Joyce Reynolds*, ed. M.M. Mackenzie and C. Rouché, 104–121. Cambridge.

———. 2005. "The Image of the Polis in Greek Tragedy." In Hansen 2005:49–72.

Ebbott. M. 2010. "Error 404: Theban Epic Not Found." *Trends in Classics* 2:239–258.

———. 2014. "Allies in Fame: Recruiting Warriors in the Theban and Trojan Epic Tradition." *Trends in Classics* 66:319–335.

Ebert, J. 1972. *Griechische Epigramme auf Sieger an gymnischen und hippischen Agonen*. Berlin.

van Eck, J. 1978. *The Homeric Hymn to Aphrodite: Introduction, Commentary, and Appendices*. Utrecht.

Edmunds, L. 1981. *The Sphinx in the Oedipus Legend*. Rudolstadt.

———. 1997. "Myth in Homer." In I. Morris and B. Powell, 415–441. Leiden.

———. 2016. "Intertextuality without Texts in Archaic Greek Verse and the Plan of Zeus." *Syllecta Classica* 27:1–27.

Edwards, A. T. 1985. *Achilles in the* Odyssey: *Ideologies of Heroism in the Homeric Epic*. Königstein.

———. 2004. *Hesiod's Ascra*. Berkeley.

Edwards, G. P. 1971. *The Language of Hesiod in its Traditional Context*. Oxford.

Edwards, M. W. 1991. *The Iliad: A Commentary*. Vol. V, Books 17–20. Cambridge.

———. 1997. "Homeric Style and Oral Poetics." In Morris and Powell 1997:261–283.

Ekroth, G. 1999. "Pausanias and the Sacrificial Rituals of Greek Hero-cults." In *Ancient Greek Hero Cult: Proceedings of the Fifth International Seminar on Ancient Cult*, ed. R. Hagg, 21–23. Stockholm.

Ellsworth, J. D. 1974. "Ἀγων Νεῶν: An Unrecognized Metaphor in the *Iliad*." *Classical Philology* 69:258–264.

Elmer, D. 2013. *The Poetics of Consent: Collective Decision-Making and the* Iliad. Baltimore.

Emlyn-Jones, C. 1986. "True and Lying Tales in the *Odyssey*." *Greece & Rome* 33:1–10.

Euben, J. P., ed. 1986. *Greek Tragedy and Political Theory*. Los Angeles.

Falkner, T. M. 1995. *The Poetics of Old Age in Greek Epic, Lyric, and Tragedy*. Norman.

Fantuzzi, M., and C. Tsagalis, eds. 2014. *The Greek Epic Cycle and its Ancient Reception: A Companion*. Cambridge.

Farenga, V. 2006. *Citizen and Self in Ancient Greece: Individuals Performing Justice and Law*. Cambridge.

Farnell, L. R. 1920. *The Cults of the Greek City-States*. Cambridge.

Faulkner, A. 2011. *The Homeric Hymn to Aphrodite: Introduction, Text and Commentary*. Oxford.

Felson, N. 2002. "Threptra and Invincible Hands: The Father-Son Relationship in *Iliad* 24." *Arethusa* 35:35–56.

Felson-Rubin, N. 1994. *Regarding Penelope: From Courtship to Poetics*. Princeton.

Fenik, B. 1968. *Typical Battle Scenes in the* Iliad. Wiesbaden.

———.1974. *Studies in the* Odyssey. Wiesbaden.

Finglass, P. J. 2014. "Thebais?" In *Stesichorus: The Poems*, ed. M. Davies and P. J. Finglass, 358–395. Cambridge.

Finkelberg, M. 1995. "Patterns of Human Error in Homer." *The Journal of Hellenic Studies* 155:15–28.

———. 2000. "The *Cypria*, the *Iliad*, and the Problem of Multiformity in Oral and Written Tradition." *Classical Philology* 95:1–11.

———. 2012. "The Canonicity of Homer." In *Kanon in Konstruktion und Dekonstruktion*, ed. E. M. Becker and S. Scholz, 137–151. Berlin.

———. 2015. "Meta-Cyclic Epic and Homeric Poetry." In Fantuzzi and Tsagalis 2015:126–138.

Finley, M. L. 1954. *The World of Odysseus*. New York.

Foley, J. M. 1988. *The Theory of Oral Composition: History and Methodology*. Bloomington.

———. 1991. *Immanent Art: From Structure to Meaning in Traditional Oral Epic*. Bloomington.

———. 1997. "Oral Tradition and its Implications." In Morris and Powell 1997:146–173.

———. 1999. *Homer's Traditional Art*. Philadelphia.

———. 2002. *How to Read an Oral Poem*. Urbana.

———. 2005. "Analogues: Modern Oral Epics." In *A Companion to Ancient Epic*, ed. J. Foley, 196–212. Oxford.

Ford, A. 1992. *Homer: The Poetry of the Past*. Ithaca.

Fowler, D. 2000. *Roman Constructions*. Oxford.

Fowler, R. L. 1998. "Genealogical Thinking, Hesiod's Catalogue, and the Creation of the Hellenes." *Proceedings of the Cambridge Philological Society* 44:1–19.

———. 2013. *Early Greek Mythography II: Commentary*. Oxford.

Frame, D. 1978. *The Myth of Return: Early Greek Epic.* New Haven.

———. 2009. *Hippota Nestor.* Hellenic Studies 37. Washington, DC.

Friedrich, P. and J. Redfield. 1978. "Speech as a Personality Symbol: The Case of Achilles." *Language* 54:263–288.

Gagarin, M. 1990 "The Ambiguity of Eris in the *Works and Days.*" In M. Griffith and D.J. Mastronarde, 173–183.

———. 1992. "The Poetry of Justice: Hesiod and the Origins of Greek Law." *Ramus* 22:61–78.

Galinsky, G. K. 1972. *The Herakles Theme.* Oxford.

Gantz, T. 1993. *Early Greek Myth: A Guide to Literary and Artistic Sources.* 2 Vols. Baltimore.

Gentili, B. 1988. *Poetry and its Public in Ancient Greece: From Homer to the Fifth Century.* Baltimore.

Gill, C. 1996. *Personality in Greek Epic, Tragedy and Philosophy.* Oxford.

Goldhill, S. 1991. *The Poet's Voice.* Cambridge.

———. 1994. "The Naive and Knowing Eye: Ecphrasis and the Culture of Viewing in the Hellenistic World." In *Art and Text in Greek Culture,* ed. S. Goldhill and R. Osborne, 197–223. Cambridge.

———. 2010. "Idealism in the *Odyssey* and the meaning of *mounos* in *Odyssey.*" In Mitsis and Tsagalis: 115–127.

González, J. 2015. *The Epic Rhapsode and His Craft.* Washington, DC.

Gottschall, J. 2012. *The Storytelling Animal: How Stories Make Us Human.* Boston.

Graziosi, B. 2002. *Inventing Homer: The Early Reception of Epic.* Cambridge.

———. 2010. "Hesiod in Classical Athens: Rhapsodes, Orators and Platonic Discourse." In Boys-Stones and Haubold: 111–132.

Graziosi, B., and J. Haubold, 2005. *Homer: The Resonance of Epic.* London.

Griffin, J. 1977. "The Epic Cycle and the Uniqueness of Homer." *The Journal of Hellenic Studies* 97:39–53.

———. 1980. *Homer on Life and Death.* Oxford.

———. 1986. "Homeric Words and Speakers." *The Journal of Hellenic Studies* 106: 36–57.

Griffith, M. 1990. "Contest and Contradiction in Early Greek Poetry." In Griffith and Mastronade 1990:185–207.

Griffith, M., and D. Mastronade, eds. 1990. *Cabinet of the Muses: Essays on Classical and Comparative Literature in Honor of Thomas G. Rosenmeyer.* Atlanta.

Haft, A. 1984. "Odysseus, Idomeneus, and Meriones: The Cretan Lies of the *Odyssey* 13–19." *The Classical Journal* 79:289–306.

Hainsworth, J. B. 1970. "The Criticism of an Oral Homer." *The Journal of Hellenic Studies* 90:90–98.

———. 1993. *The Iliad: A Commentary.* Vol. III, Books 9–12. Cambridge.

Hall, E. 1989. *Inventing the Barbarian: Greek Self-Definition through Tragedy*. Oxford.

Hall, J. 1997. *Ethnic Identity in Greek Antiquity*. Cambridge.

———. 1999. "Beyond the Polis: The Multilocality of Heroes." In *Ancient Greek Hero Cult*, ed. R. Hägg, 49–59. Stockholm.

Haller, B. 2013. "*Dolios* in *Odyssey* 4 and 24: Penelope's Plotting and Alternative Narratives of Odysseus' Νόστος." *Transactions of the American Philological Association* 143:263–292.

Halliwell, S. 1991. "Comic Satire and Freedom of Speech in Classical Athens." *The Journal of Hellenic Studies* 111: 48–70.

Halverson, J. 1986. "The Succession Issue in the *Odyssey*." *Greece and Rome* 33:119–128.

Hamilton, R. 1989. *The Architecture of Hesiodic Poetry*. Baltimore.

Hammer, D. 1997. "'Who Shall Readily Obey?' Authority and Politics in the *Iliad*." *Phoenix* 51:1–24.

———. 2002. *The Iliad as Politics: The Performance of Political Thought*. Norman.

———. 2004. "Ideology, Symposium, and Archaic Politics." *The American Journal of Philology* 125:479–515.

Hansen, M., ed. 2005. *The Imaginary Polis*. Copenhagen.

Harden, S. and A. Kelly. 2014. "Proemic Convention and Character Construction in Early Greek Epic." *Harvard Studies in Classical Philology* 107:1–34.

Harrison, J. E. 1980. *Prolegomena to the Study of Greek Religion*. London.

Haubold, J. 2000. *Homer's People: Epic Poetry and Social Formation*. Cambridge.

———. 2002. "Greek Epic: A Near Eastern Genre?" *Proceedings of the Cambridge Philological Society* 48: 1–19.

Havelock, E. A. 1966. "Thoughtful Hesiod." *Yale Classical Studies* 20:61–72.

Heath, M. 1987. *The Poetics of Greek Tragedy*. Stanford.

Hedreen, G. 1992. "The Cult of Achilles in the Euxine." *Hesperia* 60:313–330.

Heiden, B. 2008a. *Homer's Cosmic Fabrication: Choice and Design in the* Iliad. Oxford.

———. 2008b. "Common People and Leaders in *Iliad* Book 2: The Invocation of the Muses and the Catalogue of Ships." *The American Journal of Philology* 138:127–54.

Held, G. 1987. "Phoinix, Agamemnon and Achilles: Problems and Paradeigmata." *The Classical Quarterly* 36:141–154.

Henderson, J. 1997. "The Name of the Tree: Recounting *Odyssey* 24: 340–342." *The Journal of Hellenic Studies* 117: 87–116.

Heubeck, A., and A. Hoekstra. 1989. *A Commentary on Homer's* Odyssey. Vol. 2, Books 9–16. Oxford.

Heubeck, A., S. West, and J. B. Hainsworth. 1989. *A Commentary on Homer's* Odyssey. Vol. 3. Oxford.

———. 1988: *A Commentary on Homer's* Odyssey. Volume 1. Oxford.

Higbie, C. 1995. *Heroes' Names, Homeric Identities.* New York and London.

———. 1997. "The Bones of a Hero, the Ashes of a Politician: Athens, Salamis, and the Usable Past." *Classical Antiquity* 16:278–307.

Hinds, S. 1998. *Allusion and Intertext.* Cambridge.

Hogan, J. C. 1981. "Eris in Homer." *Grazer Beiträge* 10:21–58.

Holmes, B. 2007. "The *Iliad*'s Economy of Pain." *Transactions of the American Philological Association* 137:45–84.

Holoka, J. 1983. "Looking Darkly: ΥΠΟΔΡΑ ΙΔΩΝ; Reflections on Status and Decorum in Homer." *Transactions of the American Philological Association* 113:1–16.

Holt, P. 1992. "Herakles' Apotheosis in Lost Greek Literature and Art." *L'Antiquité Classique*, 38–59.

Hommel, H. 1980. *Der Gott Achilleus.* Heidelberg.

Hooker, J. T. 1988. "The Cults of Achilles." *Rheinisches Museum fur Philologie* 131:1–7.

Hornblower, S. 2013. *Lykophron: Alexandra.* Oxford.

Horrocks, G. 1997. "Homer's Dialect." In Morris and Powell 1997:192–217.

Hunter, R., ed. 2005. *The Hesiodic Catalogue of Women: Constructions and Reconstructions.* Cambridge.

Huxley, G. 1969. *Greek Epic Poetry.* London.

Irwin, E. 2005a. *Solon and Early Greek Poetry: The Politics of Exhortation.* Cambridge.

———. 2005b. "Gods Among Men? The Social and Political Dynamics of the Hesiodic Catalogue of Women." In Hunter 2005: 35–84.

Iser, W. 1974. *The Implied Reader.* Baltimore.

Janko, R. 1981. "ΑΘΑΝΑΤΟΣ ΚΑΙ ΑΓΗΡΩΣ: The Genealogy of a Formula." *Mnemosyne* 34:382–385.

———. 1982. *Homer, Hesiod, and the Hymns.* Cambridge.

———. 1992. *The Iliad: A Commentary.* Volume 4, Books 13–16. Cambridge.

———. 2012. "Πρῶτόν τε καὶ ὕστατον αἰὲν ἀείδειν: Relative Chronology and the Literary History of the Early Greek Epos." In Andersen and Haug, 20–43.

Jensen, M.S. 2011. *Writing Homer: A Study Based on Results from Modern Fieldwork.* Copenhagen.

Kakridis, J. T. 1949. *Homeric Researches.* Lund.

———. 1971. *Homer Revisited.* Lund.

Kanavou, N. 2015. *The Names of Homeric Heroes: Problems and Interpretations.* DeGruyter.

Katz, M. A. 1991. *Penelope's Renown: Meaning and Indeterminacy in the* Odyssey. Princeton.

Kearns, E. 1989. *The Heroes of Attica.* London.

Kelly, A. 2007a. "How to End an Orally-Derived Epic Poem." *Transactions of the American Philological Association* 137:371–402.

———. 2007b. *A Referential Commentary and Lexicon to Homer, Iliad VIII*. Oxford.

———. 2008. "Performance and Rivalry: Homer, Odysseus and Hesiod." In *Performance, Reception, Iconography: Studies in Honour of Oliver Taplin*, ed. M. Revermann and P. Wilson, 177–203. Oxford.

———. 2010. "Hypertexting with Homer: Tlepolemos and Sarpedon on Herakles (5.628-698)." *Trends in Classics* 2:259–276.

———. 2012. "The Mourning of Thetis: 'Allusion' and the Future in the *Iliad*." In F. Montanari, A. Rengakos, and C. Tsagalis, 211–256. Leiden.

King, B. 1999. "The Rhetoric of the Victim: Odysseus in the Swineherd's Hut." *Classical Antiquity* 18: 74–93.

Kirk, G. S. 1973. "Methodological Reflexions on the Myths of Herakles." In *Il Mito Greco: Atti del Convegno Internazionale*, ed. B. Gentili and G. Paioni, 285–297. Rome.

———. 1985. *The Iliad: A Commentary*. Vol. 1, Books 1–4. Cambridge.

Koenen, L. 1994. "Greece, the Near East, and Egypt: Cyclic Destruction in Hesiod and the Catalogue of Women." *Transactions of the American Philological Association* 124:1–34.

Koning, H. H. 2010. *Hesiod: The Other Poet*. Leiden.

Konstan, D. 2001. "*To Hellenikon Ethnos*: Ethnicity and the Construction of Ancient Greek Identity." In *Ancient Perceptions of Greek Ethnicity*, ed. I. Malkin, 29–50. Cambridge.

Kountari, E., et al. 2012. "A New Project of Surface Survey, Geophysical and Excavation Research of the Mycenaean Drainage Works of the North Kopais: The First Study Season." *IWA Specialized Conference on Water and Waste Water*, 467–476. Istanbul.

Kullmann, W. 1960. *Die Quellen der Ilias*. Wiesbaden.

———. 1984. "Oral Poetry Theory and Neoanalysis in Homeric Research." *Greek, Roman, and Byzantine Studies* 25:307–324.

———. 2002. "Nachlese zur Neoanalyse." In *Realität, Imagination und Theorie*, ed. A. Rengakos, 162–176. Stuttgart.

Kurke, L. 1992. "The Politics of *abÒrosuvnh* in Archaic Greece." *Classical Antiquity* 11:91–121.

———. 1999. *Coins, Bodies, Games, and Gold: The Politics of Meaning in Archaic Greece*. Princeton.

Lakoff, G., and M. Johnson. 1980. *Metaphors We Live By*. Chicago.

Lardinois, A. P. M. H. 2000. "Characterization through Gnomai in Homer's Iliad." *Mnemosyne* 53:641–661.

Larson, J. 2007. *Ancient Greek Cults: A Guide*. New York.

Larson, S. L. 2007. *Tales of Epic Ancestry: Boiotian Collective Identity in the Late Archaic and Early Classical Periods*. Stuttgart.

Larson, S. 2014. "Boeotia, Athens, the Peisistratids, and the *Odyssey*'s Catalogue of Heroines." *Trends in Classics* 6:412–427.

LeDoux, J. 2002. *The Synaptic Self: How Our Brains Become Who We Are*. New York.

Létoublon, F., ed. 1992. *La langue et les textes en grecque ancien: Actes du colloque Pierre Chantraine*. Amsterdam.

Levine, C. 2015. *Forms: Whole, Rhythm, Hierarchy, Network*. Princeton.

Liapis, V. 2006. "Intertextuality as Irony: Herakles in Epic and in Sophocles." *Greece and Rome* 53:48–59.

Lloyd, G. E. R. 1987. *The Revolutions in Wisdom: Studies in the Claims and Practice of Ancient Greek Science*. Berkeley.

Lloyd-Jones, H. 1971. *The Justice of Zeus*. Berkeley.

Lohmann, D. 1970. *Die Komposition der Reden in der Ilias*. Berlin.

Loraux, N. 1990. "Herakles: the Super-Male and the Feminine." In *Before Sexuality: The Construction of Erotic Experience in the Ancient Greek World*, ed. D. M. Halperin, 21–52. Princeton.

Lord, A. 1960. *The Singer of Tales*. Cambridge.

Louden, B. 1995. "Categories of Homeric Wordplay." *Transactions of the American Philological Association* 125: 27–46.

Lowe, N. 2000. *The Classical Plot and the Invention of Western Narrative*. Cambridge,

Lowenstam, S. 2000. "The Shroud of Laertes and Penelope's Guile." *The Classical Journal* 95:333–348.

Lulli, L. 2014. "Local Epics and Epic Cycles: The Anomalous Case of a Submerged Genre." In *Submerged Literature in Ancient Greek Culture*, ed. G. Colesanti and M. Giordano, 76–90. Berlin and Boston.

Lyne, R. O. A. M. 1994. "Vergil's Aeneid: Subversion by Intertextuality: Catullus 66.39-40 and other examples." *Greece and Rome* 41:187–204.

Lynn-George, M. 1988. *Epos: Word, Narrative, and the Iliad*. Atlantic Highlands.

Mackie, C. J. 1997. "Achilles' Teachers: Chiron and Phoenix in the *Iliad*." *Greece and Rome* 44:1–10.

———. 2008. *Rivers of Fire: Mythic Themes in Homer's* Iliad. Washington, DC.

Mackie, H. 1996. *Talking Trojan: Speech and Community in the* Iliad. Lanham.

Macleod, C. 1982. *Homer* Iliad XXIV. Cambridge.

Malkin, I. 1998. *The Returns of Odysseus: Colonization and Ethnicity*. Berkeley.

———. 2011. *A Small Greek World: Networks in the Ancient Mediterranean*. Oxford.

Marks, J. R. 2002. "The Junction between the Cypria and the *Iliad*." *Phoenix* 56:1–24.

———. 2008. *Zeus in the* Odyssey. Hellenic Studies 31. Washington, DC.

Martin, R. P. 1984. "Hesiod, Odysseus, and the Instruction of Princes." *Transactions of the American Philological Association* 114:29–48.

———. 1989. *The Language of Heroes: Speech and Performance in the* Iliad. Ithaca.

———. 1992. "Hesiod's Metanastic Poetics." *Ramus* 21:11–33.

———. 2005. "Pulp Epic: The Catalogue and the Shield." In R. L. Hunter 2005:153–175.

Mayer, K. 1996. "Helen and the ΔΙΟΣ ΒΟΥΛΗ." *The American Journal of Philology* 117:1–15.

McCauley, B. 1999. "Heroes and Power: The Politics of Bone Transferal." In *Ancient Greek Hero Cult*, ed. R. Hägg, 85–98. Stockholm.

Meissner, T. 2006. *S-Stem Nouns and Adjectives in Greek and Proto-European: A Diachronic Study in Word Formation*. Oxford.

Minchin, E. 2001. *Homer and the Resources of Memory: Some Applications of Cognitive Theory to the* Iliad *and the* Odyssey. Oxford.

———. 2007. *Homeric Voices: Discourse, Memory, Gender*. Oxford.

———. 2016. "Repetition in Homeric Epic: Cognitive and Linguistic Perspectives." In Antović and Cánovas 2016: 12–29.

Mitchell, L. 2007. *Panhellenism and the Barbarian in Archaic and Classical Greece*. Swansea.

Mondi, R. 1980. "ΣΚΗΠΤΟΥΧΟΙ ΒΑΣΙΛΕΙΣ: An Argument for Divine Kingship in Early Greece." *Arethusa* 13:203–216.

Montanari, F., A. Rengakos, and C. Tsagalis. 2011. *Homeric Contexts: Neoanalysis and the Interpretation of Oral Poetry*. Berlin.

Montiglio, S. 1993. "La menace du silence pour le héros de l'Iliade." *Metis* 8:161–186.

Morris, I., and B. Powell, eds. 1997. *A New Companion to Homer*. Leiden.

Morrison, J. V. 1992. *Homeric Misdirection: False Predictions in the* Iliad. Michigan.

Most, G. W. 1989. "The structure and function of Odysseus' Apologoi." *Transactions of the American Philological Association* 119:15–30.

———. 1993. "Hesiod and the Textualization of Personal Temporality." *Bibliotec di Studi Antichi* 51: 73–92.

———. 2007. *Hesiod: The Shield: Catalogue of Women and Other Fragments*. Cambridge.

Moulton, C. 1974. "The End of the *Odyssey*." *Greek, Roman, and Byzantine Studies* 15: 153–169.

Mueller, M. 2010. "Helen's Hands: Weaving for Κλέου in the *Odyssey*." *Helios* 37(1):1–21.

Muellner, L. 1976. *The Meaning of Homeric EYXOMAI through Its Formulas*. Innsbruck.

———. 1996. *The Anger of Achilles: Menis in Greek Epic*. Ithaca.

Munding, H. 1955. "Eine Anspeilung auf Hesiods Erga in der Odyssee." *Hermes* 83:51–68.

Murnaghan, S. 1987. *Disguise and Recognition in the Odyssey*. Princeton.

———. 1997. "Equal Honor and Future Glory: The Plan of Zeus in the *Iliad*." In *Classical Closure: Reading the End in Greek and Latin Literature*, ed. F. M. Dunn, D. P. Fowler, and D. H. Roberts, 23–42. Princeton.

Nagler, M. N. 1974. *Spontaneity and Tradition*. Berkeley.

———. 1990. "Odysseus: the Proem and the Problem." *Classical Antiquity* 9:335–356.

———. 1992. "Discourse and Conflict in Hesiod: Eris and the Erides." *Ramus* 21:79–96.

Nagy, G. 1990. *Pindar's Homer: the Lyric Possession of an Epic Past*. Baltimore.

———. 1992. *Greek Myth and Poetics*. Ithaca.

———. 1996a. *Homeric Questions*. Austin.

———. 1996b. *Poetry as Performance: Homer and Beyond*. Cambridge.

———. 1999. *The Best of the Achaeans: Concepts of the Hero in Archaic Greek poetry*. Baltimore.

———. 2003. *Homeric Responses*. Austin.

———. 2004. *Homer's Text and Language*. Urbana.

———. 2015. "Oral Traditions, Written Texts and Questions of Authorship." In Fantuzzi and Tsagalis 2015: 59–77.

Newton, R. M. 2015. "Eumaios Rustles Up Dinner." *The Classical Journal* 110:257–78.

Northrup, M. D. 1980. "Homer's Catalogue of Women." *Ramus* 9:150–159.

Obbink, D. 2006. "A New Archilochus Poem." *Zeitschrift für Papyrologie und Epigraphik* 156:1–9.

Olson, S. D. 1989. "The Stories of Helen and Menelaos (*Odyssey* 4.240-289) and the return of Odysseus." *The American Journal of Philology* 110: 387–389.

———. 1990. "The Stories of Agamemnon in Homer's *Odyssey*." *Transactions of the American Philological Association* 120:57–71.

———. 1995. *Blood and Iron: Stories and Storytelling in Homer's* Odyssey. Leiden.

Ormand, K. 2014. *The Hesiodic Catalogue of Women and Archaic Greece*. Cambridge.

Osborne, R. 2005. "Homer's Society." In *A Companion to Ancient Epic*, ed. J. M. Foley, 206–219. Oxford.

Pache, C. 2014. "Theban Walls in Homeric Epic." *Trends in Classics* 6:278–296.

Pade, M. 1983. "Homer's Catalogue of Women." *Classica et Mediaevalia* 34:7–15.

Papadopoulou, T. 2005. *Herakles and Euripidean Tragedy*. Cambridge.

Papakonstantinou, Z. 2004. "Justice of the Kakoi: Law and Social Crisis in Theognis." *Dike* 7:5–17.

Parks, W. 1990. *Verbal Dueling in Heroic Narrative: the Homeric and Old English Traditions*. Princeton.

Parry, A. A. 1973. *Blameless Aegisthus*. Leiden.

Parry, H. 1994. "The Apologos of Odysseus: Lies, All Lies." *Phoenix* 48:1–20.

Parry, M. 1971. *The Making of Homeric Verse*. Oxford.

Parsons, P. J. 1997. "The Lille 'Stesichorus.'" *Zeitschrift für Papyrologie und Epigraphik* 26:7–36.

Peradotto, J. 1990. *Man in the Middle Voice: Name and Narration in the* Odyssey. Princeton.

Person, R. F., Jr. 2016. "From Grammar in Everyday Conversation to Special Grammar in Oral Traditions: A Case Study of Ring Composition." In Antović and Cánovas 2016: 30–51.

Phillips, D. D. 2003. "The Bones of Orestes and Spartan Foreign Policy." In *Gestures: Essays in Ancient History, Literature, and Philosophy Presented to Alan L. Boegehold*, ed. G. W. Bakewell and J. P. Sickinger, 301–316. Oxford.

Postlethwaite, N. 1998. "Thersites in the *Iliad*." In *Homer: Greek and Roman Studies*, ed. I. McAuslan and P. Walcot, 83–95. Oxford.

Price, J. 2001. *Thucydides and Internal War*. Cambridge.

Pucci, P. 1977. *Hesiod and the Language of Poetry*. Baltimore.

———. 1987. *Odysseus Polutropos: Intertextual Readings in the* Iliad *and the* Odyssey. Ithaca.

———. 1996. "Between Narrative and Catalogue: Life and Death in the Poem." *Metis* 11:5–24.

———. 1998. *The Song of the Sirens: Essays on Homer*. New York.

Purves, A. C. 2010. *Space and Time in Ancient Greek Narrative*. Cambridge.

Rabel, R. J. 2002. "Interruption in the *Odyssey*." *The Classical Quarterly* 38:77–93.

Race, W. H. 2014. "Phaiakian Therapy in Homer's *Odyssey*." In *Combat Trauma and the Ancient Greeks*, ed. P. Meineck and D. Konstan, 47–66. New York.

Reece, S. 1994. "The Cretan Odyssey: A Lie Truer than Truth". *The American Journal of Philology* 115:157–173.

———. 2005. "Homer's *Iliad* and *Odyssey*: From Oral Performance to Written Text." In *New Directions in Oral Theory*, ed. M. Arnodio, 43–89. Tempe, AZ.

Richardson, N. J. 1993. *The Iliad: A Commentary*. Cambridge.

Richardson, S. 1996. "Truth in the Tales of the *Odyssey*." *Mnemosyne* 449(4):393–402.

Rijksbaron, A. 1992. "D'ou viennent les ἄλγεα?" In Létoublon 1992: 181–191.

Roisman, H. 2005. "Nestor the Good Counsellor." *The Classical Quarterly* 55: 17–38.

Rose, P.W. 1975. "Class Ambivalence in the *Odyssey*." *Historia* 24:129–149.

———. 1997. "Ideology in the *Iliad*: Polis, Basileus, Theoi." *Arethusa* 30:151–199.

———. 2012. *Class in Archaic Greece*. Cambridge.

Rosen, R. M. 1990. "Poetry and Sailing in Hesiod's *Works and Days*." *Classical Antiquity* 19:99–113.

———. 1997. "Homer and Hesiod." In Morris and Powell 1997:463–488.

———. 2003. "The Death of Thersites and the Sympotic Performance of Iambic Mockery." *Pallas* 61:121–136.

Ross. S. A. 2005. "Barbarophonos: Language and Panhellenism in the *Iliad*." *Classical Philology* 100:299–316.

Russo, J. A. 1968. "Homer against his Tradition." *Arion* 8:275–295.

——— A. 1997. "The Formula." In Morris and Powell 1997:238–260.

Rutherford, I. C. 2005. "Mestra at Athens: Hes. Fr. 43 and the Poetics of Panhellenism." In Hunter 2005: 99–117.

Rutherford, R. B. 1986. "The Philosophy of the *Odyssey*." *The Journal of Hellenic Studies* 106:145–162.

———. 1991. "From the *Iliad* to the *Odyssey*." *Bulletin of the Institute of Classical Studies* 38 (1991-3):37–54.

———. 2001. "Tragic Form and Feeling in the *Iliad*." In *Oxford Readings in Homer's* Iliad, ed. D.L. Cairns, 260–293. Oxford.

Saïd, S. 2011. *Homer and the* Odyssey. Oxford.

Salapata, G. 2014. *Heroic Offerings: The Terracotta Plaques from the Spartan Sanctuary of Agamemnon and Kassandra*. Ann Arbor.

Sammons, B. 2010. *The Art and Rhetoric of the Homeric Catalogue*. Oxford.

———. 2014. "A Tale of Tydeus: Exemplarity and Structure in Two Homeric Insets." *Trends in Classics* 6(2):297–318.

Scaife, R. 1995. "The Cypria and its Early Reception." *Classical Antiquity* 14:164–197.

Schachter, A. 1981. *Cults of Boeotia*. Vols. 1–4. London.

———. 2005. "The Singing Context of Kithairon and Helicon: Korinna Fr. 654 PMG Col. i and ii: Content and Context." In *Koryphaio Andri. Mélanges offerts à André Hurst*, ed. A. Kolde, A. Lukinovich, and A-L. Rey, 275–283. Geneva.

Schein, S. 1984. *The Mortal Hero: An Introduction to Homer's* Iliad. Berkeley.

———, ed. 1996. *Reading the* Odyssey: *Selected Interpretive Essays*. Princeton.

———. 2002. "Mythological Allusion in the *Odyssey*." In *Omero: Tremila Anni Dopo*, ed. F. Montanari and P. Ascheri, 185–201. Rome.

Schofield, M. 1986. "Euboulia in the *Iliad*." *The Classical Quarterly* 36:6–31.

———. 1999. *Saving the City: Philosopher Kings and Other Classical Paradigms*. London.

Scodel, R. 1982. "The Achaean Wall and the Myth of Destruction." *Harvard Studies in Classical Philology* 86:33–53.

———. 1984. "Epic Doublets and Polynices' Two Burials." *Transactions of the American Philological Association* 114:49–58.

———. 2002. *Listening to Homer: Tradition, Narrative, and Audience*. Ann Arbor.

———. 2004. "The Modesty of Homer." In *Oral Performance and its Contexts*, ed. C. J. Mackie. 1–19. Leiden.

———. 2008. *Epic Facework*. Swansea.

Scott, M. 1980. "Aidos and Nemesis in Works of Homer and their Relevance to Social or Cooperative values." *Acta Classica* 23:13–35.

Scott, W. 1997. "The Etiquette of Games in *Iliad* 23." *Greek, Roman, and Byzantine Studies* 38:213–27.

Scully, S. 1984. "The Language of Achilles: The Octhesas Formulas." *Transactions of the American Philological Association* 114: 11–27.

———. 1990. *Homer and the Sacred City*. Ithaca.

Segal, C. 1974. "The Homeric Hymn to Aphrodite: A Structuralist Approach." *The Classical World* 68:205–212.

———. 1994. *Singers, Heroes, and Gods in the* Odyssey. Ithaca.

Severyns, A. 1928. Le cycle épique dans l'école d'Aristarque, Paris.

Shapiro, H. A. 1983. "*Heros Theos*: the Death and Apotheosis of Herakles." *The Classical World* 77:7–19.

———. 1984. "Herakles and Kyknos." *American Journal of Archaeology* 88:523–529.

Shay, J. 2003. *Odysseus in America: Combat Trauma and the Trials of Homecoming*. New York.

Shive, D. 1988. *Naming Achilles*. Oxford.

Short, W. M., and W. Duffy. "Metaphor as Ideology." In Antović and Cánovas 2016: 52–78.

Sifakis, G. 1997. "Formulas and their Relatives: A Semiotic Approach to Verse Making in Homer and Modern Greek Folk Songs." *The Journal of Hellenic Studies* 117:136–153.

Silvermintz, D. 2004. "Unravelling the Shroud for Laertes and Weaving the Fabric of the City: Kingship and Politics in Homer's *Odyssey*." *Polis* 21: 26–41.

Singor, H. W. 1992. "The Achaean Wall and the Seven Gates of Thebes." *Hermes* 120:401–411.

Skempis, M., and I.V. Ziogas. 2009. "Arete's Words: Etymology, Ehoie-Poetry and Gendered Narrative in the *Odyssey*." In *Narratology and Interpretation*, ed. J. Grethlein and A. Rengakos, 213–240. Berlin.

Slatkin, L. 1991. *The Power of Thetis: Allusion and Interpretation in the* Iliad. Berkeley.

———. 1996. "Composition by theme and the *Mêtis* of the *Odyssey*." In Schein 1996:223–237.

———. 2005. "Homer's *Odyssey*." In *A Companion to Ancient Epic*, ed. Foley, 315–329.

———. 2011. *The Power of Thetis and Selected Essays*. Cambridge.

Snodgrass, A. 1971. *The Dark Age of Greece*. New York.

Solmsen, F. 1954. "The Gift of Speech in Homer and Hesiod." *Transactions of the American Philological Association* 85:1–15.

Sommerstein, A. H 1980. *The Comedies of Aristophanes. Acharnians*. London.

———. 1989. *Aeschylus. Eumenides*. Cambridge.

———. 2012. "*Atê* in Aeschylus." In *Tragedy and Archaic Greek Thought*, ed. D. Cairns, 1–15. Swansea.

Stafford, E. J. 2010. "Herakles between Gods and Heroes." In *The Gods of Ancient Greece*, ed. J. N. Bremmer and A. Erskine, 228–244. Edinburgh.

Stamatopoulou, Z. 2017. "Wounding the Gods: The Mortal Theomachos in the *Iliad* and the Hesiodic Aspis." *Mnemosyne* 70: 1–19.

Stanford, W. B. 1952. "The Homeric Etymology of the Name Odysseus." *Classical Philology* 47:209–213.

Steinbock, B. 2013. *Social Memory in Athenian Public Discourse: Uses and Meanings of the Past*. Ann Arbor.

Stewart, D. J. 1976. *The Disguised Guest: Rank, Role and Identity in the* Odyssey. Lewisburg.

Taplin, O. 1990. "Agamemnon's Role in the *Iliad*." In *Characterisation and Individuality in Greek Literature*, ed. C. B. R. Pelling, 60–82. Oxford.

———. 1992. *Homeric Soundings: The Shape of the* Iliad. Oxford.

Thalmann, W. G. 1988. "Thersites: Comedy, Scapegoats and Heroic Ideology in the *Iliad*." *Transactions of the American Philological Association* 118:1–28.

———. 1998. *The Swineherd and the Bow: Representations of Class in the* Odyssey. Ithaca.

———. 2004. "The Most Divinely Approved and Political Discord." *Classical Antiquity* 23:359–399.

Thomas, R. 1989. *Oral Tradition and Written Record in Classical Athens*. Cambridge.

Torres-Guerra, J. B. 1995a. *La Tebaida homérica como fuente de Ilíada y Odisea*. Madrid.

———. 1995b. "Die homerische Thebais und die Amphiaros-Ausfahrt." *Eranos* 93:39–45.

Torres, J. 2014. "Tiresias, The Theban Seer." *Trends in Classics* 6:339–356.

Tsagalis, C. 2008. *The Oral Palimpsest: Exploring Intertextuality in the Homeric Epics*. Washington, DC.

———. 2014a. "Preface." *Trends in Classics* 6:249.

———. 2014b. "γυναίων εἵνεκα δώρων: Interformularity and Intertraditionality in Theban and Homeric Epic." *Trends in Classics* 6:357–398.

Tsagarakis, O. 2000. *Studies in* Odyssey *11*. Stuttgart.

Turner, M. 1996. *The Literary Mind: The Origins of Thought and Language*. Oxford.

Usener, K. 1990. *Beobachtungen zum Verhältnis der Odyssee zur Ilias*. Tübingen.

van der Valk, M. 1963. *Researches on the Text and Scholia of the Iliad*. Vols. 1-2. Leiden.

van Wees, H. 1992. *Status Warriors: War, Violence, and Society in Homer and History*. Amsterdam.

Verbanck-Pierard, A. 1989. "Le double culte d'Héraklès: légende ou réalité." In *Entre Hommes et Dieux: Le convive, le héros, le prophète*, ed. A.-F. Laurens, 43–65. Paris.

Vergados, A. 2014. "Form and Function of Some Theban Resonances in Homer's *Iliad* and *Odyssey*." *Trends in Classics* 6(2):437–451.

Vernant, J.-P. 1985. *Mythe et Pensée Chez les Grecs*. Paris.

Vivante, E. 1982. *The Epithets in Homer: A Study In Poetic Values*. New Haven.

Vodoklys, E. 1992. *Blame-Expression in the Epic Tradition*. New York.

Wachter, R. 2001. *Non-Attic Greek Vase Inscriptions*. Oxford.

Walcot, P. 1977. "Odysseus and the Art of Lying." *Ancient Society* 8:1–19.

Walker, J. 1996. "Before the Beginnings of 'Poetry' and 'Rhetoric': Hesiod on Eloquence." *Rhetorica* 14:243–265.

Walsh, G. B. 1984. *Varieties of Enchantment: Early Greek Views of the Nature and Function of Poetry*. Chapel Hill.

Walsh, T. R. 2005. *Fighting Words and Feuding Words: Anger and the Homeric Poems*. Lanham.

Wehrli, F. 1957. "Oedipus." *Museum Helveticum* 14:108–117.

Wender, D. 1978. *The Last Scenes of the* Odyssey. Leiden.

West, M. L. 1966. *Hesiod. Theogony*. Oxford.

———. 1978. *Words and Days*. Oxford.

———. 1985. *The Hesiodic Catalogue of Women: Its Nature, Structure, and Origins*. Oxford.

———. 2001. *Studies in the Text and Transmission of the* Iliad. Munich.

———. 2005. "Odyssey and Argonautica." *The Classical Quarterly* 55:39–64.

———. 2007. *Greek Epic Fragments*. Cambridge, MA.

——— L. 2012. "Towards a Chronology of Early Greek Epic." In Andersen and Haug, 224–241. Cambridge.

———. 2013. *The Epic Cycle: A Commentary on the Lost Troy Epics*. Oxford.

———. 2014. *The Making of the* Odyssey. Oxford.

West, S. 1989. "Laertes Revisited." *Proceedings of the Cambridge Philological Society* 35: 113–143.

Westbrook, R. 1992. "The Trial Scene in the *Iliad*." *Harvard Studies in Classical Philology* 94:53–76.

Whallon, W. 1969. *Formula, Character and Context*. Washington, DC.

———. 2000. "How the Shroud of Laertes Became the Robe of Odysseus." *The Classical Quarterly*. 50:331–337.

Whitman, C. H. 1958. *Homer and the Heroic Tradition*. Cambridge.

Willcock, M. M. 1964. "Mythological Paradeigma in the *Iliad*." *The Classical Quarterly* 14:141–151.

———. 1977. "Ad Hoc Invention in the *Iliad*." *Harvard Studies in Classical Philology* 81:41–53.

———. 1978. *The* Iliad *of Homer*. New York.

———. 1997. "Neo-Analysis." In Morris and Powell 1997:174–189.

Wilson, D. F. 2002a. *Ransom, Revenge and Heroic Identity in the* Iliad. Cambridge.

———. 2002b. "Lion Kings: Heroes in the Epic Mirror." *Colby Quarterly* 38:231–254.

Wohl, V. 1998. *The Intimate Commerce: Exchange, Gender, and Subjectivity in Greek Tragedy.* Austin.

———. 2015. *Euripides and the Politics of Form.* Princeton.

Wyatt, W. F. 1989. "The Intermezzo of *Odyssey* 11 and the Poets Homer and Odysseus." *Studi micenei ed egeo-anatolici* 27:235–253.

———. 1996. "The Blinding of Oedipus." *New England Classical Journal* 16–18.

Zarecki, J. P. 2007. "Pandora and the Good Eris in Hesiod." *Greek, Roman, and Byzantine Studies* 47:5–29.

Zeitlin, F. 1986. "Thebes: Theater of Self and Society in Athenian Drama." In Euben 1986:101–141.

Ziehen, L. 1934. "Thebai (1)." *RE* 5A2:1492–1553.

Zlatev, J., et. al. 2008. *The Shared Mind: Perspectives on Intersubjectivity.* Amsterdam.

Zunshine, L. 2006. *Why We Read Fiction: Theory of Mind and the Novel.* Ohio.

Index Locorum

Ancient Texts and Scholia

Aeschylus
  Seven Against Thebes, 572–575, 71n69
Alcmeonis, fr.1, 200
Anacreon, fr. 2, 184
Anacreontea, fr. 26, 184; fr. 261, 1
Apollodorus, I 52, 255n33, II 67,
  258n39, 259; II 68-71, 258; II 103,
  8n16; III 5.5, 155n85; III 7, 52; III
  49–56, 134n5; III 80, 52n17; III
  57–77, 50n13
Archilochus, fr. 114, 40n86
Aristotle
  Physics, VI 9 239b10 15, 38
  Rhetoric, 1335b26-30, 267n64
Arsenius
  Apophthegmata, 7.94a, 205n3
Athenaeus
  Deipnosophists, X 83, 135; XI 783c,
  97n27; XIV 65b, 196n65; XV
  695a, 41
Bacchylides, 5.187–194, 249; 9.53–54,
  262
  fr. 33b, 256n34
Cypria, fr. 1, 164n104; fr. 1.4, 3-4, 225;
  fr. 1.5–6, 174
Contest of Homer and Hesiod, The,
  204–212, 177; 205, 169n123
Democritus, fr. B145, 129

Diodorus Siculus, IV 10.2-6, 258n39;
  IV 40, 259; IV 77, 264n55; XIX
  53.4-5, 155n85
Diogenes Laertius, I 48, 267n64
Dionysius of Halicarnassus
  On Imitation, II 2, 97n28
Epigonoi, fr.1, 195n62; fr. 4, 53n20; fr.6,
  53n20; fr.7, 53n20; fr.8.1, 53n20
Euripides
  Helen, 34 and 582, 128n130
  Herakles, 266-270, 127n125
Eustathius
  Commentary on Homer's Odyssey, I
  422.28-34, 169n123
  Commentary on Homer's Iliad, II 2.8,
  255n33; II 417, 259
FGrHist, 383 F 7, 282n26
Hellanicus
  FGrHist, 4 F 2, 8n16
Herodotus, I 67-68, 280n21, 280–281;
  II 44, 93n7; II 53, 185; IV 32, 52;
  IV 32.7, 52; V 67, 50; V 72, 281;
  VI 64.3, 165n107; VI 66.10-12,
  165n107; VIII 144.2, 246n5; IX
  18.5, 283
Hesiod
  Ehoiai (Catalogue of Women), fr. 10d,
  255n33; fr. 23a, 99n39; fr. 23.24,
  95n18; fr. 25.23-4, 100n41; fr. 25.29,
  99n40; fr. 26.31-3, 95n19; fr. 43.36-
  39, 182-183; fr. 70.18-40, 261;

Subject Index